Queer Arrangements

Lisa Barg

QUEER ARRANGEMENTS

Billy Strayhorn and Midcentury Jazz Collaboration

Wesleyan University Press   Middletown, Connecticut

Wesleyan University Press
Middletown CT 06459
www.wesleyan.edu/wespress
© 2023 Lisa Barg
All rights reserved

Manufactured in the United States of America
Designed by Mindy Basinger Hill / Typeset in Minion Pro

The Publisher gratefully acknowledges support from the General Fund
of the American Musicological Society, supported in part
by the National Endowment for the Humanities
and the Andrew W. Mellon Foundation

Library of Congress Cataloging-in-Publication Data
available at https://catalog.loc.gov/
hardback ISBN 978-0-8195-0063-2
paper ISBN 978-0-8195-0064-9
ebook ISBN 978-0-8195-0065-6

Acknowledgments for previously published material used with permission:

"Queer Encounters in the Music of Billy Strayhorn." *Journal of
the American Musicological Society* 66, no. 3 (Fall 2013): 771–824.
University of California Press.

"Working Behind the Scenes: Gender, Sexuality, and Collaboration
in the Vocal Arrangements of Billy Strayhorn." *Women and Music: A
Journal of Gender and Culture* 18, no. 1 (2014): 24–47.
University of Nebraska Press.

5   4   3   2   1

FOR DAVID

CONTENTS

Acknowledgments ix

INTRODUCTION Queer Arrangements, Queer Collaboration 1

PART I WORKING BEHIND THE SCENES: GENDER, SEXUALITY, AND COLLABORATION IN STRAYHORN'S VOCAL ARRANGEMENTS

ONE Arriving by "Flamingo" 27

TWO Difficult Beauty 45

PART II STRAYHORN'S QUEER MUSIC

THREE Strayhorn's Lorcian Encounter 85

FOUR Black Queer Moves in the Strayhorn-Ellington *Nutcracker Suite* 114

PART III STRAYHORN PERFORMING/ARRANGING STRAYHORN

FIVE Paris, Halfway to Dawn, or Listening to *The Peaceful Side* 145

EPILOGUE Ever Up and Onward: Searching for Strayhorn in the Twenty-First Century 182

Notes 191

Bibliography 241

Index 255

ACKNOWLEDGMENTS

Writing a book that explores the social and sonic dynamics of collaboration and interaction greatly heightens one's awareness of and appreciation for the contributions, great and small, of others. Over the many years of researching and writing this book, my thinking on these and countless other matters was shaped and supported by many amazing people. Due to the long journey that this book represents and my deficits of recall, I apologize in advance to all of you whose names are not included here. Another opening caveat: while it is essential to acknowledge the irreducibly collaborative and interactive process of research and writing and to credit all who have supported, impacted, and sustained my work, any shortcomings or faults in this book are mine alone.

I want to begin by thanking the family of Billy Strayhorn for their support and for granting me access to the Billy Strayhorn Collection. I am especially grateful to A. Alyce Claerbaut for generously sharing her time and memories and for her hospitality when I visited Chicago in 2015 for two unforgettable events honoring the induction of Strayhorn into the LGBTQ Legacy Walk. I'm also indebted to the support of the wider community of Strayhorn researchers, archivists, and performers—first and foremost, Walter van de Leur. Thank you, Walter, for your feedback and encouragement throughout the very long gestation of this book and for sharing your ideas, expertise, and materials. A big thanks also to David Hajdu and Krin Gabbard for supporting this project and for providing valuable materials and much jazz wisdom. I'm grateful to Liliane Terry for taking the time to speak with me at length about her remarkable life in jazz and her memories of Strayhorn. A special shout out of appreciation to the archivists, curators, and staff at the Library of Congress, Music Division—home to the Billy Strayhorn Collection—and the Duke Ellington Collection (Smithsonian Archives Center,

National Museum of American History), especially Anne McLean, Wendy Shay, and Kay Peterson for their help in locating materials and securing permissions.

I owe a considerable debt of gratitude to the material and professional support of institutions, organizations, and colleagues. At McGill University, Schulich School of Music, I'm privileged to have the support of wonderful colleagues, not to mention a stable job and a sabbatic leave that gave me precious time to think and write. The research for this book was also supported by a grant from the Social Science and Humanities Research Council (SSHRC). This project benefited immeasurably from the engagement and feedback I received through conferences and symposia, including presentations at the annual meetings of the American Musicological Society (AMS), the AMS LGBTQ Study Group, the Society for American Music, the Feminist Theory and Music Conferences, and the inaugural Rhythm Changes Conference hosted by the Amsterdam Conservatory. I benefited greatly from conversations with co-presenters and audiences at "Ellington and Strayhorn: A Celebration," Reed College; several SSHRC-funded conferences, colloquia, and meetings of the major collaborative research initiative "Improvisation, Community, and Social Practice" (ICASP); and the International Institute for Critical Studies in Improvisation (IICSI). These opportunities and other invitations to share my research opened a world of ideas and perspectives, both intellectual and creative, for which I want to thank, among others, Ajay Heble, Eric Lewis, Judy Lochhead, David Schiff, Ellen Waterman, and the larger inspiring ICASP/IICSI community.

I am very grateful to colleagues who read portions of the manuscript and provided valuable suggestions and guidance. Thank you for your time and engagement: Joseph Auner (always my sage advisor), David Brackett, Jeffrey Magee, Jeffrey Taylor, Walter van de Leur, and Lloyd Whitesell. Thanks also to Richard King and George Massenburg for sharing audio engineering and recording studio expertise. For her meticulous editorial work, help in preparing the manuscript for submission, and for cheering me on, I thank Joanne Muzak. I'm also extremely lucky to have had the support, input, and example of a brilliant and inspiring community of jazz feminist scholars, mentors, and friends, whose individual and collective work has greatly impacted this project. I owe a special debt of gratitude and appreciation to Sherrie Tucker, Tammy Kernodle, and Ellie Hisama: your intellectual generosity, care, feedback, friendship, encouragement, and laughter—even over Zoom calls—helped to sustain and motivate me through the final stages of revision. For expanding my thinking about the social and creative spaces of jazz and feminist collaboration and interaction, I thank the Melba Liston Research Collective (a collaborative historical research team I participated in alongside Tammy Kernodle, Monica Hairston O'Connell, Dianthe "Dee" Spencer, and Sherrie Tucker).

I'm honored to have had the opportunity to work with so many talented and creative graduate students and research assistants at McGill. Many thanks to: Vanessa Blais-Tremblay, Marta Beszterda, Kyle Caplan, Bruno Coulombe, Mimi Haddon, Sophie Ogilvie-Hanson, Peggy Hogan, Hester Bell Jordan, Emmanuel Majeau-Bettez, Jennifer Messelink, Meaghan Parker, Laura Risk, Kiersten van Vliet, and all the students who participated in my jazz and gender seminar. Thanks also to Houman Behzadi and the staff of the Marvin Duchow Music Library at the Schulich School of Music and to Sean Lorre and Caity Gyorgy for their assistance copying and transcribing musical examples.

This book could never have come to fruition without the support, wisdom, and camaraderie of a great many scholars, friends, and colleagues, both near and far. In Montreal (for a time, at least) big thanks to: Dorian Bandy, Shelley Butler, Giovanni Burgos, Helene Drouin, Katie Fallon, Shira Gilbert, Steven Huebner, Sara Laimon, Lisa Lorenzino, Jonathan Kimmelman, Christine Lamarre (1959–2020), Tom Lamarre, Brian Manker, Catherine Manker, Norman Ravvin, Carrie Renschler, Udayen Sen, Jonathan Sterne, Will Straw, Nandu Vadakkath, Kimberley White, Lloyd Whitesell, and Philippa Woolley. Outside of Montreal: David Ake, Georgina Born, Rashida Braggs, Mark Burford, Daniel Callahan, Susan Cook, Samantha Ege, Bernie Gendron, Bonnie Gordon, Elizabeth Keathley, Gayle Sherwood Magee, Winslow Martin, Tracy McMullen, David Metzer, Steve Meyer, Stephan Pennington, Guthrie P. Ramsey, Corinne Schippert, Van Stiefel, Caroline Lathan-Stiefel, Eileen Strempel, Judy Tsou, Anton Vishio, and Christy J. Wells.

Many thanks and appreciation to the fantastic editorial and production team at Wesleyan University Press: Suzanna Tamminen, Hannah Krasikov, Alan Berolzheimer, Mindy Basinger Hill, Jaclyn Wilson, and Stephanie Elliott Prieto. Suzanna also deserves credit for finding such excellent anonymous reviewers, whose careful comments and critical work made this a better book.

It is customary to conclude acknowledgments by honoring family. I begin with a bittersweet acknowledgment of family who passed away before the book's completion: to my late father and mother, Bernie and Helen, I am grateful for their devotion and steadfast support; and to my brother, Bruce, I'm grateful for the gift of his music and wildly creative cooking and for always inviting me to hang out at band practice. Thanks to my beloved cat, Suki, whose companionship (usually near my desktop keyboard) is sorely missed.

Last, but not least, I want to thank Marion Brackett and my brother Richard for their support. Thanks also to my Philadelphia cousins, especially Ronald and Debbie Barg, for their warm hospitality and for the care they have extended in very difficult times.

To my incredible children, Sophie and Fred, big love, joy, and gratitude for your presence in my life, and for your encouragement and patience (yes, mom's book is finally finished). My final and deepest gratitude goes to my partner, David Brackett, to whom I dedicate this book. His love, care, and unconditional support has been my greatest source of inspiration. Thank you, David, for all the many things, great and small, you contributed to this project, for your unwavering belief in me, and for lifting my spirit with humor, awesome cocktails, and jazz.

Queer Arrangements

FIGURE 0.1 Carl Van Vechten, portraits of Billy Strayhorn (August 19, 1958). Carl Van Vechten Papers. Courtesy of Yale Collection of American Literature, Beinecke Rare Book and Manuscript Library. Reproduced by permission of the Van Vechten Trust.

INTRODUCTION
Queer Arrangements, Queer Collaboration

On August 19, 1958, Billy Strayhorn (1915–1967) visited the critic, novelist, and photographer Carl Van Vechten in his famed West 55th St. apartment studio to be photographed. A black-and-white portrait of Strayhorn from their session has become a familiar, even iconic, posthumous image of the composer, arranger, and pianist, reproduced widely in popular media (figure 0.1). In classic Van Vechten style, Strayhorn is posed in near profile seated on a steel chair against a backdrop composed of pieces of gingham plaid fabric—hung at an angle to look more like diamonds than squares—which is itself layered over a patterned stone wall visible at the bottom of the frame. Slouching slightly, Strayhorn wears a loosely fitted dark wool suit. The lighting is fairly flat yet draws the eye toward two expressive details in counterpoint: Strayhorn's pensive gaze, looking away behind his signature thick black-rimmed glasses; and the musician's hand resting on top of the chair, his fingers spread out as if clutching the edge.

Van Vechten's portrait of Strayhorn exists as part of the James Weldon Johnson Memorial Collection founded by Van Vechten in 1941.[1] The collection includes other, less well-known images of Strayhorn that the photographer took on that summer day in 1958. Almost nothing is known about the specific circumstances of Strayhorn's encounter with Van Vechten. The elder Van Vechten whom Strayhorn encountered on that day in 1958 (he was seventy-eight and Strayhorn forty-three) was quite different from the (in)famous novelist and critic Van Vechten of the interwar years. As Emily Bernard has observed, "while Van Vechten's early interest in blackness was certainly inspired by sexual desire and his fascination with what he perceived as black primitivism, these features were not what sustained his interest in African American people and culture."[2] Rather, Bernard argues,

Van Vechten's primitivist investments in blackness "were matched by his conviction that blackness was a central feature of Americaness," a conviction that was "hardly a popular perspective during his lifetime."[3]

Figures 0.2a and 0.2b show two additional portraits—the first originally photographed in color, the other in black and white. In contrast to figure 0.1, these photographs show Strayhorn looking directly at the camera, a penetrating focus in his eyes. The black-and-white portrait captures Strayhorn in a more relaxed pose: he sits backwards on the chair, his hands crossed, left over right, an elegant pinky ring prominently displayed on the upper hand. The color image combines aspects of the two black-and-white portraits—profile pose as in figure 0.1 and frontal address as in figure 0.2a—but the clarity or "reality" of the image, coupled with the closer shot and warm orange and pink of the fabric, transform the visual impact. Our eye is drawn, for instance, toward the pink diamond patch in the fabric backdrop which forms a kind of halo around Strayhorn's head. In one final color image (figure 0.2c), he sits backwards on the chair, as in figure 0.2b, but here his body and gaze are oriented at a slight angle to the camera, his arms crossed, and his expression—a slight smile—enigmatic.

In his lyrical meditations on the great jazz photographs of Milt Hinton, Geoff Dyer observes that a photograph "can be as sensitive to sound as it is to light. Good photographs are there to be listened to as well as looked at; the better the photograph the more there is to hear."[4] What does Van Vechten's portrait series of Strayhorn enable us to see and hear? Like all portrait photographs, these images present a series of visual arrangements that document a silent record of interaction and dialogue between photographer and subject, one orchestrated through variations of pose, expression, composition, and perspective. A parallel can be made here between the formal, collaborative, and improvisatory elements that shape the making of these portraits and the musical practice that guided Strayhorn's career in jazz—arranging. Although musical and performance contexts vary widely, arrangers construct sonic environments that, at their best, transform and comment on the source material while also showcasing particular performers (soloists or vocalists) or facilitating improvisatory creativity and dialogue.[5] In both musical and photographic arrangements, details matter a great deal. In the tradition of jazz arranging that Strayhorn practiced, for instance, details of scoring, orchestration, and formal design play a central role not only in defining the "sound" of a chart but in crafting an expressive framework; arrangements function like dramatic or theatrical scripts, suggesting different kinds of stories, moods, or scenarios that enable (or constrain) performers/improvisers to project

FIGURES 0.2a, 0.2b, 0.2c Carl Van Vechten, portraits of Billy Strayhorn (August 19, 1958). Carl Van Vechten Papers. Courtesy of Yale Collection of American Literature, Beinecke Rare Book and Manuscript Library. Reproduced by permission of the Van Vechten Trust.

different personas, inhabit different identities, or explore different relationships to listeners.

What stories do the visual arrangements and details of the Strayhorn portraits suggest? Returning to figure 0.1, I would highlight the counterpoint between Strayhorn's pensive stare and clasped hand, details through which we might hear an echo of the affective dimension of melancholy that colors many of the scores Strayhorn wrote and arranged, a beautiful unsettling. Details of other images can be seen as capturing aspects of Strayhorn's life and identity as a Black queer artist, such as sartorial details of refinement and, in both color images, a visual emphasis on the pink diamond that frames his head in the arrangement. The pinky ring, a black star-sapphire ring, is an especially evocative detail. As a signifier of refined taste, it speaks to Strayhorn's particular embodiment of the Black queer dandy. At the same time, it also symbolizes a close personal bond: the ring was a cherished possession, a gift from his dearest of friends, Lena Horne.

In all these facets (and others I discuss later), Van Vechten's portraits of Strayhorn provide a resonant entry point for *Queer Arrangements: Billy Strayhorn and Midcentury Jazz Collaboration*. The fleeting encounter that the portraits document, their silent repertoire of interaction, the arrangement of compositional details, and the larger archival environment in which these images exist, gather together historical, affective, and formal registers that orient my own explorations of the photograph's subject. In many ways, this book is also a portrait of Billy Strayhorn. The portrait I aim to produce is one that foregrounds the relationship of Strayhorn's career and legacy to Black queer histories, paths of identification, and aesthetic practices against the background of midcentury jazz worlds. Here, the queer modernist networks collated in Van Vechten's extensive portrait archive of Black performers, artists, musicians, and writers afford a critical reference point, not least because Strayhorn's inclusion in this archive centers and materializes a linking of his career and legacy to these very networks.

Many of the figures who appear in my study, in addition to Strayhorn, also sat for Van Vechten. Not all of these figures collaborated with, or even knew, Strayhorn. These include the portraits of Black queer literary and art luminaries (Langston Hughes, Bruce Richard Nugent, Beauford Delaney, James Baldwin), pioneering queer dance world artists, such as those associated with the Katherine Dunham Troupe (Dunham herself and frequent on-stage partner Archie Savage), and other choreographers/dancers/musicians (Alvin Ailey, Arthur Mitchell, and Reginald Beane). While Strayhorn's connections to these figures play a minor role in his biography, other portraits featured in Van Vechten's collection are of legendary singers and entertainers who had deep and sustained connections with Strayhorn as friends and collaborators, such as Lena Horne and Ella Fitzgerald.

One artist, however, whose portrait does not appear in Van Vechten's archive is the one that looms largest in Strayhorn's jazz profile—that of Duke Ellington, Strayhorn's longtime employer and creative collaborator. According to one source, Van Vechten invited Ellington to sit for him, but he declined. While the reason for Ellington's absence and Strayhorn's presence in Van Vechten's archive might well be a matter of happenstance, this jazz curation constitutes a striking reversal of the historical dynamic of (in)visibility that framed Ellington and Strayhorn's partnership. The facts here are well known. Among the first openly gay Black artists working in jazz and popular music, Strayhorn joined the Ellington orchestra in 1939 and, with the exception of a short period in the early 1950s, remained in Ellington's employ until his death in 1967. Many of Strayhorn's compositions rank among the most celebrated in the jazz canon, including the Ellington orchestra's theme song after 1939, "Take the 'A' Train," the songs "Lush Life" and "Something to Live For," as well as the instrumental ballads "Chelsea Bridge" and "Passion Flower." Yet during the time Strayhorn's compositions and arrangements were actively shaping the Ellington orchestra's sound, and by extension the sound of modern jazz, he remained largely anonymous in the public sphere—"seldom seen, but always heard," as Ellington famously put it.[6]

In his biography of the artist, David Hajdu highlights the ways in which Strayhorn's ability to survive and thrive professionally hinged upon the twin conditions of his public effacement and the personal, artistic, and financial support and safe haven that his partnership with Ellington provided. He quotes the explanation of an anonymous fellow Black gay jazz musician:

> The most amazing thing of all about Billy Strayhorn to me was that he had the strength to make an extraordinary decision—that is the decision not to hide the fact that he was homosexual. And he did this in the 1940s, when nobody but nobody did that . . . Billy could have pursued a career on his own—he had the talent . . . but he'd have had to be less than honest about his sexual orientation. Or he could work behind the scenes for Duke and be open about being gay. It really was truth or consequences, and Billy went with truth.[7]

This statement—itself a legacy of the queer dilemma it names—depicts Strayhorn's choice to work behind the scenes in the Ellington orchestra as a choice of identity and safety that enabled Strayhorn to be "honest about his sexual orientation" outside the public spotlight while he pursued a vital musical career. Variations on this theme are echoed in many other posthumous interviews quoted in Hajdu's biography. George Greenlee, for example, Strayhorn's close friend from the Pittsburgh neighborhood of Homewood where they both grew up (and who is credited with arranging the historic first meeting between Strayhorn and Ellington), put it this way: "With Duke, Billy said he had security . . . Duke didn't question his manliness. It wasn't like that for him back home."[8]

A number of questions arise from these quotes that motivate my project. How do we historicize a jazz subject whose musical contributions, professional identity, and cultural legacy seem inextricably bound up with and circumscribed by the "open secret" of his homosexuality and silent authorship? How might Strayhorn's queer professional arrangement have shaped his creative practices as an arranger and composer as well as his approaches to collaboration, and his choice of and writing for specific improvising voices? In other words, what queer histories and socialities of arranging, composition, and collaboration does Strayhorn's story afford? What sonic histories of queer feeling and identities are recorded in his works, and how might these histories be positioned within larger narratives of Black queer modernist history? The chapters that follow explore these questions through diverse music-historical and theoretical angles that bring Strayhorn's work into a variety of alignments or, drawing on one of my study's guiding metaphors, *critical arrangements* with Black queer histories and jazz history. I center the socio-musical dimensions of collaborative creativity, which I will explore through Strayhorn's creative partnership with Ellington, his writing for specific improvisers in the Ellington orchestra, his vocal arranging for singers, and his work with other performers and artists in dance and music theater both in and outside of the Ellington fold.

While previous studies have claimed a gay sensibility for Strayhorn's work, little attention has been given to historicizing this sensibility within modern discourses on sexuality, race, and gender or to examining the Black queer contexts and contours of his creative labor and critical reception.[9] I want to clarify at the outset that my argument is not simply that Strayhorn's identification as an openly gay Black artist drastically limited his career opportunities in mid-century American music (which it obviously did), or that he composed music that powerfully expressed his truth (such as the classic "Lush Life"). Rather, the complex specificity of Strayhorn's lived experiences as a Black queer artist affected virtually every aspect of his career in jazz, from the creative roles he could assume and the dynamics between himself and his collaborators, to his musical sensibility, his aesthetic priorities and practices, and the types of musical and theatrical projects he conceived and undertook.

QUEERING JAZZ STUDIES THROUGH THE STRAYHORN ARCHIVE

My analyses of Strayhorn's career and the issues of queer aesthetics, history, and identity that they raise build on and complement two foundational books: the aforementioned biography by David Hajdu and Walter van de Leur's musicological study, *Something to Live For: The Music of Billy Strayhorn*.[10] As a biography and musicological monograph, Hajdu's and van de Leur's books are obviously quite different in their aims and critical agendas; however, their projects share the goal of dismantling enduring jazz myths surrounding Strayhorn's legacy, his creative partnership with Ellington, and his work for the Ellington orchestra—myths that have diminished Strayhorn's creative contributions and visibility, usually in lieu of great-man narratives of Ellington. Hajdu accomplishes this larger goal through a powerful restorative narrative of Strayhorn's life history and career that brings together a diverse community of voices from Strayhorn's personal and professional worlds. Drawing on his painstaking forensic work on extant Ellington-Strayhorn manuscripts, van de Leur's study offers a series of brilliant analyses of style and form that track and identify Strayhorn's stylistic and compositional individuality. No other author has done more to further our understanding of, and open our ears to, Strayhorn's compositional fingerprint. Along the way, van de Leur rescues from obscurity a substantial catalogue of previously undiscovered Strayhorn compositions, arrangements, and other manuscript scores which, as of 2019, are held in the Billy Strayhorn Collection at the Library of Congress (hereafter BSC).[11] Through this work, van de Leur also establishes Strayhorn's authorship on previously uncredited scores, and solves a host of other authorial "whodunits," in some cases through reconstructing the collaborative process on specific works, such as the iconic piece most (in)famously mired in authorship controversy by Strayhorn-deniers, "'A' Train."

In addition to building on and extending the biographical and musicological work of Hajdu and van de Leur, *Queer Arrangements* brings Strayhorn's life and work into dialogue with theoretical frameworks and critical modes from gender, sexuality, and critical race studies. If one of the chief historiographical myths Hajdu's and van de Leur's work undoes is that of Strayhorn as the creative "alter ego" of Ellington, then my analyses illuminate the complex gendered and raced histories and discourses through which such a myth was articulated and sustained.[12] I approach tricky questions of authorship and collaborative creativity in the Strayhorn-Ellington partnership—an arena of intense scrutiny and debate—less as a mystery or puzzle to be solved than as an opportunity to explore the social and aesthetic entanglements of artistic interaction and collaboration. I aim for a method that respects the opacity and complexity around questions of authorship in collaborative creativity while also attending to individual voice, history, and agency.

In centering the interlocking frameworks of race, gender, and sexuality in jazz, my study is most clearly aligned with and inspired by recent and emerging scholarship in jazz studies on gender and sexuality.[13] In her essay "When Did Jazz Go Straight? A Queer Question for Jazz Studies," Sherrie Tucker poses critical questions around the politics, promises, and pitfalls of doing queer history for jazz scholars. Building on Sarah Ahmed's influential book *Queer Phenomenology*, Tucker calls for an approach that theorizes queerness in terms of affective relations and differences in "orientation, alignment and directedness."[14] Such a reorientation supplies a counter to familiar and limited frameworks of sexual "object choice" and identity formation which presume (and often conflate) stable queer bodies and a homo/hetero binary. The implications that Tucker draws from Ahmed's work (and others) for jazz studies pose a critical challenge to the recuperative historical investments of a project such as this one for, as she reminds us, the "impulse . . . to exhume a queer jazz past" can all too easily reproduce the heteronormative logic of dividing jazz "into queer moments and straight moments, queer bodies and straight bodies, queer sound and straight sound."[15] While *Queer Arrangements* is guided by a search for, and the possibilities of, queer historical perspectives, sounds, and practices in jazz, such an approach need not be oriented by a divided queer/straight logic of identification but, rather, toward showing how queerness already cohabitates with straightness in jazz's past. The musical and historical analyses I undertake aim not only to trouble the normative scripts of race and sexuality in jazz history and jazz criticism (spectacularly apparent, as I chronicle later, in posthumous Strayhorn critical commentary), but also to reorient historical perspectives on the Ellington-Strayhorn partnership that have been—and continue to be—produced from within those "straight" narratives. In doing so, I expand the frames through which Strayhorn's story as a jazz historical subject have been told beyond dominant "great man" jazz narratives; my readings of his life and collaborative work track alternative interpretive possibilities and historical routes and sounds. My focus on queer arranging and, as I discuss in the next section, queer collaboration works toward foregrounding invisibilized spaces of jazz history, ones that reorganize—and queer—the normative practices and presumptions of jazz historiography.

To rearrange Strayhorn's story as a jazz historical subject, I am guided by Black queer theoretical interventions that attend to what E. Patrick Johnson and Mae Henderson in their introduction to the foundational edited volume *Black Queer Studies: A Critical Anthology* conceptualize as the "interanimation" of queerness and blackness.[16] Ellington's description of Strayhorn's sonic and creative force as "seldom seen but always heard," points toward the "interanimation" of Black and queer frequencies in Strayhorn's career and legacy. Indeed, Ellington's aphorism hails Strayhorn's invisible yet potent musical presence as a kind of queer sonic Afrodiasporic trickster, thus signifying what Fred Moten might call Strayhorn's (and Ellington's) Black radical spirit of "fugitivity."[17]

While Hajdu and other biographical accounts of Strayhorn's life honor and celebrate his extraordinary courage to live as an openly gay Black artist, and document the devotion, love, and support of colleagues, friends, and family, lingering questions and silences remain around the specific contours of this narrative, particularly in the ways it relies on an image of Strayhorn as the self-effacing and self-sacrificing "silent partner." An approach that attends to the social and historical "interanimation" of blackness and queerness would here need to ask: What do we fail to see or hear in the Strayhorn archive when narratives of invisibility guide our historical work? What assumptions are being made in this narrative about a Black queer past in relation to (in)visibility? As Marlon B. Ross reminds us, "racialized minorities may operate under different social protocols concerning what it means to be visible and invisible within normative sites like the family, the classroom, the workplace, the church, the street, and the community more generally . . . We must ask, what does it mean for African Americans to uncloset their sexuality *within* the context of a racial status already marked as an abnormal site over and against white bourgeois identity and its signifiers of racial *normativity?*"[18]

One of the dilemmas I faced in searching for alternative (queer and otherwise) jazz historical narratives on Strayhorn's career was a dearth of biographical materials and personal papers in the two major archival collections dedicated to his career—the Smithsonian Institution's Duke Ellington Collection and the Billy Strayhorn Collection in the Library of Congress, Music Division, bequeathed by the Strayhorn family in 2018.[19] Strayhorn was not a letter writer or record keeper and he gave only a few extended interviews during his lifetime, almost all of which were conducted in the early 1960s. Hajdu's biography is told largely through the voices and remembrances of colleagues, friends, and family, whom the author interviewed over eleven years beginning in the 1980s. (He conducted over three hundred interviews that involved "more than three thousand hours of conversation.")[20]

Although limited in quantity, both collections nevertheless contain valuable materials documenting Strayhorn's life and career, most prominently, oral history interviews, personal photographs, and promotional materials. In addition, the Billy Strayhorn Collection includes several letters and telegrams, a folder of newspaper clippings that Strayhorn kept, two personal address books, passports, financial documents, contracts, and royalty statements. Yet the overall scarcity of personal documents and, especially, primary biographical material greatly complicated the task of conducting original historical research focused on an individual career and life history. However, I quickly came to see the research dilemmas I was navigating as deeply entwined with the Black and queer theoretical and historical perspectives that orient my project, as well as to the specific material conditions of the Strayhorn archive.

The interpretive paths I traverse in this book are irreducibly bound to historically specific moments and contexts and engage with historicist method; however, the biographical silences and fragmented nature of the Strayhorn archive require more speculative methods of theory, interpretation, and imagination. His archive requires, in other words, a queer archival approach. Queer method in this context would caution against too easily attaching vocabularies of silence and invisibility to characterize the Strayhorn archive. There are several reasons for this. First, Strayhorn's deep catalog of extant scores and recordings is, above all else, an extraordinary sonic repository of (queer) presence, voice, and feelings. Here, following Ann Cvetkovich and other theorists of queer archival method, I engage these sonic materials as an alternative, embodied record of queer subjectivity, memory, and affect though which to construct a queer jazz archive.[21] Second, narratives of invisibility risk, as I suggested earlier, reinscribing the very categories and erasures they assume, a dynamic that is especially problematic in the case of Strayhorn, whose place in the jazz canon is itself defined by a paradox of (in)visibility.

Cvetkovich's theorizing of the queer archive as a mode to center and value ephemera and other fugitive forms of knowledge also holds relevance for interpreting Strayhorn's biographical and personal documents. As Cvetkovich puts it, "in the absence of institutionalized documentation or in opposition to official histories, memory becomes a valuable historical resource, and ephemeral and personal collections of objects stand alongside the documents of the dominant culture in order to offer alternative modes of knowledge."[22] Among a handful of ephemera I encountered in jazz archives, for instance, one object—a well-worn pencil—seemed to embody this alternative historical register of queer feeling and knowledge. The pencil (figure 0.3) was a cherished keepsake belonging to Strayhorn's (first-known) long-term partner, the pianist Aaron Bridgers, who gifted the pencil to the Duke Ellington Collection. An accompanying note, likely written in Bridgers's hand, is included with the pencil in a small plastic bag: "Billy Strayhorn's manuscript pencil (just as he left it). Donated by Aaron Bridgers."[23]

So ephemeral is this pencil's status, its existence in the Duke Ellington Collection cannot be found in any of the official finding aids. Indeed, against other rare items documenting Bridgers's relationship with Strayhorn in the Ellington Collection—including a fascinating oral history interview with Bridgers conducted by Patricia Willard in 1989 and a small collection of photographs—the pencil's "miscellaneous" status, by comparison, seems wholly justified.[24] Yet clearly for Bridgers it signified something dear, almost a kind of relic—teeth marks and all—full of queer attachment, stories, and feelings. Here, Bridgers's description of the pencil as being preserved "just as he left it" is a significant detail, as it specifies the object as an artifact of domestic intimacy, specifically from one of Strayhorn's extended postwar visits to Paris, where Bridgers lived from 1948 until his death in 2003. As is well known, before moving to Paris to take a job as the house pianist for the gay-friendly jazz club, the Mars Club, Bridgers and Strayhorn shared a home in Harlem, 315 Convent Avenue, for almost a decade.[25] In addition to the pencil, Bridgers also donated another object marked by queer resonance, a single musical manuscript for a playful love song, entitled "Oo! (You Make Me Tingle)," composed—perhaps with that pencil—in the early 1950s for an unrealized musical (with composer-arranger Luther Henderson), *Rose-Colored Glasses*.

FIGURE 0.3 "Billy Strayhorn's Manuscript Pencil (Just as he left it)." Collection of Duke Ellington Ephemera and Related Audiovisual Materials, Archives Center, National Museum of American History, Smithsonian Institution. Donated by Aaron Bridgers.

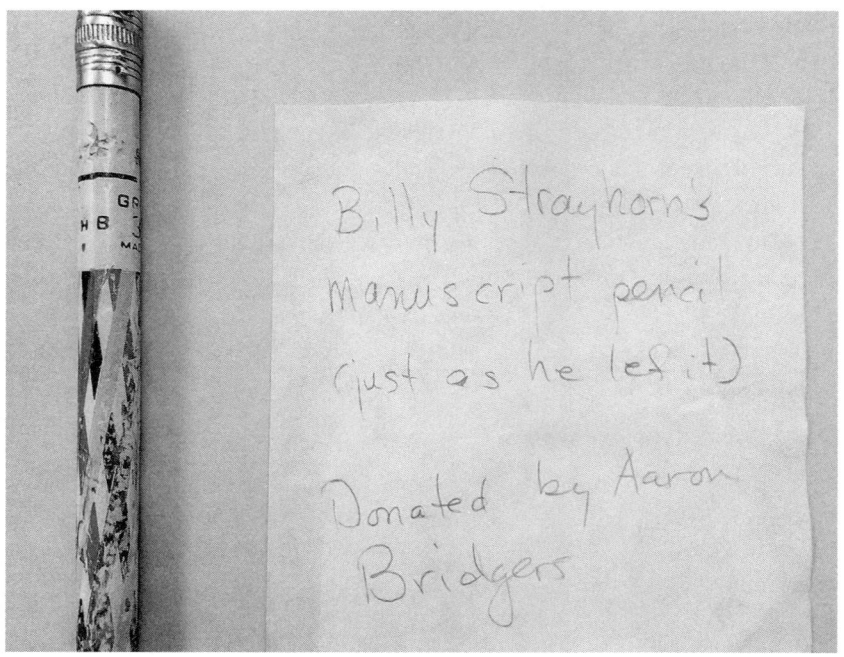

"SO NOW WHAT WOULD YOU CALL ME?"
OR QUEER COLLABORATION

> People ask me what I do, what position I have. Well, I really don't have a definable position. He [Ellington] and I work together very closely. I have arranged, and I have composed, and I've written lyrics and performed, so now what would you call me?
>
> Billy Strayhorn

This quote comes from a rare solo Strayhorn interview (that is, without Ellington). The setting is a Vancouver radio station in 1962, and the identity of the interviewer is not known; the audio tape, part of the Smithsonian's Ruth Ellington Collection of Duke Ellington Materials, is labeled "interview with unidentified male."[26] As a lead-off question, the interviewer asks Strayhorn to respond to Ellington's description of him as his "writing companion." Strayhorn's response and, in particular, his final pointed question—"so now what would you call me?"—serve as a useful provocation for my project. His response demonstrates an acute awareness that his creative labor eludes normative definition, even to Ellington; he prefaces his remarks with the quip, "that's *his* description. That's more or less what I am." Strayhorn's ambivalent response to Ellington's benign descriptor of him as a "writing companion" can also be heard as a subtle puncturing of jazz narratives that depict collaborative creativity as unburdened from networks and histories of power.

Inspired by Strayhorn's own sense of his indefinability, *Queer Arrangements* examines Strayhorn's creative labor in relation to what I call queer collaboration. On a conceptual level, queer collaboration encompasses the complex sociohistorical, biographical, sonic, and affective dimensions that guide my analyses of collaborative creativity and embodied socialities in Strayhorn's practices as an arranger, composer, and pianist. My focus on collaborative creativity in this case engages with Georgina Born's call for a sociology of music that theorizes the mediation of music in terms of complex affordances, assemblages, and events. As she argues, "music's affordances" possess the "capacity to destabilize and reorchestrate not only affect and desire but criteria of belonging and affiliation, and therefore new collective solidarities."[27]

These intersecting dimensions emerge in multiple performative modes, media, and circumstance and take diverse expressive forms. Here, queer collaboration signals ways in which queer contexts and histories came to bear on Strayhorn's collaborative relationships (real and imagined) or particular collaborative projects, arrangements, and compositions. In another register, queer collaboration points to broader analytical and historiographical issues and priorities, such as attending to—listening for—articulations of race, gender, and sexuality in Strayhorn's behind-the-scenes collaborative creativity. Like the expressive practices I engage, this approach entails close attention to details, such as the details of particular collaborative relationships and situations in relation to both broader cultural and institutional contexts and biographical scripts and circumstance. As an example of what such an analysis might look like, let's take Strayhorn's queer position in the Ellington band. Strayhorn's working arrangement as Ellington's "silent partner" functioned as a tactic to navigate and survive the "tight spaces" of possibility for an openly Black queer musician in midcentury jazz. It goes without saying that Strayhorn's life experiences growing up Black, gay, and working class in segregated Pittsburgh of the 1920s and 1930s had already demanded the honing of such skills. To refer back to George Greenlee's words, Strayhorn felt he had "security with Ellington." This security encompassed institutional, creative, personal, and social dimensions: his position not only supplied him a steady salary working for one of the top African American jazz orchestras in the music business (albeit through a very "informal" Ellingtonian financial arrangement), but also provided acceptance, respect, and belonging—in other words, alternative modes of family and community.[28]

Although the concept of queer collaboration I'm proposing is grounded in the specific circumstances and social networks of Strayhorn's career and biography, queer collaboration also takes account of the ambiguous status and practices of arranging, and the figure of the arranger in dominant jazz narratives. Notwithstanding the significant and transformative critical work in jazz studies over the past several decades, conventional jazz narratives continue to gravitate around the music's frontline players—canonic instrumental soloists and composers along with the solo achievements of a handful of "exceptional" singers. Scholars such as Mark Tucker and, more recently, John Wriggle have explored the problematic, and specifically illusive position of the arranger and arranging in the history of jazz.[29] Tucker's study of the music and legacy of Will Vodery notes that arrangers have been "viewed more as industrious artisans than creative artists" and that their public anonymity has concealed their "indispensable contributions to theater, radio, film, television, and recordings" and their centrality to the musical culture as a whole.[30] The obscurity of arrangers to the general public is paralleled by their uncertain status in jazz criticism and historiography; more often than not, the figure of the arranger exists in a kind of liminal discursive space, one that troubles normative categories of race, art, and music. As Wriggle has observed, "the perceived role of the arranger often appears to go to the very heart of the question 'what is (or is not) jazz?'"[31]

Despite (or perhaps because of) their considerable power and prestige in the swing-era entertainment industry, where arrangers were prized as style setters—highly sought after for their ability to fashion custom arrangements through which a band could communicate an identifiable sound—postwar critical perspectives have tended to view arrangers with suspicion, conflating practices of scoring (and the formal musical education associated with the development of those practices) with either or both mainstream entertainment and European classical music values. In this equation, the arranger is figured as a kind of debased agent of (white) commerce and inauthenticity.[32] An oft-cited passage on arrangers in Amiri Baraka's *Blues People* (1963) offers a particularly vivid example of this discourse. In it, Baraka faults arrangers for spoiling jazz's core blues values of spontaneity, emotionality, orality, and individualism: "Spontaneous impulse had been replaced by the arranger, and the human element of music was confined to whatever difficulties individual performers might have reading a score."[33] Arrangers (at least the ones Baraka doesn't like) are here clearly aligned with bourgeois white normativity.

Baraka's notion of arranging as the scripted other in relation to improvisation and performance continues to have traction in popular and academic writing in jazz. To be sure, elements of this discourse have a long history in jazz criticism, dating back to well before Baraka's comments; nevertheless, prewar discourse on arrangers and arranging complicates the kinds of dichotomies of race and music that Baraka's view asserts. To give one rather obscure example, in his analysis of the effect of the 1942 AFM recording ban on the development of bebop, Scott DeVeaux notes the threat that arrangers for "jazz-oriented swing bands" posed to music publishers because of the interdependence of arranging practices and improvisation. DeVeaux quotes one publisher's complaint: "Who can count on them for just one straight melody chorus to plant the refrain with those who might want to buy the song, if they could only tell what the tune was like—what with their way of going haywire after the first eight bars?"[34]

Several critical points emerge from this brief discussion of the history of arranging and arrangers. First, as noted, this publisher's comment reflects a history of the interdependence of arranging and improvisation in the practices of arranging in jazz, a history that troubled—and continues to trouble—normative distinctions between composing and arranging and their hierarchical aesthetic and legal status in relation to authorship and ownership. Here arrangers craft variegated sonic contexts (backings, formal design) that frame and facilitate improvising voices, and, in some cases, may be said to crucially shape the conditions or scripts through which improvisatory performance takes place. Arranging involves weaving together or "composing" in time and space the formal dimensions of a song or musical material and specific bodies, voices, or personalities, itself a process that fundamentally depends upon collaboration and interaction, although one typically worked out, for example, in rehearsals prior to the moment of performance or recording.[35]

Second, concepts and practices of arranging, composition, and improvisation are relational and embedded in larger racialized and gendered social, institutional, aesthetic, and juridical discourses. Extending foundational critical interventions by writers such as Baraka, jazz studies scholars have unpacked constitutive entanglements of race, gender, and sexuality in discourses around cultural difference, prestige, and value in jazz, and how, in turn, these discourses shape conceptual and embodied practices of composition, improvisation, and, more generally, performance.[36] This body of scholarship underscores the ways in which racialized and gendered jazz categories are mobilized in specific historical and performative moments—for example, how they empower or constrain jazz subjects and bodies or how, as in the quote from Baraka discussed previously, they figure as discursive anchors in debates about who and what counts as authentic jazz.

If, in some cases, arranging is positioned as the score-based and commodified "other" in relation to categories of jazz authenticity, in other cases the role and status of arranging is implicated in a different, but not unrelated, set of aesthetic distinctions between arranging and composing. At issue here is a gendered aesthetic that devalues arranging because of its focus on scored details of presentation and sound rather than generating "original" compositional material. As feminist scholars in musicology, art, and literature have long argued, the persistent devaluing of the detail, its status as what Naomi Schor would call a "bad object," can only be understood in relation to gendered (and racialized) aesthetic ideologies and histories in which the particular, the derivative, ornamental, or nonessential is attached to the feminine (or has been insistently feminized), while the original, authentic, or structural functions is considered the masculine default, and is associated with genius and authority.[37] In this gendered logic, the aesthetics of sonic details and surface presentation in arranging are rendered derivative and debased in relation to composition. Furthermore, the extension of this aesthetic discourse to institutional and legal contexts can be related to the status of arrangements themselves, which are enshrined in copyright law, where even copyrighted arrangements are defined as supplements to the original.

How to redress the aesthetic and institutional devaluing and marginalization of arrangers and arranging in jazz history remains an important project in jazz studies. Musicologists and jazz scholars have most often sought historiographical redress through documenting the careers of specific arrangers and/or identifying formal, technical, and stylistic practices and conventions, especially through analyzing individual charts or establishing lines of musical influence, innovation, and transformation. In their work on 1920s and swing-era arranging, however, jazz scholars such as John Wriggle, John Howland, Tammy Kernodle, Jeffrey Magee, and Andrew Berish have significantly expanded traditional musicological concerns to account for the larger social, cultural, political, and institutional contexts in which arrangers worked, including the impact of race, place, gender, and modernism.[38] Both Wriggle's focus on the career of swing-era arranger Chappie Willett and Howland's study of what he calls the "glorified" aesthetic of jazz arranging and composition, for example, link the marginalization of arrangers and arranging aesthetics to other (implicit) jazz historiographical biases, such as those found in sanitized narratives of jazz history that ignore the music's connection to the larger world of commerce and entertainment, including nightclub revues, variety shows, Broadway, and radio. Implicit in this critique is that erasing the entertainment contexts of jazz also disavows how these forms of entertainment—and thus the work of arrangers and composers working in these spaces—often turned upon the (eroticized) appeal of gendered and raced bodies and voices, primarily those of women dancers, singers, and entertainers.[39] On this score, the historical erasure of jazz's foundational connection to forms of entertainment, or "the popular" broadly speaking, also fails to acknowledge the co-creative participation and contributions of women performers.

In sum, big-band arranging was deeply embedded in the cultural and aesthetic practices and institutional networks of midcentury entertainment worlds. Of special pertinence to my study is to think through the ways in which the role and status of arranging as a form of collaborative backstage creative labor accommodated marginalized jazz identities and, further, to address how specific collaborative relationships came to bear on the social aesthetics of arranging practices across and between identities.[40] The treatment of the category of jazz arranging in *Queer Arrangements* is thus less about the history of jazz arranging as it has customarily been conceived than about a particular articulation—call it an arrangement—of this history, one oriented around queer historical and theoretical perspectives focused on Strayhorn's career. As such, I emphasize frameworks of race, gender, and sexuality in my analyses of the collaborative relationships between Strayhorn and the musicians with whom he worked, and I listen closely for how these relationships resonate in the final musical assemblage. If arrangers and arrangements in jazz can be said to work in the background of jazz culture both socially and aesthetically, then my analyses consider how these two senses of arranging, the social and aesthetic, emerge in Strayhorn's collaborative projects and practices as an arranger (or arranger-composer).

This final point circles back to the concept of queer collaboration, a concept that encompasses my aim to account for and theorize linkages between the social and aesthetic registers of arranging in relation to Strayhorn's work. Here, Strayhorn's long-term composing and arranging partnership with Ellington serves as a critical point of departure. Importantly, Ellington rejected the notion of Strayhorn as his "alter ego," preferring instead a more egalitarian image of a shared or, more precisely, *conjoined* body to characterize the intimacy of their musical and personal relationship: "He was not, as he was often referred to by many, my alter ego. Billy Strayhorn was my right arm, my left arm, all the eyes in the back of my head, my brainwaves in his head, and his in mine."[41] Ellington's notion of Strayhorn as the "eyes in the back of my head" not only challenges normative desires for stable, individual artistic identities, but, more importantly, names a queer perspective and/as an embodied intimacy. As I explore in this volume, such queer intimacy resounds in and around the complicated personal and professional dynamics of their creative partnership as well as in the complex sonic mix of many Ellington-Strayhorn works, which, as van de Leur has argued, can be conceived of as a mix of "different shades from the same set of colors."[42] This "same set of colors" refers to the interpretive sonic filter of the Ellington orchestra, and "different shades" refers to the individual but blended composing and arranging contributions of Ellington and Strayhorn, blends that encompass different aesthetic/formal priorities, approaches, and practices.

SEEING ALL AROUND THE MATERIAL

One of Strayhorn's earliest public statements on the art of arranging came in a 1942 column published in the periodical *Music and Rhythm* under the title "Billy Strayhorn's Arranging Hints." The far from straightforward "hints" that

Strayhorn provided must have both humored and baffled his interlocuter. Adapting language from theoretical abstractions of time and space associated more with advanced physics and popular mysticism than jazz, Strayhorn explained, "arrangers and composers must see the piece on which they are working as a complete entity. They ought to use four or five dimensions and see all around the material—over, above, and under it, and on the sides too. Then the job becomes one of transposing the physical picture into an integral and complete mental picture."[43] While Strayhorn did not elaborate on the (im)possibilities of fourth- and fifth-dimensional music theory, the metaphor is an apt description of his concept and ethos of arranging (and composing) in jazz—a multidimensional expressive practice that "transposes" the seen and unseen spatial and temporal dimensions of sonic material into a "an integral and complete mental picture." In his conversations with Hajdu, pianist Donald Shirley, who was among Strayhorn's circle of Black gay artists and friends, echoed this concept, observing that while any number of jazz composers "are very good at thinking vertically and horizontally about music," Strayhorn "could write diagonals and curves and circles . . . he was a master craftsman and pragmatic but also a romanticist."[44] Taking my cue from Strayhorn's ethos of arranging and advice to "see all around the material," my own arrangement of the Strayhorn archive traces a diverse set of narrative and analytical paths through the multiple dimensions and obscure corners of his career and music. To stretch the metaphorical comparison a bit further, the concept of queer collaboration I outlined in the previous section might be understood as a kind of transposing instrument that enables multidimensional music-historical exploration.

Several organizing frameworks anchor this exploration: conceptual, biographical, and chronological. The material covered in each chapter follows a loose chronology (with a few notable exceptions), and focuses on one particular type of (queer) collaborative role in Strayhorn's career. The material with which I engage encompasses a variety of genres (vocal arrangements, instrumental ballads, music-theater works, suites, and film music) and performance contexts and spaces. I thus attend to both the more stable visual, sonic, and documentary objects of a jazz historical archive (scores, recordings, biography, interviews, oral history, journalistic discourse, publicity material, films, photographs, and album covers) as well as the ephemeral and embodied repertoire of performance, improvisation, collaboration, and interaction.

A number of thematic threads also link the chapters, chief among them the centrality of music-theater in Strayhorn's career and creative imagination.

Music-theater works count among the major creative outputs of the Ellington-Strayhorn catalogue; yet Strayhorn's music-theatrical affinity can be traced back to his pre-Ellington projects, most notably his successful 1935 musical, *Fantastic Rhythm*, for which he wrote the entire book, including words and music for the much-admired songs "Let Nature Take Its Course" and "My Little Brown Book."[45] Indeed, it was the depth and sophistication of Strayhorn's songwriting as evidenced in these songs and others he composed during this period—including the extraordinary "Lush Life," "So This is Love," "Something to Live For," and "Your Love Has Faded"—that first impressed Ellington when the two artists met backstage at the Stanley Theatre in downtown Pittsburgh following the Ellington orchestra's performance there in 1938. For his "audition" Strayhorn played "Something to Live For" as well as other songs.[46] Following this meeting, Ellington invited Strayhorn to visit him at his Sugar Hill Harlem apartment, an occasion that Strayhorn famously immortalized in the song "Take the 'A' Train."

Strayhorn's contributions to Ellingtonia music-theater works are well known and include music composed and/or arranged for *Jump for Joy* (1941), *Beggar's Opera* (1947), and *A Drum Is a Woman* (1957). Much less known are his works created for non-Ellington music-theater projects from the early 1950s, such as a set of songs he wrote for a 1953 all-Black cast experimental theater production of Federico García-Lorca's *The Love of Don Perlimplín for Belisa in Their Garden* (*Amor de Don Perlimplín con Belisa en su jardín*), and the aforementioned unrealized 1954 musical *Rose-Colored Glasses* (both of which are explored in chapter 2). Also vital to Strayhorn's repertoire of sonic theater are theatrical, programmatic, and choreographic intertexts found in many of his vocal arrangements and instrumental works. These include essential works in the Ellington-Strayhorn canon: the stunning string of ballads he composed and arranged for Ellington's star soloist, alto saxophonist Johnny Hodges (1906–1970), which I explore in the book's central interlude, and the Ellington-Strayhorn suites *Perfume Suite* (1944), *Such Sweet Thunder* (1957), *Nutcracker Suite* (1960), and *Far East Suite* (1965).

Strayhorn's vocal arrangements and his collaborative relationships with singers are the focus of part 1. Strayhorn's vocal arranging oeuvre is extensive and varied, stretching from his hip, swinging charts for Ivie Anderson in the late 1930s and early 1940s to his lush, ethereal backings for Ella Fitzgerald in the late 1950s. I focus on selected performances and recordings from this body of work that provide critical snapshots of contrasting working conditions, collaborative relationships, and historical moments. Chapter one revisits a defining professional moment early in Strayhorn's tenure with the Ellington orchestra: his celebrated

1940 arrangement of the pop tune "Flamingo" for Ellington staff singer Herb Jeffries. My discussion of this arrangement moves through an interrelated set of queer historical and aesthetic paths surrounding the work's production and dissemination across recorded and visual media.

As a staff arranger for Ellington in the early 1940s, Strayhorn's vocal arranging assignments revolved around scoring charts for singers on the Ellington payroll such as Jeffries; however, by the mid-1950s this situation began to change significantly in ways that reflected not only the rising symbolic capital of jazz in the era of the LP, but also changes in Strayhorn's professional status and personal life. These changes set the stage for a series of more expansive and decidedly high-profile performance and recording projects from 1955 to 1958, which form the historical backdrop for chapter two. I explore Strayhorn's new arrangements of original compositions for prestige LP projects with Rosemary Clooney (*Blue Rose*, 1956) and Ella Fitzgerald (*Ella Fitzgerald Sings the Duke Ellington Songbook*, 1957), and survey Strayhorn's work as a vocal coach, arranger, and accompanist for Lena Horne. The deep, enduring personal and musical bond between Strayhorn and Horne is in many ways the most emblematic and, as such, is of special import to conceptualizing queer collaboration as it names the merging of forms of personal, professional, and musical intimacy in collaborative music making. My aim here and throughout the chapter is to describe and reflect upon these instances of collaborative intimacy and consider how they mark, enact, or embody a sociality of arranging between and across identities.

Part 2 considers issues of Black queer identity, aesthetics, and history through a close reading of several midcentury works: a set of four pieces Strayhorn composed in 1953 for an Off-Broadway production of García-Lorca's *The Love of Don Perlimplín for Belisa in Their Garden*; and his contributions to the adaptation for the Ellington Orchestra of Tchaikovsky's *Nutcracker Suite* (1960). These works (as well as other related works that I discuss) originate in specific dramatic or programmatic contexts and engage artistic figures, themes, topics, and aesthetic practices that have strong queer historical affiliations such as failed or impossible love, masking, Black queer dandyism, stylized exotica, and other liminal spheres of ambiguous identification and reversal. Despite significant differences in generic, performative, and institutional contexts, these midcentury works enact instances of queer transnational encounter, not least because two of the pieces involve a spectral gay collaborator (Lorca and Tchaikovsky), while the other is based on an artist (Shakespeare) whose work has an extensive history of queer readings. My goal is to simultaneously position Strayhorn's work within a history of Black queer modernist expressive practices and *as* a practice or poetics of Black (queer) transnationalism.

Just months following the release of the *Nutcracker Suite* in October 1960, Strayhorn set off for what would be his final extended trip to his beloved city of Paris. Two projects he worked on during this period—the film score for *Paris Blues* and his first and only solo, commercial recording, *The Peaceful Side*—are the focus of chapter 5. From his early classic "Lush Life" with its lyrical tribute to the restorative powers of "a week in Paris" to the French modernist sonic accents that pervade Strayhorn's compositions and arrangements, the City of Light loomed large in the Black queer history of Strayhorn's career and creative imagination. Beginning in 1950, Strayhorn made several extended trips to the city for both personal and professional pursuits. During his first trip to Paris in 1950, Strayhorn visited Aaron Bridgers and spent many evenings at the vibrant gay-friendly jazz bar, the Mars Club, where Bridgers worked as the staff pianist and where Strayhorn was welcomed with open arms and treated as a celebrity by the city's transnational gay cabaret subculture. The admiration, communal support, and cosmopolitan cultural energy of Strayhorn's first Parisian experience were by all accounts transformative. Yet it was his last visit that counts as his most productive: by the time Strayhorn returned to New York in mid-March 1961, he had participated in no fewer than five collaborative projects, including his work on *Paris Blues* and *The Peaceful Side*. In addition to these major efforts, Strayhorn contributed vocal arrangements for sessions featuring the Swedish singer Alice Babs and the South African singer Satima Bea Benjamin, as well as string arrangements for a trio featuring Stephane Grappelli.

Part 3 traces several routes through this period in Strayhorn's career and listens for queer collaboration and arranging in the making of the *The Peaceful Side* (1961). This unusual LP project took place during a single overnight session with Strayhorn at the piano playing arrangements of his favorite original compositions accompanied by bass (Michel Goudret), a string quartet (Paris String Quartet), and vocal choir (Paris Blue Notes). According to producer Alan Douglas, Strayhorn conceived the album "as something very introspective. He wanted to create an atmosphere and a mood and a place to go that was just quiet and alone but still complex and intelligent and mysterious."[47] Previous commentary on this recording has focused on its novelty as a solo Strayhorn effort, or what it conveys (or fails to convey) about Strayhorn's creative individuality. Yet Douglas's remembrance suggests a more conceptual register, a kind of collaborative soundscape merging notions of personal voice and modernist affect through the sensorium of a particular studio environment. Through considering the interaction of personal, social, aesthetic, and technological dimensions, I explore issues of queer collaboration in the making of *The Peaceful Side* and situate the recording within trends in the production of modern jazz during this period.

In many respects, the early 1960s gives us the best view of what we might call a public Strayhorn. In addition to the collaborative musical projects he undertook in Paris, during this period Strayhorn was also deeply engaged as both an artist and activist in the civil rights movement.[48] He also participated in at least five interviews, three of them extended solo interviews. These interviews challenge dominant narratives and images of Strayhorn as Ellington's dutiful, self-effacing, queer silent partner—what I would call Strayhorn's historiographical "invisibility blues."

The portrait of Billy Strayhorn that emerges in these chapters is not meant to be a definitive or complete accounting of its subject; rather, like Strayhorn's multidimensional arranging ethos itself, my portrait is meant to be generative and interactive. Returning to the metaphors of arranging and/as portraiture that I engaged at the outset, the varied material and archival arrangements I present and the arguments I pursue listen for queer collaborative histories and repertoires in the Strayhorn archive, a listening that itself is inspired by Strayhorn's directive to "see all around the material." In doing so, *Queer Arrangements* offers a new critical vantage point from which to examine jazz history and culture at midcentury and, more broadly, the complex relationships between social identities (race, sexuality, gender) and arrangement, composition, and collaboration in twentieth-century music. My project opens up a space for understanding Strayhorn as a versatile musician whose creative work pushes against the grain of canonical constructions of the category of jazz and therefore demands a more capacious historicized jazz frame. Indeed, Strayhorn's queer arrangements allow us to envision jazz arrangement as an alternate historiography.[49] By looking at midcentury jazz through the instrument(s) of Strayhorn's queer arrangements, we can see—and hear—jazz collaboration queerly and differently.

PART I
Working Behind the Scenes
Gender, Sexuality, and Collaboration in Strayhorn's Vocal Arrangements

ONE
Arriving by "Flamingo"

> We looked at each other, clasped hands. He sat down in the seat and
> I loved him. We became each other's alter egos. We were both at that time
> necessary to other people, me as a provider, Billy as Duke's collaborator.
> But when we were together we were free of all that . . . It was Lena and Billy,
> Billy and Lena. Everything we thought and said to each other made sense—
> and I began to talk, and it poured out of me. I was talking about me instead
> of being told about me. I could only tell it to Billy and he to me.
> I had a friend.
>
> *Lena Horne remembers Billy Strayhorn*

The ostensible topic of part 1—Strayhorn's vocal arranging—is also a journey through Strayhorn's varied relationships with singers. One relationship anchors this journey: Horne–Strayhorn. The epigraph shows how Lena Horne chose to remember the story of her first encounter and close personal bond with Strayhorn, her self-described "soulmate." Given my focus on listening for collaborative creativity and jazz intimacy in the expressive registers of song arrangements, Horne's remembrance holds a singular resonance, as a kind of song in itself, with moments of lyricism and sly comment. By the time Horne shared her memories with Strayhorn's biographer, David Hajdu, in the 1980s, she would have heard countless invocations of the Strayhorn-as-Ellington's-alter-ego trope; this is what makes her appropriation of and alternative riff on the image all the more remarkable, a move that subversively replaces Ellington to center their partnership, a partnership defined through an ethics of deep care, mutual support, and freedom. This freedom pointed in multiple directions—the freedom from feelings of personal and professional "misfit" in relation to heteropatriarchal codes of race, gender, and sexuality; freedom from their positions as "necessary to other people"; and freedom to be understood and feel an authentic sense of self through each other. In all these ways, Horne's narrative, her song to Strayhorn, is emblematic of the merging of the social and musical, personal and professional in Strayhorn's vocal arranging—a queer collaborative intimacy—that I explore in the first part of the book.

Horne described Strayhorn as a "perfect mixture of man and woman," "very strong," and "at the same time very sensitive and gentle."[1] When Horne first met Strayhorn, he was "sent" by Ellington to "keep her company": "Duke could be very possessive with women . . . so he arranged for Billy to be my chaperone. He assumed that Billy was safe, which I guess he was in the way that Duke saw me, which was as a sex object."[2] Horne credited her work with Strayhorn around this time as a formative experience in her musical training, helping her to discover her own voice: "Billy rehearsed me. He stretched me vocally. Very subtly . . . He knew what songs were right for me. He knew my personality better than I did . . . and he wrote arrangements that had my feeling in the music."[3]

Horne's remembrances of Strayhorn align strongly with the broadly held perception of Strayhorn-as-collaborator. As we shall see, these perceptions pervade the retrospective comments of many other singers (and a host of instrumentalists) with whom he worked. Here and elsewhere, I want to highlight the gendered contours of Horne's statements not only for the paths of musical meaning to which they direct us, but also for how they might connect to what film scholar Matthew Tinkcom has called in a rather different, but not unrelated, context the "queer labor" of gay male artists working behind the scenes in the US film industry.[4] In Tinkcom's work, this group includes auteur directors, songwriters, arrangers, art directors, and choreographers. Throughout his career, descriptions of Strayhorn's practices as a collaborator resonate with the title phrase of Tinkcom's book, *Working Like a Homosexual*. Tinkcom borrows this phrase from an observation made by Lela Simone, a rehearsal pianist and vocal coach who worked with stage and film director Vincente Minnelli and the legendary Arthur Freed Unit at Metro-Goldwyn-Mayer (MGM) in the 1940s and 1950s. Recalling Minnelli's working persona in a 1990 interview, Simone explained, "Vincente was not a man who was a dictator. He tried to do it in a soft and nice way. He worked in let's say . . . I don't know whether you will understand what I say . . . he worked like a homosexual."[5]

In her autobiography, Horne counted Minnelli as one of her few true allies at MGM, and her descriptions of Minnelli's sensibilities and the qualities that drew her to him resonate strongly with her remembrances of Strayhorn. According to Horne's biographer James Gavin, Minnelli "had many of the qualities that had drawn Horne to Billy Strayhorn—a soft voice, a refined air, a love of books and fine food."[6] Horne praised Minnelli in strikingly similar terms ("so wise, so ingenious, so sensitive") and described her personal bond with him as deeply connected to their shared feelings of being East Coast/New York exiles and "misfits" at MGM.[7] Horne also expressed very similar perceptions of queer Freed Unit composers and arrangers, Arthur Freed and Roger Edens: "Arthur Freed and Roger Edens were men of a certain sensitivity, and as long as I worked with them I was treated with great decency and respect."[8] In fact, it was through Horne's Hollywood network that Strayhorn came into contact with prominent white gay Broadway and Hollywood luminaries such as the Freed, Edens, and Arthur Laurents, also a close personal friend of Horne's.[9] According to Horne, Strayhorn encountered Edens at Horne's home in 1942 around the time that Horne was cast in her first big starring role in the Black-cast musical *Cabin in the Sky*, directed by Minnelli, and which is also significant for featuring the Ellington Orchestra.[10] Just months prior, Horne was famously "discovered" by Edens, who attended her debut engagement at Felix Young's nightclub, the Little Troc. This was an engagement that Strayhorn, in his roles as vocal coach and arranger, helped Horne prepare for.

Tinkcom argues that Simone's (and here, Horne's) statement about Minnelli "encourages us to theorize the possibility of a capitalist enterprise accommodating marginalized sex/gender subjects because their labor could enhance a product's appeal through its differentiated style."[11] Working behind the scenes as a vocal arranger in the Ellington organization, Strayhorn similarly cultivated a "differentiated style," and my aim in this part is to explore this "differentiated style" in relation to the conditions under which Strayhorn labored, that is in relation to his collaborative relationships (interpersonal, improvisatory, intimate) with singers and to his aesthetic practices as a vocal arranger. I want to reiterate here that my intention is not to reify Strayhorn as an exceptional Black gay subject in the world of midcentury jazz (or, accordingly, to reproduce an undifferentiated homo/hetero binary) but to describe and analyze specific collaborative situations and instances of queer affiliation, affect, and identifications surrounding Strayhorn's work as a vocal arranger and ask how such instances mark, enact, or embody a sociality of arranging.

Strayhorn's vocal arranging oeuvre is extensive and varied, stretching from his hip, swinging charts for Ivie Anderson in the late 1930s and early 1940s to lush, ethereal backings for Ella Fitzgerald in the late 1950s. My analyses of Strayhorn's vocal arranging archive is organized around four case studies and their varied historical, social, personal, and musical contexts. The first of these case studies examines Strayhorn's "differentiated style" through a deep dive into the queer histories of Strayhorn's hit vocal arrangement of the popular song "Flamingo" for singer Herb Jeffries in 1941. Where this case study prioritizes queer contexts and historical resonance in Strayhorn's aesthetic practices as a vocal arranger from his early years in the Ellington Orchestra, the other three case studies focus on Strayhorn's work with female singers on the production of midcentury jazz vocal LPs. Specifically, I consider Strayhorn's work with Lena Horne as an arranger, composer, accompanist, and vocal coach, highlighting their collaborative efforts in and outside the recording studio in 1955. Strayhorn's work with Horne was followed up by two substantial vocal arranging LP projects with the Ellington band: his work with Rosemary Clooney for the LP *Blue Rose* (1956) and his arranging for Ella Fitzgerald for *Ella Fitzgerald Sings the Duke Ellington Song Book* (1957). The four case studies explored in part 1 provide a resonant constellation of collaborative relationships and dynamics, working conditions, and historical moments that together move across a bicoastal New York-LA geography and through recording studios, a film set, nightclubs, private Hollywood parties, and domestic spaces. In reflecting on these spaces and places, I listen closely for queer collaborative dynamics at the intersection of the personal, social, and the musical.

FLAMINGO(S)

During Strayhorn's first two years with the organization, 1939 to 1941, his creative partnership with Ellington tended toward a division of musical labor in which Ellington worked out the instrumental sections and Strayhorn the vocal sections.[12] However, this situation changed rapidly. In 1941 Strayhorn co-composed and arranged many of the songs for the celebrated Black Popular Front "revusical" *Jump for Joy*.[13] By 1942 he was responsible for all the vocal arranging and was supervising a roster of singers, including Ivie Anderson (who had been with the orchestra since the early 1930s), Herb Jeffries, Kay Davis, Marie Ellington, and Joya Sherrill.[14]

To the extent that Strayhorn's work during this period revolved around creating arrangements to showcase singers for the legendary Blanton-Webster Band, his work as a vocal arranger—and that of the singers he collaborated with—were viewed largely as "commercial work," a devalued category under which the contributions of women in jazz (especially singers) have historically been marginalized.[15] At once central to the orchestra's commercial appeal yet operating at the margins, Strayhorn negotiated a similar, but in no way identical, gendered field of power as that which structured the position of many of the singers with whom he collaborated.

Notably, Strayhorn's vocal arrangements during this period were rarely recorded, and only a few made it into the Ellington book. One that did stick, and in a big way, was Strayhorn's 1940 arrangement of the Ted Grouya/Edmund Anderson pop song "Flamingo" for the baritone crooner Herb Jeffries.[16] "Flamingo" was a hit for Ellington in 1941, and a career-making song for Jeffries, who in an oft-cited remark proclaimed, "That's the bird that brought me. Most people come to this planet by stork; I came by Flamingo, and Duke Ellington delivered me."[17] Strayhorn recalled, "I think what really clinched the vocal chores for me was when Herb Jeffries came with the band [in 1939]. He was singing in a high tenor range, and I asked him whether he liked singing up there. He said he didn't, so I wrote some things for him that pulled his voice down to the natural baritone he became after 'Flamingo.'"[18] Both Jeffries's and Strayhorn's statements speak to the ways in which their collaboration on "Flamingo" facilitated a creative space in which Jeffries could explore and refashion a vocal persona, one that the singer understood as more natural, conveying a more authentic self. "That's the kind of thing he did with the singers in the band," Jeffries remembered. "He'd work very, very closely with you, and he sensed what your strengths were. Then he picked songs and did arrangements to bring out the best in you."[19] These statements, then, index a collaborative aesthetics for arranging in which the scripts of musical, social, and, personal identification work in tandem.

Yet Strayhorn's remark about Jeffries's transformation via "Flamingo" into a "natural baritone" also reflects, in part, prevailing discourses on gender/culture norms for male pop singers—especially crooners—that emerged in the early 1930s. These discourses arose in conjunction with changes in sound technology, specifically the development of new microphones that allowed for singing close to the mic. In her work on male crooners in the early twentieth century, Allison McCracken observes that the rising stardom of Bing Crosby during this period, as well as that of his rival baritone radio crooner Russ Columbo, "inaugurated the second wave of romantic crooning idols" whose lower vocal range "could be more easily promoted as properly gendered, having not an 'in-between' voice but one that was 'naturally' more potent and masculine than the tenor."[20] These associations arise in Jeffries's remembrances of the moment that led to his vocal transformation: "Backstage, I used to clown around and do some imitations. So one night... I was imitating Bing Crosby, and when Strayhorn heard me he said: 'Oh, I like you in that lower register. That's great. That's the voice I want.'"[21] McCracken's account of Crosby and the "second wave" of crooning is incisive in its analyses of the cultural discourses around voice, gender, and sexuality, demonstrating the ways in which baritone crooning voices came to be perceived as embodying heteronormative white middle-class masculinity. Yet the race-gender-voice calculus implicit in her analyses allow little space for theorizing and historicizing the repertoire, gendered embodiments, and cultural impact of Jeffries and other Black romantic crooners such as Nat "King" Cole and Billy Eckstine.[22] As Vincent L. Stephens observes, irrespective of gendered presentation, Black male popular figures navigating the Jim Crow spectatorial regime during this period all "equivocated in expressing Black male sexuality," a requirement that, he suggests, "made their expressions of masculinity queer insofar as they were discouraged from expressing virility or physical intimacy."[23] What do the historical specificities surrounding Jeffries's performance and collaboration with Strayhorn on "Flamingo" tell us about the entanglements of voice, race, and masculinity in his cultivation of the romantic and sensual Black male balladeer?

Of all the vocalists on the Ellington roster in the early 1940s, Strayhorn felt a special affinity for Jeffries who, like Strayhorn, was an avowed Francophile. The two friends enjoyed conversing in French, particularly in public spaces in which such displays of sophistication could speak back to and trouble anti-Black, racist stereotypes. As Jeffries put it, "There was a tremendous amount of discrimination, and you could show a certain amount of sophistication by the mere fact that you could speak a language that the next white person couldn't. Strayhorn and I both felt this showed you weren't that lowly person, that Amos 'n' Andy character that everybody thought you were."[24]

The registral placement and reorientation of Jeffries's voice in Strayhorn's arrangement of "Flamingo" also performs "a certain amount of sophistication," which can be fully grasped only by hearing how Jeffries's voice interacts and fits in with the musical contexts that surround it—that is, by considering the aesthetics of the arrangement as a whole. As Walter van de Leur details in his brilliant analysis of "Flamingo," Strayhorn's arrangement extends considerably and transforms the original pop song through the addition of new material—nearly a third more material—in the form of elaborate introductory, transitional, and modulatory sections.²⁵ These additions and revisions exemplify Strayhorn's innovative approach to pop tune arrangements in which "carefully worked out introductions, transitions, and codas" are used as "structuring elements to secure the internal logic of an orchestration."²⁶ The introduction for "Flamingo" is a case in point. However, these innovative features also extend to, or are animated through, the registers of affect and style. Strayhorn's newly composed introduction supplies a sonic modernist orchestral gloss on the essential generic topos of the song: Latin-tinged, tropical exotica in the "dreamy" romantic mode. A solo trombone intones the "flamingo" call, a three-note figure encompassing an octave leap upward and minor third down, echoed languidly by the trumpet.

In the next few bars, a chromatically moving theatrical "curtain-rising" passage is answered by a jarringly dissonant swift series of parallel moving saxophone chords. These chords outline notes that are sounded in the closing gesture that directly follows, a repeated, tonally ambiguous low-register brass chord (F minor over D, or dominant tritone substitution). As van de Leur observes, the closing dissonant passages as well as the flamingo call heard in the initial bars serve an expository function: the intervallic design and rhythmic profile of the flamingo call form "one of the arrangement's unifiers" while the

EXAMPLE 1.1 Strayhorn, "Flamingo" (1941). Introduction, measures 1–8.
Transcribed by author.

Arriving by "Flamingo" 33

complex dissonance foreshadows the "tonally ambiguity Strayhorn explores in the arrangement."[27]

Along with Strayhorn's sophisticated harmonic palette, his penchant for creating intricate introductory, bridging, and modulatory design in arrangements has typically been read as a sign of his French-accented modernist classicism. "The rich modern harmonies of the introduction," writes Mark Tucker, "betray the taste of someone who admitted a fondness for Ravel and Debussy."[28] Along similar lines, van de Leur credits the song's arrangement specifically with bringing a new classicism to the Ellington sound, one that departed radically from the conventions of vocal arranging of the time. As he writes, the "liquidity of its caesura-less arrangement, its structuring elements, the sophisticated modulations and integrated introductory, transitory and closing sections . . . make 'Flamingo' unique in the jazz writing of its time."[29] Van de Leur's insights echo Ellington himself, who proclaimed the arrangement "a turning point in vocal background orchestration, a renaissance in elaborate ornamentation for the accompaniment of singers."[30]

I would like to extend these comments about Strayhorn's signature classicism in a queer direction, first by returning to a path suggested by Tinkcom's model of "queer style enhancements." As mentioned at the outset, Tinkcom argues that the opulent and glamorous camp stylizations of Freed Unit production numbers for the classic MGM film musicals (what he calls "camp encodings") constituted an "extra-added labor" on the film's narrative texts, one that indexed the "emerging presence of queer metropolitan subcultures in shaping mass taste and aesthetic sensibilities."[31] In doing so, Tinkcom rethinks the visual and sonic stylistic markers of camp—artifice, excess, and performance—from the perspective of production. Camp thus functions for Tinkcom as both a form of queer labor *and* as affect or style, a coupling of social and aesthetic modes that shows "how queer subjectivity emerges within the dynamics of capitalist cultural production for audiences that extend well beyond queer male subcultures."[32] Insofar as Strayhorn's creative labor as a vocal arranger was in fact the arena in which he would most explicitly have been required to negotiate his ideas and sensibility with the popular song as commodity, Tinkcom's theory has special pertinence. However, questions arise in applying Tinkcom's model of the Freed Unit's camp sensibility to the differently located affective world of Strayhorn's "style enhancements" in an arrangement such as "Flamingo." Put another way, are the lavish camp stylizations (or "encodings") created by a privileged group of white gay male artists working for big-budget Hollywood musicals a relevant point of comparison for hearing—queerly or otherwise—Strayhorn's African American jazz-based classicisms? Yes and no. Certainly there was a considerable amount of traffic (and cultural resonance) between New York-based entertainment (e.g., Broadway and Harlem revues) and Hollywood staff composers and arrangers, but this traffic gravitated toward de facto white-only routes.[33]

Nevertheless, an argument can be made for a camp hearing, or perhaps a queerly signifyn' one, of Strayhorn's sophisticated, elaborate orchestral gloss on the popular song's cliché romantic tropical tropes. In the A-strain of the vocal chorus, this comes through the lilting melody, the beguine-like beat in the staccato brass accompaniment, and the modal sound created by major/minor mixture. Also notable here is the affect of Strayhorn's stylized orchestral additions, such as the opening "flamingo" trombone call passage with its dramatically held half-diminished seventh sax chord on the downbeat and exaggerated trumpet echo, and an almost over-the-top moment of word painting that occurs in the opening bars of the bridge—also in the form of an echo that references the melodic contour of the opening echo. As Jeffries croons through an octave leap in the first two words of the line "The wind (sings a song to you as you go)," the saxophone section sounds an undulating "wind" motive that sweeps rapidly upward, lingers for a half-measure, then languidly drops back down (example 1.2). Another stylized highlight comes through the ethereal, erotic, yet restrained affect of Jeffries's vocalese during the arrangement's most formally breathtaking addition, an elaborate thirty-bar transition section that moves through a series of complex modulations derived from the source song's material.[34] This part of the arrangement, which does not appear in Strayhorn's written arrangement, arose spontaneously during the recording session when Strayhorn directed the singer to improvise: "Do that 'Oh, oh' in there, and do that modulation down through it."[35] Even Lawrence Brown's trombone solo receives a sensuous vocal embroidery as Jeffries interjects the flamingo call in the middle of his chorus, as if whispering in the ear of the listener.

Taken together, the song's sophisticated harmonic design, complex architecture, programmatic simulations, dreamy "Oh, oh" vocal stylizations, and exotic signifiers would seem to resonate with some of the sonic idioms of camp—minus the strings—showcased in Freed Unit/MGM production numbers, as well as the ways in which such stylistic discourse served the demands of the Hollywood fantasy industry. Yet a theory of camp from the perspective of production such as Tinkcom's depends on the potentially problematic claim of ironic intent, and, as Lloyd Whitesell has argued, stylistic extravagance does not need to be ironic

EXAMPLE 1.2 Strayhorn, "Flamingo" (1941). Bridge, measures 17–24. Transcribed by author.

to count as queer.[36] Whitesell's work on glamour and stylistic extravagance in the Hollywood musical helps to clarify this queer interpretive line both for its careful theoretical framing and for its specific historical pertinence. That is, Whitesell considers an iconic number from the Freed Unit, one whose elaborate design and sonic tropes provide a particularly resonant counterpoint to "Flamingo": Leo Arnaud and Connie Salinger's arrangement for Tony Martin's crooning of the pop song "You Stepped Out of a Dream," which was featured in the hit 1941 backstage musical *Ziegfeld Girl*. The song, composed by Nacio Herb Brown with lyrics by Gus Kahn, was published the same year—1940—that Strayhorn arranged "Flamingo." Big band recordings soon followed, most notably sides by Glenn Miller (singer Ray Eberle) and Kay Kyser (singer Harry Babbitt), whose version

36 *Working Behind the Scenes*

had a modest success, reaching number twenty-two on the charts. However, it was the film version of the song, released in April 1941—just as "Flamingo" was flying high on the popular song charts—that had the far greater and lasting pop-cultural impact.

Arnaud and Salinger's arrangement of "You Stepped Out of a Dream" propels the musical's first big production number, a Busby Berkeley walk-down extravaganza showcasing the Ziegfeld female triumvirate of Lana Turner, Judy Garland, and Hedy Lamarr. As with "Flamingo," "You Stepped Out of a Dream" projects an air of sophistication and debonair charm, delivered by the suave crooning of a male baritone(ish) singer in a languorous low-medium tempo/groove. Both arrangements feature complex pop song formal architecture, lush harmonic backings, and ornate sonic detailing in service of a lyric extolling the intoxicating potential of luxuriant fantasy and yearning for a feminine object of desire. In both cases, these affects are projected with touches of exotica; in "You Stepped Out of a Dream" this comes in the form of a modulation into unabashed sonic exotica that cues Hedy Lamarr's walk-down turn.

With its Latin-tinged groove and luxe modernist jazz stylings, however, "Flamingo" can be heard as a camp comment on precisely the kind of extravagant Freed Unit pop confection that is "You Stepped Out of a Dream."[37] But this idea begs that question of camp posture in "You Stepped Out of a Dream"; indeed, the visual and sonic stylistic excesses and over-the-top performances of femininity in the number seem ready-made for camp interpretation. As Whitesell puts it, the number's "ultrafemme quality in so stylized a form is bound to trigger a camp response in modern viewers." Yet Whitesell, like Tinkcom, focuses on the production front, and rejects the possibility of queer critique via an ironizing perspective or posture. Whitesell argues that "in its time this kind of hyperbole carried the force of an ideal . . . Womanhood was elevated to a peak of virtue and attractiveness by heightening the aesthetic impact of the display to impossible degrees . . . The performers in this number never drop their careful bodily and facial comportment; they sustain the expressive ideal by maintaining a perfect façade."[38] The sonic extravagances of Salinger's orchestral arrangement support and amplify this heightened display of white femininity.

Although ironized intention and camp possibility in this instance are foreclosed, Whitesell advocates importantly for other forms and modes of queer creativity—principally queer postures of aestheticism—as a framework to connect stylistic extravagance to queer subjectivity.[39] As he argues, this "dedication to pure, extravagant style for its own sake" enables a queer subject to retreat from or escape a "stigmatized position in reality to a perfect world governed by abstract aesthetic rules."[40] What of "Flamingo?" The evidence for a (Black) queer ironic posture in Strayhorn's arrangement of "Flamingo" is at once elusive and compelling. It is helpful here to set it alongside other Strayhorn vocal arrangements of standards from this period—arrangements of notably more weighty songbook fare. These include his arrangements of "Where or When" (Rodgers and Hart), "The Man I Love" (George and Ira Gershwin), "I'll Remember April" (de Paul/Johnston/Raye), "Skylark" (Mercer/Carmichael), and "Lover Man" (Davis/Ramirez/Sherman; Strayhorn's arrangement was written in 1945, as Billie Holiday's version was charting).[41] All of these arrangements stand out, like "Flamingo," for their formal and affective sophistication, sensuousness, and complexity; however, unlike "Flamingo" they unambiguously project a serious nonironic posture, one that resonates strongly with Whitesell's category of queer sonic aestheticism. An argument could be made that this point of difference conveys differences in Strayhorn's aesthetic regard for the original materials, that he attached a higher artistic stature to the work of Rodgers/Hart, the Gershwins, and others.

Of these arrangements, Strayhorn's inspired take on the romantic déjà vu song "Where or When" seems particularly pertinent. Its dreamy introduction moves through extended modulatory passages, and its unorthodox/irregular phrase lengths create a beguiling sonic narrative that perfectly captures the erotic overtones of uncanny encounter evoked in the lyric. The arrangement's sense of narrative is most dramatically projected in the elegance and sophistication of the design: a kind of sonic parallel of the aforementioned film musical walk-down number, a sequence of entrances with solo instrumental voices and instrumental choirs taking turns as they "alternately emerge from and submerge into the orchestral background."[42] Another innovative feature of this chart is an unusual midform modulation that, as van de Leur observes, effectively creates "a ternary form" in which the middle section acts as "a miniature development of the work's musical material."[43] These features can also work to heighten the queer registers and queer afterlife of Hart's lyric, which can be heard as giving furtive voice to illicit desire. (Hart, a tortured, closeted gay man, lived a double life.[44]) The varied background rhythmic figuration in brass—a characteristic feature of Strayhorn's vocal arranging oeuvre—enhance the sense of yearning, passion, and illusive feelings.

In sum, as with "Flamingo," Strayhorn's arrangement of "Where or When" exhibits a jazz modernist blend of sophistication, sensuousness, and refinement but with serious affect, investment in the emotional depth and erotic possibilities of the lyric, all of which connect this arrangement to the bittersweet queer expressive beauty of Strayhorn's original songs.[45] For the moment I will defer the question of camp and "Flamingo" to pursue a different story of queer affiliation between a film musical production number and Strayhorn's arrangement(s), one that places "Flamingo" on the stages of minor Hollywood studio.

This story begins on January 3, 1941, the day the Ellington Orchestra kicked off a West Coast tour with a seven-week gig at the Casa Mañana Ballroom. Thus also began Strayhorn's encounter with white and Black Hollywood from 1941 to 1942. "He got into the whole exotic trip of the West Coast," Jeffries remembered. "It was a kind of mecca to us—all the glamour . . . Strayhorn bought into all that."[46] A highlight of Strayhorn's Hollywood experience was the opportunity to attend celebrity parties. About three weeks into the Casa Mañana gig, Strayhorn accompanied Ellington to one such party at the Hollywood home of Sid Kuller, an MGM "gag writer." The two were invited back the following weekend along with other members of the Ellington Orchestra. According to Hajdu, it was at this party that Strayhorn met and befriended Lana Turner, arguably the most "glorified" of the three Ziegfeld girls to take her walk-down in "You Stepped Out of a Dream." Turner recalled that she danced with Ellington band drummer/percussionist Sonny Greer: "He was cute . . . but not as cute as Billy, but he [Billy] wouldn't dance with me. That was okay. We talked and became great friends."[47] The details and extent of their friendship is not known; however, sometime in 1944, Strayhorn composed a trumpet concerto, eponymously titled "Lana Turner." This instrumental portrait of the star conjures a very different sonic take on her trademark glamour and "sexy ordinary" image: a warm and sensuous midtempo swing arrangement infused with sophistication, a restrained bluesy lyricism, and an affectionate touch of the burlesque.[48]

That Saturday night Hollywood party would hold far greater significance for music history: it was there that Kuller and Ellington first discussed working together on a music-theater project. This project was quickly realized as the groundbreaking "revusical" *Jump for Joy*, which premiered at the Mayan Theater in the summer of 1941. In many ways, the opportunity to collaborate on *Jump for Joy* represented the artistic culmination of Strayhorn's glamour year in Hollywood. Yet, during the last two months of 1941, after the close of *Jump for Joy*, Strayhorn's arrangement of "Flamingo" was given filmic realization as one of five Ellington soundies produced by a Hollywood-based company (RCM) that was then managed primarily by the songwriter Sam Coslow (of Cotton Club fame).

These soundies enabled Strayhorn to work behind the scenes as an arranger in the Hollywood film industry.[49]

A short-lived phenomenon of the early 1940s, soundies were three-minute, low-budget performance films made for coin-operated automated viewing machines—or "visual jukeboxes"—primarily under the trade name Panorams. RCM and other film production companies marketed soundies in reels containing eight different film segments, which together formed a *Soundies Miniature Revue*. Customers paid ten cents per soundie, but had no choice as to which of the eight possible segments—or part of the revue—they would see. Like jukeboxes, Panorams operated in entertainment spaces such as bars and amusement parlors, as well as the lobbies of upscale hotels and theaters.[50]

Klaus Stratemann's detailed commentary on the Ellington soundies, all of which were directed by Josef Berne, categorizes "Flamingo" as the "exotic dance number" in *Soundies Miniature Revue*, No. 1049 (seventh position), sandwiched between two patriotic numbers. This reel, which was released in January 1942, also featured Ellington's "Bli-Blip" from *Jump for Joy*, with Marie Bryant and Paul White.[51] The "exotic dancing" in "Flamingo" is delivered by Janet Collins and Talley Beatty in two quasi-narrative dance sequences set in a generic Afro-Caribbean "tropical" mise-en-scène. This secondary footage is intercut with Jeffries and the Ellington Orchestra performing "Flamingo" on a studio-constructed "nightclub" stage. Stratemann, along with virtually every other source on this soundie, identifies Collins and Beatty as "two members from Katherine Dunham's famous black dance troupe."[52] Although Janet Collins, who would a decade later become the first African American prima ballerina to be hired into the corps of the New York Metropolitan Opera Ballet, probably was not dancing for Dunham at the time the soundie was filmed, she had performed in her company for a brief period that year. Talley Beatty, however, was in fact a principal dancer with Dunham, and one of a number of gay male members of her troupe, a group that included Dunham's frequent on-stage partner Archie Savage, who was also associated with the queer interracial social circle around Carl Van Vechten.[53] Indeed, this queer connection is enshrined in the Van Vechten archive, as evidenced in his 1942 portraits of Dunham and Savage (his images of Savage are explicitly homoerotic).

According to dance historian Susan Manning (by way of George Chauncey), the Dunham Company was a center for gay life in Harlem during the 1940s and 1950s. Gordon Heath, a Black gay actor, for example, characterized Dunham's productions as "the highest prancing camp in the business."[54] Manning argues that Dunham's particular amalgam of techniques from classical ballet and modern dance with Black Atlantic vernacular and Africanist dance forms "presented legibly queer images for gay spectators."[55] She develops her argument with reference to the type of images and movements featured in Dunham's early 1940s breakthrough program *Tropics and Le Jazz "Hot,"* which premiered at the Windsor Theatre in New York to critical and popular acclaim. The middle section of this work, "Tropics" (subtitled "Shore Excursions" and set in Martinique), featured Dunham dancing in her celebrated "Woman with Cigar" role; one critic described the scenario as Dunham "meets dockhand and flirts with him and his companions."[56] The dockhand in question was danced by the aforementioned Archie Savage. Through their association with Dunham's troupe during this period and through the influence of Dunham's work (as evidenced in aspects of dance technique, the scenario, and costuming), Beatty's and Collins's work in the soundie's dance sequences links up to this queerly inflected choreographic discourse of stylistic and stylized fusion. It is highly unlikely, however, that Dunham had a direct hand in the choreography for the soundie. While she was on the West Coast at this time, having just finished a cross-country tour of *Cabin in the Sky* (in fact, Ellington is reported to have attended a November performance of the LA run), the fees that would have been incurred for both the Ellington Orchestra and Dunham were almost certainly beyond the limited budgets of soundie productions. In any case, the sequences themselves were not substantial enough to require her participation or presence. More likely, the choreography versioned a night club act that Collins and Beatty toured during the early 1940s. (They billed themselves as "Rea and Rico DeGard.")[57]

Yet a queer reading of the dance sequences is perhaps most convincingly secured through its placement in and interaction with Strayhorn's arrangement. Indeed, the larger visual, choreographic, and sonic assemblage in the soundie, as well as details of the editing work, actually heighten the arrangement's registers of stylistic extravagance and classicisms discussed previously. For example, in the second vocal chorus, we see a series of striking close-ups of Jeffries and Ellington, initiated through a frontal close-up of Jeffries as he croons the flamingo call. The camera then cuts quickly to a close-up of Ellington: he smiles, eyes sparkling, gazing admiringly at Jeffries. Our gaze replaces Ellington's as the camera cuts back to Jeffries for the line, "For it's you I rely on, and a love that is true"; the dramatic visual frontality of this image coupled with Jeffries's suave crooning and handsome, urbane visage, gives a special charge to this part of the arrangement, amplifying the aura of sophistication, cool sensuality, and exotic-romantic fantasy.

FIGURE 1.1A Still from "Flamingo" (1941).
Jeffries, frontal close-up.

FIGURE 1.1B Still from "Flamingo" (1941).
Ellington gazes at Jeffries.

FIGURE 1.2 Stills from "Flamingo" (1941). Collins and Beatty's pas de deux.

At the bridge, the camera crosscuts from its close-up on Jeffries to Collins: she is clad in an ornate, ruffle-laden Caribbean dress and bandana and is balancing a large tray of fruit with one hand. On the plain white backdrop behind her we see a somewhat menacing shadow of a giant flamingo. In sync with Jeffries's octave leap on the words "the wind," Collins arches her back and sweeps her arm melodramatically over her head, heightening the already theatrical affect of the wind motive. The camera pulls back to reveal a tiny and bare patch of "beach" upon which we see Beatty dressed as a native "sailor" or dockhand replete with head wrap, a striped shirt with a pattern of circular cut-outs, and loose cropped white pants. In the dance sequence that ensues, the longest and most substantial of the two, Collins and Beatty perform an erotic barefoot pas de deux. The first part of the sequence lasts from the bridge through the intricate "Oh, Oh" modulatory/transition section: in it they dance slowly around each other, with undulating, swaying hip movements and other choreographic gestures associated with Afro-Caribbean and African American vernacular and theater dance. At one point, Collins lifts the billowy, sheer white "picnic" cloth off the ground and wraps it seductively around her body as she writhes and undulates around in a kind of brief Salome-esque veil dance.

For the trombone solo, the choreography shifts stylistic gears and the two dancers present an extended ballet sequence: Beatty executes a series of quick turns (chaînés) around Collins punctuated by delicate jumps (sissone) and leg extensions, while Collins continues her undulating hip movements. The two

Arriving by "Flamingo" 43

dancers then perform variation-like exchanges of turns, jumps, and leg extensions such as attitude and arabesque. As the trombone solo moves toward the cadence, Collins and Beatty slowly drop to their knees, arching their torsos back to the ground into an extreme limbo position. This ends the sequence and the camera crosscuts back to the performance just as alto saxophonist Johnny Hodges stands to take his solo. As we shall see in chapter 3, the move to Hodges, indeed the choice to feature Hodges in this arrangement, initiates another queer collaborative register, one that reflects Strayhorn's special attachment to Hodges's improvising voice.

My reading of the soundie as a scene of collaboration brings together bodies, sounds, and movements that make legible an historical network of Black gay cultural production, community, and art worlds. This network of queer affiliation coexisted within and was obviously shaped by the larger worlds of Black entertainment that flourished on the peripheries of Hollywood in the early 1940s, the same networks that would, just one month prior to the soundie production, bring together Strayhorn and Lena Horne. As I chronicle in the following chapter, their professional and personal relationship traverse pathways of queer collaboration, ones that center gender-expansive forms of jazz intimacy and co-creativity.

TWO

Difficult Beauty

In 1993, at the age of seventy-six, Lena Horne performed at the JVC Jazz Festival for a program called *A Tribute to Billy Strayhorn: Lena Horne Sings for Swee'pea*. It was her first significant public performance since the close of her extraordinary one-woman autobiographical musical revue, *Lena Horne: The Lady and Her Music*, in 1981. At the JVC Jazz Festival performance, Horne was backed by a band led by Mercer Ellington, featuring Bobby Short and Joe Henderson—all musicians with close connections to Strayhorn and his music. According to her biographer James Gavin, Horne had turned down a string of prior invitations from festival director George Wein. Despite her deep reservations, Horne felt compelled to perform as a tribute to Strayhorn: "I came out for Billy."[1] As an opener for the performance, she sang "Maybe," a song Strayhorn wrote for her that was also featured as an opener on the 1961 LP *Lena at the Sands* (Live). The JVC concert precipitated a remarkable string of new projects over the following years, the centerpiece of which was a Blue Note studio recording, *We'll Be Together Again*. The album's liner notes describe her chosen repertoire as "intimate messages . . . to lost friends and family, most of all Strayhorn, her closest friend and soulmate." For this memorial LP, Horne included five Strayhorn originals: "Maybe," "Something to Live For," "Love Like This Can't Last," "A Flower Is a Lovesome Thing," and "You're the One" (another of Strayhorn's custom songs for Horne). Writing of "A Flower Is a Lovesome Thing," which she learned after Strayhorn's death, Horne explained, "It's difficult, but it's *so* beautiful . . . The words he uses, his changes. I saw the whole picture."[2] In 1996 Horne rerecorded three of these Strayhorn songs again for her *American Masters* documentary, *Lena Horne: In Her Own Voice*. These recordings were movingly rearranged for an intimate small group with pianist Geri Allen and saxophonist Joe Lovano. In the studio, synthesized strings were added to the mix.

What might be called the posthumous archive of the Horne-Strayhorn collaboration is substantial: a deep repository of memories, feelings, and attachments embodied in Horne's voice, her choice of repertoire, and her engagement with and performances of Strayhorn's original songs. However, material documenting their collaboration during Strayhorn's lifetime is sparse, comprising, in addition to Horne's 1965 autobiography, the following: a few press reviews from several Chicago engagements they did together early in 1955, and a handful of sides recorded over six months, from March to July 1955, for the RCA Victor label (under the direction of Lennie Hayton). One of these tracks was the song Horne featured on *We'll Be Together Again*, "You're the One." The archival scarcity of the Horne-Strayhorn collaboration makes it an elusive music-historical object. Yet I contend that Horne's posthumous musical tributes to Strayhorn and, importantly, her concept of these performances as a mode of sonic remembrance, care, and intimate, spiritual connection, offers a useable guide for accessing this elusive past. On this point, I'm drawn to her evocation of Strayhorn's gorgeous Black queer modernist ballad "A Flower Is a Lovesome Thing": a "difficult" but "so beautiful" arrangement of "words" and "changes" through which she perceived a "whole picture." Horne's conjoining of the words "difficult" and "beautiful" resonates toward the expressive and formal registers of Strayhorn's song and, by extension, to the power of songs to contain worlds and connect or transport us to the past.

The mixture of difficulty and beauty that Horne summons in her description of "A Flower Is a Lovesome Thing" can also be heard as a kind of metonym for the historical and biographical contexts and feelings that shaped the Horne-Strayhorn collaboration. Throughout her 1965 autobiography, *Lena*, and in numerous interviews, Horne eloquently names and reflects on these contexts and feelings. In the epigraph that opens chapter 1, for example, Horne explained her relationship with Strayhorn as enabling deep forms of human connection, understanding, and communication that provided a space of freedom from social expectations and personal obligations: "When we were together we were free . . . Everything we thought and said to each other made sense . . . I was talking about me instead of being told about me."[3] These reflections on her relationship with Strayhorn—and the gender-expansive forms of jazz intimacy their relationship activated—echo in her interpretation of "A Flower Is a Lovesome Thing," which she described as an "ode to natural physical beauty, from someone who could appreciate something beautiful without needing to possess it."[4] Here, the conceptual and musical power of Horne's homage to Strayhorn sits alongside her post-1960s archive of Black feminist sound and thought.

This sense of intersubjective affirmation, understanding, and freedom was inseparable from and, indeed, provided the framework for their musical and professional collaborations. Summarizing the qualities of Horne's relationship with Strayhorn, Gavin writes, "But no one, not even [her spouse] Lennie Hayton, made her feel safer than Billy Strayhorn. His voice, firm but soothing, calmed her when she was ready to break. They could finish each other's sentences or sit together for hours and hardly talk. Strayhorn stayed in the room while she put on her makeup; if there was a piano there he played it."[5] Implied in Gavin's reference to Horne's feelings of safety and connection with Strayhorn are the ways in which their personal and musical relationship acted as a crucial refuge in and through difficult times and circumstances. In 1993 she recalled this aspect of her relationship with Strayhorn, telling a reporter for the *Los Angeles Sentinel*: "Every time there's a musical crisis in my life, I dream about Billy. He comes in the dream."[6] As well, Horne's autobiography chronicles with great power and insight how networks of professional support (close friends, family, collaborators) enabled her to survive the pain, isolation, and daily indignities of performing as a Black woman across the color line in the era of Jim Crow.[7]

The image Gavin gives us also calls attention to the significance of small acts, intimate socialities, and safe spaces—a soothing voice, hours spent together in silence, backstage companionship, a played piano. Such small acts are crucial for creating forms of trust and connection vital to collaborative relationships and practices. Here the Horne-Strayhorn partnership—its multifaceted difficult beauty—stands as both a starting point and a conceptual guide for exploring jazz intimacy and collaborative histories in Strayhorn's vocal arranging projects. This chapter looks at Strayhorn's relationship to and arranging for three "star" midcentury jazz singers: Lena Horne, Rosemary Clooney, and Ella Fitzgerald. I first trace intersecting paths of personal and professional support and musical intimacy in Strayhorn's work with Horne as an arranger, composer, accompanist, and vocal coach, focusing on their collaborations in and outside the recording studio in 1955. Strayhorn's work with Horne was followed up by two substantial vocal arranging LP projects with the Ellington band: Strayhorn's collaboration with Rosemary Clooney for the LP *Blue Rose* (1956) and his arranging for Ella Fitzgerald for *Ella Fitzgerald Sings the Duke Ellington Song Book* (1958). My analyses of these projects aim to identify and think through how different social, musical, and interpersonal histories and scripts came to bear on Strayhorn's collaborative work with Horne, Clooney, and Fitzgerald and how these collaborations either imagined and practiced new forms of gendered relationships or revised old ones. Indeed, the three collaborative relationships, and the contrasting moments of (queer) collaborative dynamics they prompted, underscore how jazz intimacy is performed across formations of race, gender, and sexuality. In highlighting the intersections of the social, interpersonal, and musical in jazz collaboration, my analyses of these diverse collaborations also expand historical narratives around the production of popular vocal jazz LPs in the mid-twentieth century through closely attending to the types of gendered relationships these collaborations archive.

IT'S LOVE

The Horne-Strayhorn relationship occupies a unique space in the biographies of both artists, at once central and peripheral to the jazz narrative told about their lives and careers. Origin stories are (as always) particularly telling in this regard, and for Horne-Strayhorn that story began in Los Angeles during the intermission of *Jump for Joy* at the Mayan Theater in November 1941. Their bond was immediate and intense: in the weeks following, they kept constant company as Horne, with the support of Strayhorn, prepared for her debut auditions and performing engagements in LA. In this support role, Strayhorn served as Horne's accompanist and vocal coach, helping her to shape and refine her sound. As she remembered, "I wasn't a born singer . . . I had to learn a lot. Billy rehearsed me. He stretched me vocally. Very subtly, he made me stretch—he raised keys on me without telling me. He taught me the basics of music . . . He went around with me to auditions and played piano for me. I was terrified, but he kept me calm and made me good."[8]

One performance engagement that Strayhorn and Horne worked collaboratively to prepare for looms large in Horne's Hollywood story: her breakout gig at nightclub impresario Felix Young's newly opened establishment, the Little Troc.[9] As a venue, the Little Troc was a considerably scaled-down version of Young's initial plan for a lavish Hollywood nightclub called the Trocadero, which was to feature a debut revue showcasing Horne. (It failed to materialize due to the outbreak of World War II.) The show at the Little Troc, which premiered in January 1942, also featured dancers Talley Beatty and Katherine Dunham, who opened for Horne. The special closeness between Horne and Strayhorn was apparent to Beatty, who later recalled, "Billy and Lena were working together in her dressing room, which was really a closet. They were right up against each other, but it didn't matter to them. They only needed the space of one person, they were so close."[10]

Strayhorn and Horne collaborated to compile her set list for the show. This new list combined Horne's established nightclub repertoire, which she had developed during her New York/East Coast engagements (most famously for her performances at Barney Josephson's Café Society), alongside new material. The latter included four new charts that Strayhorn scored for Horne and her accompanist Phil Moore. As Horne remembered it, "that small room was perfect for me. I had some material that I had used at Café Society and Billy fixed up two or three things for me—'There'll Be Some Changes Made,' and a couple of Harold Arlen things, 'When the Sun Comes Out,' and 'Blues in the Night' which was a very famous song at the time."[11] Strayhorn also worked with Horne as she prepared for her debut recording sessions for RCA Victor in mid-December 1941. (These sessions took place less than two weeks after the production of the "Flamingo" soundie.)

Outside (or, more aptly, alongside) their professional activities, Strayhorn took on the role of music-cultural ambassador for Horne, introducing her to the vibrant South Central LA nightclubs, including one of the city's first gay bars, Brothers. Horne recalled, "Billy and I would often wind up at a little after-hour joint called Brothers. It would be crowded and hot and funky, and yet muted and wonderful, and I know those were some of my happiest, most feeling moments."[12] The "hot and funky" atmosphere of Brothers also inspired Chester Himes's short story "A Night of New Roses," which depicts the club as an alluring underworld of smoky, perfumed exotica. In his cultural history of Black LA during the 1940s, R. J. Smith describes Brothers as a "secret temple of exotica." The Black queer owner, Henry "Brother" Williams, "greeted people at the door dressed in a Chinese silk robe," with his partner—the other brother in Brothers—Aristide Chapman by his side.[13]

Horne and Strayhorn continued to keep constant company over the ensuing months; however, their next significant documented period of collaborative work did not take place until over a decade later in 1955. When Horne's and Strayhorn's career paths intersected that year, it was at a difficult and uncertain time in their professional lives. For Horne this difficulty came in the form of professional frustration, alienation, and burnout stemming from a punishing schedule of joyless nightclub touring, performing night after night before largely

Difficult Beauty **49**

white wealthy audiences. (She later called all nightclubs "toilets.") At the same time, she felt increasingly disconnected from and dissatisfied with her repertoire, which she was coming to view as trite and irrelevant to urgent issues of racial justice and equality. Indeed, Horne's deep dissatisfaction would, by the decade's end, culminate in her radical shift toward outspoken support of civil rights issues and prioritizing performance projects that brought her into close contact with communities and networks of Black activism.

Strayhorn's career was at a different kind of crossroads. Toward the end of a crucial period in his career, from 1953 to 1956, Strayhorn set out to establish his own professional identity.[14] Horne, Hayton, and others in their orbit supported and encouraged Strayhorn in his quest for professional independence. This move was buoyed by and realized through new artistic ventures and associations, such as his close collaborative work with the celebrated Black tap troupe/fraternity, the Copasetics, and his composing for and collaborative efforts with theater projects in 1953 and 1954 (explored in chapter 3). In addition to his work with Horne during 1955, Strayhorn also contributed several string arrangements for Ben Webster's solo LP *Music for Loving* and accompanied Carmen McRae on an outstanding studio recording of "Something to Live For" on June 14, released on the Decca LP *By Special Request*.[15]

Strayhorn also pursued new independent professional arrangements. One of the more shocking stories in David Hajdu's biography concerns Ellington's role in undermining one such new, promising professional avenue that Strayhorn pursued at this time—a partnership with the composer, arranger, and Black entertainment impresario Luther Henderson, who Strayhorn came to know through the Horne-Hayton network. As Henderson explained to Hajdu, the two musicians had pinned their hopes on a lucrative plan for a partnership that would encompass the full spectrum of the music business: composing/arranging, recording, A&R (artists and repertoire), and production work. However, Ellington called a meeting alone with Henderson, during which he raised serious doubts about Strayhorn's abilities while also flattering Henderson's "superior" talents. Upon meeting with Strayhorn soon after his encounter with Ellington, Henderson suddenly found Strayhorn to be "equally hesitant to proceed with their agreement," a fact that Henderson attributed to Ellington's machinations.[16] In other words, Ellington reprised his doubt-sowing performance with Strayhorn, expressing his misgivings about Henderson's abilities.

Already before this event, at the urging of Hayton, Strayhorn had looked into his royalties and other financial dealings related to his partnership with Ellington and was dismayed by what he discovered. These unpleasant surprises included a host of financial inequities, missing author attributions, and other "irregularities" in the copyright records at Tempo Music, Inc., Ellington's company.[17] Yet the significance of such revelations and their role in Strayhorn's estrangement from Ellington during this period is quite complicated, not least because Ellington was a very generous employer, covering Strayhorn's rent and a level of living expenses that paid for a "vast and lavish wardrobe, the finest food and drink, travel—anything that Strayhorn seemed to need or want."[18] Thus, while Strayhorn apparently expressed anger and frustration privately about the financial inequities stemming from his uncredited and unremunerated creative labor, it was the larger problem—the relations of dependence that structured his professional arrangement with Ellington—that led to the tangle of accumulated artistic, social, and personal frustrations.[19] As Leonard Feather astutely observed, "Money wasn't quite the problem ... The problem was the lack of independence that his business problems represented ... He knew he wasn't being acknowledged for many of the things he was doing. He was obviously frustrated as an artist. He decided it was time to do something about it."[20] Strayhorn's moves toward independence at this moment were also arguably furthered by the severe downturn in the fame and fortunes of the Ellington Orchestra during this period.[21]

For both Strayhorn and Horne, then, the opportunity to work together at such a vulnerable and uncertain period in their careers provided some measure of connection and support, a refuge in music making, a way of coping with precarious and difficult feelings and circumstances. As Horne would later say, "being with other musicians, it is when I feel the most free."[22] Their collaboration began in January 1955 when Strayhorn went on tour with Horne as her accompanist, forming part of a trio with drummer Chico Hamilton and bassist George Duvivier. Little is known about the details of their tour outside of their most high-profile gigs. At the top of this short list was a three-week engagement at the posh Chicago nightclub Chez Paree, which received a brief, celebratory press review in the *Chicago Defender*. The reviewer noted that the show began with a set of small-group song arrangements (described as Horne's "regular singing stint"), including the Strayhorn original "Ooo, You Make Me Tingle." An elaborate revue-like production followed as the trio was joined by the full Chez Paree orchestra. The reviewer, for example, described the finale as a "miniature" Hollywood production number with Horne reprising her 1940s-era film performances.[23]

A couple of weeks after the Chez Paree gig, the trio of Strayhorn, Hamilton, and Duvivier accompanied Horne for a very different performance engagement: a benefit show for the first Joint Negro Appeal fundraising campaign at the Trianon Ballroom on Cottage Grove Avenue (the benefit also featured Sarah Vaughan). Tellingly, a review of the performance appeared not in the pages of the jazz press but in Marion B. Campfield's society column for the *Chicago Defender*, "Mostly about Women," and is the only mass media document in which Strayhorn is named:

> 'NOTHER IMPRESSIVE date on the weekend past's jam-packed calendar was the JOINT NEGRO APPEAL's first fund-raising fete to aid 18 Windy City's Red Feather agencies. "Salute to Lena Horne" dazzler lured fashionable throng to Trianon ballroom . . . but 'twas La Lena herself who captured the hearts of every one with her scintillating personality, her breathtaking beauty and the grace, poise and refreshingly sincere charm . . . Bouquets are also due . . . Miss Horne's pianist-arranger BILLY STRAYHORN . . . whose sensitive support proved [he] enjoyed that assignment.[24]

Campfield highlighted Strayhorn's participation in the fundraiser, praising his sensitive sonic support as Horne's "pianist-arranger." The descriptor "pianist-arranger" here neatly (if generically) foregrounds the porous boundaries between the roles and artistry of accompanist and arranger. Indeed, the sonic support of an accompanist can be conceived of as a kind of "real-time," improvisatory or intuitive realization of arranging practices—both create the framework for interaction and dialogue, for collaborative exploration and projection of lyric and music, sonic meaning, and feeling.[25] Horne described Strayhorn's sensitive sonic support as rooted in forms of trust, love, and understanding, and ability channeled through his skill of anticipating and accommodating her breath and phrasing: "He was a great accompanist for me because he understood me and loved me . . . But he was also musically great for me; he had a trick of hearing the breath. When you sing, you need air, and he made a soft little bed right there to support the structure, so while you're taking your breath, nobody knows. It takes an awful lot of sensitivity."[26]

During the months they were on tour in 1955, Chico Hamilton observed how their personal bond translated as musical reciprocity, empathy, and deep connection: "A lot of the time that year, when Billy was the pianist in the trio, it was like he had a direct psychic link to Lena . . . When she was singing, he translated what she was feeling on the piano and sent back to her in his music at the same time. It went both ways."[27] I want to make two broad points here. First,

Hamilton's notion of a "direct psychic link" between Horne and Strayhorn—one that activated extraordinary powers of musical communication, interaction, and understanding—pays witness to how these two artists embodied and translated affective and sonic channels of support and empathy. It bears (re)emphasizing here the irreducible ephemerality of the dynamics and repertoire of musical interaction and communication as it manifests across the entire process of musical production, from the informal spaces of conversation and practice to the formal spaces of rehearsal and performance. And, in the context of recording studio sessions, this ephemerality adheres across multiple takes, filtered through technological mediations of sound capture and editing.

A second point provides critical context to Hamilton's observation: for Horne, the "direct psychic link" to Strayhorn linked up to a broader network of professional support and artistic survival. Especially during this difficult and unhappy period of her career, an intense and intentional focus on the materiality and formal dimensions of songs and singing became for Horne a protective strategy, a way of distancing herself from the racialized and gendered objectifications and expectations of her audiences. Put another way, Horne's masterful song styling was her stage armor (along with a formidable stage presence), a shield forged through precise musicianship and concentration on the sonic dimensions and dynamics of a song—crisp, angular enunciation; penetrating attack and tone; sharp, controlled phrasing; deliberate and imposing gazes and gestures. Such performative protections have typically figured in critical and journalistic discourse as a posture of aloofness, self-absorption, and cool distance, a posture that performance studies scholar Shane Vogel has theorized as a strategic Black feminist performance mode, what he calls Horne's "impersona."[28] As Vogel argues, Horne's "performative impersona" reflects a strategy "that enabled her to create a psychic space in which she could resist the spectatorial violences of Jim Crow cabaret," while also managing the complicated pressures and demands of performing her role as symbol and voice of Black female middle-class respectability, or, as she put it later in life, "a good little symbol."[29] Importantly, Vogel's account of Horne's performance stylistics takes its cue from Horne's intellectual work, as articulated in her autobiographies and oral history. For a *New York Times* piece in 1994 written by her biographer, she quipped, "People kept saying, 'There's so much mystery about her. What is she thinking? And she's so sexy.' And I wasn't. I just didn't like them. So I had this kind of grand attitude, which went very well in the nightclubs."[30] Horne expressed a more pointed version in her 1965 autobiography: "I rarely spoke on stage. I was too proud to let them think they could have any personal contact with me. They got the singer, but not the woman."[31]

If, as Vogel argues, Horne's performative impersona "created a [distanced] psychic space" for resistance and survival, this creative labor was not a solo project, but one that she pursued through collaboration both on and off the stage. Indeed, as Nichole Rustin-Paschal has written, Horne's autobiography makes clear "that her development as a singer had as much to do with the quality of the musicians she worked with as it did with her changing political and racial consciousness and her parental responsibilities."[32] It goes without saying that Strayhorn was one among many important and close musical collaborators who worked with Horne in support roles; Horne's pianist and arranger Phil Moore, and arranger, conductor, and pianist Lennie Hayton also played key roles.[33] In May 1955, Horne and the trio entered the studio, joining Hayton and a roster of other musicians to record her first studio LP for the RCA Victor label, *It's Love*. The LP's title showcased the title track (composed by Leonard Bernstein on lyrics by Betty Comden and Adolph Green) from the 1953 musical *Wonderful Town*. As was conventional for pop vocal recording at that time, session musicians, apart from the leader (Hayton), were uncredited. According to Hajdu, Strayhorn accompanied Horne on fourteen sides recorded during these sessions, not all of which were included on the LP. However, extant recording session ledgers, which are incomplete, identify Strayhorn as the pianist on only five sides: two with full band arrangements—"It's All Right with Me" (Cole Porter) and "Fun to Be Fooled" (with strings, Harold Arlen/Ira Gershwin/E. Y. Harburg)—and three small group arrangements—"Love Me or Leave Me" (Gus Kahn/Walter Donaldson), "Let Me Love You" (Bart Howard, released as a single), and "It's Love."[34] *It's Love* also features one of Strayhorn's original songs for Horne, "You're the One," and, given his authorship, it is reasonable to speculate that he played on that side as well, although Hayton is credited with the arrangement, scored for big band.

Yet the most convincing and compelling evidence for Strayhorn's vital role as a collaborator on these sessions emerges from the retrospective testaments of other session musicians. Trumpeter Jimmy Maxwell, who played on seven of the sessions, recalled, "She was real comfortable with Strayhorn at the piano. She was nervous and shy, and she wouldn't do a take without Strayhorn, even though her own husband was the leader and a hell of a pianist."[35] The takes that feature small-group arrangements are of special relevance to this discussion, as they come closest to capturing the sound and collaborative dynamics of Horne backed by the trio. Indeed, one side from these sessions, Horne's version of song "Love Me or Leave Me," was included in the trio's opening Chez Paree set. Released as a stand-alone single, "Love Me or Leave Me" was a hit for Horne. It reached number nineteen on the pop charts in July 1955 riding a wave of popularity generated by another hit—an MGM biopic based on the life and career of torch singer Ruth Etting, who had popularized the song in 1929. Titled *Love Me or Leave Me*, the film musical featured Doris Day as Etting, and her version of the song was included in the film soundtrack LP released by Columbia Records (and became Day's best-selling single). But Horne's version, with its cool swing and thinly veiled simmering rage, stood in striking contrast to the sultry sweetness of Day's version. The reviewer for *Metronome* called Horne's version "a daring presentation," and gushed that it showed Horne "at her most exciting."[36]

Apart from some playful pianistic "cushions" in the form of bluesy staccato fills between phrases, Strayhorn's accompanying work on the side is largely buried in the mix of what, on the whole, is a routine swing arrangement. A more audible record of interaction and dialogue between singer and pianist comes on a side from *It's Love*: an intimate arrangement of the ballad "Let Me Love You." Both in sound and affect, this song hails a different (although not unrelated) constellation of performative and cultural associations than "Love Me or Leave Me." Importantly, "Let Me Love You" stands out on the LP for the ways in which it evokes the (jazz-adjacent) sonic and performative affects of queer intimacy and theatricality associated with the midcentury nightclub. In the case of "Let Me Love You," these associations gravitate toward a specific site: New York's Blue Angel cabaret, where the tune's queer songwriter, Bart Howard, hosted and played piano from 1951 to 1959.[37] During this period, Howard was known for his collaborations with iconic cabaret singer Mabel Mercer, who recorded "Let Me Love You" in 1953.[38]

The Horne-Strayhorn version of "Let Me Love You" translates—in real time—the song's cabaret aesthetic into jazz terms. Through the first four stanzas of the lyrics, the performance closely replicates the piano-vocal arrangement and expressive template of Mercer's version; Strayhorn's accompaniment, a lilting left-hand ostinato that alternates with gently rolled chords in E major, faithfully reproduces the artful café pianism of its model (although a guitar doubling Strayhorn's rolled chords can be heard faintly in the mix). Against this continuous backing, Horne murmurs a series of teasing propositions: "If you lend me your ear, I'll make it clear the way that I do / Let me whisper it; Let me sigh it; Let me sing it, my dear . . . Let me do a million impossible things." At the close of the fourth stanza on the words "And if that's not enough / I'll buy you the first of May," the recording shifts stylistic gears: Horne, Strayhorn, and bassist Duvivier are joined by Hamilton on drums as the arrangement moves into a medium-tempo swing groove much more typical of hipper-leaning midcentury popular vocal jazz sides.[39] Strayhorn is freed up to interact with Horne and the rhythm section, drawing on a varied stock of responsorial rhythmic fills, riffs, countermelodies, and rich chordal accents. One other side on *It's Love*—Strayhorn's first original song for Horne, "You're the One"—also stands out for its repertoire of sonic interaction between singer and pianist.

After their tour and recording dates in 1955, Horne and Strayhorn continued to collaborate sporadically. According to Duvivier, Strayhorn—whose nickname for Duvivier was "The Professor"—assisted Horne in preparation for what would prove her most successful LP to date, the celebrated 1957 *Lena Horne at the Waldorf Astoria* (Live), by offering suggestions for the arrangements, including the vocal/bass duet versions of the Ellington medley of "Mood Indigo" and "I'm Beginning to See the Light": "We were rehearsing at Lena's and Billy Strayhorn was there. He used to come by whenever Duke's band was in town. He did some arranging for Lena and would come up to listen and make suggestions. He heard us and said, 'Why not let George just play behind her for a while?' RCA wanted to record one of Lena's shows live, which was a rather daring thing in those days. So we did an Ellington medley as a vocal/bass duet."[40] The LP charted for two weeks on the *Billboard* LP Top 40 list in 1957.

Late in 1960 Horne performed the second song Strayhorn composed for her, "Maybe." Notably, Strayhorn chose to publish the song with Hayton-Horne Music Co. (registered copyright on March 7, 1961), rather than Tempo Music. With its playful attitude and cynical take on romantic promise, the lyric and minimalist structure of the song perfectly suited Horne's supper club repertoire and, indeed, Horne featured the song as an opener for her second live LP for RCA Victor, *Lena Horne at the Sands*. For her 1993 Strayhorn tribute, *We'll Be Together Again*, Horne reprised this arrangement commenting, "I like an opening number that shakes people up, and this is definitely in your face."[41] It bears emphasis here that both "Maybe" and "You're the One" not only capture Strayhorn's ability to craft a song custom tailored to Horne's voice, but also, crucially, archive how in these moments Horne's voice, vocal stylistics, and persona motivated and directed Strayhorn's songwriting, arranging, and collaborative practices. Listening to Horne's original recording alongside Strayhorn's manuscript drafts for the song as well as an origin story about the song's first performance helps to further illuminate the latter point. The autograph manuscript materials for "Maybe" consist of three items: a partial score and two handwritten drafts of the lyric.[42]

The origin story is included in Hajdu's biography. The interlocutor is one of Strayhorn's inner circle of New York friends, Bill Patterson, who gives an account of witnessing the song's private debut in Strayhorn's Riverside Drive apartment.

> I was lying on the coach reading while Billy was writing "Maybe" . . . He [Strayhorn] said, "I'm working on a new song for Lena—what do you think?" And he played me some of it and sang it for me. And to be perfectly honest, I thought it was awful. There wasn't very much there. It wasn't much of anything . . . Lena came in a little while later. She sat down with him on the piano stool and they went over it, and then she stood up and she sang the song, and I couldn't believe it. It sounded like a completely different song. He had written this thing perfectly for her and her attitude.[43]

Although Hajdu does not give a precise date for the event chronicled in Patterson's story, its placement in Hajdu's narrative implies that "Maybe" was written during the mid-1950s; however, the song's recording date of November 3–5, 1960, and its 1961 publication copyright, would suggest a later composition date, likely in 1960 (by contrast, the earlier Horne-Strayhorn song "You're the One" was registered for copyright in 1955).

Further complicating the dating of the song's genesis is one of the two handwritten drafts of the lyric shown as figure 2.1. This version is written on the back of an empty manila envelope and gives the verses of the song that correspond to the AABA sections, along with the first line of a short C section (the lyric for the final verse/A section is missing). The draft lyric was inscribed with a green pen, supplemented by additional shorthand penciled-in musical notations. The latter include cues for the number of bars per specific line of text, and rhythmic patterns. The complication this sketch introduces concerns the information that appears on the front of the manila envelope: the name and workplace address, written in a faded red pencil, of Bill Grove, Strayhorn's partner for the last four years of his life. According to Hajdu's biography, Strayhorn and Grove's relationship began in the winter of 1964, shortly after Strayhorn's diagnosis with esophageal cancer, although the two apparently knew each other through mutual friends associated with the Neal Salon. (Hajdu describes Grove as being on the "periphery" of Strayhorn's queer social network.) The wording on the front of the envelope uses "for" rather than "to" "Wm Grove" and there is no sign of postage, which might suggest that the envelope functioned as a scrap piece of paper that Strayhorn repurposed as manuscript. If so, we could speculate that perhaps Strayhorn was reworking the song for a performance, maybe even for one in which he was to serve as Horne's accompanist. We know, for instance, that Horne and Strayhorn performed a song that Strayhorn contributed to Ellington's Sacred Concert, "A Christmas Song" (also known as "A Christmas Surprise"), in December 1965 at Grace Cathedral.[44] It is also possible, although less plausible, that Strayhorn (or someone else) intended to give the handwritten lyrics or, alternately, the missing contents of the envelope to Grove (if the latter, the draft lyric might be the scrap, not the envelope).

Whatever the case, adding to the uncertainty surrounding the song's composition are the two other primary documents: another handwritten draft of the lyric for "Maybe," penned on stationary from the Sherman Hotel in Chicago (undated), and an autograph draft manuscript score. The hotel stationary draft for the lyric spans seven pages and shows Strayhorn developing and working out the lyric. The sketch-like nature of this draft suggests strongly that it is the prior or original document.[45] There is nothing special or unusual about the existence of various and disparate sketches for a song lyric in Strayhorn's papers—he left multiple sketches for lyrics of other songs. However, returning to Patterson's story about the song's creation, in this case I would argue that the representational field of these drafts are usefully conceived or, more precisely, listened to, in dialogue with Patterson's story describing the song's dramatic transformations in its two living-room debut performances. In Strayhorn's initial solo rendition, Patterson was left puzzled and unimpressed by what he perceived as thin material. Yet, later, as Strayhorn rehearsed it with Horne, the song suddenly came alive, dramatically and critically transformed through her singing and performance.[46] Listening to Horne's live recording alongside these two versions of the lyric as well as reading the partial autograph manuscript score foreground two key elements: the improvisatory nature of these materials, and the primacy of the lyric—its content, syntax, rhythm, and temporal unfolding. Together these materials present resonant traces of their collaborative creative process, cueing the intimate, ephemeral spaces of co-creation.

Some two years after their work on "Maybe," a very different kind of musical event would bring the two artists together, an event that channeled their collaborative energies toward explicitly political and activist ends. As recounted in Horne's autobiography, Strayhorn and Horne traveled together to Jackson, Mississippi in June 1963 and participated in a National Association for the Ad-

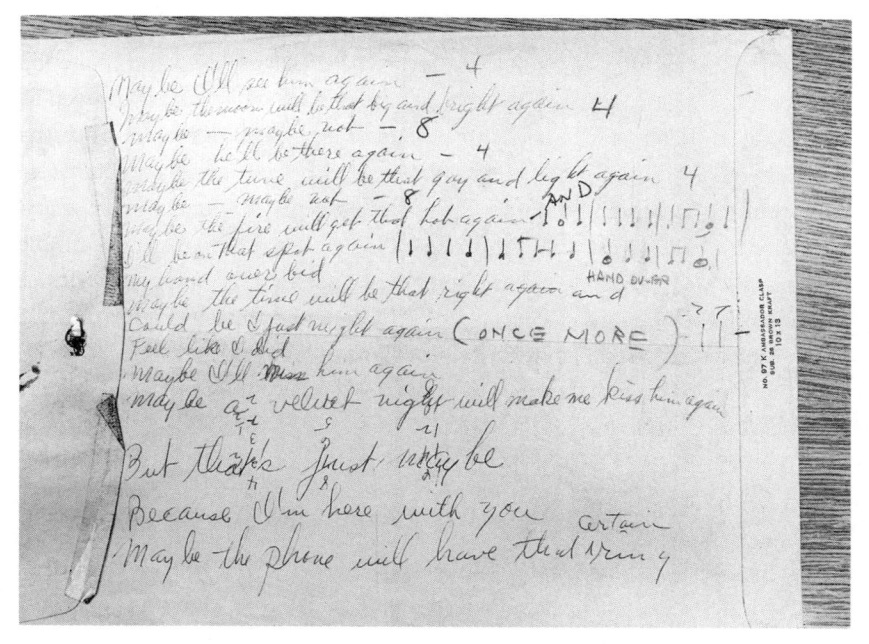

FIGURE 2.1 Strayhorn's drafted lyrics for "Maybe." Billy Strayhorn Collection, Library of Congress, Music Division. Reproduced by permission of Billy Strayhorn Songs, Inc.

vancement of Colored People (NAACP) rally spearheaded by the organization's Jackson representative, Medgar Evers, and performed at a Southern Christian Leadership Conference church concert. Horne narrates this event as a decisive one, representing a momentous break in which she dropped her former defenses and rejected her distanced function as a purely symbolic civil rights figure to engage in direct activism for racial justice: "I invited Jean Noble to come with me and rounded up Billy Strayhorn to play for me and off we went."[47] Vogel persuasively traces Horne's political awakening during this moment to her experiences performing in the 1956 Broadway musical *Jamaica*, particularly the "networks of professional support" and communal bond that developed while performing alongside the work's cast of young African American dancers.[48]

Evers welcomed Strayhorn and Horne at the Jackson airport on the morning of June 7. At the afternoon rally, Horne delivered a short speech collaboratively written with Strayhorn, and sang two a cappella spirituals that she and Strayhorn had prepared: "This Little Light of Mine" and "Amazing Grace." The rally was the largest NAACP demonstration to date and was held "in defiance of a state court

Difficult Beauty 59

injunction barring racial protests."[49] Horne later recalled her feelings of unease and panic, fearing that her status and style as a Black celebrity and nightclub singer would be a liability and create an insurmountable obstacle to musical and social connection and solidarity with the southern Black communities she would be performing for.[50] She credited Strayhorn's calming presence, musical support, and words of assurance for giving her the confidence she needed. As Bruce Rastrelli wrote about this event, "Lena craved her brave friend Billy Strayhorn to go with her . . . She desired his eloquent words for her speech, and wanted his soulful arrangements and beautiful accompaniment."[51] That evening at the church benefit, held at the Negro Masonic Temple on Lynch Street in Jackson, they performed a set of freedom songs that Strayhorn arranged for the occasion.[52]

BLUE ROSE

In mid-January 1956, the year following Strayhorn's work with Horne and the trio, Strayhorn flew to Los Angeles from New York to begin a collaborative recording project with pop singer Rosemary Clooney. Although Clooney was an experienced band singer, having recorded with Harry James and Benny Goodman, her stardom was most closely associated in the pop imagination with a string of hits she cut in the early 1950s for Columbia Records, notably the Mitch Miller ethnic novelty songs "Come On-a My House" and "Mambo Italiano," as well as for her featured role alongside Bing Crosby and Danny Kaye in Paramount's Technicolor blockbuster *White Christmas*.[53] The collaboration with Clooney was the first of its kind for both Strayhorn and the Ellington Orchestra: not only did it mark Ellington's first collaboration with a singer for a full-length prestige jazz LP, but for the first time in his seventeen-year relationship with Ellington, Strayhorn was offered full creative autonomy on a major recording project, one that (also among the first) daringly paired a star white female pop singer with an African American jazz orchestra. Even with a band as illustrious as the Ellington outfit, this pairing must have raised a few red flags for executives at Columbia, or at least it would seem so judging by the evidence of the cover art for the resulting LP, *Blue Rose* (figure 2.2). Images of Ellington and Clooney appear on the cover in a split visual space that juxtaposes, collage-like, a large filmic image of Ellington with a much smaller photographic image of Clooney. In the background, placed directly under the title "Blue Rose: Rosemary Clooney and Duke Ellington and his Orchestra," a grainy smoke-filled, black-and-white image of Ellington's face

FIGURE 2.2 Rosemary Clooney and Duke Ellington and His Orchestra, *Blue Rose* LP cover, Columbia Records (1956). Reproduced by permission of Sony Music.

appears as if being projected onto an art-house movie screen. He smiles gently, his eyes cast downward toward a color photo, pasted-on headshot of Clooney floating in the foreground; she, in turn, innocently gazes outward toward an unseen camera seemingly unaware of the celluloid Ellington looming behind her. This stylized separation of Ellington and Clooney in the visual field delineates, however satirically, racial and sexual boundaries through a technologically mediated, safe distance.

Yet the LP cover design, with its contrast of Clooney's "in-color" head against the "black-and-white" Ellington, also referenced the real-life "virtual" conditions involved in recording the LP—just one of a set of unusual conditions surrounding Strayhorn and Clooney's working relationship. At the time, Clooney was pregnant with her second child and was suffering from extreme nausea and vomiting, which precluded her from traveling from Los Angeles to New York to record the session.[54] On top of this challenge, the two collaborators had to work under a very tight deadline. As the story goes, producer Irving Townsend initially pitched the idea for *Blue Rose* to Ellington and Strayhorn on January 12, during the opening night of the Ellington Orchestra's engagement at Café Society Uptown. Strayhorn immediately expressed enthusiasm for the project, saying he considered Clooney "an underrated singer." At the end of their initial discussion, "Strayhorn, Townsend, and Ellington had agreed on a basic approach to the album: whatever Clooney and Strayhorn wanted to do."[55] However, "whatever [they] wanted to do" was set to begin on January 23—and in New York, not LA.

Difficult Beauty 61

Townsend overcame this obstacle by making use of the relatively novel (at least for jazz) technology of multitrack recording; Strayhorn would fly to New York to direct the session for the instrumental tracks then travel back to LA to record the vocal overdubbing with Clooney. Originally, Ellington and Strayhorn wanted to title the LP *Inter-Continental* to highlight the bicoastal recording process, but that concept was nixed by Columbia in favor of the more pop-friendly *Blue Rose*. This title accommodated the intended commercial appeal of the LP with its play on Rose(mary), "blues," and associations of the blue rose flower with ideas of feminine elegance and mystery.[56] But as a sought-after yet unattainable natural object, the blue rose also holds an intriguing (queer) symbolic history as a figure for fantasy and the impossible.[57]

With Townsend's plan in place, Strayhorn, armed with records, manuscript paper, and pen, arrived at Clooney's Beverly Hills home on Roxbury Drive, where he stayed for more than a week in her older child's bedroom doing double duty as caregiver and musical collaborator (often simultaneously). Clooney's husband, director-actor-singer José Ferrer, was abroad working on a film project. In Hajdu's biography of Strayhorn, Clooney recalled the ensuing mix of musical, personal, and domestic intimacy:

> He made me breakfast in bed. We didn't know each other at all before that, and we became incredibly close immediately. I was having a very difficult pregnancy. I was really suffering and he got me through it. I'd say, "Oh God, I'm going to throw up again," and he would say, "Okay, now. It's okay," and he would take care of me. He said, "Don't get up, honey," and he'd make me crackers and milk. I felt a bit better one day, and he baked me an apple pie. He cared about that baby. He cared about the fact that I couldn't afford to get tired, and he watched out for me. I would just stay in bed and talk about things. Most of the time, we didn't even talk much about music. We did work on the music, it was like I was working with my best friend. I wanted to do my best for him, and I would do anything he wanted . . . I was never associated with a man who was so completely unthreatening and uncontrolling and so completely in charge.[58]

While Clooney's memory conveys her genuine affection and respect for Strayhorn, it is difficult to ignore the troubling histories of race, gender, sexuality, and power that haunt her story of Strayhorn as trusted domestic caregiver. That this tale of a white woman served by a caring and "unthreatening" Black man takes place in a Hollywood mansion only underscores the proximity of Clooney's narrative to the racialized and sexualized legacies of the subservient Black domestic worker in popular culture.[59] In this context, the way Clooney narrates her memory of Strayhorn's actions as domestic caregiver, coupled with her characterization of Strayhorn's nonnormative masculinity, hails Strayhorn's Black queer body according to the scripts of historical white affection for gendered asexualized Black service.[60] Yet as a description of her working relationship with her collaborator, particularly as it marks socio-musical practices and effects of empathy, support, and nurturing, Clooney's memory aligns strongly with the broadly held perception of Strayhorn-as-collaborator. Indeed, her description of him as a commanding but not controlling collaborator can arguably be read as destabilizing racialized gender scripts.

After Strayhorn arrived at Clooney's home, the two collaborators set to work selecting their songs for the LP and, when time and health permitted, rehearsing the arrangements at the piano, which, presumably, Strayhorn worked out with the singer over that same week.[61] In addition to haunting versions of Ellington classics such as "Sophisticated Lady" and "I Got It Bad (and That Ain't Good)" and a newly composed Ellington original, the eponymous "Blue Rose" (an instrumental with vocalese), the LP included two original Strayhorn songs from 1939, "Grievin'" and "I'm Checkin' Out, Goom Bye," along with one Strayhorn instrumental, significantly a full-band arrangement (of film-noir-like proportions) of his great ballad for alto saxophonist Johnny Hodges, "Passion Flower." As Clooney explained it, "Having 'Passion Flower' on there was sort of a wink, an inside thing to those in the know that this was basically Billy's record."[62] With the inclusion of an instrumental arrangement, the Ellington Orchestra–Clooney collaboration departs from the conventions of most "star" pop vocal jazz LPS from this period. Rather, *Blue Rose* is a hybrid format of featured singer and bandleader/composer. This mixture of vocal and instrumental tracks reflects both live performance formats of swing/big bands and pre-LP era recording practices. At the same time, *Blue Rose* also importantly aligns with the mixture of vocal and instrumental tracks featured on LP film soundtracks, which were very popular during this early LP period.

The tracks for *Blue Rose* were cut in four sessions: the instrumental tracks were recorded in New York on January 23 and 27, and the vocal overdubs in LA on February 8 and 11. Of the new arrangements of Strayhorn's two songs, Clooney's version of the blues-based ballad "Grievin'" stands out. Notably, the manuscript for the vocal arrangement—the first and only recording of the song with Strayhorn's lyric—bears a dedication under the title "For Rosemary Clooney," and Strayhorn made extensive alterations to the original 1939 instrumental arrangement of the tune (an effective but largely conventional swing-band arrangement credited to Ellington), including the addition of a newly composed introduction.[63]

Strayhorn's new introduction immediately announces the ballad's orchestrally lush stylistic updating in relation to the expressive and formal lexicon of the blues. Harry Carney (baritone sax) states the A-strain of the melody in a slow swing tempo backed by a dissonant-charged, dark plunger-mute "wha-wha" chordal texture that unfolds over a truncated blues chorus. A particularly interesting feature of the melody is how Strayhorn maps the conventional two-bar symmetrical phrase structure onto a series of rhythmic displacements that begin on the upbeat to the first full bar with a three-note pattern (two eighths followed by a dotted half note), rising upward C♯–D–F. In measures 1–4, the pattern expands melodically with pendular leaps ascending a ninth from F–G before descending downward through the tonic triad via an eighth-note triplet figure that leads to A♭ on the downbeat at m. 4. The triplet figure reverses in m. 5 (B♭–C–D) landing on F, where the melody lingers for the final two measures over an E♭ minor seventh (functioning as the dominant), before cadencing in B♭ with the "grievin'" figure, a bluesy half-note pendular leap.

With her signature warm, sensuous yet light sound, Clooney delivers the lyric in a stylish, rhythmically subtle yet straightforward manner, backed for the first two vocal choruses (AA) by riff figures that respond in rhythmic unison. These riff figures are derived from rhythmic and melodic features described previously (e.g., repeating triplet pattern, pendular contour, blue notes) and appear throughout the arrangement in various guises. By far the most dramatic incarnation occurs in the third vocal chorus after the bridge: the texture thickens with reeds and brass playing the riff figure in unison behind Clooney as she pleads, "Every day, every night, how I pray that you'll treat me right." The emotional tension spills into the next bar as the riff figures give way to a trombone trio playing a half-note chromatic step in octaves (C–D♭–C) below Clooney's climactic ultimatum: "You will regret and you'll cry some, If I die from grievin,'" a moment that itself suddenly morphs into an expressive, improvisatory rupture in the form of a particularly memorable (and perfectly timed) wailing, coloratura trumpet solo by Cat Anderson. While truly astounding, the full force of Anderson's blowing on this chorus depends, nevertheless, on the sonic backing that frames, or more accurately, propels him.

Directly after Clooney intones the grievin' figure at the cadence, the full band lurches upward in unison through a syncopated, chromatically inflected two-bar climb, a kind of sonic launching pad for Anderson. As the trumpet part takes

EXAMPLE 2.1 Strayhorn, "Grievin'"; measures 9–16. Transcribed by author.

EXAMPLE 2.2 Strayhorn, "Grievin'"; measures 27–34. Transcribed by author.

off, the reeds and brass choir continue in the upper register, but now in an extravagant call-and-response pattern punctuated by a chromatically rising and rousing full-throated rhythmic ostinato based on a variation of the riff figure (a tied-quarter-note triplet ostinato, which we first hear sung in the B-section of the melody). With Anderson's trumpet climbing further into the stratosphere for the final jaw-dropping measures of his solo, the backing instrumental choir intones fragments from the first half of the melody.

The collective dramatic force of Anderson's chorus is so startling that we might conclude it overwhelms Clooney, as if stealing her emotional spotlight through an affect of improvisatory combustion. But such an interpretation would only be possible if we ignore the larger expressive and musical arc of the arrangement. Here, Anderson's solo functions theatrically, amplifying—quite literally—the feeling that Clooney authorizes in the lyric of the preceding climactic vocal chorus. This blues-saturated emotional transference might also be heard as a kind of erotic excess beyond the racialized and gendered proprieties of Clooney's vocal persona. Formally, Strayhorn weaves Anderson's solo chorus into a quasi-through-composed architecture that unfolds in the latter part of the arrangement and leads the modulation, moving the song as if through sheer propulsion, from B♭ to D♭.[64]

Taken as a whole, the foregoing discussion of form, style, and sonic affect in Strayhorn's vocal arrangement for "Grievin'" suggests how the practices of composers/arrangers, singers, and players collaboratively refashion the formal and affective layers of a song from within. Strayhorn conceived the process of arranging as a kind of co-text: "You really need to write something you think fits his sound and is your sound, too—a combination of what you do and what he does."[65] Strayhorn's notion of sonic fit implies that tailoring an arrangement around the technical abilities and stylistic persona of a singer (or soloist) creates a comfortable space for a performer to discover or imagine "her space" within the music—in other words, a fit that facilitates rather than dictates and thus helps to create spaces for effective improvisations. From this perspective, it is possible to hear Strayhorn's elaborate, blues-tinged arrangement as enabling a sonic space for Clooney to fashion a new vocal persona, one that she understood as helping her to break free from the limiting racial and sexual codes of the 1950s novelty song (an argument that can, of course, also be extended to most, if not all, of the other arrangements on the LP).

Indeed, in her 1999 autobiography, *Girl Singer*, Clooney associated the experience of collaborating on *Blue Rose* with artistic self-discovery and empowerment.

Her comments on the subject arose in the context of recalling a memorable evening she spent with Billie Holiday just a few months after the Strayhorn-Ellington session: "Billie said it wasn't work to do a song she could feel—the only kind of song she would do—and I felt 'Blue Rose' and all the songs on that album in a way I could never feel 'Come On [-a My House].' I wasn't in a position to change my material, and had I been, I might not have had the confidence to do it. Now I did."[66]

In terms of vocal persona, Clooney's sound on *Blue Rose* aligns with the hipper, jazz-influenced, mainstream, white big band singers of the day such as Peggy Lee and Frank Sinatra. Yet, as I noted earlier, Clooney had already cut more than a few sides in the early 1950s (including a Columbia disc with Frank Sinatra) in which we can also hear this stylistic orientation (and in fact some critical assessments of these sides compared Clooney to Ella Fitzgerald).[67] Beyond these larger stylistic references and associations, however, I am also interested in what it meant for Clooney to "do a song she could feel" in relation to the specific working conditions and set of constraints surrounding her collaboration with Strayhorn. The sociality of the arranging process on *Blue Rose* required forms of intimacy improvised within both domestic/private and public/professional spaces and across lines of gender, race, and class. How might we, then, connect such forms of improvised intimacy to the collaborators' personal engagement with the affective registers of specific song arrangements?

To return again to the example of the blues ballad "Grievin'," for Clooney, the choice of this song may have been guided by her ability to "feel" the song (a choice itself guided by Strayhorn's own sense that the song would fit her well). The lyric ("I") expresses the pain of a lover dealing with an unfaithful and callous partner, a theme that animates another song on the LP, Strayhorn's poignant, slow-tempo, dissonant-tinged arrangement of Ellington's "I Got It Bad (and That Ain't Good)." Although generic with respect to the thematic conventions of pop/jazz ballads (and blues), both songs would have had a particular personal resonance for Clooney and thus could have provided a vehicle for her to address difficult personal feelings surrounding her life circumstances. During this period, Clooney struggled to maintain the heteropatriarchal image of, in her words, "the perfect Fifties Wife" in the face of her husband's flagrant philandering (which began shortly after their honeymoon) and intimidating temper tantrums—all while she paid the bills and worked tirelessly to support their rapidly growing family.[68] Her pregnancy during the *Blue Rose* collaboration led to the second of five children born between 1955 and 1960, all of whom she was left to support after she and Ferrer first split up in 1961.[69]

Blue Rose also signaled a new direction in Strayhorn's career with respect to his partnership with Ellington. Handing Strayhorn the creative reins for the project amounted to a kind of peace offering from Ellington following several years of estrangement between the composing partners, as discussed earlier. Clooney seems to have been aware of the tension between them over authorship and visibility, given her comment about the inclusion of "Passion Flower" as a covert tactic to mark Strayhorn's largely uncredited public authorship.[70]

In the days leading up to Strayhorn's meeting with Ellington and Townsend at Café Society Uptown at which they first discussed the Clooney LP project, Strayhorn visited the club with a small group of close friends to celebrate his homecoming to New York after a liberating extended trip to Paris. While in Paris, Strayhorn visited Aaron Bridgers, and spent many evenings at the Left Bank jazz bar, the Mars Club, where Bridgers worked as the staff pianist, and where Strayhorn was treated as a celebrity by the city's expatriate gay cabaret subculture. The singer-pianist Blossom Dearie, whom Strayhorn befriended, performed regularly at the Mars Club during this period and would later fondly recall the pleasures of singing for the club's gay patrons, telling Hajdu "a majority of the audience was like dear Aaron and Billy, brilliant listeners."[71] Returning home to New York from Paris meant leaving behind the transforming cultural energy, communal support, and warm admiration he found in the City of Lights for professional uncertainty and reckoning. Strayhorn's hard feelings about his return can be gleaned in Hajdu's account of his homecoming party at Café Society Uptown. With a group of friends, including his soon-to-be boyfriend Francis Goldberg, Strayhorn "bought a few rounds in salute to Bridgers, and charmed the group with droll descriptions of the Mars Club."[72] At one point, he noticed a bill plastered on the wall advertising the upcoming January 12 Ellington engagement. According to a musician friend, Strayhorn responded with a shady comment: "'Well, I'll have to come to see Duke Ellington—and hear all those Billy Strayhorn songs,' after which he looked around the tiny little club . . . puffed on a cigarette and quipped, 'If there's room for them.'"[73]

In recounting these stories, I'm not suggesting that we can unproblematically impute (auto)biographical meaning into the music or claim a reified homology between the social and musical. Nor am I simply pointing to the generalized affective power of songs to sonically embody or project personal feelings and fantasies. What I am arguing is that such specific everyday life circumstances and contexts acted as a constellation of social "texts" (among others) that framed their collaboration and, as such, played a role, however ineffable, in the selection of songs and in shaping the arranging process, specifically along paths of cross-gender projection and identification. Sometimes these paths emerged through creative directorial advice given during the vocal overdubbing in the studio.[74] When Clooney was recording Strayhorn's other original number, a charmingly "retro" arrangement of the up-tempo swinger "I'm Checkin' Out, Goom Bye," she recalled Strayhorn's direction for realizing the lyrics, with its lighthearted yet pointed message to a deceptive lover, this way: "He told me not to do it angry. He said, 'Just because you're leaving the other person, it doesn't mean you're angry. You're in charge. You're leaving, because you're the strong one. You might even come back. Who knows?'" Clooney concluded, "It was almost like he was giving me his whole philosophy."[75] In her autobiography, Clooney also recalled how Strayhorn helped her overcome extreme nerves at the overdubbing sessions in LA: "'I want you to imagine you're living in New York and you've got a really hot date and you're ready to go,' Billy said to me through his big square glasses. 'You're a beautiful woman, looking into the mirror and combing your hair, and there's Duke Ellington and there's no band. The radio is playing the record, and you just sing along with the orchestra, and we overhear it.'"[76]

Clooney's recollections of working with Strayhorn in the studio vividly capture a practice of collaboration and creative labor rooted in an ethics of care, support, and human connection. Widening the lens, Clooney's accounts of their interactions also stand as relatively rare documentation of Strayhorn directing a recording session in which he was free to assume a kind of authorial independence and autonomy without having to either play the submissive "right-hand man" to Ellington or, as we shall see in the final case study, run interference for an underprepared Ellington. Indeed, the story I tell about the collaborative dynamics in the recording studio during the production of *Ella Fitzgerald Sings the Duke Ellington Song Book* is in some ways a narrative of failed communication and disempowerment. Where my discussion of Strayhorn's work with Horne and Clooney privileged the (queer) collaborative dyad between arranger-composer and singer, my analyses of Strayhorn's work with Ella Fitzgerald on the behind-the-scenes collaborative dynamics in the recording studio take account of a third featured collaborator, one whose presence in this chapter has been decidedly spectral—Ellington.

"WE TRY": RECORDING "CHELSEA BRIDGE"

The *Blue Rose* sessions in January of 1956 were the starting point for what would be an extremely busy and productive creative period for Strayhorn and Ellington. Their heavy workload only increased in the wake of the Ellington Orchestra's "born-again" legendary Newport Jazz Festival performance in the summer of that year.[77] Among the major collaborative efforts they undertook were the jazz musical-historical fantasia *A Drum Is a Woman* and the Shakespeare-themed suite *Such Sweet Thunder*. While *A Drum Is a Woman* was originally recorded in the fall of 1956 and released on a Columbia Label LP with singers Joya Sherrill, Margaret Tynes, and Ozzie Bailey, the first (and only) staged performance of the work was produced for television the following year in a groundbreaking broadcast on CBS (*US Steel Hour*) on May 8, 1957, featuring an all-Black cast including dancers Talley Beatty and Carmen DeLavallade in the lead roles.[78] In between (and alongside) the 1956 sessions and the CBS televised staging, Ellington and Strayhorn composed and recorded *Such Sweet Thunder*, which was premiered in an early version at Town Hall on April 28, 1957, followed by a second performance at the Ravinia Festival on July 1 and, in its final version, at the Stratford Shakespeare Festival (Stratford, Ontario) on September 5. Amidst all this flurry of composing, arranging, and recording, the Ellington-Strayhorn team began work on *Ella Fitzgerald Sings the Duke Ellington Songbook*, a project that comprised two recording sessions in June and September 1957.

My discussion of collaboration on this project takes a granular look at the studio dynamics as captured on eight rehearsal tracks for Strayhorn's vocal arrangement of "Chelsea Bridge." These tracks, which were commercially released as part of the 1999 reissue of *Ella Fitzgerald Sings the Duke Ellington Song Book*, afford a rare behind-the-scenes sonic record of collaborative social and musical dynamics in the making of a prestige jazz LP in a midcentury recording studio. Listening closely to the interaction of social and musical scripts in these tracks complicates the benign sociality and canonical images evoked both in the original liner notes, and those for the deluxe 3-CD reissue in 1999. My argument, however, is not simply to illuminate the contradiction between the hagiography of liner notes and the far more complicated reality of what goes on in the recording studio; rather, my aim is to address how these complications unfold in relation to issues of authorship and across dynamics of power, gender, and jazz.

To better appreciate these social and musical dynamics, let me step back briefly to situate the *Ella Fitzgerald Sings the Ellington Song Book* project alongside Ella

Fitzgerald's other iconic *Song Book* recordings produced by Norman Granz for the Verve label. In many ways, the *Ellington Song Book* stands out from the two *Song Book* LPs that directly preceded it—Cole Porter and Rodgers and Hart—and the five that followed from 1956 to 1964.[79] The *Ellington Song Book* was the first and only opportunity that Fitzgerald would have to interpret a *Song Book* catalog dedicated to the works of an African American artist who was also a treasured colleague and friend. As well, unlike the other *Song Book* sessions that were both dedicated to white songwriters (or songwriting teams) and featured the charts of white "name" arrangers (Buddy Bregman, Paul Weston, Nelson Riddle, and Billy May), the *Ellington Song Book* sessions were led by an African American creative team and featured a predominately African American jazz orchestra. This latter fact points perhaps to another obvious difference: the Fitzgerald-Ellington *Song Book* sessions were the only sessions in which the songwriter—or rather songwriters—whose works Fitzgerald was interpreting were also the performers, arrangers, and musical directors.[80] In either case, the differences between the *Ellington Song Book* project and the other *Song Book* sessions accentuate a clear misfit between Granz's concept and the aesthetic and working methods of the Ellington-Strayhorn creative partnership (if not the Ellington outfit more generally). The original 1957 release sought to elide the most glaring dimension of this misfit—the Ellington-Strayhorn "authorship problem"—by packaging the two authors as essentially "interchangeable" (as always, the default in this exchange requires, to some extent, the invisibilizing of Strayhorn).[81] There are multiple ramifications here, one of which is especially salient to my focus: how this clash—a dissonance that encompassed aesthetic, social, and interpersonal matters—framed expectations and impacted the collaborative process and dynamics in the studio environment.

In one sense, the rehearsal tracks for "Chelsea Bridge" capture an aural image of collaborative dynamics and a division of creative labor that presents Ellington in his canonical role as the auteur-artist-bandleader.[82] For example, Ellington's voice dominates the verbal exchanges as he is heard directing the rehearsal and revising the arrangement while the band, Strayhorn, and Fitzgerald follow. Of these takes, the liner notes for the reissue, written by Patricia Willard, explain, "In the studio, Ellington and Strayhorn together built the music, adding and subtracting sound specifications from their own blueprints, as they constructed with Fitzgerald, an exquisite 'Chelsea Bridge' . . . Duke and Billy are mutually respectful. Ella, for all her stature as a star, is heard humbly in awe of the company she's in."[83]

Although virtually all of the newly scored arrangements for Fitzgerald and a large chunk of the original compositions comprising the LP are credited (or co-credited) to Strayhorn, Ellington's exchanges with Strayhorn, as Strayhorn is heard working with Fitzgerald and the band from the piano, cast Strayhorn's creative labor in the familiar role of "right-hand man" or, as producer Norman Granz put it in the original LP liner notes (written by Leonard Feather), Ellington's "perennial associate."[84] Yet listening closely to the aural transcripts of the rehearsal tracks tells other stories—alternate takes, if you wish. Musically, the tapes afford listening in to the process through which Fitzgerald and the musicians in the band shape and embody the music through listening to each other, interacting with the mics, their scored parts, and the overall soundscape of the studio. Especially audible, for example, is how Fitzgerald accompanied by Strayhorn listens closely and develops her interpretation over the course of the many takes. A clear example of this occurs in listening to how Fitzgerald with Strayhorn's support navigates the piece's tricky pick-up entrance and first A section. In an early take, Strayhorn plays an upper register figuration to cue Fitzgerald for the entrance, but Fitzgerald falters after an unsuccessful attempt to execute the pick-up, which involves lining up the vocalese with the rising B♭ minor phrase. In the second try, Strayhorn loudly plays the pick-up in the upper register as a cue, which Fitzgerald "answers." Once Fitzgerald is secure with the pick-up, Strayhorn returns to the more subtle high-register piano cue for subsequent takes while Fitzgerald experiments with different open and closed vowel sounds for the vocalese, eventually settling for the master take on a closed "ooo."

The rehearsal takes also document the intersection of musical and social scripts in the collaboration. These registers emerge through listening for the affective dimensions of voice and sound in the verbal exchanges, including pauses and silences, which capture dissonant layers of emotion and resonant tension. As Monica Hairston O'Connell and Sherrie Tucker argue in their analyses of Melba Liston's oral histories, attending to what they call the "information-rich" registers of aurality and voice means listening for "how the voice evokes, undoes or evades a shared sense of what means what—the voice going one way—the words another."[85] Here, knowledge of the chaotic circumstances and complicated social dynamics surrounding this recording session helps us to tune in to these affective registers. As Fitzgerald recalled in a 1965 *DownBeat* article, "It was a panic scene with Duke almost making up the arrangements as we went along. Duke is a genius—I admire him as much as anyone in the world—but doing it that way, even though it was fun at times, got to be kind of nerve-racking."[86]

While Ellington arrived for the session unprepared, Strayhorn did not come empty-handed. In fact, he arrived with thirteen new charts, including a soaring and powerful vocal arrangement of his ballad "Day Dream" with lyrics by John Latouche, which I will return to later.

According to Granz, "When we got to the studio, Strays had some arrangements, but nothing close to what we needed . . . Duke came without anything done . . . Ella really was very upset, and she didn't want to do it. She wanted to walk out . . . Strays spent a lot of time holding Ella's hand and saying, 'There, there, it's going to be okay. Don't worry.'"[87] The gendered stereotypes that shape Granz's image of an emotionally distraught, helpless "Ella" in need of "Strays's" reassurances and managing is worth foregrounding; as a commentary on the interaction of social and musical scripts surrounding this studio collaboration, it also is an image that suggests a precarious situation in relation to Fitzgerald's agency as a collaborator and professional.

Two moments stand out in the verbal and musical interactions documented in rehearsal tracks, which I identify as: 1) the "we try" exchange and 2) the "fuzzy moment." As shown in the transcription, at the open of the rehearsal track of "Chelsea Bridge" we hear Fitzgerald, Strayhorn, and Ellington discussing the performance of the second B/bridge section, which immediately follows the final A of the first AABA chorus. Fitzgerald is closest to the mic and the three are acoustically separate from the background chatter of the band. Ellington initially addresses Fitzgerald directly but Strayhorn quickly intervenes to reassure Ellington that Fitzgerald knows what to do, they have worked it out ("she's alright, she's alright"). A more extended exchange in the warmup between Ellington and Strayhorn in which they discuss Fitzgerald's part illustrates a complicated gendered dynamic between the leader and his assistant assigned to prepare Fitzgerald.

FITZGERALD: I'll try . . . do my best; I can't do no more.
ELLINGTON: Uh . . . the whazzizname . . . I would say when you get to the bridge—I mean you have a general idea, right?
FITZGERALD: We're getting it . . . [*Strayhorn interrupts*]
STRAYHORN: —She's alright, she's alright . . . In the middle it says here, so I told her to let me play the thing and then she answers me . . . [*inaudible*].
ELLINGTON: Why don't you make the entrance back into the [*inaudible*] . . .
STRAYHORN: That's what I'm doing . . .
ELLINGTON: Yeah.
STRAYHORN: That's exactly what . . . she answers me . . .

Difficult Beauty **73**

ELLINGTON: She [*scats a bit of theme*], then you [*scats more*], then she picks it up from there.

STRAYHORN: She answers me . . . [*starts singing a different part*].

[*Ellington walks away to lead band. Strayhorn and Fitzgerald continue the discussion. We hear Ellington clap his hands to call the band to attention.*]

FITZGERALD [*to Strayhorn*]: I sing a chorus and then what else?

STRAYHORN: Uh, you sing a chorus, and then a half-chorus.

FITZGERALD: Yeah, then I come back in to [*sings opening note of theme*].

STRAYHORN: Yeah.

[*In background we hear Ellington and band joking around.*]

FITZGERALD: Thank you, [Vera?].

[*Tape cuts out for a moment.*]

FITZGERALD: Which entrance are you talking about now?

STRAYHORN: This right here [*sings the part after second bridge (B) section*] . . . Let me make both times, because, see, the second time it will be coming out of here . . .

FITZGERALD: Yeah.

STRAYHORN: Out of that, so just let me make it and then you . . . you answer and then the second time we . . .

FITZGERALD: We try.

In the first half of the exchange, Strayhorn and Ellington discuss Fitzgerald in the third person, a discomforting gendered dynamic that can be heard as undermining Fitzgerald's agency. But the situation is complicated by the particular pressures of the session, a condition that modulates how we hear Strayhorn's tone and delivery as he moves to assert his voice and navigate the situation: his job is to facilitate the collaboration, to produce a good outcome. And, crucially, they are rehearsing an arrangement *done by Strayhorn of his own composition*. Notwithstanding her considerable star power during this period and the tremendous respect for her artistry among her collaborators, as the singer, Fitzgerald is in a position of vulnerability: her voice stands apart from the band (which the position of the mic emphasizes), exposed, and the success of her vocal performance depends upon the band. She has to prepare, and to be prepared in a way that is different from instrumentalists. It is "nerve-racking," to use her own words, and the rehearsal tapes document that feeling.

Bassist Jimmy Woode later told Hajdu, "Ella and Billy had a rough time. That wasn't the way either one of them like to work. They were perfectionists. They were accustomed to planning and having the work fine-tuned to perfection."[88] While Woode may well be overstating the notion that Strayhorn and Fitzgerald would always be allotted the time to "fine-tune" their work to perfection in studio situations (with or without Ellington), his account of difficult feelings and ways in which such feelings shaped the micro-interactions of social scripts and music making in the studio accords with the sonic and affective record of the rehearsal tapes. As for Ellington, we hear the voice of someone trying to put the best spin on a difficult situation as he attempts to introduce a note of levity to the proceedings with sardonic humor ("we all know *exactly* what we're doing, right"). The joking between Ellington and the band (minus Fitzgerald and Strayhorn) continues for a bit in the opening tracks; however, moments of tension and complication unfold in subsequent tracks.

The most significant of these moments—what I call the "fuzzy moment"— comes in the middle of the rehearsal tracks when Ellington makes an executive decision to cut a newly composed eight-bar introduction that Strayhorn scored for the vocal arrangement. Leading up to this moment, Ellington voices dissatisfaction with the reading of the introduction in the first two run-throughs. He tells Strayhorn, "Hey, this introduction, Strayhorn, is not coming off as fuzzy as I thought it would." After this, we hear Strayhorn attempting to rectify the problems from the piano—he works on the inner voicing, fixes some wrong notes in the brass section. As they prepare for another take, Ellington says, "Alright, let's take the whole thing. Ready. Now look, in the introduction, the very beginning, in the very beginning, ah, we're not . . . we're getting a much too robust sound out of everybody as they make the individual entrances and what we're trying to do is get a fuzzy thing here." They try again and, in the subsequent takes, we hear Ellington's impatience grow. After working with drummer Sam Woodyard to create more variety in the percussion, this is how the "fuzzy moment" dialogue ends:

ELLINGTON: Let's get something beside the brushes . . .
WOODYARD: Want some mallets? [*plays hand drum*]
ELLINGTON: Strays I think we're going to take out the first introduction.
STRAYHORN: [*silence*]

As a studio practice in Ellington band recording sessions, the editorial decision to cut Strayhorn's newly scored introduction seems hardly worth commenting on—merely a routine part of the recording process in which a bandleader must make tough calls in relation to the time-versus-effort calculations that are demanded in the studio. In this case, the calculation concerned a bad fit between the complexity of the writing and the amount of time they had to work on the chart. But I hear in Strayhorn's silence, in the "fuzzy moment," a sonic archive documenting their very long and conflicted history around issues of power, authorship, and aesthetics. As emphasized earlier, Ellington's repeated failures to respect the formal integrity and intentions of Strayhorn's scores were a primary source of hard feelings and frustration for Strayhorn. In this case, Ellington's cutting of his newly and beautifully scored introduction to "Chelsea Bridge" for this session occurred within an already precarious and frustrating situation for both Strayhorn and Fitzgerald as they had to bear the fallout for Ellington's lack of preparation.[89] Indeed, Ellington's editorial decision directly impacted Fitzgerald's performance, depriving her of a skillfully conceived and custom-composed instrumental entrance—a sonic frame and platform for her extraordinary artistry.

Another dissonant interpersonal script that is crucial to include here involves circumstances beyond the recording studio. Although this was a creatively productive time in the Ellington-Strayhorn partnership, for Strayhorn it proved also to be a challenging and painful time as an employee in the Ellington orbit. Early in 1957, Ellington hired a virulently homophobic publicist, Joe Morgan, whose extreme animus toward Strayhorn not only created a toxic work environment for Strayhorn but also led to a de facto policy of withholding authorial credit to Strayhorn whenever and wherever possible, including, most spectacularly, in a feature profile of Ellington for *Look* magazine that Morgan engineered, published in August 1957. Publicist Phoebe Jacobs told Hajdu, "Joe Morgan hated Billy with a passion that was beyond all understanding. For one thing, Morgan thought that Billy represented competition for Duke's attention . . . And Billy was gay, which threw Morgan completely off the deep end. Just the mention of Billy Strayhorn's name drove Joe Morgan crazy. The very idea of Billy made him nuts."[90]

The dramatic centerpiece in Hajdu's account of Morgan's homophobic PR regime during this moment is an agonizing story of a dinner encounter in the summer of 1957 between the tap dancer Honi Coles and Strayhorn at the Flash Inn, an Italian restaurant that Strayhorn frequented, located "on the northern edge of Harlem."[91] Both Coles and Strayhorn were core members of the legendary fraternal tap group, the Copasetics. In his own words: "I got to know Billy very well though the club we were in together, the Copasetics. We were so close he called me 'Father.'"[92] As Hajdu sets the scene, the *Look* profile of Ellington had just hit the newsstands, but their discussion was prompted by Coles's mention of another PR piece on Ellington published in the May 7 issue of *Newsweek* in the lead-up to the CBS *US Steel Hour* televised broadcast of *A Drum Is a Woman*. This piece credited Ellington as the "the author, composer, lyrist, narrator, conductor, piano player," and gushed that the event would count "as one of the few times a great name in jazz has had a full hour of prime evening TV time to himself."[93] The piece also highlighted the Town Hall premiere, a week prior, of *Such Sweet Thunder*, crediting it as Ellington's "twelve-part suite in honor of Shakespeare." Coles confronted Strayhorn directly about his feelings, pressing him to respond to questions about his authorship being absented in the press coverage of these two high-profile performances: "Why weren't you mentioned? You wrote every bit as much of that music they're fussing all over as Ellington, and they didn't even mention your name. Why do you let them get away with that?" Despite several rounds of Strayhorn's dissembling responses ("'Oh Father, you know I don't need all that. I'm better off without all that. Let him have his articles. I'm better off this way.'"), Coles pushed on:

> I don't believe you. I think you do care or you wouldn't be drinking like a fucking fish every fucking time I see you. That got him. Billy said: "Be careful, Father. Some day, I may get angry with you" . . . I understood what he was saying. Because he wasn't a celebrity, he didn't have to answer to anybody about his lifestyle. So I said, "I understand. The main thing is that you're happy." And I asked him straight out, "Are you?" And he went into his Father routine—"oh Father . . ." And he started to cry. I sat there with him, and Billy sat there, and he cried like a baby.[94]

This story is gut wrenching and, it is important to say, its inclusion in Hajdu's biography could be read as highly problematic for the way it discloses Strayhorn's very private pain, while also combining that disclosure with an abject image of Strayhorn's alcoholism. Yet, in the context of Strayhorn's archive of feeling, the story serves a critical purpose, a queering counterforce to the countless complacent representations of Strayhorn as the gentle, submissive collaborator, happy to cede the spotlight to Ellington.[95] As such, Coles's story—and his position as "Father" in Strayhorn's chosen family—opens up a critical space for hearing the dissonant layers at the intersection of the personal and musical in Ellington's cavalier and insensitive attitude toward Strayhorn's chart. Implicit in Coles's story is a larger truth that Strayhorn did indeed desire public recognition of his artistry, a recognition that, in the case of his creative labor, would also extend to desire for Ellington to respect the integrity of his charts. On this point, Coles's story also provides a useful pivot for listening to other *Song Book* sessions for which no rehearsal tapes were recorded.

The "Chelsea Bridge" session took place on the fourth and final day of the recording dates at Fine Recording in New York City. On the first day of the session, the band cut two other Strayhorn originals—new vocal arrangements of "Day Dream" and "Take the 'A' Train" (Dizzy Gillespie sat in for the latter side). Trombonist and copyist John Sanders remembered that Strayhorn took on a directorial role for this session. Importantly, no major cuts were made to Strayhorn's charts, including an elaborate and luminous introduction for the ballad "Day Dream," a fact that would seem to undermine the rationale for Ellington's decision to cut the introduction of "Chelsea Bridge." Strayhorn's arrangement of "Day Dream" for Fitzgerald stands as one of his most powerful and emotionally complex charts and shares with "Chelsea Bridge" formal and affective features, including a warm, lush backing, and chromatic voicing. Strayhorn's arrangement parallels the ethereal and sensual atmosphere of Latouche's lyric; as Walter van de Leur has observed, the introduction simulates the direct experience of the dreaming subject with a breathing backing that moves through hazy textures and clarinet bird calls delivered by Jimmy Hamilton.

As is well known, "Day Dream" was among the earliest works Strayhorn scored for the Ellington Orchestra, composed in 1939 as a showcase for Johnny Hodges. Little is known about the specific contexts or circumstances in 1941 under which the words, credited to the white queer lyricist, composer, and book writer John Latouche, were added. The work was originally copyrighted in 1940 under the names of Ellington and Strayhorn and, then, in the following year, newly registered with Latouche credited for the words. Almost certainly, Strayhorn would not have been involved in commissioning Latouche for the lyric so early in his tenure with Ellington. And the fact that Strayhorn declined to produce a vocal arrangement of the song between 1941 and 1957 raises the possibility that he may initially not have welcomed Latouche's added lyric. In a biography of Latouche, however, Howard Pollack claims that Latouche "developed a warm friendship with both Strayhorn and Ellington" and "likely collaborated in person with either Strayhorn or Ellington, or both."[96] While there is no evidence of collaboration between Strayhorn and Latouche in the early 1940s, in 1946 Strayhorn and Latouche came into contact through their collaborative work on the music-theater production of *Beggar's Holiday*, a Broadway-jazz reworking of John Gay's *The Beggar's Opera*, for which Latouche wrote the book and lyrics. The production broke ground on several fronts, most radically in featuring an interracial cast and creative team. As the story goes, Ellington was away on tour (with Django Reinhardt) and thus largely absent from rehearsals. Although he was the titular composer for the production, Ellington "dispatched Strayhorn who wrote and arranged large portions of the show, occasionally conferring with Ellington over the phone."[97] Along with his musical contributions, during the rehearsals Strayhorn played a key role in the backstage creative team, working closely with the large cast of actors, singers, and dancers. It is very likely that Strayhorn befriended Latouche during the production. A telegram from Strayhorn to Latouche dated March 11, 1954, is strong documentary evidence of a "warm friendship" developed during this collaboration. The occasion for the telegram was the Off-Broadway premiere of the musical *The Golden Apple*, for which Latouche wrote the lyrics. Strayhorn's message reads, "A million bushels and pecks of Golden Apples to You, Swee' Pea."[98] Still, the most important queer backstage story from *The Beggar's Opera* collaboration concerns Strayhorn's relationship to the production's dancers. In the words of Albert Popwell, one of the dancers in the production, "He always came around us and delighted in being around us . . . This was unusual, because we were more or less a clan—they called us the gypsies, because were really in a world of our own. And Billy always seemed to merge toward us, one because so many of us were gay, and that was a very important connection, especially if you were black *and* gay."[99]

While any collaboration between Strayhorn and Latouche for "Day Dream" remains a mystery, one thing is certain: Strayhorn's 1957 setting of Latouche's lyric in the extraordinary arrangement for Fitzgerald bears witness to a deep engagement with Latouche's words.[100] Here, the affective frequencies that orient Strayhorn's arrangement of "Day Dream," its mix of sonic beauty, dissonant underscore, and lyrical meditation on the ineffable power of romantic fantasy echo back to the music-poetic environment in which this chapter began—the "difficult beauty" that Lena Horne heard in and through her performance of Strayhorn's "A Flower Is a Lovesome Thing." In her interpretation of the ballad for the tribute album *We'll Be Together Again*, this emerges with a quiet, meditative, almost prayerful energy. Strayhorn composed both works—sublime vehicles for Hodges's ballad voice—in the same year, 1939 (although "A Flower Is a Lovesome Thing" was first recorded by Hodges under the title "Lovesome Thing" and copyrighted in 1941). Unlike "Day Dream," however, the added words for "A Flower Is a Lovesome Thing" came from Strayhorn's pen, probably around the time of its copyright registration in 1954.[101] In both its newer texted incarnation and in the original Hodges version—a song without words—"A Flower Is a Lovesome Thing" evokes the sensuous yet fragile poetry of flowers: "Azaleas drinking pale moonbeams / Gardenias floating through daydreams." Odes to the "luscious living lovesome" qualities of flowers abound in Strayhorn's oeuvre, most definitively in his catalog of original ballads for Hodges that he wrote over the course of his entire career.

Strayhorn's special attachment to flowers was first cultivated in his youth. Between the ages of eight to eleven, Strayhorn's mother, Lillian, with whom he was extremely close, sent him on extended visits to the home of his grandparents in Hillsborough, North Carolina. She did so, in large part, to protect him from the dire precarity and domestic violence surrounding his life in Homewood (Strayhorn was a target of his father's alcohol-fueled rage and abuse).[102] Strayhorn's time with his grandparents provided a space of peaceful refuge where he spent his days playing his grandmother's piano, taking long solitary walks along the river and through town, and learning about the fine points of flowers from his grandmother, Lizzie, who, according to Strayhorn's sister, Lillian Strayhorn Dicks, "had a special affection for flowers" and would "spend hours discussing them with Bill."[103] Throughout his adult life Strayhorn would gift bouquets of flowers to the women in his family as well as close female friends and acquaintances.

Strayhorn's sonic and lyrical evocations of flowers resonate toward these biographical contexts, or, more precisely, the archive of memories and feelings these experiences enabled: freedom to be oneself and to wander and imagine in calm, safe spaces; maternal bonds and communal connection; contemplation and communion with natural beauty; aesthetic and spiritual cultivation and reflection. At the same time, the queer aesthetic and affective registers I explored earlier in relation to "Flamingo" also critically orient Strayhorn's flower-themed compositions, the titles of which conjure sensual objects, delicate beauty, and the utopian spaces of dreams and fantasy—what I refer to in the chapters that follow as Strayhorn's queer music. Through their interaction with and embodied performances of his vocal arrangements, the singers profiled in part 1—Herb Jeffries, Lena Horne, Rosemary Clooney, and Ella Fitzgerald—all engaged to some extent with this repertoire of queer feeling and sound. Strayhorn's queerness required that he work behind the scenes, a space from which his voice facilitated spaces and created contexts for other voices to be heard, to discover new vocal personas and new ways of sounding and being.

As my exploration of Strayhorn's vocal arranging and collaborative projects with singers has shown, these contexts and spaces merged the personal and musical, private and professional, across scripts of race, gender, and sexuality within and against the patriarchal spaces of midcentury jazz. To be sure, a critical element in the art of arranging revolves around cultivating skills of musical sensitivity and empathy in collaborative music making; yet for Strayhorn, as with any number of gay male artists working behind the scenes, this talent for sonic empathy in collaborative efforts was deeply shaped by and through his queer identity. Assigned to "manage" and score charts for singers in the Ellington organization, Strayhorn practiced an intimate care ethics—a queer collaborative practice that, in the cases I've examined (and in many more), was guided by a deep sensitivity to the vocal qualities, abilities, affective ranges, and performative personas of the singers dually with a deep sensitivity to the precarious position of women vocalists navigating male-dominated jazz spaces.[104]

PART II
Strayhorn's Queer Music

THREE
Strayhorn's Lorcian Encounter

In a 1966 interview, critic Stanley Dance asked Billy Strayhorn to comment on his and Duke Ellington's approach to their collaborative composing of the Shakespearean-themed 1957 suite *Such Sweet Thunder* and their 1960 arrangement of Tchaikovsky's *Nutcracker Suite*. As Strayhorn described it, both projects involved an extended precompositional process. In the case of *Such Sweet Thunder*, this took the form of intensive study, dialogue, and research over a six-month period: "We read all of Shakespeare!" Strayhorn told Dance. Despite significant differences between the two works—an original composition versus an arrangement of a preexisting piece—Strayhorn argued that the creative challenge for both pieces was essentially the same, namely that of interpretation and adaptation. "The only difference with Shakespeare," he added, "was that we had to interpret his *words*."[1]

As it happened, the Shakespearean words on which Strayhorn had focused his creative energies came in the suite's seventh movement, "Up and Down, Up and Down (I Will Lead Them Up and Down)," what the composing partners called an instrumental "parallel" to the character Puck from *A Midsummer Night's Dream*: a musical parallel to the erotic disorder that the elf Puck, servant to the fairy king Oberon, unleashes in act 2 of the play. After incurring the wrath of Oberon, Puck is ordered to conjure a dark fog and lead the two pairs of mismatched young Athenian lovers (Helena and Demetrius; Hermia and Lysander) astray. Puck carries out this order with perverse pleasure, confusing the two men by imitating their voices in turn. While Strayhorn cast Clark Terry (flugelhorn) in the lead role, it is Strayhorn as composer who is the real Puckish agent as he leads the instrumental couples—Hermia and Lysander

(Johnny Hodges, alto saxophone, and John Sanders, trombone), Titania and Oberon (Ray Nance, violin, and Jimmy Hamilton, clarinet), and Demetrius and Helena (Russell Procope, alto sax, and Paul Gonsalves, tenor sax)—far afield through rapidly shifting cross-section instrumental combinations that move along elaborate, polyphonic paths of sonic mirroring and inversion. Terry's flugelhorn weaves through these complex textures and voicings, commenting and responding, and at key points establishes illusory moments of tonal order; the scene ends famously as Terry's instrument "speaks" one of Puck's lines: "Lord what fools these mortals be."[2]

Strayhorn's choice to "parallel" Puck and the erotic disorder he animates serves as a resonant starting point for exploring queer aesthetic and historical contexts in Strayhorn's compositions.[3] Besides the sexual mischief that Puck orchestrates, other queer topics in *A Midsummer Night's Dream* are signaled in Puck's outsider perspective, his servant role, and the larger fairy/mortal divide that structures the play.[4] Queer contexts for Strayhorn's Puckish encounter surface in aspects of his biography. Strayhorn had an abiding, deep affection for the Bard and expressed a deep attachment particularly to one of Shakespeare's "Fair Youth" sonnets, a body of work that has inspired an extensive history of queer readings and attachments.[5] Strayhorn's identification with Shakespeare informed his enthusiasm for composing *Such Sweet Thunder*: "he took it on excitedly, glowing to his friends about having an Ellington Orchestra project geared especially to him."[6] Strayhorn's love of Shakespeare was well known among the Ellington band and, according to Jimmy Hamilton, surfaced as a (somewhat affectionately mocking) nickname for Strayhorn during this period: "We used to call him Shakespeare—that was one of his nicknames . . . Not when he was around, I'm talking about."[7]

Yet the most intriguing biographical link comes through the metaphorical parallels between character and composer that Strayhorn's choice of Puck invites us to consider. As David Schiff observes, "Strayhorn's self-portrait as the impish fairy Puck suavely symbolized multiple aspects of his life. He was openly gay, and at the same time was often an invisible instigator of musical spells; he usually remained in New York while the band toured, phoning in musical fixes as needed."[8] While I would not want to elide Strayhorn's "musical spells" with last-minute telephonic "musical fixes," the notion of Puck as a self-portrait of Strayhorn is apt, particularly with respect to the supportive role he played in his partnership with Ellington (here filling the role of Oberon) and, during this period, his frequent outsider or "virtual" position in the band.

How might we link queer identity and history to the Puck-like invisibility under which Strayhorn worked, to his compositions and arrangements, and to his choice of and writing for specific improvising voices? The paired chapters in this section are concerned with elaborating how Strayhorn's identity and communal affiliation with Black queer artistic networks informed and supported his creative engagement with and expressive treatment of queer material and figures. This focus rearranges the concept of queer collaboration to center issues of queer aesthetics and modernist history; that is, whereas part 1 attended to Strayhorn's collaborative relationships and his positionality and practices as a vocal arranger, my exploration of queer collaboration in part 2 foregrounds the conceptual, historical, formal, and affective facets of Strayhorn's creative or imaginary encounters with queer material and histories. I offer a close reading of two midcentury works as case studies: a set of four pieces Strayhorn composed in 1953 for an Off-Broadway production of Federico García Lorca's *The Love of Don Perlimplín for Belisa in Their Garden*, and several movements from the aforementioned Strayhorn-Ellington adaptation of Tchaikovsky's *Nutcracker Suite*. My study of these two works will track several central issues. First, as with *Such Sweet Thunder*, I consider how similar dramatic and programmatic constellations found in both works engage artistic figures, themes, topics, and aesthetic practices that have strong queer historical affiliations. The latter include failed or impossible love, masking, stylized exotica, and other liminal spheres of identification and reversal. Second, in discussing these queer topics, I highlight a shared (queer) transnational orientation that involves a fictive collaboration with gay male artists from the past, specifically Lorca and Tchaikovsky.[9] Finally, I argue that the two works address issues around the representation of Black queer identity and desire that, taken together, position Strayhorn's translations within modernist queer cultural history and, more specifically, within the history of Black gay cultural production, history, and aesthetic practices.[10]

To be sure, the *Don Perlimplín* pieces and the *Nutcracker Suite* arrangements differ significantly in relation to genre, performance, and historical and institutional contexts. And the *Nutcracker Suite* arrangements, co-created with Ellington, fit easily into jazz/Ellingtonian history. By contrast, the *Don Perlimplín* pieces were composed for a queer experimental theater production, one of several non-Ellington music-theater projects Strayhorn pursued in the early 1950s, the most significant of which was an unrealized 1954 musical, *Rose-Colored Glasses*. Strayhorn's concept for this unfinished work—perception and invention through the eponymous rose-colored glasses—and the disparate archive of surviving materials offers a useful framing for my focus in this chapter on queer collaboration in Strayhorn's music for the *Don Perlimplín* production.

BROTHER BIG EYES

A number from the first act of *Rose-Colored Glasses* introduces the character Brother Big Eyes, a mysterious denizen of the surreally hip "Land of Ool-Ya-Coo."[11] Brother Big Eyes makes his living forging "magic glasses" out of a "little trailer." As described in Strayhorn's lyrics, he offers a variety of products to suit the needs of his customers: some magic glasses are "ready-made" and others tailored to fit the "individual psyche" of their wearers:

> Once upon a time there was a man named Brother Big Eyes,
> At least that's what everybody called him.
> He was a queer-looking duck:
> Kinda funny
> Kinda sad
> Kinda quiet
> Kinda . . . well, kinda MA-A-AD!
>
> Well, Brother Big Eyes had a little trailer
> Hitched to the back of his bicycle
> And from this trailer he conducted his business,
> Quite a business it was, for, you see,
> Brother Big Eyes made magic glasses.
>
> He ground them, tinted them
> And polished them himself
> You could get them ready-made,
> Right off the rack,
> Or tailor-fitted
> To suit your own individual psyche.

With his "quiet-funny-mad-sad" ways, the figure of Brother Big Eyes bears a striking metaphorical resemblance to Strayhorn himself. As if to emphasize this whimsical autobiographical trace, the stage directions for the musical called for a set dominated by a gigantic pair of horn-rimmed glasses. The symbolic parallels between character and author are not hard to find: Strayhorn conducted his musical business, as it were, in something like a "little trailer"—that is, behind the scenes of the Ellington outfit; and, not unlike Brother Big Eyes's enchanted glasses, Strayhorn's musical products manifest seemingly magical registers of musical empathy and transformation, whether in composing for the Ellington Orchestra or in crafting and arranging songs "tailor-fitted" for the vocal personas of particular singers.

Strayhorn's description of Brother Big Eyes as a "queer-looking duck" constitutes a further parallel, one that is, I want to argue, of a piece with the affective force of Brother Big Eyes's ocular power to alter—with Puck-like magic—the perceptions of his "customers." The use of "queer" obviously marks Brother Big Eyes as "strange" or "eccentric," yet it also may allude to the gay male subcultural use of the term under the cover of Broadway polish.[12] Such cryptic queer topics surface in several of Strayhorn's earliest songwriting efforts: critics and listeners have long speculated about double coding in his 1935 youthful, pre-Ellington classic "Lush Life" (and, interestingly, he wanted this song to close out the musical's finale). Much of this speculation has revolved around the historical possibility of queer resonance in the opening couplet "I used to visit all the very gay places, / Those come what may places." Whether or not the adolescent Strayhorn was aware of the newly circulating underground use of the word *gay* (and it is plausible given Strayhorn's sophisticated, urbane tastes and sensibilities, and his early self-awareness of his own nonnormative sexual identity), the lyric of "Lush Life" gives voice to a potent mixture of topics and affects with a distinct queer historical lineage—failed, impossible love, Paris as a fantasy destination, scenes of slumming, underworld decadence, and intense loneliness. Strayhorn himself would remark in a *DownBeat* piece from 1949, "It's a song most persons have to listen to twice before they understand it, and then lots of them don't know what it's about."[13]

According to Strayhorn's collaborator for the musical, Luther Henderson, a Black modernist poetics of coded scripts pervaded the fantastical bebop-inflected narrative of *Rose-Colored Glasses*: as he travels around the Land of Ool-Ya-Coo, Brother Big Eyes encounters "these crazy characters like Papa Doo Dah and Johnny No Love . . . It was supposed to be like a dream. Very cryptic, very weird."[14] Yet the queer moment that most interests me in the lyric for "Brother Big Eyes" resides in the ambiguously hyphenated space of the phrase "queer-looking"; for coupled with the professional practices of Brother Big Eyes, the joining of "queer" and "looking" evokes at once both a "queer-looking" visage and "looking queerly," a different way of seeing the world that Strayhorn's character imparts to others through the medium of magic glasses. Indeed, Henderson recalled that the musical was all about the implications of an altered, strange perception of the world, in particular as it affects erotic desire: "What's reality? What's perception? What's the difference? And what does love mean with this going on?"[15] The power of the magic glasses thus exists in their capacity to alter perception, yet the source of this power and the specific form such alternations may take depends upon the ability of Brother Big Eyes to craft a product that skillfully reads and reflects the psychic interiority and desires of its users. Understood as a metaphor for the relationship between composer/arranger and musician, the transformative potential of the magic glasses suggests a queer modernist matrix of affect, empathy, perception, and practice.

"Brother Big Eyes" was one of eleven new songs Strayhorn wrote for *Rose-Colored Glasses* (at least four other numbers have been credited to Henderson).[16] Strayhorn's collaboration with Henderson coincided with the period from 1953 to 1956 when Strayhorn left the Ellington fold and set out to establish his own professional identity. His desire to separate from Ellington began after a series of personal and professional losses and disappointments. In 1950 Ellington dispatched Strayhorn to Paris to work on his behalf on what turned out to be a disastrous Orson Welles production of *Faust*, titled *The Blessed and the Damned*; although Strayhorn sketched out four works for the production, only one piece, a song for Helen of Troy (played by a young Eartha Kitt) survived Welles's compulsive cuts and changes to the production.[17] During this same trip, Strayhorn found out that Aaron Bridgers had accepted the gig as bar pianist at the Mars Club and thus would not be coming back to New York. Yet, as I discussed in chapter 2, Strayhorn's quest for independence was most directly precipitated by frustration over uncredited creative labor and an "accumulations of grievances, from copyright issues to artistic conflicts." As van de Leur emphasizes, it was especially the latter—artistic conflicts—that most frustrated Strayhorn.[18] These conflicts arose most glaringly in Ellington's repeated failures to respect the formal integrity and intentions of his collaborator's scores. Indeed, one of the last Ellington projects to which Strayhorn contributed before the separation was a series of recording sessions for Capitol Records in April 1953. According to van de Leur, Ellington "vigorously went to work with Strayhorn's scores, taking out sections and incidentally reshuffling the order of pieces."[19]

When Strayhorn returned to New York late in 1950 after the Welles debacle, he sought out alliances with a largely Black gay artistic community. He regularly attended salon gatherings at the home of dancer Frank Neal and his spouse, Dorcas, where he came into contact with many young Black gay artists, musicians, choreographers/dancers, and writers, such as Talley Beatty, Charles Sebree, and, on occasion, James Baldwin.[20] Neal, Sebree (painter, illustrator, set/costume designer, dancer, playwright), and Beatty (dancer/choreographer) all began their careers in the vibrant Chicago Black arts scene in the 1930s and 1940s. The three artists probably first met through their participation in the Katherine Dunham Company during this period. Beatty performed as a principal dancer in the Dunham troupe on and off from 1937 to 1942, while Sebree worked as a set/costume designer and (briefly) dancer, and Neal as a dancer. Neal and Sebree were also active in and around the historic South Side Community Arts Center during its inaugural years in the early 1940s. By 1950, all three artists had relocated in New York.

The Neal salon meetings and the sense of community and affirmation they provided proved to be tremendously empowering for Strayhorn, encouraging him to seek creative projects outside the Ellington fold. "For those in the group who were Black and gay," observed Dorcas Neal, "it meant the world just to see that there were others like them in the arts." Dancer and choreographer Talley Beatty would remember Neal salon evenings as "great socio-political meetings to ease the pain." Neal remembered Strayhorn proclaiming, "There are some things I want to do for myself for a change, I think I'm going to do them."[21]

If the Neal salon provided a queer communal network of support during this period, it was another closely related gay-friendly environment, the world of theater, that served as Strayhorn's creative forum.[22] For the musician, theater meant primarily Broadway: he was an avid theatergoer and envisioned the musical *Rose-Colored Glasses* for the Broadway stage. The reasons for the production's failure to move beyond the planning stages are not entirely clear, but evidence suggests it was a casualty of Ellington's machinations to prevent Strayhorn and Henderson from forming a musical partnership.[23] Because *Rose-Colored Glasses* never made it into production (and because only three of eleven of his songs survive), a detailed discussion is not possible. However, less than a year prior to *Rose-Colored Glasses*, in the fall of 1953, Strayhorn composed four pieces—all of which survive—for an Off-Broadway production of Federico García Lorca's experimental play *The Love of Don Perlimplín for Belisa in Their Garden*, subtitled *An Erotic Alleluya in Four Scenes* (*Amor de Don Perlimplín con Belisa en su jardín: Aleluya erotica en un prologo y tres escenas*). Mounted by the vanguardist Artists' Theater collective in November of that year, the one-act play was staged with an all-Black cast and played to sold-out audiences for three performances at the Amato Theater in Greenwich Village, a small venue of approximately four hundred seats. The Artists' Theatre was founded in the late 1940s by Herbert Machiz with the financial backing of influential art dealer John Bernard Myers. Its mission, as stated in the performance flyer for the Lorca production, included advancing new opportunities for collaboration among artists in the theater, "to experiment with new production methods," and "to allow actors to work with unconventional scripts."[24] Strayhorn first met Machiz while working with him in Paris on the Welles production of *Faust*; Machiz was the production manager. During its first years, the group mounted productions of new works by queer playwrights Tennessee Williams, Frank O'Hara, John Ashbery, and James Merrill, all under the direction of Machiz. The Lorca production was performed as the first half of a double bill with Lionel Abels's *The Death of Odysseus* during the fledgling company's premiere season.

Working closely with Machiz, Strayhorn conceived of the production of *The Love of Don Perlimplín for Belisa in Their Garden* (hereafter *Perlimplín*) as an opportunity to address issues of Black gay identity or, at any rate, to make a statement that would give a level of recognition and visibility to that experience. While the music Strayhorn composed for this project has been the subject of critical commentary, its connections to the production's interpretation of Lorca's tragicomedy in Black or queer terms remains unexplored.[25]

I present multiple contexts that illuminate such connections, proposing a queer hearing of—and tracing a transnational queer history for—Strayhorn's musical contributions. These include the choice of play and playwright, themes, and formal devices enacted in the text itself, the performative contexts of the Artists' Theatre production, and, crucially, the transformative role of Strayhorn's setting of three lyric texts in the play. I understand Strayhorn's musical contributions as a critical reading and translation of Lorca's drama, one that fully engages with the text at the level of both form and content.[26] In doing so, my analyses shed light on what, following Brent Hayes Edwards, we might call the "literary imperative" in Strayhorn's work. Strayhorn's incidental music stands as the first among an impressively long list of subsequent musical realizations of the play, including six ballets and a dozen operas, most notably Bruno Maderna's radio opera version from 1962.

QUEER DISGUISES: "LOVE, LOVE" AND "SPRITE MUSIC"

Strayhorn's concept for a Black gay-themed music-theater production actually preceded the Lorca project; he first voiced the idea while working on a slightly earlier and decidedly less challenging Machiz project, a summer-stock production of Vernon Duke and John Latouche's *Cabin in the Sky*. As recounted by cast member Bill Dillard, the idea emerged during a backstage conversation between the two artists about what would be Strayhorn's "dream project": "And Strayhorn started talking. He had this idea about doing this all-Black show, and it had something to do with homosexuality."[27]

Even without knowing the specifics of Strayhorn's "dream project," his idea to create and stage a show explicitly representing Black gay identity at this moment—just as the Cold War "lavender scare" was gearing up—was itself a radical Black queer vision for music-theater. On this point, Strayhorn's idea engaged the ambiguities and contradictions around discourses of sexuality in the postwar period which, as historian John D'Emilio and many others have argued, gave rise, simultaneously, to radical, liberatory visions and activism alongside violently oppressive and conformist forces.[28] In his analysis of the reception of James Baldwin's pioneering queer novel, *Giovanni's Room* (1956), Douglas Field observes that the publication of Alfred Kinsey's reports on "male and female sexual behavior in 1948 and 1953, respectively, shattered pervasive conceptions of sexual practice," while also raising anxieties around the policing of sexual and racial-gender boundaries.[29] Although Kinsey's work was intended to counter homophobia by exposing, for example, the fallacy that gay men and women could be visibly identified by stereotypical gender-deviant or "sexual invert" self-presentation, it "in fact contributed to a national homosexual panic."[30] The circulation of this discourse around sexual/gender deviancy and homosexual "passing" in the postwar Black press is here a case in point. Extending Field's work on the reception of *Giovanni's Room* to include and center coverage in the Black press, Rachel Corbman has argued that "a unique cluster of sociopolitical forces—including the Cold War, the Civil Rights Movement, and the birth of the modern concept of homosexuality—caused the black press to amplify its vehement and vocal opposition to homosexuality at the same historical moment that James Baldwin published *Giovanni's Room*."[31] Corbman discusses coverage of homosexuality in a wide range of Black press publications during the 1950s, including the "lower-brow" publication *Jet* magazine, which between 1951 and 1954 published "four full-length feature articles on black homosexuals or homosexuality," including a piece on the "moral charges" against Bayard Rustin, and, in April 1954, homophobic fear-mongering reporting ("Are Homosexuals Becoming Respectable?????") that told readers: "Prominent Negroes whose strange sex lives are whispered conversation [include] a celebrated writer, a successful actor, a noted educator, two members of a nationally known quartet, a West Coast newspaperman, a classical pianist, a late boxing champion, several male choreographers and a now-deceased composer."[32]

Clearly, Strayhorn and his collaborator Machiz were not among these unnamed subjects whose "sex lives are whispered in conversation"; yet, the homophobic tropes that organized such coverage bring into sharp focus the radical concept and possibilities of their work together on the *Perlimplín* production. While Strayhorn initiated the collaborative project, it was almost certainly Machiz who decided on a "nontraditional" staging of Lorca's *Perlimplín*. It is not hard to see why Machiz thought his choice would be an appropriate match for Strayhorn's concept. Both playwright and play would have evoked associations of sexual deviance, most obviously through the figure of Lorca himself, whose homosexuality was known to the entire creative team. As costume designer Bernard Oshei remembered, "Of course everybody thought of Lorca as the great gay Martyr."[33] Furthermore, the play itself had been censored as "pornographic" in Spain for its erotic content. The first attempted production in 1929 by the theater group El Caracol at the Sala Rex in Madrid was shut down by the government.[34] The state authorities did not object to the erotic content per se, but rather to the subversive nature of the erotic content in relation to heteronormativity. For as in many of Lorca's plays, the rejection of social morality and conventions surrounding gender and sexuality in *Perlimplín* is enacted through modes of male fantasy, masking, and masochism.[35] To understand how Strayhorn's pieces sonically engage with such Lorcian theatrical modes and devices and, by extension, the network of queer discourse and contexts from which these emerged, a brief overview of the play and its critical literary history is necessary.

Lorca's *Perlimplín* takes a stock comedic theme—the marriage of an old man to a young woman—and refashions it through a set of surrealistic, highly stylized, and overtly artificial frames.[36] The title of the play itself evokes a kind of cutting-and-pasting of historical stock characters, themes, images, and genres. Both the figure of Don Perlimplín as protagonist and the reference to the *alleluya* in the subtitle (which in the version used for the production was translated as "lace paper valentine") originate from the worlds of eighteenth- and nineteenth-century Spanish popular culture; the genre of the *alleluya* was a type of eighteenth-century comic strip.[37] The mixture of comic and tragic modes through which Lorca realizes the characters and action in the play are animated by the sense of stylized historical and generic montage. Even his stage directions foreground this quality: for example, the directions for the third scene (set in Perlimplín's dining room) specify that "the perspectives are deliciously wrong." In an oft-cited letter, Lorca referred to the characters in the play as "ampliaciones fotográficas" (photographic enlargements).[38] As Paul McDermid observes, Lorca "mimics the photographic process, 'developing' the character and scenario of the alleluya version of don Perlimplín into a stage play."[39] In this sense, the self-consciously outmoded forms and genres generate a set of masks—artificial conventions, images, and roles that literally and figuratively conceal or contain the characters.[40]

Echoing in particular the frames of historical pastiche in the play, Alfred Leslie's sets for the 1953 production consisted of a series of five large panels (reaching eighteen feet high by ten feet wide) that were used as rotating backdrops on top of the small revolving stage. Each panel featured a stylized version of a canonical art-historical image. As Leslie recalled, "I was thinking of all the Western artists of the past and using elements of their work in order to create the ambience of a particular space."[41] For the interior scenes that dominate the first half of the play, Leslie's oversized images, framed in eye-popping greens, formed a surrealistic counterpoint to the opulent golds of the period furniture and the ornate eighteenth-century costumes chosen by Bernard Oshei (Lorca specifies green walls and a "green dress coat" for the first scene).

In the play's prologue we are introduced to Perlimplín, a shy, bookish, confirmed bachelor of around fifty, and his faithful, motherly maid, Marcolfa. Marcolfa convinces Perlimplín that he should marry Belisa, a young, beautiful woman with, we soon learn, an avid sexual appetite. On his wedding night, Perlimplín is unable to consummate the marriage and when he awakes the next morning, a giant pair of golden horns sits atop his head, itself encased (as specified by Lorca) in a "white wig full of curls." For as we (and he) soon learn, during the night, Belisa has had sex with five men, representing "five different races." Perlimplín then enacts a macabre plan: disguised as a young suitor, he appears under Belisa's balcony hidden beneath a red cloak and sends her passionate, erotic notes. Belisa is drawn to the mysterious stranger and her attraction soon—through the encouragement of her husband—develops into an obsession. In the final scene, Perlimplín tells Belisa that he intends to murder her lover not out of a machismo code of honor ("Don Perlimplín has no honor! No honor!" he declares moments before), but so that "he will love you with the infinite love of the dead, and I will be free of this dark little nightmare of your magnificent body." As he looks around the garden, he directs Belisa to "look from whence he comes" and exclaims, "Dear God, how beautiful, how beautiful he is!" He exits and soon after staggers in, wrapped in the red cloak, with a bejeweled dagger he has thrust into his own breast.

With Perlimplín's elaborately orchestrated suicide, the play completes a formal transformation from farce to, if not tragedy, then a kind of melodramatic pathos. In the final moment, Perlimplín seems to morph from a tortured, sexually frustrated figure with a cruel imagination into a kind of queer Christ figure, sacrificing himself, in a characteristically Lorcian blood ritual, so that Belisa could be made to understand—and be transformed by—his psychic and bodily wounds. This ritualized moment emerges from, and comes as a resolution to, the splitting of Perlimplín's consciousness in the second half of the play, itself an element rich in irony and self-reflexivity.[42] Perlimplín directs the action through devices of fantasy and masking, and attempts to transcend his identity and body through fugitive acts of imagination, desire, and ritual sacrifice.[43] Just before his death, for example, he tells Belisa that her love for the young man is a "triumph of my imagination." Sarah Wright suggests that this "further twist on the theme of deceptiveness of appearances" raises the question of disguised homoerotic love. As she observes, "behind Belisa, who appears to be the archetypal sensual young woman, we find a beautiful young man."[44] On another level, however, Perlimplín's authorial role turns his sexual frustration into (misogynist) mechanisms he can control—first words and sadistic fantasy, then violence.

These themes and theatrical devices are poetically condensed in three lyric texts that Strayhorn set.[45] The first of these lyrics, "Love, Love," is explicitly interpolated as a "song" sung by Belisa offstage in the play's prologue.[46] Perlimplín's first encounter with Belisa, then, comes through her disembodied voice, which while comical, nevertheless creates a resonant field of ambiguously gendered desire. From its opening bars, Strayhorn's setting takes full advantage of this queer contrast between Belisa's unseen voice and the overheated eroticism of the text, the opening line of which hails the phallic pleasures of fish and/in thighs: "Enclosed within my thighs / the sun swims like a fish" (example 3.1, [a]). Strayhorn animates the erotic/aquatic metaphors in Belisa's lyric with a halting yet liquid vocal melody, while the waltz-time accompaniment shapes a simple alternation of two chords (the B major tonic and a minor-seventh chord built on the dominant, F♯), an affect redolent of Erik Satie—a three-beat dance looping around itself. Together melody and accompaniment create a delicately stylized atmosphere that amplifies both the puppet-like, reflexive nature of the characters—the sense of people hiding behind masks—and its ambiguously gendered frames.[47] With the none-too-subtle double entendre on the words "morning cock," the mood abruptly shifts into Andalusian exoticism replete with flamenco Phrygian coloring against a recitative-like vocal line. The song's affect of queer erotic wit reaches completion in Strayhorn's coy setting of the line "don't let it vanish, no," which he deliciously extends through the reiteration of the word "no" (example 3.1, [b]).[48]

Strayhorn's musical translation of Lorca's theatrical sensibility in "Love, Love" proposes a diverse network of transatlantic modernist affiliations—French, Spanish, and African American. The articulation of this modernist confluence through rhetorical modes of irony, stylization, and masking marks and extends a field of cross-cultural affinity between African American modernism and Lorcian modernist drama, a perceived affinity that was a part of the reception of Lorca by African American artists (a topic to which I will return). Both traditions draw heavily from folk and vernacular repertoire; of particular importance here is the centrality of (queer) trickster figures in Lorca's theater during this period. These take the form of harlequins, magicians, puppeteers, and, most pertinent to Perlimplín, the Puck-like figure of the duende.[49] Translated literally as "lord of the house," the duende comes from Spanish folklore and appears as a "puckish figure capable of intervening for better or for worse in the life of ordinary mortals."[50]

In *Perlimplín* two decidedly "puckish" duendes appear onstage in the guise of sprites, who literally cloak the wedding night scene (they "run a curtain of misty gray" over it). For the 1953 production, the sprites appeared as two opulently costumed Moors, who stood at the proscenium arches. With Perlimplín and Belisa safely hidden from the audience's prying eyes, the sprites directly address the play's spectators with droll metacommentary about the voyeuristic desire propelled by the act of spectating itself:

> FIRST SPRITE: And how do you like it? It's always nice to cover other people's failings . . .
> SECOND SPRITE: And then to let the audience take care of uncovering them.[51]

Strayhorn's incidental music for this scene, "Sprite Music," transmutes the trickster-like linguistic prowess and cutting commentary of the sprites through a harmonically disjunct, almost atonal virtuosic pianistic display. A rapid triplet figuration and shifts in register effectively convey, at once, the fantasia of the sprites and the play's abrupt fracturing of the theatrical conventions of realism

EXAMPLE 3.1 Strayhorn, "Love, Love"; (a) measures 1–12, (b) measures 21–24. From Walter van de Leur, *Something to Live For*, 123.

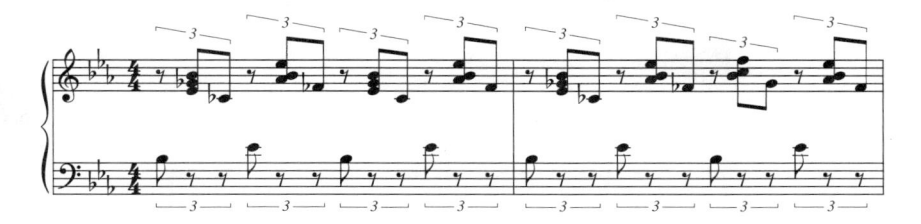

EXAMPLE 3.2 Strayhorn, "Sprite Music"; measures 1–2. Transcribed by author.

(example 3.2). As in "Love, Love," a French modernist voice is invoked, this time strongly reminiscent of the pianism of Ravel. The distinct accent of these two Strayhorn settings itself has queer implications, not only in terms of its use of queer expressive modes of irony, eroticism, and masking (and the inclusion of puckish figures), but also with respect to Strayhorn's real-life identification with French art and culture. For much like his white gay American counterparts, Strayhorn's Francophilia signaled queer affiliation.[52]

EROTIC (IM)POSSIBILITY: "WOUNDED LOVE" AND "THE FLOWERS DIE OF LOVE"

With their non-jazz modernist musical language and associations, "Love, Love" and "Sprite Music" may have come as a surprise to listeners familiar with Strayhorn's work. By contrast, "Wounded Love," which is sung by Don Perlimplín following his comically failed wedding night and foreshadowing his suicide, evokes both in style and feeling Strayhorn's lush, expressive jazz ballads and songs. As van de Leur has observed, the setting features "a harmonic progression more conventional for Strayhorn, including chromatic passing chords and a middle section in the parallel minor."[53] By taking up the formal and emotional vocabularies associated with his instrumental and vocal ballads to set a queerly resonant lyric of erotic impossibility and alienation, Strayhorn brings into close proximity this queer thematic and a soundscape of lyrical beauty, bittersweet expressivity and interiority—a coupling that recalls both early Strayhorn songs such as "Lush Life" and "Something to Live For" and, as we shall see, Strayhorn's ballads for Johnny Hodges.[54] Indeed, both "Wounded Love" and "Lush Life" meditate on a very similar queer topic—the experience of intense pain, loss, and loneliness wrought by a failed, impossible love. "Same-sex desire," as Heather Love writes, "is marked by a long history of association with failure, impossibility, and loss," an association which, she observes, "historically, has given queers special insight into love's failures and impossibilities."[55]

The mix of erotic longing and impending doom in "Wounded Love," as well as details of text setting and form, underscore these queer themes and, in doing so, realize the merger of artifice, lyricism, and lament in Lorca's verses.

> Love, Love
> That here lies wounded
> So wounded by love's going;
> so wounded,
> dying of love.
> Tell everyone that it was just
> the nightingale.
> A surgeon's knife with four sharp edges;
> The bleeding heart—forgetfulness.
> Take me by the hand, my love,
> for I come badly wounded,
> So wounded by love's going.
> So wounded!
> Dying of love!

The opening vocal gesture is a dramatic descending minor seventh leap on the words "Love, Love," a gesture that seems to encapsulate Perlimplín's sexual frustration and confusion—Belisa awakens his desire (and the powers of fantasy and imagination) but he is unable to respond to her physically.[56] Indeed, as can be seen in example 3.3 (m. 3), this descending minor seventh leap mirrors Perlimplín's abjectly mocking reference to the opening words in Belisa's prior song through the process of inversion; that is, the descending minor seventh leap inverts Belisa's ascending major second heard on the same words "Love, Love" (this connection is also signaled in the extant manuscript, which bears the title "Love–Love WOUNDED LOVE"). Strayhorn also makes use of a simple vocal motive, a repeated A♭, to convey the linking of love and death in the poem, most vividly encapsulated in the two iterations of the line "dying of love" in which the A♭ motive takes the shape of a quarter-note triplet on the words "dying of" followed by a whole note for "love."[57]

In addition to these formal and motivic procedures, Strayhorn's setting mirrors Lorca's use of speech rhythms and visual imagery to intensify the dramatic arch of the lyric. The shift to parallel minor in the B section, for example, features a

EXAMPLE 3.3 Strayhorn, "Wounded Love;" measures 1–12. Transcribed by author.

declamatory vocal line against an increasingly active and chromatic accompaniment. This build in tension highlights a succession of images: first "nightingale," then, "surgeon's knife," with a climax on "Four sharp edges," which dissolves into the achingly expressive setting of the phrases "Bleeding heart" and "Forgetfulness" that reiterate the descending minor seventh in the left hand and the repeated A♭ vocal motive.

Through such close attention to meaning, affect, and lyrical form, Strayhorn's "Wounded Love" draws out the deep, emotionally fraught layers of the poem, a musical-dramatic statement that orients Strayhorn's darkly sensuous song stylistics to the queer topics and affects voiced in Lorca's text: thwarted desire, melancholy, erotic melodramatics. In the play, "Wounded Love" closes scene two and functions as a transformative moment in the dramatic shift from farce to tragedy; when scene three opens in Perlimplín's surreally designed dining room (in which the "perspectives are deliciously wrong"), Belisa is already taken with Jovan, the passionate young lover imagined by Perlimplín. Here "Wounded Love" seems to initiate another queerly resonant topic in the play—namely, a "closet" dialectic of disguise and revelation that structures the second half of the dramatic action.

The larger contexts surrounding Strayhorn's engagement with these coded closet dynamics warrant additional comment, for the queer territory explored in Lorca's drama gestures toward other pre-Stonewall gay-authored representations of queer themes in McCarthyite America by such playwrights and writers as Tennessee Williams, Robert Anderson, Jane Auer Bowles, William Inge, and James Baldwin.[58] In fact, in the fall of 1953, Strayhorn repeatedly took friends to see Anderson's melodrama *Tea and Sympathy*, which opened on Broadway in September just at the time when Strayhorn was working on the Lorca project.[59] Set in the environs of a New England private boys' school, Anderson's play tells the story of a young sexually frustrated wife, Laura (played by Deborah Kerr in her New York theatrical debut), who leaves her brutish, closeted husband, Bill (the school's homophobic headmaster), to seduce a sad, sensitive, effeminate, book-loving, acoustic guitar-playing student who is "deeply confused about his sexual identity."[60] Anderson's play—not the 1956 film version—foregrounded the close relationship between homophobia and anti-communist persecution: the action begins, for example, with the public accusation and expulsion of the boy, Tom, on suspicion of being a homosexual. The evidence marshaled to confirm his "perversion" includes his love for classical music and poetry and his enthusiasm for playing the part of Lady Teazle in the school's production of

The School for Scandal. Most damningly, Tom has been seen in the company of another suspected homosexual in the story, a teacher at the school with whom he was spotted skinny-dipping.

Thus, the dramatic arc of both *Tea and Sympathy* and Lorca's *Perlimplín* revolve around the tortured and confused sexuality of (at least one) male protagonist, and the disruptive or unconventional sexual behavior of a female lead. Whereas Anderson's hugely successful Broadway production ultimately disavows heteronormative fears of homosexuality, Lorca's drama is critical and transformative.[61] For in *Perlimplín*, as in all of his works for theater, Lorca seeks, as McDermid eloquently argues, "to promote a spiritual dimension of Love that is always denied to the queer who loves, the one who desires the same sex and finds that the dominant (hetero)culture circumscribes her desire as merely physical."[62] Comparing the different dramatic outcomes staged in the final scene of each play underscores such differences. In *Tea and Sympathy*, Laura's seduction of the young boy is framed as a (scandalous) act of maternal sexual charity meant to dispel questions about sexual deviance. In Lorca's work, by contrast, the gendered terms are inverted: it is Perlimplín who sacrifices himself and thus serves as a figure of, if not feminized, then ambiguously gendered identification.

The metaphysical dimensions of this moment are dependent, however, on its framing as a "performative rite" replete with a "sung liturgy,"[63] a function that both Lorca and Strayhorn assign to Belisa's song "The Flowers Die of Love." In his stage directions, Lorca calls for a "sweet serenade" cast in a chorus-stanza form to establish the mood. Referencing—with dark irony—details of Belisa's first comically erotic song, "Love, Love," this deceptively simple song of yearning passion is heard from offstage, while Perlimplín hides behind a rosebush onstage.[64] At several points in Belisa's song, we hear his voice, recitative-like, intoning the refrain "the flowers die of love." As specified in the play's text, between Belisa's and Perlimplín's parts, choral voices echo the second line of each of Belisa's free verse couplets.

Critical discussions of this final scene focus on the ways in which Lorca's lyric references the vernacular form of the serenade, juxtaposing the simplicity and innocence of Belisa's passion—and the form itself—with the foreboding darkness of the impending suicide.[65] Strayhorn's setting both establishes the ritual mood for this complex scene and interprets its formal-expressive juxtapositions into a jazz-inflected fantasy of a Spanish folk song. For the opening verses, a simple E♭ major triadic melody moves against a modal accompaniment anchored by a drone ostinato in the left hand whose rhythmic profile evokes a slow habanera,

EXAMPLE 3.4 Strayhorn, "The Flowers Die of Love"; (a) measures 1–11, (b) measures 25–28. Transcribed by author.

while the refrain "the flowers die of love" is underscored by a shift to the parallel minor (example 3.4, [a]). Perlimplín's echoing of the refrain does not appear in the manuscript score; yet at each of the three iterations of the refrain, Strayhorn substitutes a measure in which the voice rests and the right hand plays three high-register open sonorities (B♭–E♭–B♭), the last of which ends the song, imparting a delicate, otherworldly feel. This feature suggests, I would argue, if not a space for Perlimplín's spoken refrain, then a ghostly sonic signifier of it.

At measure 21, we hear what initially appears to be a third strophe, but this breaks off after four measures for the climactic couplet, "silver of streams and mirrors, anise of your white thighs." The setting for the first half of the couplet simulates its own subtle sonic streams and mirrors: against pedal tones in the outer voices, we hear an undulating wave of parallel harmonies in the inner voices—C minor moves down to a (quirkily spelled) C♭ minor then back up to C minor, with a biting dissonance created by the C♭ minor triad against the E♭ and B♭ pedal tones occurring with the word "mirrors" (example 3.4, [b]). Unmoored from its tonal surroundings, this moment concentrates the verse's paradoxical affect of "sweet popular form and its dark content," of stylized surface and tortured, melancholic depths, as it amplifies the topic of erotic deception and disguise.

BLACK QUEER LORQUISMO

My discussion of Strayhorn's music for the Artists' Theatre production of *Perlimplín* has thus far been based largely on a close reading of the original manuscript scores. In the absence of contrary evidence concerning details of musical performance or direction, it is fair to assume that the performance forces were limited to piano and voices and that the scores represent more or less what was heard by the audiences. The roles of Perlimplín and Belisa were played, respectively, by Elwood Smith and Gladys Bruce. Smith's resume was particularly well matched for the lead role: a Julliard-trained actor-singer and an experienced Broadway performer, he had appeared in two all-Black-cast Broadway productions: he was cast in a supporting role for the 1946 musical *St. Louis Woman* and, in 1952, he performed in the first postwar revival of Virgil Thomson/Gertrude Stein's modernist opera *Four Saints in Three Acts* (which shares with *Perlimplín* a Spanish mis-en-scène and rich queer modernist subtexts).[66] Bruce, on the other hand, was an up-and-coming jazz/popular music singer. In 1951 she collaborated with her husband, the arranger and bandleader Jimmy Mundy, on two R&B sides,

"The Right Kind of Feeling" and "I've Got the Blues for My Baby," and during the fall of 1953 was a headliner at New York's L'Onyx Club.[67]

Of the two brief New York press reviews the production received—both by prominent theater critics—only one mentions Strayhorn's music. Writing for the *Saturday Review of Literature*, Henry Hewes characterized the performance as "delicate and not too expert." Hewes nevertheless found that Lorca's "sad poetic story . . . still manages to come through," praising the "bright scenery by Alfred Leslie" and the "haunting music by Billy Strayhorn."[68] A perfunctory notice in the *New York Times* had nothing positive to say about the production under Machiz, whose direction is disparaged as "hesitant and restrained" where it should be "fleet-footed and more integrated."[69] Some sixteen years later, John Myers would recall the production as "appalling," but, unlike the other reviewers, his critique, which leans heavily on a kind of campy racial paternalism, lays the blame entirely on the cast: "Alfred Leslie created a beautiful rococo decor and a stage which was a turntable; and he had two beautiful blackmoors pulling on the ropes changing the sets and so on—every avant-garde device you could think of, and these poor darling blacks just didn't know where they were with Lorca . . . how to manage their skirts, their fans . . . it's very hard to explain."[70]

Myers's memory of the production stands in stark contrast to Strayhorn's vision of the production as a vehicle for Black gay communal identification. As for Strayhorn's memory, the archive is silent. Yet, as I argued at the outset, the queer collaborative act of performing Lorca with an all-Black and largely gay male cast (and queer theatrical troupe) in McCarthyite America carried a powerful symbolic currency all its own—recall here designer Oshei's earlier comment: "Of course everybody thought of Lorca as the great gay Martyr."[71] Oshei's characterization of Lorca reflects a wider awareness of the homophobic contexts of Lorca's execution by Nationalist insurgents in his native Granada at the start of the Spanish Civil War. While the primary reason for Lorca's murder in 1936 was political (his outspoken stance against Franco), the "open secret" of his sexual dissidence was bound up with his political dissidence. In his book *The Death of Lorca*, for example, Ian Gibson quotes one of the Falangist killers: "We have just killed Federico García Lorca. We left him in a ditch and I fired two bullets into his arse for being a queer."[72]

Viewed in this context, the 1953 production of *Perlimplín* stands as a queer revision of previous African American expressions of political solidarity with the Spanish left. As is well known, the cause of the Spanish Civil War galvanized leftist African American intellectuals and artists in the late 1930s, such as Langston Hughes and Paul Robeson. Strayhorn's Lorcian encounter, although an anomaly in his career, nevertheless connects to (and, in fact, is a largely overlooked instance of) the history of African American cultural engagement with and translations of the artist. Langston Hughes, for example, translated Lorca's *Blood Wedding* in 1938 (although it was not published until 1991); and his commanding translation of Lorca's *Gypsy Ballads* (1951) introduced Lorca to a postwar generation of African American poets and artists. Postwar odes to Lorca by African American artists include those by the radical poets Bob Kaufman and Amiri Baraka, and Romare Bearden's celebrated early series of paintings *The Death of the Bullfighter* were inspired by Lorcian themes.[73] This engagement was in some senses initiated by Lorca himself. In 1929 Lorca came to New York under the pretense of studying English at Columbia University, an experience that led to his celebrated poetic homage to Harlem in *Poet in New York*. While Lorca's poems on Black Harlem life invoke primitivist tropes, they also go beyond such romantic, apolitical discourse, probing the dynamics of American racism and addressing themes of social justice.

Yet this history of African American Lorquismo was itself bound up with the larger history of the US reception of the artist during the Cold War period, when, as Jonathan Mayhew has observed, the influence of Lorca's work peaked.[74] Lorca's image and work became a locus for varied forms of "resistance to the conformity and repression of cold war America" and for imagining alternative "versions of American exceptionalism" founded upon perceived affinities between progressive American and Spanish discourses of nation.[75] In the African American context, this discourse invoked cultural and historical parallels between Andalusian culture and expressive practices (gypsies, flamenco, *cante hondo*) and African American culture (blues, spirituals, jazz), similarities which, in the case of poets such as Kaufman, Baraka, and later Nathaniel Mackey, were explicitly theorized through the Lorcian figure of the duende.[76] Of most significance to the topic at hand, however, is how this history of Black and white North American Lorquismo intersected with—and was thus shaped by—queer subcultures. Indeed, many of the male poets Mayhew cites hailed from interracial queer subcultures, from the Harlem Renaissance (Hughes) and the Beats (Kaufman, Ginsberg, Burroughs) as well as other Bay Area queer poets (Jack Spicer and Robert Duncan).[77] The 1953 *Perlimplín* production stands as a critical predecessor of this historical intersection in New York (and San Francisco) of Beat, gay, and Black culture, bringing together diverse modernist worlds and transatlantic networks: New York jazz and avant-garde theater and art, white and Black queer subculture, and Broadway.[78]

SONGS WITHOUT WORDS, OR ARRANGING "WOUNDED LOVE" FOR JOHNNY HODGES

Although no recordings were ever made of Strayhorn's pieces for the *Perlimplín* production, in 1958, some two years after he resumed his partnership with Ellington, Strayhorn arranged "Wounded Love" as an instrumental ballad for Johnny Hodges, recorded under the title "Three and Six." The meaning of this cryptic title, which appears on the lead sheet for the arrangement, is unknown; of more importance is that a manuscript sketch for the arrangement bears the original song title and, apart from a few minor alterations that serve to streamline and simplify the phrasing and form, the recording hews closely to the original music.[79] While Hodges may not have known the original words for the song, the sonic dialectics of his improvising voice, with its uncanny lyrical blend of melodic stylization and deep expressivity, detached refinement and earthy soul, powerfully translate Lorca's lyric lament into a ballad of remarkable beauty and feeling.

Strayhorn's decision to arrange this song as a ballad for Hodges has particular relevance for this study. Along with Strayhorn's songs, his ballads for Hodges stand out as his most intimate, personal, and certainly most sensuous lyrical statements. The close musical relationship between Strayhorn and Hodges was established almost from the beginning of Strayhorn's tenure with the Ellington band in 1939 with pieces such as "Passion Flower," "A Flower Is a Lovesome Thing," "After All," and "Day Dream." These works share a modernist sonic conception rooted in the use of altered dominant chords with upper extensions, chromaticism, slow tempo, sustained backings, and static harmonic fields, a sound complex that is frequently heard—as in his Lorca songs and, perhaps most famously in his ballad "Chelsea Bridge"—in relation to the harmonic procedures and nocturnal "mood" programs of French musical impressionism.[80] Yet it is Hodges's playing, with his languorous "liquid" glissandi, that stages Strayhorn's modernist take on the instrumental ballad, amplifying its sense of suspended dream-like temporality, tonal ambiguity, and lush chromaticism. His voice performs a kind of sonic alchemy, blending and transforming the modernist abstractions and expressive or programmatic components of Strayhorn's conception.

During this period, Hodges's consistent popularity with the public—over the decade he won almost every *DownBeat* poll for his category—made him

Ellington's premiere star soloist. Like Strayhorn, Hodges left the Ellington outfit in the early 1950s (his absence roughly paralleled Strayhorn's); when he returned in 1955, Strayhorn composed the stunning "Pretty Girl" and, a year later, "The Ballad for Very Tired and Very Sad Lotus Eaters." Not long after, Strayhorn also featured Hodges in two magnificent arrangements of Ellington ballads, "I Got It Bad (and That Ain't Good)," and "Prelude to a Kiss." His arrangement of "I Got It Bad" for Hodges is especially notable in this context: although Ellington composed the melody of the song, Strayhorn created the original *Jump for Joy* arrangement for the great Ivie Anderson, and, over the course of his career, produced over a dozen arrangements of the tune, arguably culminating in his arrangement showcasing Hodges.[81] Their musical relationship continued until the end of Strayhorn's life in 1967, a collaboration that resulted in a large body of recorded Strayhorn compositions and arrangements featuring Hodges. Among the late Strayhorn-Hodges collaborations, standouts include "Elf" (retitled "Isfahan" for the *Far East Suite*), and his final dark, cancer ballad "Blood Count."[82] The Strayhorn-Hodges collaboration, what Jack Chambers has memorably dubbed their "spectral alliance," stands as a distinct, even unique, genre and creative energy within Ellingtonia—if not also in the wider field of jazz—"momentary but somehow momentous."[83] As Chambers writes, listening to the "lotus-eating, dream-like music Johnny Hodges and Billy Strayhorn made together for all those years, there can be no doubt that they were soul-mates."[84]

The close identification of Strayhorn with Hodges pervades critical and journalistic commentary on Strayhorn both during his lifetime and posthumously. Furthermore, the special muse-like musical relationship between Strayhorn and Hodges emerges as a dominant theme in the recollections of several long-time Ellingtonians. In an interview with Stanley Dance, for example, Cootie Williams responded to questions about Strayhorn's music by saying, "All the beautiful things. All the pretty things. He wrote those with Johnny . . . Everything he did was for Johnny Hodges."[85] Strayhorn scored a great many gorgeous charts for other great Ellington soloists. Nevertheless, Williams's statements speak to the indelible association of Strayhorn's compositional voice in the key of Hodges, as it were, and with the sonic power of "all the beautiful" and "pretty things." It was not for nothing that Charlie Parker referred to Hodges with the pointedly feminized (and Euro-classicized) moniker, Johnny "Lily Pons" Hodges. Both Williams's comments and Parker's comparison of the qualities of Hodges's alto saxophone sound (especially, we can assume, in the interpretation of love songs) to that of a star Euro-American coloratura soprano point to a larger network of associations around voice and identity that defined the genre of the instrumental ballad in jazz and popular music during this time. Specifically, such statements index the ways in which codes of feminized (and racialized) sexuality fundamentally shaped the genre's affects of intimacy and its power to communicate or give voice to a desiring self—affects and expressive modes that Hodges, starting with his extraordinary 1941 recordings of "Day Dream" and "Passion Flower," both referenced and refigured.

By the mid to late 1950s, Strayhorn and Ellington were themselves exploiting these associations in diverse programmatic contexts, including *Such Sweet Thunder* (1957), *A Drum Is a Woman* (1957), and *Far East Suite* (1963). Strayhorn's showcasing of Hodges in the Afrofuturistic number "Ballet of the Flying Saucers" from *A Drum Is a Woman* is here exemplary. In the 1957 televised broadcast of *A Drum Is a Woman* for CBS's *US Steel Hour*, Hodges, backed by ethereal harp arpeggios, takes center stage in the interlude sections of "Ballet of the Flying Saucers."[86] In *Such Sweet Thunder*, two Strayhorn-Hodges ballads were repurposed: under the title "Star-Crossed Lovers," "Pretty Girl" became the sonic parallel for *Romeo and Juliet*, with Hodges cast in the role of Juliet; while the ballad "Lately" was revamped as a piece of moody, sensuous exotica titled "Half the Fun," a reimagining of Cleopatra (half of *Anthony and Cleopatra*). Both tragedies, it bears emphasizing, have had rich queer afterlives; indeed, the composition and premiere of *Such Sweet Thunder* occurred five months prior to perhaps the most famous queer American reworking of *Romeo and Juliet*—*West Side Story* (Bernstein/Robbins/Sondheim/Laurents). Several years later, in 1959, "Star-Crossed Lovers" and "Half the Fun" would have their own queerly inflected afterlife as the accompaniment for two central duets in Talley Beatty's 1959 ballet *The Road of the Phoebe Snow*.[87] Beatty's ballet centers on a story of doomed youthful love set in a Black working-class community struggling with the effects of racism, violence, and poverty, a scenario that bears striking parallels to *West Side Story*.

In these contexts, as well as in the context of the instrumental ballad version of "Wounded Love," what codes of gender and sexuality in Hodges's sound made his voice a resonant vehicle for expressing moments of queer desire or identification? To address this question I pursue first an argument about the queer historical potential inscribed within the grooves of Hodges's recording of "Wounded Love." To return to an argument I rehearsed in the previous chapter in relation to the ballads "A Flower Is a Lovesome Thing" and "Day Dream," this recording not only archives the sonic traces of Black queer desire as thematized in the original song, but it makes legible (or audible) the queer affective registers and sounds that inhabit the Strayhorn-Hodges's instrumental ballads. Indeed, the recording of "Wounded Love" is suggestive of the ways in which we might hear his ballads for Hodges as a continuation and transformation of the lyrical modes and affects of the early pre-Ellington queer-themed songs, "Lush Life" and "Something to Live For." For the Strayhorn-Hodges ballads seem at once to sing *something*, a type of song without words and, at the same time, obscure or displace linguistic specificity into a dreamy, sensuous, and singing reverie of longing, beauty, and intimacy.

The queer links between Strayhorn's songs and his ballad writing for Hodges invites a closer consideration of personal and musical circumstances and contexts that came to bear on their collaboration. Biographical and critical commentary has centered on the striking differences in personality and public persona between the two artists. According to Hajdu, in contrast to Strayhorn's outward affability and his erudition, Hodges's "modest vocabulary and often shaky grammar" caused him acute embarrassment and led him to create "a protective shell of taciturnity." Hodges avoided encounters with the public, declined to sit for interviews or sign autographs, "even for the most ardent fans, because he could scarcely write his name."[88] Onstage in performance, an outward coolness—he famously maintained an aloof, stone-faced, non-emotive bodily posture—set against the extravagant lyricism, soulfulness, and emotive eloquence of his playing created an incongruous spectacle of sight and sound. Almost without exception, he would sit stock still, devoid of bodily movement or legible expressive gesture, his eyes glancing right or left as if scanning the audience.[89] Ultimately, Hajdu argues, the musical alliance of Strayhorn and Hodges is best understood as "a model of compatible contrasts": in his playing Hodges throws off the "gruff" veneer to express a warm "impeccable musical eloquence"; Strayhorn, by comparison, carefully maintained a genial, even "exuberant" public persona, while creating "works of tortured discontent." Together these complementary energies generated a mix of "gut musical feeling and conservatory acuity united in artistic fidelity."[90]

I'm drawn to Hajdu's notion of "compatible contrasts," but I would argue that defining the Strayhorn-Hodges collaboration in these terms does not account for a deeper connection that may have "united" them in "artistic fidelity," a connection that dwells at the intersection of race, class, queerness, and shame. Cue Hodges, Johnny's spouse, told Hajdu that her husband needing to conceal his fear, particularly in social situations that might "reveal" his limited formal education and literacy skills (Hodges dropped out of school at age fourteen), directs us to these deeper connections. Although the sources and manifestations of their stigmatization differed, the lived social and psychic experiences of stigmatization impacted their careers and, I would argue, oriented their relationship to musical creativity.[91] What role, if any, their shared orientation to intersecting forms of stigma may have played in their personal bond or musical collaboration is unknowable; however, this observation offers a space for theorizing further queer collaboration in the Strayhorn-Hodges archive. Take, for example, another interlocutor quoted in Hajdu's biography, the jazz organist "Wild Bill" (William Strethen) Davis: "Neither one of them guys was really who they seemed . . . Johnny was just as mushy inside as Strayhorn was froufrouy."[92] Davis's statement strikingly queers Hodges by way of Strayhorn through the gendered codes of the descriptors "mushy" and "froufrouy," aligning both collaborators with a kind of feminized masculinity (one carefully disguised by a veil of, respectively, affability and aloofness). Though Davis's comments take aim at the personal, they could just as easily be applied to the Strayhorn-Hodges musical alliance as practiced in their principal collaborative musical medium—the ballad. Indeed, although it was not his intention, Davis's use of the word "mushy" for Hodges might be heard against the iconic and sardonic ode to queer loneliness in the final verse of "Lush Life": "Romance is mush / Stifling those who strive / I'll live a lush life in some small dive / And there I'll be, while I rot with the rest / of those whose lives are lonely too." Although theirs were songs without words, over the course of nearly three decades, the collaborators' unique take on the genre's defining romantic associations and intimate sonic affects—a blend of eloquence, stylized extravagance, and soulful longing—may, like Strayhorn's songs, be heard as a kind of categorical rupture. The slow-burn, romantic soundings of the ballad offered an ideal creative forum to give voice to vulnerable selves and fashion lush sonic fantasies full of languid, intoxicated melodic musings, or, as Chambers would have it, "late-night absinthe reveries."[93]

Yet to identify too closely expressions of queer desire and feeling in Strayhorn's music—his "differentiated style"—with the special affective world of the Strayhorn-Hodges ballads risks obscuring the larger record of Strayhorn's engagement with other queer topics, themes, practices, and affects in diverse generic settings. Indeed, my focus in this chapter on how a larger history of queer affiliation emerges in transnational programmatic contexts already underscores this varied queer historical archive and its circuits of desire and identification.[94] Where my tracing of this archive in Strayhorn's *Perlimplín* project examined queer connections in Strayhorn's musical translations of and engagement with Lorca's text, my discussion of Strayhorn's contributions to the Strayhorn-Ellington *Nutcracker Suite* in the chapter that follows draws out linkages between Strayhorn's imaginative translations of Tchaikovsky's suite and historic artistic figurations of Black queer identity and exotica, such as those exemplified in the works of gay Harlem Renaissance artists. My goal is to position simultaneously Strayhorn's work within a history of Black gay expressive practices and *as* a practice or poetics of Black (queer) transnationalism. At the same time, I attend to how these practices intersect with and are meditated by multiple cultural and interpretive contexts, including the history of North American stagings of *The Nutcracker* (ballet), the changing symbolic capital of midcentury jazz in the era of the LP, and the critical perceptions of the Ellington-Strayhorn partnership.

FOUR

Black Queer Moves in the Strayhorn-Ellington *Nutcracker Suite*

In the spring of 1960 Strayhorn began working on his and Ellington's adaptation of Tchaikovsky's *Nutcracker Suite* for jazz orchestra. Plans for the LP arose during a period in Strayhorn's life in which "he was becoming prone to periods of isolation and delay unless he found a particular musical project inspiring."[1] *The Nutcracker Suite* was just such a project and it served as a reparative creative outlet, providing a sorely needed emotional boost as he struggled with personal and professional issues. From Hajdu's vivid recounting of the work's genesis we know that Strayhorn forcefully pitched the idea for the project during a group meeting in Los Angeles that included Ellington, producer Irving Townsend, and several band members (Harry Carney, Ray Nance, and Jimmy Hamilton). Apart from the evident rhetorical eloquence of Strayhorn's proposal, it is easy enough to imagine why such a prestige project would have found receptive ears: a complete LP jazz version of a popular classical work could be sold to executives at Columbia for its potential to generate crossover appeal, thus attracting the coveted "middle-of-the road" demographic of the adult record-buying public. Moreover, the form of the suite, with its historical connections to dance and programmatic expressivity, was an established favorite of the composing partners and well suited to the Ellingtonian jazz idiom.[2]

Yet economic, aesthetic, and cultural prestige factors alone do not fully explain Strayhorn's choice of Tchaikovsky's ballet suite as a vehicle for exploring extended form in jazz, nor do they justify his enthusiasm for and personal investment in the project. A glimpse of the latter can be garnered in a story about the work's genesis, which places Strayhorn in the posh upper Manhattan brownstone of Marian and Arthur Logan, a gathering place for the city's Black elite, where he spent a weekend immersed in composing the work.[3] As Ellington's personal physician and close friend, Arthur Logan was by then a familiar fixture in the Ellington world; yet it was Marian, a former nightclub singer, with whom Strayhorn had forged an especially close bond. That weekend, she observed Strayhorn as he composed, humming, whistling, and occasionally dancing a few steps. She remembered the scene this way:

> It was a beautiful springtime, but you would have thought it was Christmas, he was carrying on so with that *Nutcracker* . . . I said, "Bitty [short for Itty Bitty Buddy], you were born at the wrong time. I think you're really an old Russian." "Oh really?" [Strayhorn replied,] "do you really think so?" I said, "Well you're certainly acting like one." Strays said, "Well, then, I think I should have a vodka." And he did. We toasted Tchaikovsky and had a grand old time. . . . But he really worked on that music. He loved doing that music. Strays liked to have a collaborator. He liked somebody to hide behind. Now he had the greatest collaborator of them all, a dead man. Duke was always removed—he was never around, and when he was, he never told Strays what to do—but he was still there.[4]

Logan's narrative highlights multiple contexts and issues of history and identity that speak to Strayhorn's choice of Tchaikovsky as well as his approach to the arrangements. These include the encounter between the cosmopolitan cultural milieus of postwar African American modernism and nineteenth-century Russian imperial concert music, the association of the *Nutcracker* and North American Christmas, the linking of Strayhorn's compositional imagination and aesthetic sensibility with dance and classical music, and, finally, Strayhorn's apparent need for a collaborator as a kind of protective catalyst enabling creativity. While I would complicate the notion that Strayhorn "liked" to "hide behind" a collaborator, Logan's story suggests a number of significant contexts for exploring queer collaboration in Strayhorn's project, not least of which is that his spectral collaborator was also a gay man.

I begin my discussion of the Strayhorn-Ellington *Nutcracker Suite* with Logan's remark that Strayhorn was "born at the wrong time" and "acting" like an "old Russian." While affectionately teasing, this image nevertheless conveys a perception of Strayhorn's artistic self as somehow anachronistic or out of temporal sync. Allied with Logan's observation concerning Strayhorn's desire for a shadowy or removed (preferably dead) collaborator, her portrait of the artist at work alone in an uptown Black bourgeois salon speaks to specifically queer forms of asynchrony—or queer temporality—that shaped Strayhorn's professional experience and position vis-à-vis Ellington and the band, as well as his musical encounter with Tchaikovsky's score.[5] However, assuming the "old Russian" in question is, if not Tchaikovsky himself, then some similarly imagined antique Russian composer, the anachronistic image also gestures toward queer spaces of affinity, or, rather, a play of affective, musical, temporal, and socio-historical relations of affinity and difference.

In what follows, I explore how these relations of affinity and difference emerge in Strayhorn's personal identification with the project, in his and Ellington's collaborative concept, and, most crucially, in Strayhorn's musical work. Walter van de Leur has identified Strayhorn as the principal creative agent in at least six of the nine movements, a division of creative labor typical of their collaboratively composed works during this period.[6] Also typical of their composing partnership at this time was the centrality of conversation in the "precompositional" phase of a project. That is, Ellington and Strayhorn's collaborative practice on the Tchaikovsky project, like all their collaborations, "consisted of *discussion*, an exchange of musical ideas, and a quest for solutions to compositional problems, which led to mutual inspiration, but not necessarily to joint compositions . . . Especially in later years, when Strayhorn rarely toured with the band, the collaboration boiled down to conversation."[7] Significantly, the metaphor of conversation surfaces in Strayhorn's statements about the particular challenges he faced as an arranger in adapting Tchaikovsky's *Nutcracker Suite* for the Ellington orchestra. As he explained:

> It's always a struggle . . . to present [the music of] someone of the stature of Peter Ilych Tchaikovsky, adapting it to our flavor without distorting him. . . . Actually, it sort of felt like we were talking to him, because we didn't want him turning over any more than he already was.[8]

These comments speak to Strayhorn's complex understanding of arranging as a practice of translation, transformation, and reception, as well as his evident respect for and identification with his spectral collaborator. In his book *Listen: A History of Our Ears*, Peter Szendy has provocatively considered arranging and arrangements as an act of critical listening and translation, a process that he describes (channeling the writings of Robert Schumann) as a "critique of a music in music."[9] As he writes: "arrangers may even be the only listeners in the history of music to write down their listenings, rather than describe them (as critics do). And that is why I love them, I who so love to listen to someone listening. I love hearing them hear."[10] Szendy's notion of arrangements as a sounding record of critical listening resonates with Strayhorn's own ideas about the critical practice of arranging; in his comments to Stanley Dance on the art of arranging (which included a discussion of his approach to "translating" Tchaikovsky), Strayhorn summed it up by saying, "You have to say *what* you feel about *this* tune to the people."[11]

The opportunity to directly engage with a classical score by a composer Strayhorn held in high esteem also linked up to aspects of Strayhorn's biography, such as his youthful passion for classical music and his unfulfilled dream of becoming a concert pianist. At the same time, much like the Shakespearean allure of *Such Sweet Thunder*, the high cultural orientation of the project in the context of the United States appealed to Strayhorn's cosmopolitan sensibility and his persona as an aesthete and intellectual, qualities that, as noted earlier, he began cultivating during his youth in Pittsburgh's Black working-class neighborhood of Homewood. According to Hajdu, the adolescent Strayhorn "embraced all the era's standard symbols of refinement: studying French, classical piano, sartorial fastidiousness."[12] In other words, he cultivated a practice of dandyism (a topic to which I shall return later). For Strayhorn, as for any number of queer children, such deep investments in artistic pursuits provided both refuge and forms of compensatory pleasure.[13] Jazz percussionist Michael (Micky) Scrima, who became a close friend of Strayhorn's at Westinghouse High, remembered:

> He was in a shell. You got to remember, those Pittsburghers were tough. How can I say this? He had a hard time making friends. To tell you the truth, people used to call him a sissy . . . All he did day and night was concentrate on the only thing he cared about, the one thing he wanted—to . . . be a classical concert pianist.[14]

Marion Logan's comments on the genesis of the *Nutcracker Suite* capture something else vital about the musical character of Strayhorn's—and Ellington's—adaptation of their model: its charm and sophistication; its evocation of the personal, humorous, and familial; and its combination of irony and homage as well as of modernist and vernacular voices. This mixture comes through also in Strayhorn and Ellington's renaming, or as they put it "reorchestrating," of Tchaikovsky's dance titles—"Peanut Brittle Brigade," "Sugar Rum Cherry," and "Arabesque Cookie"—combining a sense of quasi homage and signifyin' wit that reconfigure the ballet's imperial culinary commodities (marzipan, tea, coffee) in terms of popular American holiday products: cocktails, cookies, and peanut brittle. Similarly, the renaming of the suite's ethnic and supernatural (or nonhuman) characters transforms and refigures Tchaikovsky's sonic depiction of difference and otherness.[15]

Yet Strayhorn and Ellington's programmatic and musical translations of Tchaikovsky into US vernacular should not be construed as some kind of unmediated encounter with Tchaikovsky's score and the late nineteenth-century imperial fantasies of otherness that shaped it. Rather I want to emphasize the ways in which their alterations not only addressed personal and contemporary concerns, but also reflected and responded to a specifically North American field of cultural and social meanings that had accrued to the work—and indeed made it an appealing project in the first place. On this point, George Balanchine's enormously influential midcentury staging of *The Nutcracker* for the New York City Ballet stands as the most significant referent. As dance historian Jennifer Fischer argues, it was the 1957 and 1958 nationally televised CBS broadcasts of Balanchine's version that captured the popular imagination, cementing the now-indelible association of the ballet with the domestic rituals of North American Christmas (as well as the seemingly permanent need for its annual performances).[16] Directed by John Houseman for the prestigious series *Playhouse 90*, Balanchine's staging for the opening scene's Christmas-night family gathering projected a cozy, Americanized image of "home and hearth" that suited perfectly the context of its medium and widespread notions of an idealized, 1950s-styled white middle-class domesticity. The opening scene ("Overture") featured actress June Lockhart, of newly minted *Lassie* fame, as Clara's mother.[17] As the opening bars of the "Overture" sounded, viewers were treated to the image of mother (Lockhart) tenderly reading to her daughter, the two cuddling warmly on a couch in front of the fireplace. This scene captures vividly how the ballet's postwar popularity was secured through its proximity to heteronormative Anglo American family values, associations that would make *The Nutcracker* a rich cultural text for subcultural or countercultural appropriation.

Given the work's popular currency, it is not surprising that 1960 saw the release of more than one jazz *Nutcracker Suite*: the second one, *The Swingin' Nutcracker*, featured arrangements by the West Coast trumpet virtuoso Shorty Rogers. Like Ellington and Strayhorn's recording, Rogers's version for the RCA Victor label was released in November, timed to capitalize on the holiday market. The two recordings share common elements such as general jazz-arranging practices and humorous retitling of Tchaikovsky's dances (although Rogers's titles rely on rather contrived word plays drawing on hip jazz lingo, e.g., "Like Nutty Overture" and "Flowers for the Cats"). The Strayhorn-Ellington version, by contrast, is far more engaged with the program. For instance, the reordering of dances in the Ellington-Strayhorn LP coupled with the role and choices of improvising solo voices, heightens the genre's referencing to a live, staged performance—albeit one experienced through the medium of the LP. Where Tchaikovsky divides the *Suite* into three sections (*Overture miniature, Danses caractéristiques, Valse des fleurs*), Strayhorn and Ellington's two-part/two-side plan would seem to allude more to the two-act dramatic form of the full-length ballet. That is, sides one and two of the LP are presented as a quasi two-act performance for which Strayhorn composed a new addition, a musical intermission entitled "Entr'acte" that closes side one of the LP. This new addition takes the form of an up-tempo swing arrangement based on the "Overture," and functions as a showcase for a string of solos (Johnny Hodges, Harry Carney, Paul Gonsalves, Lawrence Brown, and Jimmy Hamilton). Another significant change on side two concerns the ethnic transformation and placement of "Waltz of the Flowers"; with its new title "Waltz of the Floreodores" and its placement directly prior to the Arabian Dance ("Arabesque Cookie"), it programmatically, although not musically, evokes the Spanish Dance or "Chocolate" from the ballet (which Tchaikovsky did not include among the *Danses caractéristiques* in the *Nutcracker Suite*).

For many listeners at the time, Ellington and Strayhorn's reworkings could, like those in Shorty Rogers's version, be construed simply as either an uncomplicated parody or as an act of musical uplift, and thus confined to that rather bland category of "swinging the classics" (or classicizing jazz).[18] As it turned out, the former interpretation surfaces in Gene Lee's highly negative review of the LP in *DownBeat*, in which he accused the composing partners of producing a degrading "crude parody" of a beloved classical work.[19] To be sure, strategies of parody (and irony) figure into the mix (particularly taking into account the mediating contexts of Balanchine's televised *Nutcracker*), but two other contexts are crucial for a full accounting on this issue. First, the cultural prestige of jazz circa 1960 coupled with the postwar status of African American artists in the public sphere had reached a point where the album cover for the original recording could give—without irony—equal authorial billing to Ellington, Strayhorn, and Tchaikovsky.[20] Second, Ellington and Strayhorn's adaptations trouble the assumed high/low aesthetic hierarchy that has historically been central to the practice of "ragging" or "swinging the classics." As van de Leur points out in his editor's note to his edition of the score, Strayhorn (and Ellington) consciously eschewed straightforward "jazzed-up renditions" and instead "virtually recomposed the ballet, using a wide array of techniques to take the original to a new and strikingly personal level."[21] Far from making the rarified sounds of high culture more accessible, or using Tchaikovsky to score easy parodic points, several of the movements, as we shall see, do just the reverse, approaching their classical model as a vehicle for (queer) modernist experimentation. That Rogers himself appreciated these qualities is evidenced in comments he made to Leonard Feather for a 1961 *DownBeat* "Blindfold Test." His response after listening to "Sugar Rum Cherry": "I want to get this album; it's very interesting, because for instance I had the Sugar Plum Fairy in my album, and I approached it quite differently . . . whether Swee' Pea or Duke wrote this interpretation, it was a very high creative level. Five stars" (Feather correctly gave arranging credits to Strayhorn).[22]

Strayhorn and Ellington conceived of their approach as a musical dialogue across and between the boundaries of race, nation, and time. Their arrangements stage a sympathetic encounter with the past(s) that delineates new sonic worlds of signification and identification, ones that critically comment on the present. Indeed, each movement weaves a varied fabric of formal, stylistic, and expressive *correspondences*, or, to use Ellingtonian language, *parallels*, that reimagine the social-musical associations structuring both Tchaikovsky and Balanchine's vision of an Americanized *Nutcracker*. The aforementioned "Overture" scenario is a case in point: Strayhorn's reworked version proposes alternative domestic images of family and community.[23] Channeling the jovial formality of the Christmas dance through a singing, sophisticated, medium-swing arrangement, Strayhorn (re)locates Tchaikovsky to an urban, cosmopolitan, multicultural domestic space—one perhaps not unlike the Logans' apartment where he worked on the arrangements. At a moment in which the civil rights movement was linking the color and culture of family values to demands for racial justice—activist causes to which Strayhorn was passionately devoted—such tactics, no matter how lighthearted, could have a pointed symbolic resonance.[24]

The swinging and convivial cosmopolitan domesticity of the "Overture" can also be heard in relation to the domestic gay social spaces Strayhorn inhabited. Although he apparently eschewed the gay New York private party networks of the postwar years, Strayhorn hosted parties regularly in his home for a core group of (mostly) gay friends, particularly during the 1940s when he was living with Aaron Bridgers. He often spent the better part of a day (or two) cooking "mounds and pots of home-style dishes like fried chicken and beans with rice." Fellow gay arranger and composer Ralph Burns fondly remembered these intimate gatherings for their relaxed, improvised sociality and sense of communal affirmation:

> It would be great, because a lot of us had so much in common. A lot of us were in the music business, and we were gay, of course—not that we would stand and talk about being gay. That wasn't it. It was just really good to be in each other's company. Billy would put these parties together, and they were just a great, easy, natural good time.[25]

In keeping with the suite's program, the "Overture" accordingly functions like a party soundtrack or background music for the Christmas Eve festivities—the "real world" that sets the scene for Clara's fantastical journey. Tchaikovsky's stagings of the supernatural and exotic in the movements that follow afforded especially rich material, and, indeed, it is the atmospheric, slow-tempo arrangements of several of the subsequent character dances—"Sugar Rum Cherry" ("Sugar Plum Fairy"), "Chinoiserie" ("Chinese Dance"), and "Arabesque Cookie" ("Arabian Dance")—that show Strayhorn (and Ellington) in their most adventurous, imaginative, and personal (re)compositional mode.

BETWEEN THE SUGAR PLUM FAIRY AND SUGAR RUM CHERRY

Enter Sugar Rum Cherry: a tenor and baritone saxophone duet, consisting of Paul Gonsalves and Harry Carney, intones Tchaikovsky's famous theme (durations doubled), conjuring a hefty, bluesy apparition who struts in amidst low register, and intoxicated growls (example 4.1, [a]). In place of Tchaikovsky's delicate string pizzicato accompaniment, Strayhorn substitutes a syncopated, atmospheric drum figure played by Sam Woodyard; its evocative 12/8 Afro-Cubanesque groove, which opens the movement and adds a patina of "cool," sets the scene for Strayhorn's fleshy riff on Tchaikovsky's celesta-animated heroine. As the first half of the theme cadences, Strayhorn amplifies Tchaikovsky's descending four-note clarinet figure with the addition of an alto sax duet; the trio continues through the subsequent four bars as backing to the theme's second phrase (now for Carney alone), which Strayhorn arranges as a series of diminished triads in the reeds pitted against an F♯ pedal in the bass. At the unison cadence on E, the reeds abruptly drop out—the sonic equivalent of stage blackout—leaving only Woodyard's groove to fill the sonic void. A varied second statement ensues as the theme is passed between a clarinet/alto sax duet then back to Gonsalves and Carney to complete the A section.

Strayhorn's "Sugar Rum Cherry" projects a dramatic sense of difference with respect to his model, and an argument could be made for his approach as a mode of signifyin', an ironic "repetition with a critical difference."[26] However, the play of difference in "Sugar Rum Cherry" also reflects a sincere effort on Strayhorn's part to "adapt" Tchaikovsky's fairy and her other-worldly aura to his own cultural "flavor without distorting." Thus, while Strayhorn's version reflexively engages coded oppositions or contrasts of style, voice, and idiom (classical music vs. jazz, European vs. African American, feminine vs. masculine, and so on), it cannot be

EXAMPLE 4.1 Strayhorn, "Sugar Rum Cherry"; (a) measures 5–13, (b) measures 25–28. Transcribed by author.

reduced to, and in fact confounds, simple, stable binaries of musical and social difference. Accordingly, the movement's transformation of the delicate, flowing turns and intricate on-point footwork of the Sugar Plum Fairy into the growling, strutting, hip-swaying Sugar Rum Cherry is less a send-up of its (white, feminine) model, than a reimagining and recoding of the formal and expressive materials of her magical dance in modernist vernacular African American terms. In the B section (which parallels the "quasi arpa" celesta solo in the original), the arrangement shifts gears to a slow-swing tempo (example 4.1, [b]). A haunting, muted, wha-wha brass trio plays a rising chromatic line (derived from a two-bar ascending celesta motive in the original) as Paul Gonsalves comes in for a twenty-four-measure tenor saxophone solo, introducing a feeling of mystery and quiet lyricism to the dance. The melancholic moans of the trio recur throughout this section as Gonsalves's bob-inflected phrasing fills the silences.

Strayhorn's gloss on the return of the A section similarly extends and reframes the formal logic of his model, turning a relatively closed ABA form into a more open-ended and fragmentary structure. While a clear sense of return is signaled in the recurrence of the opening saxophone duet and accompaniment, the arrangement now focuses on a two-bar melodic fragment from the beginning of the theme, which is repeated seven times. The effect is essentially a written-out fade-out; yet it imbues the close with a feeling of a kind of jazzy fantasia. I hear the ending as a poetic rendering of the variations in the accompaniment and dynamics, and gradual fragmentation of the theme that Tchaikovsky employs to conclude "Sugar Plum Fairy."

As my observations have already implied, Strayhorn filters the programmatic associations of Tchaikovsky's dance through a field of social and musical signification rooted in African American, and, more specifically, Ellingtonian practices and voices. With its muted, growling horns, its mysterious, atmospheric drum ostinato, and its dark-hued, blues-based chromaticism, "Sugar Rum Cherry" derives its rhetorical flavor from sonic tropes associated with "jungle style." From its origins in the Ellington band's performances in the late 1920s at Harlem's Cotton Club, through seemingly infinite incarnations and mutations, jungle style functioned as the primary Ellingtonian musical mode for conjuring, both in ironic and sincere ways, liminal realms of fantasy and primitivist otherness capable of summoning, sometimes all at once, the uncanny and the gutbucket.

Strayhorn's use of these sonic signifiers for this arrangement, coupled with the formal revisions and reversals in timbre, texture, register, and tempo, stage musical and affective crossings marked by histories of race, sexuality, gender, and nation. In particular, the movement's assemblage of gendered and racialized sounds and styles recalls just the sort of theatricalized spectacle in which a performer like Sugar Rum Cherry could be imagined to have appeared, namely the stage of a jazz-age Harlem nightclub or speakeasy. In this context, Strayhorn's bluesy, husky-voiced, gender-expansive heroine can be heard as a spectral remembrance of the queer performative pleasures associated with the great 1920s female entertainers and blues queens such as Bessie Smith, "Ma" Rainey, Ethel Waters, and Gladys Bentley.[27] Such a linking can be productively illuminated via critical work on the queer poetics of gay Harlem Renaissance artists in whose texts and images the era's classic blues and drag culture was celebrated and recorded. Strayhorn's practice of translation in "Sugar Rum Cherry," for example, resonates with what Sam See has theorized as a queer aesthetic of "primitive drag" in the Harlem-based poems of Langston Hughes. This term fuses "the two dominant historical tropes, primitivism and cross-dressing, that Hughes employed in his work." Drawing out connections between critical studies on the queer historical and performative affinities of jazz-age blues and drag cultures on the one hand, and, on the other, Hughes's own literary homages to those cultures, See examines "crossings of form, race, gender and sexuality" in Hughes's 1926 collection, *The Weary Blues*. Hughes's poetics of crossing and use of "chiastic" blues forms unsettle on a performative level, even as they inhabit naturally, familiar "visual and epistemological taxonomies of identity." In this way, "the poems represent the historical feeling of non-normative, disidentificatory experience"; they not only amplify a "queer practice of drag performance" but stand as an embodied history of that era's queer subculture.[28]

See's notion of "primitive drag" in Hughes's blues poems has something in common with Elisa Glick's analysis of Black queer dandyism in the fiction of Wallace Thurman and art of Richard Bruce Nugent. Like Strayhorn, Nugent was openly gay and cultivated a specifically African American form of dandyism (although much more in the mode of bohemian flamboyance).[29] Both Thurman and Nugent's constructions of the Black queer dandy can be seen as "making legible a distinctly African-American incarnation of queer forms of desire, identity, and community emerging in modern, urban culture."[30] In her discussion of Nugent's 1927 series *Drawings for Mulattoes* (published in Charles S. Johnson's collection *Ebony and Topaz*), for example, Glick observes the ways in which Nugent's four drawings employ an Aubrey Beardsley-inspired language of "stylization and linear abstraction . . . to complicate the oppositions of black/white and female/male, creating androgynous figures who often seem to blur gender and racial

FIGURE 4.1 Richard Bruce Nugent, *Drawings for Mulattos, Number 4*. From Charles S. Johnson, *Ebony and Topaz* (ca. 1927).

polarities." For instance, the final image, *Number Four*, features a complex play of black-on-white and white-on-black silhouettes meant to represent the racial and sexual admixture of Harlem cabarets: androgynous, naked dancing bodies and masked facial images are assembled against phallic palm trees and a treble clef with two rising pitches A ("African?") and B ("Black"?) (figure 4.1). Glick links these images compellingly to Nugent's queer modernist vision of Harlem culture and to a performatively fluid "dialectic of primitivism and decadence" that characterizes the expressive idiom of the black dandy.[31]

My argument here is that the stylized race and gender reversals and crossings in these images and their historical reference to the signs of Harlem cabaret and practices of Black dandyism stand as a salient queer visual counterpoint to—and provide a queer history for—the sonic gender/racial admixture and jungle style accents in Strayhorn's aural depiction of his titular heroine. Like Hughes's blues poems and Nugent's drawings, Strayhorn's reading of Tchaikovsky in "Sugar Rum Cherry" performs difference, but not in the service of reifying it; rather, various crossings of identity and sounds that structure Strayhorn's reimagining of Tchaikovsky's "Sugar Plum Fairy" move through the spaces of difference in a sonically animated dance that unsettles and discloses, albeit with a large chaser of charm and signifying wit, the patriarchal heteronormative binaries around which arrangements of difference are organized.[32]

Finally, extending the frames for queer arrangements of difference to those of temporality and setting brings our attention back to Sugar Rum Cherry as, specifically, a musical character of the night, and of the Harlem nightclub. In his analysis of Hughes's poetic remembrance of the "queer space and time" of the 1920s Harlem nightclub in the 1951 poem "Café: 3 a.m.," Shane Vogel argues that the "central role of musicians and performers in the afterhours economy suggests that the queer temporality of such spaces is also a kind of *musical time*."[33] A parallel can be drawn between the varieties of temporal asynchrony and ambiguity that I've explored in Strayhorn's Black queer historical reimagining of Tchaikovsky's score and Vogel's analyses of the queer temporal and spatial histories of the Harlem nightclub as lyrically archived in Hughes's "Café: 3 a.m." Observing that Hughes's "Café: 3 a.m." is "the only poem in his oeuvre where Hughes explicitly references the terminology of homosexual deviance ('degenerates,' 'fairies,' and 'Lesbians')," Vogel reads the text as a "poem out of time, harkening back, on the eve of a sexually and politically conservative decade, to an earlier moment."[34] Similarly, Strayhorn's engagement with (and reconfiguration of) the racial-gender sonic tropes of jungle style in "Sugar Rum Cherry" stages a kind of queer temporal "return" to what Vogel would call "the scenes" and "musical time" of the Cotton Club and the queer blues culture and sociality of the 1920s and 1930s.

NAIBARA: STRAYHORN'S ARABIAN DANCE

Situating Strayhorn's work as part of a set of larger practices, as I've been arguing, enables a critical positioning and historical recovery of Strayhorn's music within a Black queer artistic usable past. The final and longest movement of the suite "Arabeseque Cookie" is in many ways the most radical of Strayhorn's arrangements to invite such a positioning. Notwithstanding the tongue-in-cheek wordplay of its title, this slow-tempo, evocative "mood" piece reinterprets the dreamy orientalist languor of Tchaikovsky's "Arabian Dance." As in "Sugar Rum Cherry," jungle style scoring is part of the recipe, but it is only one ingredient of sonic otherness in the complex and emotionally charged mix of "Arabesque Cookie."

A newly composed ten-measure introduction scored for bamboo flute and

EXAMPLE 4.2 Strayhorn, "Arabesque Cookie," aka "Naibara"; measures 1–10. Transcribed by author.

EXAMPLE 4.3 Tchaikovsky, "Danse arabe" ("Arabian Dance"), oboe theme. Transcribed by author.

bass opens the movement. The bamboo flute quotes an oboe passage from the middle of "Arabian Dance," a variation on the main theme's ornamental quintuplet figure (examples 4.2 and 4.3). Strayhorn's arrangement develops this thematic variation, transforming it into an extended, piercing wail richly suggestive of a North African soundscape. Expanding this sonic geography and mournful affect, a bass ostinato echoes the flute's descent and leads into a trombone-trio setting of the first (A) of Tchaikovsky's two "Arabian" thematic figures. Strayhorn retains the G-minor modal flavor of the original as well as the three-bar construction of the A theme, but reworks the formal, rhythmic, and timbral layers of his model. In place of Tchaikovsky's largely homophonic setting, we hear a polyphonic succession of three overlapping melodic statements, the final one of which Strayhorn scores for a plunger-muted wha-wha trombone—its pendular minor-third wails create a ghostly echo. Both the dark affect and multidimensional scoring of the opening intensify as the arrangement unfolds. Driving this unfolding is a tambourine ostinato playing constant sixteenth notes, which acts in counterpoint both to the loping gait of a muted drum figure and to the aforementioned bass

EXAMPLE 4.4 Strayhorn, "Arabesque Cookie," A theme; measures 11–22. Transcribed by author.

ostinato, saturating the sonic space. Strayhorn's structural use of the tambourine to provide a dynamic temporal feel and textural variety contrasts strikingly with its role in the Tchaikovsky's original, where it functions as a static, decorative detail (example 4.4).

After the last echoes of the final trombone wha-wha fade, the B theme enters, scored for clarinet and bass clarinet. Strayhorn's arrangement of this section at once references and telescopes Tchaikovsky's distinctive orchestration in which two B♭ clarinets provide a drone-like accompaniment for the statements of the B theme, scored for violins/violas (example 4.5). That is, Strayhorn's orchestration neatly combines the drone and thematic/melodic features of his model, an alteration that weds formal and expressive effect. Playing over three octaves apart, the hollow, haunting sound of the clarinets extends and deepens the movement's

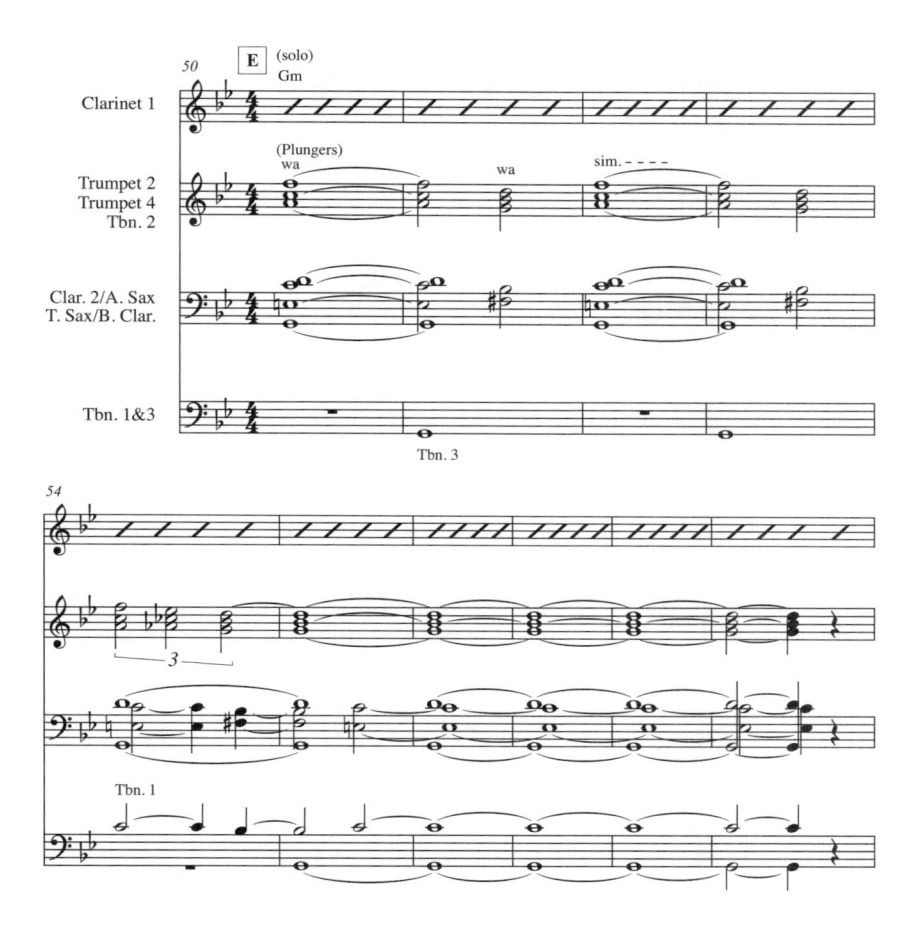

EXAMPLE 4.5 Strayhorn, "Arabesque Cookie"; measures 50–59. Transcribed by author.

mournful affect, as does the overall sparse texture with only the tambourine's rhythmic drone, the bass ostinato, and the muted drum lick as backing.

As many commentators have observed, the rhythmic propulsion provided by the tambourine as well as the sound of the muted drum (and the Latin-tinge quality of its groove) evoke the exotic "Arabian" strains of what is arguably Ellington's most enduring hit tune, "Caravan" (co-composed by Juan Tizol and first recorded in 1936).[35] This referencing can be interpreted on a number of levels: it obviously contributes to the arrangement's unmistakable Ellingtonian flavor and positions it in the lineage of Ellington exotic "mood" pieces; yet as a mode of translation it also calls attention to the representational practices of all three pieces ("Caravan," "Arabian Dance," and "Arabesque Cookie") with respect to the depiction of orientalist fantasy.[36] Importantly, Strayhorn himself had already given a modernist imprint to "Caravan" for a masterful 1945 arrangement he scored in collaboration with Ellington. Commenting on the partial manuscript for this arrangement (a sixteen-bar A section of the AABA form), van de Leur has pointed to the overall conceptual planning of the arrangement, as well as the locked parallel dissonant chords of its six-part voicings, as evidence of Strayhorn's distinctive contributions. Another piece of crucial circumstantial evidence for Strayhorn's authorship is that this manuscript was found in the holdings of the Strayhorn family, pulled from the locked special file cabinets in his apartment where he kept many of the pieces that were dear to him (rather than store them in the Ellington library).[37]

One final intriguing music-dance intertext: two years before his "Caravan" arrangement, Strayhorn co-composed with Ellington the song "Strange Feeling" for a midnight floor show at New York's Hurricane nightclub (it ran from May to September 1943).[38] The lavish production number (bearing the same name) was the featured finale and showcased the "quasi-oriental styling" of dancer Leticia Jay, who marketed herself as an "East Indian/primitive dancer" and was then known by her stage name Leticia. The musical and programmatic association of dancer and song—with its a dark, dissonant-laced sonic atmosphere and foreboding lyric—is reinforced by the original manuscript for the piece, which bears the title "Leticia."[39] In its review, *Variety* hailed the "versatile, sexy, terper" and "torso gyrations" of her performance, while *Billboard* noted her "exotic get-up" in "the fanciest production number of the show," describing her "cooches from every possible position" as "sexy, not dirty." In her short biography of the dancer, Constance Valis Hill recounted her "specialty act" as consisting of "fast turns, back bends, high kicks and graceful veil work."[40] Other significant elements of the production number included its interracial mix of six white female backup dancers—from the June Taylor dance troupe—and the blues vocalist Beverly White performing with the Ellington orchestra. "Strange Feeling," of course, is best known not from this original theatrical version, but from the version Strayhorn and Ellington created a year later (featuring male vocalist Al Hibbler) for their first collaborative suite, *Perfume Suite* (premiered in the Ellington orchestra's 1944 Carnegie Hall performance).[41]

What would it mean for Strayhorn to engage with the field of representation created by these works? What (queer) histories and practices of exoticism are inscribed or critiqued in the specific formal and expressive vocabularies of the "Arabian Dance" arrangement? Strayhorn's arrangement of Tchaikovsky simultaneously expands the temporal and spatial dimensions of his model and reduces or condenses its melodic material. This approach not only serves practical purposes—for example, it facilitates the movement's two solo improvisation sections—but also interpretive and poetic ones. Strayhorn's translation of Tchaikovsky's "Arabian Dance" into the Black modernist Ellingtonian vernacular unveils and amplifies a vast expanse of sonic territory and affect not explored, but suggested in the original. The passages from the opening of the movement described previously can be usefully heard from this perspective; yet probably the most visceral example of this process of sonic magnification occurs in the transition from the first to the second section (from rehearsal letter D to E). After some twenty-five bars, the sparse, melancholic setting of the first section suddenly gives way to an expansive, lush soundscape as the full reed and horn choirs enter for the first time and the tonality shifts to F major. A series of elaborate alterations and passages ensues: cross-section voicings and chromatic waves derived from Tchaikovsky's unusual parallel harmonies are set among nearly constant trumpet and trombone plunger-mute held notes, creating a layered backing for Jimmy Hamilton's clarinet solo. While the sheer density of the backing could threaten to overwhelm Hamilton's voice, Strayhorn's careful voicings enable the clarinet to stand out in the texture, creating a space for Hamilton's intricate solo work to take off—his agile, rapid flights of melodic embroidery move swiftly like a bird through (or above) Strayhorn's haunting, richly colored sonic landscape.

Here as elsewhere, Strayhorn's translations of Tchaikovsky's sonic exotica propose a modernist play of affinity and difference with respect to his classical model. In the movement, however, Strayhorn's approach also has something in common with neoclassical practices, particularly those of French modernism. From this perspective, Ravel's dance hit *Bolero* (1928), with its neo-(Spanish) Arabian melodies, which the composer described famously as "impersonal folk-tunes of the usual Spanish-Arabian kind," is a useful model for comparison.[42] Indeed, Strayhorn's setting shares with *Bolero* the stylized use of a preexistent dance in the context of a ballet, the continual reorchestration of an exotic "Arabesque" melody, and a formal buildup through increases and contrasts in density and loudness over a rhythmic ostinato. Yet the automatized ostinato figure that drives Ravel's dance stylizations is foreign to Strayhorn's dance, as is, for that matter, the essentially static rhythmic conception of Tchaikovsky. Rather, Strayhorn continuously reorchestrates, revoices, and augments the rhythmic profile of his model. Moreover, his version interpolates a newly composed contrasting

B section, a platform for Johnny Hodges's sensually voiced alto to take center stage. Strayhorn frames this section with a shift into a medium-swing tempo and modulation to G minor as the tambourine, bass ostinato, and drum groove drop out. Hodges obbligato-like, blues-based improvisation is surrounded by a backing that both contrasts with and extends the opening alchemy of sounds. For instance, the full ensemble continues the lush, layered voicings of the previous section, but Strayhorn varies the texture and timbre: the reeds—now with the bamboo flute joining the two clarinets, tenor sax, and bass clarinet—play repeated unison statements of the opening thematic variation for bamboo flute, while a trombone trio intones the distinct descending figure from the A theme (with a lone plunger-mute trumpet periodically adding a coloristic accent).

Turning now to the questions posed earlier, how might my reading address issues of exoticist representation in the movement as well as those of Black queer history and identity? I argue that—as in the case of "Sugar Rum Cherry"—the formal, sonic, and programmatic features in "Arabesque Cookie" can be allied with figurations by gay Harlem Renaissance artists of queer desire and identity. The musical assemblage just described, for example, realizes—especially as translated through Hodges's improvising voice—the fusion of primitivism and stylized modernity central to the aesthetic of the Black queer dandy as theorized by Glick in relation to the visual art of Nugent. At the same time, Strayhorn's engagement with an orientalist subject in "Arabesque Cookie" invites a link to the dissident racial and sexual codes found in literary representations of the Black queer dandy. As Monica A. Miller has argued, these literary Black dandies "perform a black modernism that places modernism in conversation with the Harlem Renaissance while at the same time proposing a black modernist discursive practice that finds its specificity in heterogeneity, not authenticity or imitation."[43] This heterogeneous field also gravitates around Nugent: perhaps the most famous Harlem Renaissance literary representation of the Black queer dandy, the character Paul Arbian in Wallace Thurman's 1932 roman à clef *Infants of the Spring*, was directly modeled on Nugent (Thurman derived the last name of his character from Nugent's initials, Richard Bruce Nugent). In the novel, Arbian's transgressive performances of racial and sexual identity and, in particular, his open, unapologetic expressions of same-sex desire are embroidered with the vocabularies of exotica and "perfumed decadence" in the Wildean mode.[44] For instance, we are told that Arbian is working on a novel entitled *Wu Sing: The Geisha Man* (the dedication reads: "to Huysmans' Des Esseintes and Oscar Wilde's Oscar Wilde"), and an intense, extended dream scene in the novel closely simulates Nugent's 1926 queer modernist stream-of-consciousness text "Smoke, Lilies, and Jade." In this scene, Arbian recounts a homoerotic dream set in an intoxicating field of exotic flowers: "white lilies, red lilies, pale narcissi, slender orchids, polychromatic pansies, jaundiced daffodils, soporific lotus blossoms."[45] Of relevance here is the close proximity of Black queer dandyism (and perhaps the name "Arbian") to the tradition of homoerotic orientalism, a coupling that is at issue in Strayhorn's arrangement of the "Arabian Dance."[46]

Intriguingly, Balanchine's 1950s staging of the "Arabian Dance" relied on a related form of (queer) Afro-orientalist imagery. The dance was choreographed as a solo for Arthur Mitchell, who had recently become the first African American male dancer to become a permanent member of a major ballet company. In the 1958 CBS telecast, Mitchell appears in stereotypical "arab" theatrical drag: bare chest, punjabi pants (sirwal), white turban, heavily khol-smeared eyes. As June Lockhart intones "this is how coffee tasted best, on sugar lumps," Mitchell bows and presses his palms together in a greeting gesture. A series of vigorous yet sensuous moves follows: Mitchell undulates, swirls, and stretches across the set for several minutes before sitting down next to a large, decorative hookah. As the camera zooms in for a frontal close-up, Mitchell picks up the hose of the hookah, puffs on it, inhaling deeply, and blows the smoke into the camera. Another round of brisk pseudo-Arab undulations and upper body movements ensues; these "arabesques" (to borrow Strayhorn and Ellington's wordplay) end as Mitchell sits down in front of four children costumed as parrots. The latter echo his arm movements while he gradually falls into a sleepy, presumably drug-induced, reverie. Compared to the tradition of the "classically exotic Arabian [dance]," Balanchine's almost campy version seems to "have been inspired by watching a . . . Hollywood epic full of romantic 'sheiks' and midnights at the oasis."[47] Similarly, a rather less glamorous (but no less commodified) pop "sheik" image, in fact adorned the original LP cover for the Strayhorn-Ellington *Nutcracker Suite* (figure 4.2). Among the color storybook-like illustrations of the characters from *The Nutcracker*, we see a hookah-smoking, turbaned, brown-skinned "moor" with gold hoop earrings and delicate, boyish features.

Of course, the representation of Arab locales as a zone for "sexual border crossing," and the polyerotic appeal of Hollywood "sheiks"—from Rudolf Valentino in the 1920s to Peter O'Toole's T. E. Lawrence in *Lawrence of Arabia* (1962)—has been bound up throughout Hollywood history with ambiguous or "veiled" performances of gender, racial and sexual identification, and desire.[48] Beyond the generalized "Arabian" mis-en-scène, Strayhorn's choice to frame his arrangement

FIGURE 4.2 Ellington-Strayhorn-Tchaikovsky, *The Nutcracker Suite* (ca. 1960), original LP cover. Photo by Gordon Parks. Reproduced by permission of the Gordon Parks Foundation.

with a distinctive North African gloss (as heard in the opening bamboo flute line for example) could resonate in this queer direction given the historic primacy of the Maghreb as a site for homoerotic orientalist adventure and imagining among gay male artists and writers.[49] However, while Strayhorn's take on his "Arabian" subject may be positioned within this context, I want to propose a more critical standpoint with respect to the colonial relations of power that authorize such erotic fantasies. We need to consider here the ways in which Strayhorn's identity as an openly gay Black man, living in the intensely homophobic and highly racialized social order of Cold War America, enabled a specific form of critical consciousness, one that arguably came to bear his sonic animation of an orientalized/feminized subject. This critical program, in fact, oriented the antiracist political and social concerns and practices of Black transnationalism, which during this period voiced a specifically anticolonialist consciousness.[50] I contend that we can hear in the movement's multilayered forms and dark affects—its complex mix of the personal and stylized, sensual and melancholy, African American and French modernist sounds—a displacement of colonialist narratives of pure exoticism of both the hetero- and homoerotic varieties.[51] Originally given a reverse-coded title, "Naibara" (Arabian spelled backwards), as the concluding number in the suite, Strayhorn's version critically expands in scope and significance beyond its original role in—and as—a series of "ethnic" *divertissements*. Amplifying the idea of reversal signaled in his original title for the movement, Strayhorn reverses in the final section of the arrangement (and in a somewhat abbreviated form) the textural/sonic buildup that structures the first part of the arrangement. As the suite nears the close, the texture is gradually liquidated: the tambourine figure and melancholic trombone wha-whas from the opening give way to a series of iterations of a solo bass ostinato lick. The bass's two-bar octave descent is left unresolved, hanging plaintively on the implied dominant (D), after which a final tambourine-shake sounds.

Thus far I have considered the critical soundings of sonic exotica in "Arabesque Cookie" in relation to a diverse set of intertexts that situate these soundings in the contexts of colonial and (Black) queer histories as well as to the oeuvre of Strayhorn-Ellington. By way of conclusion, I want to take up one additional musical intertext: the penultimate movement from *Such Sweet Thunder*, "Half the Fun," conceived as an instrumental ode to Cleopatra (a reference to the African female "half" of *Anthony and Cleopatra*). "Half the Fun" was itself an arrangement of a prior work, although in this case the prior work was Strayhorn's own composition—significantly a ballad for Hodges titled "Lately" from 1956. Both in terms of sound and form, this movement stands as the most striking precursor and relative of Strayhorn's critical Black modernist take on Tchaikovsky's "Arabian Dance," exhibiting close similarities in groove, mood, affect, texture, and pitch material (the latter rich in dissonance and harmonic ambiguity). With evocative effects created by drummer Sam Woodyard, the opening section of "Half the Fun" unfolds over what David Schiff has described as an "exoticized D♭ ostinato" and projects a Latin-tinged rhythmic groove ("a habanera slowed down to the tempo of a beguine").[52] Paralleling "Arabesque Cookie," Hodges performs the sensually voiced solo—the titular Cleopatra—and his solo similarly comes in the middle of the three-part form with a distinct harmonic shift to a G♭ ostinato (in "Arabesque Cookie" it is G minor, and the solo itself is more distinct and adventuresome).

"Half the Fun" is the conceptual and musical companion of the suite's opening movement, a parallel to *Othello*, although the movement's title, the eponymous "Such Sweet Thunder," is somewhat confusingly a reference to the Shakespearean comedy *A Midsummer Night's Dream*. The pairing of these two Shakespearian tragedies foregrounds the theme of interracial love; as Schiff observes, the plots of both plays revolve around "a high-stakes romance between European and African lovers." At a time in which civil rights protests against systemic and violent anti-Black racism were occurring across the southern states (where "antimiscegenation" laws were still on the books), Strayhorn and Ellington's Black modernist sonic take on interracial intimacies, as imagined explicitly from the point of view of two North African protagonists, Othello and Cleopatra, delivered potent critical-political comment.[53] That Strayhorn would draw on this sonic template in translating Tchaikovsky's North African "Arabian" dance suggests a very similar relationship toward the material, one that engages colonial histories, exoticist representation, and a Black (queer) transnational imaginary.[54]

QUEER INTIMACY

In a late-1957 article entitled "The Race for Space," Ellington voiced publicly what stands as one of his most explicit comments on racism in the US. Writing in the wake of the controversy following the Soviet Union's launching of Sputnik, Ellington plays on the use of the terms "race" and "space" in the debate, arguing that the Soviet Union's achievement was made possible because, in his words, the nation "doesn't permit race prejudice as we know it inside Russia to interfere with scientific progress." Conversely, Ellington links the US's inability to keep up with Soviets to its preoccupation with the then-increasing national spectacle of racial violence and surveillance surrounding civil rights agitation. Thus, rather than denounce the Soviets Ellington concludes: "Those who write the great symphonies and those who write jazz classics are of the same creative mold of the men who put Sputnik into space and those who will follow this mighty Russian achievement with other space satellites and miracles."[55] Ellington's commentary shows an acute awareness of the ways in which the rhetoric of anticommunism served as a cover for US racism. Moreover, he situates the "miracle" of musical creation and scientific discovery within a universal sphere of racial and musical equality; and this rhetorical tactic was central to the discourses of Black internationalism and its diverse musical expressions.[56] As with my analysis of Strayhorn's Lorcian encounter in the previous chapter, my reading of Strayhorn's contributions to the jazz *Nutcracker* traces a queer Black transnational imaginary within the "miracle" of this "classic" of jazz translation.[57] In both works, these queer transnational frequencies amplify a sonic history of queer feeling and a range of distinct queer topics, themes, aesthetic practices, and affective modes.[58] Along with ballads for Hodges, and vocal arrangements such as "Flamingo" explored earlier, these works are infused with sounds, and adorned with titles, that summon, in the tradition of the Black queer dandy, the intoxicating pleasures of taste, sensual objects, feelings, colors, and the liminal spaces of dreams and fantasy.[59]

136 *Strayhorn's Queer Music*

In critical assessments of Strayhorn after his death in 1967, this queer sonic terrain is often figured as perverse excess in terms of both race and gender. Gunther Schuller, for example, voiced discomfort with "a certain effeteness" in Strayhorn's ballad "Chelsea Bridge," which "was to mar much of Strayhorn's work," while James Lincoln Collier charged Strayhorn with "encouraging [Ellington's] . . . tendency towards lushness [and] prettiness at the expense of the masculine leanness and strength of his best work, the most 'jazzlike' pieces."[60] From the other side of the Atlantic, British critic Eddie Lambert counterposed Strayhorn's "soft, feminine" writing to Ellington's "rugged masculinity" and, in fact, singled out Strayhorn's works for Hodges as "overly scented confections" in which Strayhorn "pushed his art to the very limit of sensualism and, at times sentimentality."[61] The commentary of these critics performs a double move: it devalues aesthetic qualities associated with the feminine while linking notions of Black masculinity and authentic jazz so that Strayhorn's influence leads, in effect, to a type of deracialized feminized cosmopolitanism, an abject lack and thus a loss of racial roots.[62] Critical reception of Strayhorn during his lifetime also commented on his "different" sound but only rarely in such overtly gender-racialized terms. In 1952, Strayhorn voiced his awareness of this perception, comparing negative critical comments that Ellington was receiving at that time due to personnel changes to comments "that accompanied my arrival." This was also the interview in which Strayhorn himself asserted, "I think my playing and writing style is totally different from Ellington's."[63]

Notwithstanding the homophobic investments that organize these comments, I want to suggest that this "overly scented"—which is to say ambiguously gendered and raced—notion of beauty be revisioned as a figure for a Black queer erotics of sound and a site of queer desire and pleasure.[64] On this point, the history of homophobic reception of Strayhorn's queer music is suggestive of the ways in which his sonic erotics resisted or exceeded the codes of legibility in dominant, largely white critical jazz discourse. Yet with Strayhorn this queer sonic beauty is, as I emphasized earlier, almost always shadowed by the tension of dark affect, a bittersweet, often melancholic underscore that can take many forms, from the mix of delicate, plaintive lyricism and harmonic sophistication expressed in the Lorca songs "Wounded Love" and "The Flowers Die of Love" (or in the emblematic "Lush Life" and "A Flower Is a Lovesome Thing"), to the sensual soul of his instrumental ballads for Hodges, and the haunting layers of mournful dissonance that underpin the elaborately designed backings of an arrangement such as "Arabesque Cookie."[65] Van de Leur interprets Strayhorn's aesthetic of multilayered formal design during this period—with its open orchestral textures, intricate harmonic and thematic scoring, and polyphonic writing—convincingly in terms of its expressive functions, that is, the ways in which these multiple layers activate and develop "emotional subtexts" and registers of dissonant interiority.[66] Such expressive and programmatic use of multilayered formal design can be identified to some degree in almost all of Strayhorn's scores where, as van de Leur explains, it often functions to stage a type of narrative in which "the listener is drawn into a gradually unraveling musical adventure that places him or her in a different time and space. The ensuing sections tell a story, introduce new perspectives on the song's melody, and start subplots."[67] Writing of three Strayhorn works composed in 1957—the exquisitely orchestrated vocal arrangement of "Day Dream" for Ella Fitzgerald, "Up and Down, Up and Down" from *Such Sweet Thunder*, and another elaborate through-composed instrumental, "Cashmere Cutie," (which was not performed or recorded until 1995)—van de Leur eloquently observes: "Through this more polyphonic writing, Strayhorn created multiple musical layers . . . It opened up even more emotional subtexts than before, as if he allowed the tension and conflict that had always been present in his music to come to the surface."[68]

The analyses presented in part 2 provide a new set of queer historical and aesthetic frames for situating the various "emotional subtexts" and the "tension and conflict" in Strayhorn's practice of dissonant underscoring. I would argue, finally, that these tensions and dissonances can productively be related to Strayhorn's "queer position" in the Ellington Orchestra, a position that, as I argued earlier, has always haunted critical perceptions of the Strayhorn-Ellington partnership. In his book *Duke Ellington's America*, for instance, historian Harvey G. Cohen presents a narrative that contrasts the hard-working, consummate professionalism of Ellington to the gay aesthete Strayhorn, whose "hedonistic lifestyle" tragically diminished his productivity. Yet Cohen quotes Ellington as saying, "Strayhorn lives the life I'd love to live . . . He is the pure artist," a comment Cohen interprets as Ellington's expression of a desire for, even a voyeuristic pleasure in, the kind of bohemian artistic life of creativity, travel, and leisure that Strayhorn the "pure artist" lived—thanks to the largesse of the industrious Ellington. As he puts it, "Strayhorn got paid more money per week than any Ellington band members during this period and also enjoyed royalties from Tempo Music. While the band slogged it out on the road night after night, Strayhorn usually did not accompany them, remaining in New York City and Paris for long stretches, living an openly

FIGURE 4.3 Original photo used in the Ellington-Strayhorn-Tchaikovsky *Nutcracker Suite* (ca. 1960) LP cover. Photo by Gordon Parks. Reproduced by permission of the Gordon Parks Foundation.

gay lifestyle . . . doing his writing, and always being on call for Ellington when he needed help composing and arranging."⁶⁹

Whether in overt or subtle forms, driving the need for this critical straightening is perhaps less anxiety about Strayhorn's queerness or his position as Ellington's silent partner, than the fact of the extraordinary intimacy of the Ellington-Strayhorn partnership itself, "beyond category" to use Ellington's favorite honorific. This elusive and, I would argue, queer intimacy is suggested in the LP cover art for the original recording of the Ellington-Strayhorn *Nutcracker Suite* (figure 4.2), the central focal point of which is a photograph of Strayhorn and Ellington in a circular frame (an image that counts as the first time in the history of their partnership that Strayhorn was given prominent visibility and authorial credit). The photograph of the two partners comes from a series of images shot by the pioneering African American photographer, director, and novelist Gordon Parks. On an assignment for *Life* magazine, Parks visited Ellington and Strayhorn in a San Francisco hotel room while the two were preparing for the Los Angeles recording session on which the *Nutcracker Suite* was cut (figure 4.3). Clearly composed with reference to the genre of domestic portraiture, the photograph captures, literally brings into a single frame, multiple layers of domestic associations—of the medium of the LP, the ballet, and, most strikingly, the gendered dimensions and intimacy of the Ellington-Strayhorn partnership.

The couple wear matching white knit polo sweaters in the fashion of bachelor-pad hipsters; yet Ellington (the "husband") gazes directly at the viewer, his chin resting casually on his hand, while Strayhorn (his "wife") stands behind Ellington, looking demurely downward.[70]

As well, the illustrated figures that circle the photograph reinforce a gendered visual economy. For instance, the feminized (or ambiguously gendered) illustrated figures arranged on Strayhorn's side of the cover feature from top to bottom a Sugar Plum Fairy; a Turban-wearing, hookah-smoking North African character; what appears to be a flamenco-styled Spanish female figure; and a bejeweled Chinese character. Ellington's side, by contrast, is dominated by the more normative (and white) gender figures, including a phallic-looking soldier on top just above Ellington's head, across from the Sugar Plum Fairy. Despite the implications of the illustrated figures, however, the LP cover captures the ways in which Strayhorn's nonnormative Black masculinity made Ellington's own figurations of Black dandyism seem somehow less threatening.

The recording of the Nutcracker session in LA in June 1960 was quickly followed up with a reworking of the *Peer Gynt Suites Nos. 1 and 2* (Strayhorn composed four of five movements).[71] That same summer, Strayhorn and Ellington began work on a major collaboration scoring music for the film *Paris Blues*. The composing partners initially worked together on the score—a notice in the *Hollywood Reporter* from July 21, 1960, cites a "pre-recording" session for the film music; however, in October 1960, Strayhorn travelled to Paris ahead of Ellington to work on location with the cast and director Martin Ritt (Ellington joined Strayhorn on set in early December). An unintended, yet momentous, outcome of Strayhorn's participation in *Paris Blues* was a chance opportunity to record his first and only solo LP project, given the title *The Peaceful Side*, at Barclay Studios in January 1961.

These, and other projects from around this time, make the early 1960s a remarkable and, I would argue, understudied period in Strayhorn's career. In addition to major collaborations with Ellington, Strayhorn sat for a number of extended interviews, including an oral history session with the Duke Ellington Society of New York. He was also deeply engaged as both an artist and activist in the civil rights movement: as discussed in chapter 2, he travelled to Mississippi with Lena Horne as her accompanist for a series of NAACP fundraising performances, attended NAACP fundraising events in New York, and participated in voter registration drives. As well, he collaborated with Ellington on civil rights-themed pieces for *My People* (1963). Perhaps his most critically celebrated achievement during this period came with his contributions, from 1964 to 1966, to the Ellington-Strayhorn LP *Far East Suite* (released in 1967), a collaboration that grew out of Strayhorn's travels to India and the Middle East in conjunction with the Ellington Band State Department Tours. In many respects, this varied archive of sound recordings, film music, oral history, and interviews from the final years of Strayhorn's life provides the most extensively documented view of a public-facing Strayhorn.

PART III
Strayhorn Performing / Arranging Strayhorn

FIVE

Paris, Halfway to Dawn, or Listening to *The Peaceful Side*

A two-minute sequence of footage titled "Harlem in Paris" is preserved in a collection of historical newsreels held in the Gaumont-Pathé Archives. This footage—which was released on January 15, 1961, as part of the Gaumont weekly newsreel magazine, *Gaumont Actualité*—captures a hastily edited series of three fragmentary scenes focusing on Black nightlife and African American jazz musicians in Paris. According to the catalogue description in the Gaumont-Pathé record, the footage was shot on a winter evening sometime in the early weeks of January 1961 and records the experience of an unnamed Black student as they explore small jazz clubs in Paris—a short montage toward the end displays the street signs for Whisky A Gogo, Jockey Club, Mars Club, and Blue Note. In the first sequence, we see footage of Ellington and Louis Armstrong playing a duet on a tiny nightclub stage, Ellington seated at an upright piano. A quick cut then takes us to a crowded bar scene that opens with a close-up shot of Ellington seated at the bar and being served a pot of tea. And as the camera pulls back, for a six-second sequence Strayhorn comes into view seated on a barstool next to Ellington.[1] Strayhorn is wearing a suit and dark aviator glasses and sits quietly drinking his beer, a plate of food in hand. The newsreel footage of this scene also captures Aaron Bridgers, who stands between Strayhorn and Ellington. The few seconds of footage show Ellington and Bridgers actively engaged in the conversation: Bridgers turns toward Strayhorn, addressing him as he leans in close toward Strayhorn's face; Ellington appears to say something about or directed to Strayhorn (he points at him). Unsurprisingly, neither Strayhorn or

Bridgers are identified in the archival record—only the names of Ellington and Armstrong are included; yet it is precisely their unintentional, fleeting presence that interests me, particularly for the way these newsreel moments collate scenes, relationships, and contexts surrounding the concurrent production and recording of this chapter's focal objects—Strayhorn's collaboration on the film music for *Paris Blues* and his piano solo LP project *The Peaceful Side*.[2]

Produced by Alan Douglas for the United Artists' label and recorded at Barclay Studios Paris, *The Peaceful Side* was initiated by Douglas during a chance encounter with Strayhorn at the Mars Club in the same month that the newsreel footage was shot—January 1961. Several days of swift planning ensued and culminated in an overnight recording session (two back-to-back three-hour sessions) with Strayhorn at the piano playing novel arrangements of original compositions he selected for the occasion accompanied by, variously, bass, a string quartet, and vocal choir. According to Douglas, Strayhorn conceived the LP "as something very introspective. He wanted to create an atmosphere and a mood and a place to go that was just quiet and alone but still complex and intelligent and mysterious."[3] Previous commentary on this recording has focused on its novelty as Strayhorn's first and only solo studio LP—a long-overdue institutional moment of jazz recognition—or in terms of what it conveys (or fails to convey) about Strayhorn's creative individuality and approach to the piano. Yet Douglas's remembrance suggests a more conceptual register, a collaborative, experimental soundscape merging notions of personal voice and autobiography with modernist affect as these elements are filtered through the sensorium of a particular studio environment. In this context, *The Peaceful Side* aligns with creative and technological trends in the production of modern jazz and, more generally, the sonic culture of the midcentury LP. This chapter listens for queer collaboration and jazz intimacy in *The Peaceful Side* through attending to these conceptual, affective, and technological registers of the recording alongside its (auto)biographical impulses and other significant contexts and histories. My starting point for discussing Strayhorn's recording project puts this project in relation to his collaborative work on the film music for *Paris Blues* as well other Paris-related projects during this moment. A central queer current running through and, indeed, orienting my analysis is Strayhorn's deep attachments to Paris as a site of fantasy, nocturnal exploration, sophistication, personal independence, and belonging. Bridgers described the social freedom, however illusory, that Paris represented for him and Strayhorn this way: "Nobody cared who you were or what you were . . . There was no judgment. That's one of the reasons Billy and I loved it here [in Paris]."[4]

The story I tell about Strayhorn, queer collaboration, and postwar Paris is, of course, part of the larger and richly documented history of African American musicians, performers, artists, writers, and entrepreneurs living and working in Paris during this period. Black queer artists were a significant presence in this vibrant and diverse community, including, most famously and importantly, James Baldwin. Writing specifically about Baldwin, Tyler Stovall has noted that this African American gay subculture was integrated within "the life of both black expatriates and the French intelligentsia."[5] Stovall's observation accords with Hajdu's description of Strayhorn's Paris at this moment: "Strayhorn had an address book with the names and addresses of friends and colleagues around the globe and one book just for Paris, a separate world for him . . . His Paris book was a checklist, and every evening a friendship flourished over food and drink: with the music writer Claude Carriérre at Gaby and Haynes's soul-food restaurant, with the jazz buff Alexandre Rado at the Club Saint-Germain, with the expatriate American saxophonist Johnny Griffin at the Montana bar."[6] The friendships and Parisian jazz clubs highlighted here convey a vivid snapshot of Strayhorn's social life, adding much to the images furtively captured in the Gaumont newsreel.

It goes without saying that Strayhorn's "Paris book" (along with his "regular" address book) also lovingly included one of the people he appears with in the footage, Aaron Bridgers. Indeed, after checking into his hotel in Paris early in October 1960, Strayhorn headed directly to see Bridgers at the Mars Club where he was performing.[7] It seems both striking and somehow fated that Strayhorn would undertake his only solo project in the city he famously hailed in his first and, for many listeners, his most significant queer lyrical statement, "Lush Life." We can hear in *The Peaceful Side* a performance and arrangement of his compositional self, one that is oriented by Black queer frequencies—a low-key, quiet meditation on and a novel arrangement of Strayhorn's sophisticated, Black Parisian modernism. The recording archives queer collaboration in its transatlantic assemblage of bodies, sounds, and voices and its improvisational combination of quiet remembrance, deep reflection, subtle humor, and sonic experimentation.

PARIS BLUES

That Duke Ellington, Louis Armstrong, Billy Strayhorn, and Aaron Bridgers were all captured in the *Gaumont Actualité* newsreel was due in large part to their mutual participation at that moment in the making of the film *Paris Blues*.

Based on a 1957 novel by Harold Flender, the film was shot on location from November 1960 to January 1961. Armstrong and Bridgers had on-screen roles as Black expatriate jazz musicians; Strayhorn and Ellington collaboratively scored the soundtrack, although Strayhorn's name was not included with Ellington's name in the film credits. There are further links between the newsreel footage and feature film: the opening scene of *Paris Blues* takes place in a fictionalized version of the small Parisian jazz clubs, or *caves* as they were known, featured in the newsreel. Importantly, the most resonant reference for the opening scene was the American-owned *cave* at the center of Strayhorn's Parisian jazz universe, the Mars Club. Several visual elements support this referencing, first and foremost of which is that Bridgers—the nonfictional Mars Club pianist during this period—appears in the scene. At the recommendation of Strayhorn, Bridgers was cast as the "black expatriate pianist" in the band of the film's central white (also expatriate) character, a jazz trombonist and aspiring "serious" composer played by Paul Newman.[8] We see but don't hear Bridgers as the filmmakers dubbed over Ellington's playing in the soundtrack (an editing decision that Bridgers would later complain about bitterly).

A more significant visual reference to the social life of the Mars Club in the opening scene, however, is its inclusion, daring for its time, of queer and interracial couples.[9] As Krin Gabbard has observed, the scene hails the queer and interracial contexts of Strayhorn's Parisian social world: "We see people of all ages and ethnicities, including male and female homosexuals, interracial couples, and a young man with a much older woman. Intentionally or not, this multiply integrated scene was also an idealized reflection of the milieu inhabited by Billy Strayhorn."[10] Indeed, what attracted Ellington and Strayhorn to the project in the first instance was a film script that centered on the romance of two interracial couples, each pairing a male expatriate musician with a female American tourist—Paul Newman (Ram Bowen) with Diahann Carroll (Connie Lampson) and Sidney Poitier (Eddie Cook, a tenor saxophonist) with Joanne Woodward (Lillian Corning). As the producer Sam Shaw recalled, "Duke thought that [interracial romance] was an important statement to make at the time. He liked the idea of expressing racial equality in romantic terms . . . That aspect of the film appealed to Billy, too, metaphorically for a gay relationship. Billy was also interested in the artistic struggle. One of the guys wanted to compose concert music but wasn't accepted by the classical establishment. This issue was of great importance to Billy."[11] These progressive racial-sexual themes in the original film script, however, were abandoned soon after the filming began, apparently in response to pressure from executives at United Artists who demanded the script be rewritten to remove the interracial storyline, while also maintaining what Rashida Braggs has called the "folklore" of Paris as a liberatory, racially progressive alternative to the United States. As she puts it, *Paris Blues* and films like it show "black musicians as receiving respect and honor as they worked alongside white musicians in Paris. The American-produced film brought African American performers together while also maintaining onscreen the illusion of Paris as a color-blind place for African American musicians."[12]

Mirroring this narrative straightening in the racial alignment of the couples along (white) normative same-race lines, the film's jazz-as-art narrative was also revised in ways that reinforced, rather than displaced, Eurocentric cultural and racial norms. For instance, Paul Newman's character's quest for artistic legitimacy positions jazz and, by implication, the Black music tradition represented in the film through the sound/body of Louis Armstrong (Wild Man Moore), as an alluring yet ultimately limited (read nonserious) music for the "true" (read white) artist-composer. As Braggs observes, the film "deemphasizes race relations as the core struggle of the story, by foregrounding Ram Bowen's desire for his jazz compositions to be recognized by classical musicians."[13] Gabbard makes a compelling argument, however, that Ellington and Strayhorn's background music—which, as is customary in film-scoring practice, was worked out and recorded in postproduction—implicitly critiques and undermines the film's Eurocentric logic.[14] Gabbard's argument revolves around a close reading of details of scoring, sound, style, and form in Ellington and Strayhorn's handling of the "Paris Blues" theme, which is heard at key moments, in varying versions, throughout the film. The "Paris Blues" theme is put to multiple uses diegetically and extradiegetically: it is literally the title/music of a composition the Newman/Ram Bowen character is working on; it is associated with the love story and struggles of Newman/Ram and Woodward/Lillian; and, most salient to this discussion, it is bound up with the film's jazz-as-art narrative trope.

These multiple uses and significations come together in the film's closing, a climactic scene set on the platform of a Parisian train station with the two central couples. In previous scenes, we learn that Lillian and Connie are returning to the United States. We also know that Eddie will return home to be with Connie at a later time (several weeks later), and that Ram plans to leave with Lillian and Connie, giving up on his dreams of becoming a "serious" composer. However, when Ram shows up late at the platform, Lillian realizes he has changed his mind: he has decided to forgo his lover and, it is strongly implied, his career as a jazz trombonist, to pursue the life of suffering and deprivation required to compose classical ("serious") music. For this final bittersweet dialogue between Ram and Lillian, Strayhorn and Ellington scored an elaborate arrangement of the "Paris Blues" theme showcasing first the alto saxophone of Johnny Hodges followed by the trombone of Murray McEachern. As Lillian and Ram (along with Eddie) part with their lovers and the train is set to leave the station, the "Paris Blues" underscore is gradually but jarringly superseded by the assertive, hard-swinging rhythms of distinctly Ellingtonian train music, its dissonant-laced brass arrangement conjuring the literal and figurative equivalent to an incoming train. In terms of its filmic or narrative function, the underscore for the final scene brings together the varied significations of the "Paris Blues" theme with a sonic landscape appropriate to the scene's setting on a train station platform. In this case, the decision to end with the train music could signal Ram's resolve, the sense that he is moving on or past the romantic entanglements that threaten his artistic ambition. Going beyond this more obvious function, Gabbard argues that both the rich, intricate soundings of the "Paris Blues" arrangement and its sonic and stylistic juxtaposition with the train music can be heard as displacing the film's tacit message, which, in demanding that Newman/Ram Bowen choose between jazz and "serious" music, excludes jazz from the timeless, privileged category of art.[15]

In a 1961 piece on the film published in *DownBeat*, critic John Tynan praised the Ellington-Strayhorn underscore, calling it the only music in the film of "genuine interest."[16] Although Tynan dismissed the film's story as "dramatic nonsense," his comments on the music show him to be a perceptive listener, recognizing Strayhorn's vital contributions to the underscore, a recognition that, although controversial at the time, is supported by the surviving manuscript scores for the film music, which are largely in Strayhorn's hand.[17] Despite Strayhorn's self-effacing statements about his contributions, which seemed to give all credit to Ellington's "powerful stuff," Tynan wrote he was "sure the orchestration credits are Billy's, though he gets no billing. Under his pen the orchestra comes through in full splendor as the cinematic action shifts through Parisian locales. There are delicate, subdued nocturnal voicings behind a late night street scene . . . scoring for flute, oboe, and clarinet in a wispy impressionistic vein as the actors stroll by the Seine, the music developing on a broader palette during a boat ride on the river."[18]

For Gabbard, the background music accompanying the final scene can also be listened to for what it says about Strayhorn's un- or undercredited authorship and, more generally, the fraught collaborative dynamics that shaped the Ellington-Strayhorn partnership. Attuned to the history surrounding questions of authorship and power in their partnership, Gabbard interprets the juxtaposition of the lyrical, romantic "Paris Blues" theme with the assertive, hard-driving Ellingtonian train music as amplifying Ellington's (unconscious) desire to neutralize Strayhorn's voice (which he sees as rooted in Ellington's creative and psychic dependence on Strayhorn): "At the finale of 'Paris Blues,' the lovely Parisian music of Strayhorn—at its most ravishing thanks to the alto saxophone of that single greatest interpreter of Strayhorn's music, Johnny Hodges—is overpowered by the Ellington Express."[19] Although I'm sympathetic with this interpretive scenario, I would argue that, in this instance, Gabbard's reading risks substituting one set of problematic dichotomies for another. First, as Gabbard's commentary itself implies, Strayhorn's lyrical arrangement of the "Paris Blues" theme for Hodges, as well as the theme's scoring for solo trombone that follows, already undermines the film's racialized gendering of jazz as reducible to attractive melody bereft of form, harmonic complexity, and deep structure. Second, the arrangement's thematic entanglements and its affective, formal, and stylistic juxtapositions need not be heard in terms of a gendered program of creative conflict in which Ellington's driving train music takes over—literally drowns out—Strayhorn's delicate Paris-accented musical voice; rather, we can listen to the underscore for its queer collaborative energies, for its multivoiced and multilayered sonic assemblage, an expressive figuration of and for the music's Black modernist aesthetic. Indeed, as I discuss later, a similar type of modernist musical assemblage plays a prominent role in several of Strayhorn's more adventuresome arrangements for *The Peaceful Side*, all of which were recorded prior to the postproduction New York recording sessions for the underscore.

At the same time, the decision to conclude the film score with the train music can also be heard as a call back or bookend to the other train music—Strayhorn's own "'A' Train"—which opens the film. In this scenario, the train music heard in the final scene functions as counterpoint or extradiegetic Ellingtonian double to the diegetic performance of "'A' Train" we hear the jazz sextet play from the stage of the jazz club in the film's opening minutes. With the opening credits running, the camera scans the club scene, capturing interracial and queer couples dancing and socializing while Ram and Eddie mime a version of "'A' Train" that the Ellington band recorded for the film. The Paris sessions for this side as well as another side heard diegetically in the club scene, "Mood Indigo," were likely directed by Strayhorn. Intriguingly, the action and dialogue in the first scene after the credits dramatizes a tense encounter between a composer and his arranger—Ram and Eddie, respectively. This exchange warrants closer consideration in relation to Strayhorn's collaboration on the project.

An establishing shot of Paris rooftops and streets at dawn precedes the scene. From an aerial view, we follow the club owner Marie Séoul (Barbara Laage) as she walks toward and descends the stairs into her club to deliver a basket of food from an early morning trip to the market. As she enters the club, we see Ram and Eddie on the stage where they have been working all night on Ram's eponymous "Paris Blues" composition. Eddie listens closely to Ram play the lyrical, melancholic "Paris Blues" melody on the trombone from an upright piano, pencil in mouth, feet propped up on the piano's edge. As the last plaintive notes of the theme sound, Eddie takes his feet down and begins writing on the manuscript paper placed on the piano's music rack, presumably transcribing the melody Ram is playing; Ram moves closer to the piano, looking anxiously at Eddie as he is at work and asks, "What did you think?" Eddie continues writing, refusing to respond to Ram's question; instead, he tells Ram of his intention to score the part for oboe: "Play it against your horn. It'll lighten up the melody and give it a nice effect." Ram persists in his questioning ("Eddie, now what do you think?"), seemingly uninterested in Eddie's scoring idea. When Eddie finally responds flatly, "It's good, man," Ram is clearly dissatisfied and continues to prod Eddie into voicing his approval ("Just good, huh?"). Growing annoyed, Eddie quips, "That's better than bad." With Ram's insecurity on full display, the composer accuses his arranger of thinking his composition "not good enough to show," and for judging the melody as "too heavy" (to which Eddie correctly, if peevishly, responds, "I didn't say that … "). As tensions escalate, Eddie attempts unsuccessfully to defuse the conflict, blaming it on exhaustion ("Man, we've been at this too long. We both need some shuteye."). The ensuing exchanges become more pointed and acrimonious: "Yeah, I hear the way you said it," Ram tells Eddie as he packs up his trombone, to which Eddie responds sardonically, "What do you want me to say? It's great? All right, you're Gershwin, you're Ravel and Debussy." The dialogue continues:

RAM: What's wrong with that?
EDDIE: You write a piece of music, I listen to it, and that's what it says. Ram Bowen, all by itself. Now, what more than that do you want? Besides, what's my opinion, man? A court of law?
RAM [*petulantly*]: I don't want an oboe playing that melody. What do you think of that, man?

EDDIE: I think you're tired, you've been up all night . . . [*voice raised and forceful*] So give it to a tuba . . . Look, I need sleep, man. I give up my nights . . . I sit here, morning after morning, arranging your music, eh?
RAM: What do you want, a medal?

At this, Eddie threatens to walk out; Eddie demonstrates his anger by first throwing the manuscript pages in his hand violently to the floor and then knocking over some chairs that are stacked on the club's tables. Marie Séoul, the owner of the cabaret, suddenly appears, defusing the tension in the room. This interruption prompts a conciliatory parting exchange between the two collaborators; Ram admits to being disturbed about something (although he can't articulate what it is), and Eddie finally gives Ram the sincere endorsement he craves: "I like the music, man, I like it fine."

The conflict between Ram and Eddie clearly functions as the film's opening gambit on the central jazz/art narrative arch, a confrontation between Ram, the sensitive, tortured artist, and the pragmatic Eddie, a hard-working, no-nonsense jazz musician with little patience for Ram's artistic pretentions. Yet what interests me about this this confrontation is the ways in which it stages the complicated creative and emotional role of Eddie specifically as arranger. Although the conflict between Eddie and Ram ultimately reinforces the Eurocentrism of the film's positioning of jazz (and arranging) as outside of "authentic" art (a move that, unsurprisingly, is closely linked to the film's Hollywood racial narrative of heroic whiteness), the casting of Poitier's Eddie as an arranger/orchestrator whose collaborator fails to respect or comprehend his creative labor while also demanding his emotional support and approval, would surely not have been lost on—and likely amused—Strayhorn (although to be clear, I'm not arguing for Ram as a proxy Ellingtonian figure in this scenario). That Strayhorn and Ellington were paying attention to Eddie's arranging idea comes later in the film: in the middle of the first section of the background music, some thirty minutes into the film, we hear the "Paris Blues" theme played on a solo oboe, a sly but distinct endorsement of Eddie's position. As Gabbard argues, the composing partners "could be using an oboe to wink at those in the audience who recall that Eddie Cook, the black musician, had suggested an oboe as a way of correcting the heaviness of a theme that a white musician had played on his trombone."[20]

THE PARIS ALBUM

Months before Strayhorn and Ellington recorded the background music for *Paris Blues* in a New York studio, Strayhorn explored a very different, although not wholly unrelated, musical concept in the making of his only solo LP, *The Peaceful Side*. As he would do for the film score, Strayhorn sought to engage the qualities of a scene, place, or environment—in this case, the ambience of a small Parisian recording studio during the overnight hours, a nocturnal environment that Strayhorn favored and memorably named "halfway to dawn." The recording sessions took place over two consecutive nights and resulted in a musical self-portrait expressed through a set of intimate piano arrangements of his own compositions. Of the ten tracks, five arrangements ("Lush Life," "Take the 'A' Train," "Day Dream," "Multi-Colored Blue," and "A Flower Is a Lovesome Thing") feature unusual backings scored for string quartet and wordless vocal choir/vocalese. The other five tracks alternate Strayhorn alone at the piano ("Strange Feeling" and "Chelsea Bridge") or with just a minimal bass accompaniment ("Just A-Settin' and A-Rockin'," "Passion Flower," and "Something to Live For"). While sonic environment and setting were central to Strayhorn's concept for the album, its creatively expansive soundings, self-reflection, and experimental energies differ starkly from the *Paris Blues* film music. As Brian Priestly observes, "Billy at the piano, virtually alone except for some boldly minimal backings . . . contrasts markedly with the project that had brought Strayhorn to Paris . . . and the kind of music he was concurrently contributing on Ellington's behalf to the underscore of the movie *Paris Blues* . . . What Billy does here using just a string quartet and four or five wordless voices—but not simultaneously—is quite stunning in its subtlety and restraint."[21]

On this point, Strayhorn's album, as well as the conditions of its production, present an alternate take on, and critical counterpoint to, the Hollywood framing of jazz sound, culture, and collaboration in postwar Paris. While the low-key mood and late-night ambience of the recording led producer Alan Douglas to title the LP *The Peaceful Side*, Strayhorn referred to it simply as the "Paris Album." As Douglas told it to Hajdu: "It was my title, and it never seemed right . . . It was really the *inside* of Billy Strayhorn. What was really peaceful was the actual recording."[22] As his words imply, the LP was very much a studio-specific project, one that made creative use of technological affordances of the studio.[23] While Douglas seems to draw a categorical distinction between the expressive work of the LP—an intensely personal vehicle for Strayhorn to tell his truth at that moment—and the specific conditions of production—the "actual recording"—my analyses seek to relate these two factors, which I conceive of as different sides of Strayhorn's practice of collaborative jazz intimacy. In what follows, I explore queer collaboration and jazz intimacy in the album's varied and idiosyncratic soundings—the first studio recording of Strayhorn's compositional voice "unplugged" from the orchestral filters of the Ellington orchestra.

If for *Paris Blues* the Mars Club functioned as a reference or prototype for the fictional jazz cave depicted in the film, the jazz club's role in the making of *The Peaceful Side* was far more tangible. As noted at the outset, the project was set in motion by a serendipitous encounter at the club between Douglas and Strayhorn one evening in early January 1961. In his account of the scene, Douglas remembered asking, "Billy, when are you going to sit down and record something yourself? . . . We know how your stuff sounds when Duke plays it. Why not let us hear how it sounds when you play it?" Strayhorn's response was plain (and not without irony): "Why not?"[24] When, several days later, they entered Barclay Studios, Strayhorn's collaborators included the Mars Club regular, white French bassist Michel Gaudry. During this period, Gaudry could be heard most evenings at the Mars Club, accompanying the club's house pianists, Aaron Bridgers and another expatriate African American pianist, Art Simmons, a luminary of the Paris jazz world (the two pianists played on alternate nights). Joining them frequently to form a trio was the Hungarian/Romani guitarist and violinist Elek Bacsik. According to Bridgers, Bacsik, who studied classical violin at the Budapest Conservatory, contributed to the string quartet arrangements for "Take the 'A' Train" and "A Flower Is a Lovesome Thing," but his precise role is unclear.[25] Other collaborators with ties to the Mars Club scene, and whose contributions were key to the "boldly minimal backings," were members of the French vocal jazz group Les Doubles Six, led by white French jazz vocalese specialist, pianist, and translator Mimi Perrin. Perrin and several members of Les Doubles Six performed the vocal arrangements on the album under the name the Paris Blue Notes.[26] Although the identities of the musicians heard in the string quartet backings were not included in the album's credits and remain unknown, Strayhorn's decision to collaborate with French classical musicians in itself reflects the particular constellation of diverse jazz sounds and community in and around the Mars Club.

Like many other Parisian jazz clubs, the Mars Club counted among its jazzophile patrons professional musicians working in the city's postwar popular and classical musical scenes. A case in point concerns the hard-living, jazz-loving

French pianist and composer Samson François, an artist whom Strayhorn greatly admired and whom he met one evening at the Mars Club sometime over the six-month period Strayhorn was in France from October 1960 to March 1961. Since Samson François's death in 1970 at age forty-six (he suffered a heart attack on the concert stage in 1968), his idiosyncratic and passionate interpretations of Chopin, Ravel, Debussy, Schumann, and Liszt have garnered him a near-cult status (most notably in France), despite numerous uneven and erratic recordings. In interviews as well as in liner notes for his albums, François likened his playing and interpretive approach to the improvisatory ethos of jazz ("It must be that there is never the impression of being obliged to play the next note"), and what he perceived as expressive and formal affinities linking certain repertoires of modern jazz and classical music.[27] François's relationship to jazz practice was a major theme in critical reviews of his performances and recordings. A review of his 1960 recording of Ravel's *Piano Concerto in G Major* published in *Billboard*, for example, praised François's interpretation for its "wit, gaiety and near-jazz technique."[28]

I want to dwell for a moment on the story of Strayhorn and François—their mutual admiration of each other's artistry, and their Mars Club encounter. This story would seem only a minor footnote (if that) in any accounting of Strayhorn's Parisian works and recordings during this period. Yet the story interests me in some ways because of its peripheral, minor nature in relation to the more obvious or "relevant" jazz historical contexts for Strayhorn's Parisian works, *The Peaceful Side* in particular (I will have more to say about those more relevant contexts soon). Furthermore, the story of the Mars Club encounter between Strayhorn and François comes from Bridgers, who recounted it in an oral history interview with Patricia Willard for the Smithsonian in 1989 and, more extensively, in a subsequent interview conducted in French with François's son, Maximilien Samson François, for his biography, *Samson François, Histoires de . . . Mille Vies, 1924–1970*. In the latter interview, Bridgers explained that he first learned of Samson François's admiration for Strayhorn's works when he met the pianist in 1959. As he put it, the two hit it off right away, "talking like old friends" about their shared interests:

> We discovered that we shared many common interests, although I was a bar pianist and he was a classical pianist. For example, our passion for Ravel, Chopin, Liszt and Duke Ellington! While we were talking about Duke Ellington, he told me that he had a particular admiration for the compositions of Billy

Strayhorn... I told him that Strayhorn was my best friend, that we shared an apartment in New York and that meeting him had motivated me to become a jazz pianist. Shortly after that first meeting [1959], while I was in New York, I discovered that Strayhorn had just bought a series of records by Samson François. He asked me if I knew him and when I said "yes" and told him about our meeting, he was very happy. One or two years later, in Paris... Strayhorn came to listen to me at the Mars Club one night when I saw Samson François come in, and I exclaimed, "At last, it's my privilege to introduce you two to each other!" Their mutual sympathy was immediate and they soon engaged in an intellectual conversation about music, exchanging views on Bartók etc. which, I must say, went completely over my head.[29]

In the earlier version of this story told during his Smithsonian interview, Bridgers specified that Strayhorn owned "a complete collection of Samson François," and that Samson François loved Strayhorn's works "because of the Ravelian/Debussy side and Chopin," noting that François was "a great interpreter of Ravel and Chopin."[30] Bridgers's linking of the French modernism of Ravel and Debussy with Chopin in this quote reflects perceptions of that time (and since), especially in relation to the programmatic, atmospheric, and expressive use of chromaticism in the work of all three composers. The influence of classical techniques and Chopin-esque expressive affinities, as well as French modernist sound and refined affect also deeply shaped Strayhorn's pianism—as it did the queer jazz modernist classicism of his compositional imagination. As evidenced starting in his early-1940s recordings with the Ellington Orchestra, Strayhorn's playing and technique stood out for the way in which he combined influences from Art Tatum and Teddy Wilson with the French modernist pianism of Debussy, Ravel, and Satie, while also drawing on techniques and expressive devices of the Romantic piano repertoire, which pianists like François specialized in. As Walter van de Leur explains, while the influence of French modernist sound on Strayhorn's playing—as with his compositions—can be heard in his "choice of chords, in their often high registration and their colorist weight," his "often florid fills hint at nineteenth-century European piano literature—composers who come to mind are Franz Liszt and Frédéric Chopin—and thus link his playing to piano techniques outside the jazz idiom."[31] In Bridgers's repeated telling of the story of the encounter between Strayhorn and François, he ascribes significance to what the story conveys about these musical and aesthetic affinities, which he credits for making their Mars Club meeting one of immediate "mutual sympathy." At

Listening to The Peaceful Side 157

the end of his account, Bridgers briefly mentions their "intellectual conversation about music," which centered partly on their shared enthusiasm for and interest in the compositional techniques of Béla Bartók. Beyond the context of Strayhorn's connection with François, Bridgers's commentary on these musical affinities also index the queer coordinates of his and Strayhorn's shared Francophilia. In remembering his initial attraction to Strayhorn, for example, Bridgers explained, "We had the same favorite musicians, especially Tatum and Teddy Wilson. And we both loved the French classical composers. I had always had a love for all things French, and I discovered that Billy did too."[32]

To return to *The Peaceful Side*, these affinities and sympathies call attention to a distinctly cosmopolitan arrangement of sound and sensibility, one that resonates across the LP's expansive lexicon of piano jazz modernism, embracing both the pop and classical sides of the midcentury jazz sound. It goes without saying that this resonance comes through the material itself (that is, Strayhorn's compositions) and through the technical skill set and expressive resources of Strayhorn's playing, including his refined tone, sophisticated voicings, cascading fills, and improvisatory wit and elegance. Indeed, the novelty of hearing Strayhorn performing Strayhorn without Ellington or musicians from the Ellington band was the ostensible catalyst for making the LP and, for many listeners and critics at the time (and since), this represents the chief value of the recording. Despite (or perhaps because of) Ellington's absence, critical evaluations of Strayhorn's playing on both *The Peaceful Side* and other recordings invariably prompt comparisons to Ellington's piano playing. Not surprisingly, this comparative critical discourse amplifies the same sorts of gendered and racialized tropes that I discussed in the previous chapter, for example, counterposing feminine-associated qualities of Strayhorn's playing such as his lighter touch, classical sensibility, and "pretty" harmonic palette with the sonic signifiers of Ellington's jazz piano masculinity—weighty sonorities, percussive attack, and heavy swing.

A version of this discourse from this period appears in John S. Wilson's review of another landmark in the solo Strayhorn archive: his first solo concert performance in the summer of 1965 for the New York chapter of the Duke Ellington Jazz Society. Held in the auditorium of the New School for Social Research auditorium, Strayhorn put together a small group, dubbed the Riverside Drive Five, for a program that he meticulously curated, comprised largely of original works covering his entire career that mixed new arrangements of familiar pieces with recent or lesser-known compositions.[33] In his review for the *New York Times*, with the by-line "Pianist Echoes Mentor in Pastels and Wit," Wilson wrote: "As a composer, Mr. Strayhorn concentrates on the soft, pastel colors in the Ellington spectrum. Much of his program was devoted to gentle, reflective melodies ... His style as a solo pianist is of a piece with his composing, soft and gentle, making his melodies drift dreamily along ... he was never the flamboyant striker of sparks at the keyboard Mr. Ellington often chooses to be."[34] An updated iteration on these discursive tropes appears in critic Kevin Whitehead's 2015 essay "Strayhorn the Pianist." In it, Whitehead hails Strayhorn as "jazz's quiet man" whose playing "never quite got the Ellington effect at the keyboard" and whose touch "was more even, less idiosyncratic."[35] To further develop this idea, Whitehead cites the views of composer and pianist Anthony Coleman, who draws a sharp distinction between Ellington's forceful "steely" playing and "jagged attack" and Strayhorn's "prettiness" and pop-classical influences. As Coleman (via Whitehead) sees it, Ellington's playing "is about the weight of sonorities ... rather than harmony, which is Strayhorn's strength ... Listening to him [Strayhorn] play, I'm not sure how deep his jazz roots really are. But the jazz aesthetic has something to do with prettiness ... and Strayhorn makes the case for that prettiness."[36]

While Strayhorn's performances on *The Peaceful Side* confirm and expand Coleman's "case" for jazz "prettiness," I contend that to listen to the LP primarily as a solo jazz piano performance captured on record occludes the conceptual and creatively expansive registers of the LP. To return to a point made at the outset, Strayhorn's concept for his solo LP framed the idea of the "solo" in terms of affect, mood, and environment, a being alone or "place to go," which, as described by producer Douglas, enabled and embodied ideal forms of introspection as complex, intelligent, and mysterious.[37] Sound engineer Gerhart Lehner remembered the special ambiance of the sessions as akin "to a dream ... Billy's music just poured out, like the recordings already existed and he was miming to a tape."[38] There is in Strayhorn's sonic dream a kind of utopian, and I would argue a distinctly queer utopian, impulse or concept at work.

From this perspective, Strayhorn's "Paris Album" might provocatively be described as a musical self-portrait in the form of a Black queer concept album. Strayhorn's interpretations and arrangements embrace the exploratory and the beautifully weird. Through the LP's ten sides, he collaboratively reimagines, remixes, and reframes the formal, expressive, and programmatic registers of his works in ways that specifically engage the affordances of the LP format and studio environment to create a nocturnal fantasia, a destination of (im)possibility and dreaming "halfway to dawn." Here Strayhorn's choice of repertoire, representing his "favorite" original compositions—ones that, importantly, he frequently performed for friends and small audiences at private parties and other personal, informal settings—links the specific conceptual priorities of the LP with the larger themes of jazz intimacy and queer collaboration central to my project.[39] Crucially, Strayhorn's self-portrait is dominated by versions of the same set of songs and ballads that expressively, lyrically, and affectively organize Strayhorn's queer music: "Lush Life" and "Something to Live For," as well as the Strayhorn-Hodges ballads "Passion Flower," "Day Dream," and "A Flower Is a Lovesome Thing." Even the most famous nonballad instrumental included on the LP, "Take the 'A' Train," is re-sounded as an urbane ballad with murmuring strings underscoring Strayhorn's at turns wistful and playful interpretation (in the tune's introduction, Strayhorn subtly and humorously mimics Ellington's playing). As Douglas remembered, "It was him saying, 'Here are these songs that mean a lot to me, and this is what they happen to mean at this particular point.'"[40]

THE PEACEFUL SIDE IN/AND THE JAZZ FIELD

Thus far my discussion of *The Peaceful Side* has focused on the specific constellation of biographical, conceptual, and creative contexts of the recording. To dig deeper into this constellation requires widening my lens to situate *The Peaceful Side* in the larger field of modern jazz and jazz-adjacent LPs of the 1950s and early 1960s. Positioning the LP within this wider field not only clarifies its relationship to postwar recording trends, but also, more specifically, foregrounds the ways in which Strayhorn's project interacted with these trends. I'm interested in considering how Strayhorn's work on the Paris album can be heard as actively engaging these trends, that is, how Strayhorn listens to and arranges these various and varied trends. Let's begin with what is perhaps the most apparent point (or points) of connection: the proliferation of piano trio recordings during this period, for example those led by Bud Powell, Ahmad Jamal, Bill Evans, Oscar Peterson and—in 1951 for a series of eight piano duets with Ellington, accompanied by bass—Strayhorn himself. The duets with Ellington, which included versions of "Flamingo" and "Tonk," were recorded toward the end of 1950 and released on the short-lived Mercer label (a joint project of Mercer Ellington and Leonard Feather) under the title *Mercer Records Presents the Billy Strayhorn Trio*.[41]

Given the absence of drums and the inclusion of vocal choir and string quartet in the arrangements, obviously the LP is not technically a trio; however the imprint of the midcentury piano trio LP on *The Peaceful Side*—and, by extension, the "mainstream" small-group jazz sound—is evident in multiple ways, including the improvisatory and performative intimacy of the recording, aspects of the mixing and style, and, perhaps most importantly, in how Strayhorn exploits the interpretive and expressive possibilities of these elements. As well, five of the ten tracks follow the conventions of any number of piano trio recordings, interspersing small-group arrangements with piano solos.[42] Strayhorn's piano-bass duets with Michel Gaudry on "Just A-Settin' and A-Rockin'" and "Something to Live For" especially stand out in relation to the trio aesthetic and sound, and Strayhorn's similar placement of these two songs, two and nine respectively, reinforce this connection.

Of the two, Strayhorn's version of "Just A-Settin' and A-Rockin'" is the most striking for the ways it reworks the affective and sonic frameworks of the original tune, a midtempo riff-based (or proto-jump) tune, first recorded in 1941 as a vehicle for Ben Webster's warm tenor sax. Of significance here are both the interpretive and embodied details of Strayhorn's reworkings as well as how these reworkings reference the composition's authorship and recorded history outside of the Ellington orchestra. While the original instrumental version was co-credited to Strayhorn and Ellington, Strayhorn's inclusion of it on the LP could, as van de Leur suggests, be interpreted as a de facto claim (or reclamation) of individual authorship—and this claim is supported by the existence of untitled sketches of the tune in Strayhorn's hand.[43] The question of the tune's authorship, however, is a complicated matter: in 1944, it was issued a copyright under the slightly altered title, "Just A-Sittin' and A-Rockin'," with a third authorship credit given to Lee Gaines, who composed a lyric for the song. Along with his fellow members of the all-male jubilee-style vocal quartet, the Delta Rhythm Boys, Gaines participated in the first recording of a vocal version of "Just A-Sittin' and A-Rockin'" for the Decca label in July 1945. Early in 1946, the Delta Rhythm Boys recording appeared on the "Juke Box Race Records" popularity chart several times, peaking at #3 on January 26. By the next month, their recording crossed over into the pop charts, where it reached #17.[44] As was typical for pop tunes during this period, multiple labels released vocal big band versions under the copyrighted title "Just A-Sittin' and A-Rockin'" around the same time. In September 1945, for example, jazz singer and chanteuse Thelma Carpenter recorded a version for the Majestic label (backed by the Earl Sheldon Orchestra). Most salient for Strayhorn's reworked version, however, was the (minor) hit version of the tune recorded by the Stan Kenton Orchestra with vocalist June Christy for Capitol in October 1945 (it charted during the same period as the Delta Rhythm Boys version).

Listening to The Peaceful Side **161**

The Kenton/Christy recording is distinguished by an added sung vocal introduction, one that Strayhorn appropriates and richly harmonizes in his eight-bar introduction of the tune for *The Peaceful Side*. Importantly, Strayhorn's only known vocal arrangement of the tune, for Rosemary Clooney in 1956—which preserves the original title "Just A-Settin' and A-Rockin'"—does not include this added introductory vocal verse, a fact that makes his use of it as a framing device for the version on *The Peaceful Side* particularly intriguing and evocative. Why would Strayhorn recall this added verse from a recording made fifteen years prior? Beyond the easy answer that he did so because he liked it, is the fact that Christy herself recalled it for her 1959 updated version of the tune, arranged by Pete Rugolo for the Capitol LP *June Christy Recalls Those Stan Kenton Years*.[45] Strayhorn's (double) recollection here signifies in several directions: 1) to the sound and affect of Christy's controlled vocal sensuality; 2) to the unsung "intertext" of the added words for the introductory verse; and 3) more speculatively, as a sly way of commenting on the tune's multiple authorial interlocuters. As for this last signifying context, Strayhorn's incorporation of the introduction points toward the authorship of Rugolo, the "name" arranger who most likely scored the original 1945 Kenton/Christy chart, and who also was for Strayhorn once the source of difficult feelings. The cause of these difficult feelings was Rugolo's authorship of a "luxe pop" arrangement of "Lush Life" for Nat "King" Cole's recording of the song in 1949, an event—and specifically an arrangement—that greatly angered Strayhorn. In fact, The Cole/Rugolo "Lush Life" stands as the first studio recording of the song and was done without Strayhorn's involvement or, apparently, his consent. According to Bridgers, Strayhorn's animus toward their version triggered a rare moment of anger: "that was the only time I ever, ever heard Billy really upset . . . I never heard him talk like that. He was screaming, 'Why the fuck didn't they leave it alone?'"[46]

With this context in mind, Strayhorn's reworking of Rugolo's introduction to his (similarly) "luxe pop" "Just A-Sittin' and A-Rockin'" arrangement into a quiet, reflective prelude of pointedly unstylized, impromptu lushness, resounds as a subtle act of reclamation (if not reappropriation). This counterinterpretive framework brings me back to the other two signifying possibilities—Christy's voice and the lyric—both of which, I want to argue, help us to tune into the details of Strayhorn's (re)interpretation and performance and the relation of these embodied details to the LP's queer collaborative ethos as manifest in its conceptual, autobiographical, and aesthetic programs.

The lyric for "Just A-Sittin' and A-Rockin'" expresses with a lighthearted and sophisticated tongue-in-cheek attitude the frustration and loneliness of a neglected lover (the "I") waiting for "him" to return. An interesting detail of the added introductory lyric concerns its form of address, specifically the way it picks up on and expands a change in the form of address from an "I" to a "you" in Gaines's original lyric. This narrative move happens in the fifth verse of the original lyric when the protagonist shifts from a first-person internal monologue to addressing a "you": "Now if I don't find him / I hope you'll remind him." The added lyric for the introductory verse identifies this "you" as a friend or audience of friends who the protagonist is preparing to address: "I know I should go out / Be seen here and there / But my friends have found out / My baby don't care." I hear Strayhorn's interpretation of this introductory verse as a kind of wordless doubling that pianistically translates the direct address to a listener—a you— before the performance begins. In Strayhorn's rendition, this intimate effect is enhanced by the lyrical profile and elastic (rubato) playing of the melody, and the expressivity of the aforementioned lush harmonies and impromptu ornamental fills. At the same time, we can listen to this moment for its autobiographical registers, that is, in relation to Strayhorn's reflective pianistic evocation of the words which, however lightheartedly, address conflicted feelings around public visibility and personal revelation. These sonic mixtures are further developed in Strayhorn's interpretation of the AABA tune: the rhythmic profile of the original A sections with its playful forward-driving swing and call-and-response unfolding, are reworked and varied in Strayhorn's rubato treatment of the melody and abstract modernist offbeat left-hand accents. The reworkings are also carried through in the A sections through subtle yet dynamic interaction with Gaudry on bass; and in the B sections, which modulate from B♭ major to D minor and feature a more lyrical melodic line. Strayhorn amplifies these shifts, giving an urgent and plaintive expressivity with sophisticated, quasirhapsodic passages (which also do double duty as replacements for the solo choruses).

Alongside the piano trio, Strayhorn's collaboration with Mimi Perrin and a subset of her group Les Doubles Six documents his engagement with the midcentury trend of jazz vocalese recordings. Perrin modelled her group after the first wave of influential jazz vocalese artists, principally Lambert, Hendricks, and Ross.[47] As I noted earlier, for *The Peaceful Side* sessions, Perrin's group is identified as the Paris Blue Notes, a change that was most likely done to avoid contractual issues with Columbia Records and Philips Records, the labels on which Les Double Six recorded a string of albums from 1960 to 1964. Like *The Peaceful Side* and many other Barclay Studio recording projects, these LPs involved transnational and interracial collaboration. These included *The Double Six Meet Quincy Jones* (Columbia, 1960), *The Double Six of Paris: Swingin' Singin'* (Philips, recorded 1960–61), *Dizzy Gillespie and the Double Six of Paris* (Philips, 1963), and *The Double Six of Paris Sing Ray Charles* (Philips, 1964). While there is no documentation regarding Strayhorn's thoughts on jazz vocalese, in an interview during this period he singled out for praise the pop-jazz vocal group The Four Freshman (the vocal quartet recorded "Chelsea Bridge" for their 1958 Capitol LP *Voices in Latin*, with added lyrics written by group member Bill Comstock). However, Strayhorn's treatment of jazz vocalese in his arrangements differs significantly from the vocalese practices on these recordings, a topic on which I have more to say later. The one important exception is Strayhorn's arrangement for the blues ballad "Multi-Colored Blue," which features up-tempo call-and-response choruses with the vocal choir. In the A section, a twelve-bar blues, the choir sings response riffs, while in the eight-bar B chorus they "shout" for the first four bars.

Strayhorn's jazz vocalese arrangement for "Multi-Colored Blue" provides an occasion to hear his LP project in conversation with the pop end of the mainstream jazz spectrum; however, the more relevant midcentury jazz context for most of the other arrangements—and, more broadly for Strayhorn's compositional sensibility—is the LP's relationship to the emergence of "chamber jazz," "third-stream" and related jazz recordings (such as the Modern Jazz Quartet recordings for Prestige and Atlantic labels). Now often (and confusingly) associated with so-called "West Coast" jazz, many of these recordings involved novel instrumental ensembles, often without piano, and featured compositions and arrangements that combined or attempted to "fuse" jazz and classical vocabularies and sound. Among the most prominent artists/bandleaders here: Stan Kenton, George Russell, Chico Hamilton, Jimmy Giuffre, Gerry Mulligan, Shorty Rogers, and Chet Baker. One specific example with special pertinence for Strayhorn's career would be the LP *Chico Hamilton Quintet Featuring Buddy Collette* recorded in 1955, the same year that Hamilton and Strayhorn went on tour with Lena Horne, forming part of a trio with Hamilton and bassist George Duvivier. Hamilton's quintet LP featured arrangements scored for (in addition to flute, Buddy Collette), cello (Fred Katz), guitar (Jim Hall), and bass (Carson Smith).

On *The Peaceful Side*, Strayhorn's use of a classical string quartet backing in combination with a harmonically advanced and composition-focused aesthetic clearly connects his project to the broader "chamber jazz" and "third-stream" concept. However, it is also the case, as van de Leur has observed, that Strayhorn's (and Ellington's) own prior compositions and arrangements were in many ways the original inspiration and thus, in some cases, the primary source of influence for the wave of midcentury classical-jazz fusions.[48] For the purposes of this discussion, I consider Strayhorn's version of his exquisite ballad "Passion Flower" and the foreboding song "Strange Feeling," tracks three and five respectively. "Passion Flower," which counts as the first of four Strayhorn-Hodges ballads that Strayhorn selected for the LP (the other three, in order of appearance, are "Day Dream," "Multi-Colored Blue" [aka "Violet Blue"], and "A Flower Is a Lovesome Thing"), is the most sophisticated in terms of its concept, harmony, and melody of the two compositions.[49] Notably it is the one ballad that maintained—through a rich and varied body of arrangements—its original instrumental conception; even the elaborately reworked 1956 version Strayhorn created for the Clooney-Ellington Orchestra LP *Blue Rose* retained its identity as a showcase for the erotics of Hodges's alto sax sound.[50] To be sure, this history informs Strayhorn's version of "Passion Flower" on *The Peaceful Side*; at the same time, however, the minimalism and quiet intimacy of his interpretation, accompanied by Gaudry, brings out or foregrounds the piece's complex musical concept and structure while also revoicing its sensual mood and lyrical, quasioperatic melodic exploration. As Gaudry would remember the collaboration: "he was serious but nice and easy . . . That was his secret—he made you feel comfortable. He was so honest. His playing was so honest, and it was emotional. It just happened. He gave me a little advice, like colors he wanted, some moods."[51]

A close counterpart to "Passion Flower" both in mood and in amplifying what Gaudry describes as the honesty and emotional truth of Strayhorn's playing, is Strayhorn's treatment of the foreboding and theatrical mood piece "Strange Feeling," the midpoint work and quasi-interlude on the LP. The extant manuscript for this arrangement bears the title "Feeling," a shortened title which, although conventional, signals for me something profound about Strayhorn's reconception of the work, one that radically recontextualizes the "mood" of its original versions. These versions originate in two performance contexts: first as an accompaniment to an "exotic" dance number under the title "Leticia" in 1943, and, in the following year, as the second movement of the Ellington-Strayhorn *Perfume Suite* (for Ellington's 1944 Carnegie Hall concert). Strayhorn's version of "Strange Feeling" for the LP transforms the exoticized dark-hued programs of the originals (as dance/perfumed feminized mood) into an atmospheric piano miniature of austere beauty and mystery. As if channeling the core repertoire and interpretive poetics of Samson François, Strayhorn's "Feeling" explores a sonic-dramatic landscape reminiscent of a Debussy prelude or, to be more specific, one prelude in particular: *La cathédrale engloutie* (The Sunken Cathedral, Preludes Book 1, no. 10, 1910). I hear in Strayhorn's whole-tone saturated atmospheric introduction and in his forceful striking of dense, sonorous minor-mode block chords against the blues-tinged melody, embodied traces of this prelude as interpreted by a pianist such as François (as, for example, documented on the LP *Samson François: Piano Recital 1960*), thus at once affirming the affinities that attracted François and Strayhorn to each other's work, and Strayhorn's "Feeling" as a work imagining and claiming its own stream of "chamber jazz."

THE STRAYHORN EFFECT, OR LISTENING TO "LUSH LIFE"

If key musical features of the *The Peaceful Side*, including its format, performative intimacy, and the compositional profile and interpretive poetics of Strayhorn's arrangements of his original works, engage musical trends of the midcentury modern jazz LP such as the piano trio and "chamber jazz" or "third-stream" projects, these same defining elements as well as others—technological, sonic, and programmatic—put Strayhorn's work in conversation with a wider field of musical trends and studio recording and production practices, including trends usually excluded from the privileged and "respectable" categories of jazz historiography. This dialogue is reflected, although somewhat obliquely, through the LP's incorporation of arrangements featuring dreamy studio special effects and wordless vocal choir; these and other atmospheric sounds put *The Peaceful Side* in proximity to the original postwar LP fad, namely the proliferation of mood music, easy-listening (or "background music") albums. Jazz recording projects from various aesthetic orientations participated to some extent in this trend.[52] To be sure, this participation was partly motivated by commercial considerations as record labels struggled to find ways to market jazz LPs to (largely white middle-class) consumers. In fact, the particular intersection of aesthetics and commerce is what connects the trends I've discussed thus far—piano trio, jazz/classical concept "chamber jazz," and "third-stream" LPs—with the mood music fad; that is, what these trends have in common comes in the search for new (jazz) sounds, stylistic blends, expressive possibilities and forms that could also accommodate (or, perhaps more aptly, create) new modes of listening and musical consumption in the postwar era.

This broader perspective positions *The Peaceful Side* within a diverse range of artists and projects: from early and mid-1950s ballad-centric recordings of the "with strings" variety showcasing top jazz instrumental soloists, to early-1960s recordings such as the Miles Davis/Gil Evans collaborations, especially *Sketches of Spain* (1960), and Bill Evans's *Portrait in Jazz* (1960), *Explorations* (1961), and *Conversations with Myself* (1963). Strayhorn contributed several charts to one of the standard-bearer LPs in the former category, *Music for Loving: Ben Webster with Strings* (1954).[53] Another provocative precursor here, not only for its Black classical music orientation and its focus on sonic and melodic exploration and/ as mood, but for Black queer cosmopolitan histories of this aesthetic, is Donald Shirley's first LP, *Tonal Expressions* (1955). Like *The Peaceful Side*, *Tonal Expressions* does not include drums, featuring only a duo of piano and bass, and digs deeply into the romantic and erotic terrain of the ballad (including "Secret Love," "The Man I Love," and, that most midcentury ballad, "My Funny Valentine").[54]

While its classical-jazz blends, ballad-heavy material, and nocturnal, dreamy atmosphere of some sides align *The Peaceful Side* with trends at the intersection of the midcentury jazz LP and mood music, the most audible instances of connection to mood music LPs comes in the treatment of the vocal and string quartet backings that Strayhorn deploys on "Lush Life," "Take the 'A' Train," "Day Dream," and "A Flower Is a Lovesome Thing." Crucially, in contrast to virtually all the other jazz albums cited here, these backings are treated with heavy reverb and other studio-driven special effects. These technological mediations conjure associations with the mood music mainstream as exemplified by the midcentury wave of easy-listening and exotica LPs featuring arrangements and compositions by artists such as Les Baxter, Paul Westin, Martin Denny, Harry Revel, (Juan García) Esquivel, and others. White big band "name" arrangers such as Billy May also participated in this recording trend, crafting LPs combining jazz with the mood music sound. In the same year as *The Peaceful Side*, for instance, May, in collaboration with Charlie Barnet and a small group dubbed the Out-Islanders, released an "exotica" LP under the title *Polynesian Fantasy*, which featured an impressionistically audacious "ultra-lounge" arrangement with wordless vocals of Mercer Ellington's "Moon Mist" (first recorded by the Ellington Orchestra in 1942).[55]

Yet Strayhorn's incorporation of mood music's sonic tropes—the special effects/reverb, strings, and wordless vocal choir—signal other formal, affective, and programmatic ends. Against the up-close and first-person quiet "realness" of Strayhorn's solo performance, the backings activate multiple sonic and semiotic registers (often simultaneously), from the ambient, abstract, and liminal—sudden splashes of color or dream-like textures and atmospheric sensations—to the narrative or quasicinematic. Take Strayhorn's arrangement for "Lush Life," significantly the LP's opening statement: the changing, at times volatile and unsettling layers of sound, affect, and mood critically differentiate the arranging/recording concept and aesthetic from midcentury exotica or "mood wax" sound. Rather than a series of individual tracks presenting a singular, stable mood—a sonic bath that allows the ear to listen and luxuriate undisturbed—Strayhorn's treatment of mood music materials, like his arrangements and performance writ large, arrange the wordless choir and strings as part of an experimental and conceptual matrix, digging into what, borrowing from Fred Moten, can be called the LP's Black "fugitive" improvisatory soundings.[56] Indeed, his arrangement of "Lush Life"—Strayhorn's first and only formal studio recording of this extremely personal song—invites a hearing in dialogue with Moten's own "fugitive" improvisatory take on a second solo Strayhorn version of the song, an extraordinary vocal performance with Strayhorn accompanying himself on piano, captured live in a January 14, 1964, performance at the Basin Street East club in New York. That Moten's engagement with this second solo "Lush Life" foregrounds the song's Harlem-Paris sonic geography as well as its Black queer aesthetic coordinates and forms of "lyrical surplus," makes such a comparative hearing all the more instructive.[57]

For Moten, the Harlem-Paris routes or migratory "itineraries" of the historical Black avant-garde act as a "chain of renaissance," a kind of underground Black Atlantic or "multiply sited encounter between the European and African diasporas." Such racialized encounters and cosmopolitan geopolitics birth a constellation of "forces/voices" that drive and amplify a "sentimental avant-garde," a "dense erotics" embodied in Black performance as well as in "texts and canvases" of the Black radical tradition. In Moten's account, these insurgent, improvisatory "forces/voices"—elsewhere called the "the erotics of the cut"—are sonically materialized in what Moten terms Ellington's "sound of love," a formulation he borrows from the title of Charles Mingus's 1974 composition, "Duke Ellington's Sound of Love." Ellington's "sound of love" encompasses "the weight and energy in and of sound—of Ellington's life and love, Ellington's eros, (the Ellington) ensemble."[58]

Although the privileged artist here is Ellington, I would argue that Moten's theorization of Ellington's "sound of love" in relation to Mingus's homage to Ellington implicitly includes Strayhorn's queer collaborative voice—call it the "Strayhorn effect." This arises most strikingly through Mingus's incorporation of Strayhorn's works in his composition; that is, Mingus's "Duke Ellington's Sound of Love" contains audible traces of "Lush Life" and "A Flower Is a Lovesome Thing," the balladic bookends of *The Peaceful Side*.[59] These sonic intertexts sound in the harmonic and melodic elements of the composition and are developed with stunning beauty and depth in Don Pullen's piano work on the original 1974 recording, which remixes and refashions the "dense erotics" of Strayhorn's lyricism. Perhaps that is Moten's point: his engagement with Strayhorn and "Lush Life" emerges as part of a theoretically complex riff on the "surplus" sonic/erotic movements, encounters, and "instruments" that connect various Harlem-Paris modernist itineraries and migrations (which in Moten's reading can involve an alternate stop in Greenwich Village). Strayhorn's voice is imagined as part of a "small ensemble" of Harlem-Paris "forces/voices"—a trio to be exact. Specifically, Strayhorn is paired with the great Black queer modernist painter Beauford Delaney, who moved to Paris in 1953 and remained there until his death in 1979.[60] Speculating on their (fugitive) Black queer connections, Moten writes: "Of course Delaney and Strayhorn—whose name is so suggestive especially when we hear him sing, the outness . . . of his voice or horn, itinerant, stray like the brass and winds of Ellington's (and Strayhorn's) 'instrument'—share . . . in the outness of their (homo)sexuality and their movements, on the A-train and more widely, as 'Lush Life' suggests, what it is to be driven by the paradoxically hidden extremity and necessary unrequitedness of love."[61]

Circling back to Moten's commentary on Strayhorn's 1964 solo version of "Lush Life," Moten hears the "outness" of these "forces/voices" materialized in two moments, the first of which comes in what he describes as an instance of "tonal breakdown" that occurs "when the word 'madness' is uttered with some uncontrollable accompaniment."[62] This moment arises in Strayhorn's execution of the opening of the lyric's third stanza: "Then you came along / with your siren song / to tempt me to madness." The other moment hails the "lyrical surplus" in Strayhorn's delivery of the song's famous opening line: "I used to visit all the very gay places / those come what may places / relaxing on the axis of the wheel of life to get the feel of life / from jazz and cocktails."[63] Moten identifies the sonic surplus here as "too much rhyme . . . the voice is all over, strained or fragile"; in Moten's hearing this unruly or "stray" vocal and lyrical moment inscribes and amplifies a history of sonic and phonic rupture or, in his words, "a long apprenticeship to the *materi*ality of voices that the music represents" and within which "lies universality: in this break, this cut, this rupture."[64]

Strayhorn's performance of "Lush Life" on the opening track of *The Peaceful Side* activates interrelated forms and affective histories of Black modernist sonic "surplus," but through an alternate constellation of means and materials, namely as filtered through the space of the studio environment and the "instrument" of the arrangement. The arrangement here is a capacious category, an "instrument" that encompasses: 1) Strayhorn's handwritten manuscript short score for the vocal choir and bass accompaniment parts, written in the song's principal key of D♭; 2) the exigencies of the song's recorded performance in relation to the specific ensemble of bodies, instruments, and technological mediations—the interactions between the solo Strayhorn and the vocal choir and the mono mix and studio effects facilitated by the Barclay sound engineer, Gerhard Lehner; 3) the formal and quasinarrative structures of the arrangement; and 4) the emotional and (auto)biographical (or "lived") registers of the song as both object and subject, that is as manifest in the interpretive details and embodied Black queer jazz history of Strayhorn's playing.

Strayhorn's concept of arranging as a multidimensional practice of "seeing all around the material" is subtly manifest in the manuscript short score for the "Lush Life" arrangement (figure 5.1).[65] The score is minimal and sketch-like, covering three and a half minutes of music compressed into eight staff systems. After an instruction to "Ad Lib" for the piano introduction, only the choral parts and bass accompaniment are notated—although, significantly, Strayhorn sketched out his "ad lib" introduction on a separate piece of manuscript paper with the title "L. L. Intro." While the notation and title are written in pencil, Strayhorn marked the rehearsal letters A through C in red pen. The vocal parts move through various combinations of scoring involving voicings with two to six pitches; however, the way the voices are mixed on the recording—specifically the heavy use of reverb (the singers most likely were isolated from the piano in an echo chamber) makes it extremely difficult to hear the precise number of voices performing in any one moment on the recording. The short score is clear and detailed enough for the singers to have read directly off of it for the recording session; however, the extant manuscript materials for this session (BSC) include six vocal parts and a bass part. Either way, the absence of notated vocables in the short score as well as their absence in the extracted vocal parts suggests that Strayhorn's directions for the vocables were communicated during session rehearsals.

Regardless of its largely functional nature, the short score is a valuable instrument; its remarkable economy of means and concomitant minimalist aesthetics create a blueprint for listening to the arrangement's multidimensionality. One way this works comes in how the short score represents the multidimensional—formal, affective, narrative—relationships between Strayhorn's solo performance

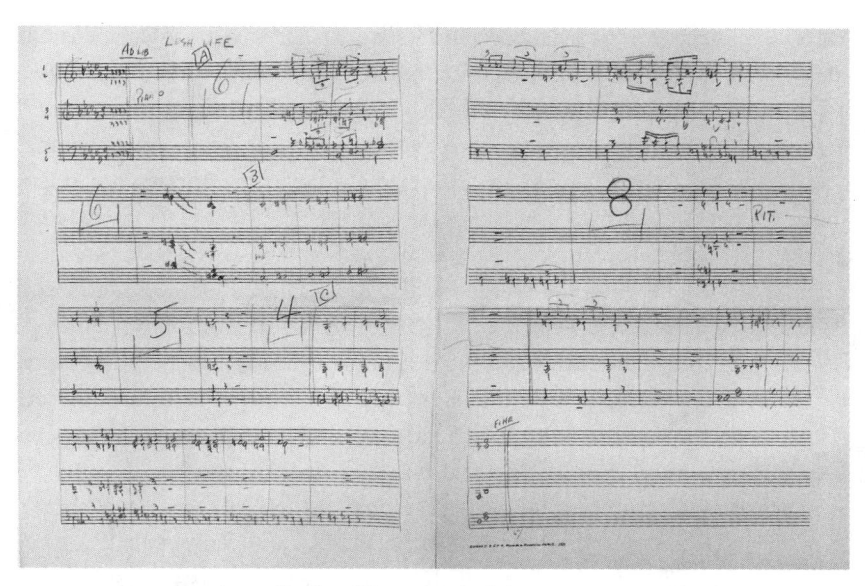

FIGURE 5.1 Strayhorn, "Lush Life" autographed short score manuscript (choir and bass parts). Billy Strayhorn Collection, Library of Congress, Music Division. Reproduced by permission of Billy Strayhorn Songs, Inc.

of the song and the wordless vocal choir. On the most basic level, Strayhorn's concept for the wordless choral backings is structured by an array of arranging conventions, what could be called the convention-dimension of his arranging practice. That is, Strayhorn deploys the vocal backings to create variety in sound and mood, both momentary—as in abstract bursts of color and dreamy atmospheric affect—and on a larger scale, in relation to the song's concerto-like formal unfolding, that is, as a means of underscoring the song's contrasting (yet through-composed) formal divisions. For example, Strayhorn varies the vocal arrangement to differentiate and create affective contrast between the first section (A) of the song, which features a recitative-like melodic contour, and the openings of B and C, which present the legato, melodically expansive sections. In the former (A), the wordless vocal choir provides responsorial utterances with fast-moving scat vocables passages, or sudden quarter-note interjections, such as the downward vocal slide/sigh two measures before rehearsal B. In the B and C sections, by contrast, the choir joins the piano, singing a series of half-note sustained chords on an open "oo" vowel.

Let's now take these same materials and sections and look (and listen) through

Listening to The Peaceful Side **171**

the arrangement's more conceptual and creative dimensions. In these dimensions the voices act as liminal sound, as programmatic figuration, and as characters in a subterranean music-drama—all of which Strayhorn collaboratively arranges and embodies to underscore the song's expressive registers. This requires, I contend, listening to and for how Strayhorn's arrangement sonically translates and stages the song's lyric, a dimension of wordless song that is inscribed in the short score. More than any of the other "songs without words" on the LP, Strayhorn's arrangement of "Lush Life" interpolates the vocal choir as part a dramatic conception cued to the implied lyric.

This implied wordless text (figure 5.1) is a kind of ghostly presence that orients the varied and unfolding music-dramatic relationships between Strayhorn—the soloist—and the voices. The choral backings assume multiple roles in these relationships, from jazz modernist word-painting, and dramatic vocal "sighs," to Greek chorus-like comment on the lyric's iconic tortured tale of failed romance, longing, and loneliness. These roles, then, encompass and play out along a spectrum of meaning and affect from the literal or illustrative to the gestural and abstract, a spectrum that is itself reflected in and structured by the richly evocative images and metaphors of the (wordless) lyric. For example, the first scat passage with its burst of eight-note chromatically altered chords and swing profile represents the urbane sound-image of "jazz and cocktails" that ends the first verse.[66]

A related sound-image recurs in the opening two measures of the fifth system but here the vocal backing—now with audible bass accompaniment—performs a dual formal and expressive role. In the moment, the passage acts as a vocal figuration or sonic projection of the queer compensatory powers of "a week in Paris" to heal the protagonist's existential feelings of loneliness and disappointment—indeed the vocal scoring is bright and soothing. At the same time, however, the voices participate in the unfolding music-dramatic fabric of the full stanza, a terrain of intense and conflicted emotions:

A week in Paris will ease the bite of it.
All I care is to smile in spite of it.
I'll forget you I will,
While yet you are still,
Burning inside my brain.

Here and throughout the arrangement, Strayhorn's multidimensional approach amplifies the "always already" extraordinary synthesis of word and music that is "Lush Life." For in this passage, the silencing of the "hope" and brightness that the voices seem to offer after the first line propels the performance toward its most outwardly emotional climax: Strayhorn's rhapsodic piano solo—represented in the short score in the space of the "8"—which, as the cadenza-like improvisational proxy for the protagonist, metamorphizes the tortured feelings of the "I" in the final three lines.

Picking back up an analytical context discussed earlier, the sensorial and sonic power of these musical-narrative devices are crucially enabled by and filtered through the technological affordances of the recording studio. Three moments—three responsorial "ahs" to be precise—strikingly illustrate the role of studio-engineered special effects in shaping the sound and music-dramatic dimensions of "Lush Life." Occurring the in the second, third, and sixth systems, the moments of Greek chorus "ah" responses are treated with especially heavy reverb, a technological enhancement that imbues these moments with liminality and a particularly cinematic quality, while also bringing a tinge of avant-garde sonic experimentation into the mix. The first occurrence in the second system comes in the form of a whole-tone collection performed in a vocal slide, moving in quarter notes from a minor seventh spanning B♭ to A♭ to a minor seventh spanning D to C; the downward trajectory of the slide turns the open vocable into an almost sardonic sigh, as if responding in faux sympathy to the "sullen gray faces" and their "twelve o'clock tales." A similar affective note arises in the second "ah" iteration as the choir "responds" to Strayhorn's playing of the penultimate passage of the B section, as if both commenting on his illusory hope of "a great love" and anticipating the stanza/section punch line—"Ah, yes, I was wrong, Again I was wrong." In between these two "ahs," at the start of the B section, the choir shifts roles, becoming a continuous vocal backing moving upward in half-note octaves—a siren song of temptation. The third and final responsorial "ah" is a far more sober interjection than the two that precede it, coloring the word "rot" in the drastically fatalistic final stanza: "And there I'll be / While I rot with the rest." This moment is followed by a two-measure dramatic ritardando that pianistically delivers the final line "of those whose lives are lonely, too."

The treatment of the vocal choir in "Lush Life," while unusual and, I would argue, queer in relation to mainstream jazz recording protocols, nevertheless partially aligns with larger shifts in midcentury recording studio practice and aesthetics. Such shifts had an outsized influence on public tastes and the changing perceptions of genre, style, and identity.[67] As Albin Zak has argued, these shifts owe a great deal to the studio innovations and creativity of arrangers such as

EXAMPLE 5.1 Strayhorn, short score (choir and bass arrangement) with "silent" lyrics for "Lush Life," *The Peaceful Side*. Transcribed by author.

V.
V.
V.
DB
Ooh
Ooh
Ooh
Ooh
Everything seemed so sure.
Now life is awful again,/ A trough full of heart/ Could only be a bore.
Ooh ooh
Doo doo doo doo doo doo doo doo
Doo doo doo
Doo doo doo doo doo doo
A week
in Paris
will ease
the bite of it.
All I care is to smile in spite of it.
rit.
Ah
I'll forget you I will, /While yet you are still
Burning inside my brain.
Romance is mush/ Stifling those who strive.
I'll live a lush life in some small dive.
And there I'll be
while I rot
with the rest
Of those whose lives are lonely, too.
Fine
Ooh
Ooh
Ah
Ah
Ah
Ah

Gordon Jenkins and producers such as Mitch Miller, who viewed the studio and artifice of recording as technologies and spaces "to construct miniature audio dramas," or "fashion music that underscored drama, emotion, and narrative."[68] As my close reading of "Lush Life" illustrates, Strayhorn's arrangement—one conceived and realized in collaboration with the studio environment and sound engineer Lehner—nods toward these larger commercial pop studio practices. Yet, as I've been arguing, the deployment of studio-mediated dramatic sonic devices in "Lush Life" belies the conventional, straight-narrative trajectories to which these innovative studio practices were aimed. Strayhorn's arrangement, its emotional and formal complexity and integrated multidimensions, and its Black queer contexts and histories, appropriates these devices to tell a different story, one that ends in a dream-like ambiguous space, almost a prayer: the choir sings its final "ah," now open and serene, joining with Strayhorn as they together "sing" a series of slowly rising open major 6/9 chords based on quartal harmonies.

Beyond its function as a coda or closing frame, the ending's luminous open chord and rich ambiguity also provide—metaphorically and musically—a transition to the fuller musical self-portrait that ensues. As observed earlier, Strayhorn's set list for the LP conveys another dimension or register of his arranging concept; this is nowhere more apparent and poetic than in his choice for the LP's closing track, a deeply elegant and Parisian-accented version of "A Flower Is a Lovesome Thing" arranged for string quartet and bass. The positioning of "Lush Life" and "A Flower Is a Lovesome Thing," as the opening and closing frames for the LP foregrounds their contrasting yet complementary sonic, lyrical, and affective programs.[69] The contrast in backings—vocal choir and bass for "Lush Life," string quartet and bass for "A Flower Is a Lovesome Thing"—alone is worth highlighting, and is consistent with Strayhorn's long-standing conviction that a string quartet would not be "the right way to do 'Lush Life.'"[70] Where the wordless lyric for "Lush Life" gives voice to psychic conflict, pain, loneliness, and impossible love—as performed in the city that the song hails for its ameliorative promise—a "A Flower Is a Lovesome Thing" evokes a far more serene and utopic object and mood: the fragile, miraculous beauty of a single flower, a "luscious, living lovesome thing." As an ending to his musical portrait, Strayhorn's arrangement of the song is an optimistic and graceful closing gesture, a kind of parting musical bouquet that evokes not only his signature saying "ever up and onwards" but also his lifelong practice of gifting flowers to family (especially his beloved mother Lillian) and friends, old and new.

CONCLUSION: PRODUCING THE SOLO STRAYHORN

My analyses of Strayhorn's work on *The Peaceful Side* have advanced an expansive, queer collaborative notion of the "solo" in listening to Strayhorn's piano album. By way of conclusion, however, I want to critically reflect on the network of race and power that made Strayhorn a "solo act" in relation to the social conditions and institutional contexts of the recording sessions. As I argued earlier, the collaboration between Strayhorn and the white Parisian musicians and production team both archives and reflects the interracial networks of postwar Parisian jazz culture, especially as it gravitated around the Mars Club. At the same time, these networks of interracial community existed within or alongside histories of racialized power structures, in this case most glaringly in relation to those that organized jazz labels and came to bear in the dynamics of recording studio collaboration. As virtually the only Black body in the studio, then, Strayhorn's creative voice and performing body were positioned as a solo act within the racialized institutional histories and practices of independent labels in the postwar period.

Any accounting of the impact of these networks of race and power on the production history of *The Peaceful Side* begins with the LP's label United Artists, which, at the time, was new to jazz production and marketing. The label was founded in 1957, primarily to distribute Hollywood movie soundtracks, and Alan Douglas was hired in 1960 to oversee the label's fledgling jazz division. To some extent, Douglas's role in the making of *The Peaceful Side* for United Artists exemplifies the complicated racial (and gender) arrangements that regularly framed the production of postwar jazz recordings of Black jazz artists for independent record labels.[71] In these arrangements, white producers and record label owners acted as both the directors and beneficiaries of a kind of racial colonialism rooted in the extractive white jazz love of well-intentioned fans, record collectors, critics, and musicians.[72] As Nichole Rustin, John Gennari, and others have shown, white jazz producers, critics, and promoters presented themselves as benevolent patrons and entrepreneurs while also acting as gatekeepers and tastemakers.[73] For instance, in her nuanced intersectional analysis of Charles Mingus's conflicts with producer Bob Thiele in the making of *The Black Saint and Sinner Lady* (1963) and *Mingus Plays Piano* (1964), Rustin observes that Thiele "embraced a discourse that valued black jazzmen as vessels for emotion but not as self-determining architects of creative and economically sustaining careers."[74]

Rustin's analyses of Mingus's early-1960s recordings also consider another

Listening to The Peaceful Side

FIGURE 5.2 United Artists advertisement in *Down Beat* (March 28, 1963). Copyright Universal Music.

recording of special pertinence to my project, both by virtue of its close chronological proximity, and for its direct jazz-world connection to Ellington and the United Artists label: the 1962 Ellington-Mingus-Max Roach collaboration, *Money Jungle*. Produced by Douglas, the sessions for *Money Jungle* took place in New York at Sound Makers Studios a year after *The Peaceful Side* Paris sessions. However, due to an extended—and for Strayhorn frustrating—delay in release, the two LPs came out around the same time in January and February 1963. In fact, the two albums were featured together in a United Artists advertisement that appeared in the March 28, 1963, issue of *DownBeat*. As shown in figure 5.2, *Money Jungle*, as would be expected, gets top billing, with the ad copy proclaiming it "one of the greatest piano trio recordings in Jazz History."[75]

The *DownBeat* ad for *The Peaceful Side* supplies an entry point to think about the LP cover image of Strayhorn, particularly in relation to the LP's branding and marketing. We see Strayhorn's face in a close-up partial profile; a cloud of smoke from a lit cigarette, held in between his fingers on his left, fills the space, swirling around the right side of his head, glasses, and cheek. On one level, this hip intellectual jazzman image of Strayhorn seems somewhat generic for the way it evokes midcentury jazz racialized associations of jazz with bohemian sophistication, mystery, and authenticity (and based on the two other LPs advertised alongside *The Peaceful Side*—Ken McIntyre's *Year of the Iron Sheep* and Kenny Durham's *Matador*—the profile head shot seems to have been a favorite at United Artists). However, in the context of the one and only previous LP image of Strayhorn—the one for the Ellington-Strayhorn *Nutcracker* LP released a year prior—the image is striking, even radical; rather than gazing down submissively behind Ellington's shoulder, here he peers out directly at the camera, projecting a far more personal and authoritative image. From this perspective, the LP image of Strayhorn signals the ways in which Strayhorn engaged the LP as a singular forum for creative autonomy and visibility. Although the need to record the LP over two consecutive overnight sessions was undoubtedly necessitated by pragmatic (specifically economic) constraints, Strayhorn's concept for the LP and his intimate performances and arrangements framed the conditions of production—the sensorium of the nocturnal studio environment—in artistic and expressive terms.

To be sure, Douglas deserves credit for his admirable efforts in giving Strayhorn the opportunity to have that forum and realize his concept. However, there were significant failures in the postproduction promotion and marketing of the LP, including a protracted release, careless errors in the LP's back-cover information, and lackluster marketing.[76] In addition to modest sales and narrow distribution (it sold less than 3,000 copies) the LP credits misattributed Strayhorn's "Passion Flower" to the songwriting partners E. Coates and G. Wiskin (they composed a different song with the same title), a mistake that Strayhorn had to manually correct, in block print, for copies he lovingly gifted to close friends in New York.[77] Aware of the importance of the solo LP, he spelled his name "Strayhorne," the added "e" a subtle but powerful symbol of the solo creative self. As Hajdu observes, Strayhorn "block-printed his own name next to 'Passion Flower'... and he spelled it Strayhorne, just as he had twice earlier, before he met Duke Ellington and when he tried to leave him."[78] The error in authorial attribution was reproduced in John S. Wilson's laudatory but very brief review of *The Peaceful Side* for *DownBeat* (he awarded the LP four stars, hailing Strayhorn's arrangements for their discrete "discernment" and for the "simplicity and directness" of his playing).[79]

Strayhorn clearly thought highly enough of his solo LP to gift it to close friends; however, he also apparently aimed his highly (self) critical eye toward his own performance. When asked about the forthcoming solo album during his interview with the New York chapter of the Duke Ellington Society in March 1962, Strayhorn replied: "In Paris I made an album, and I'm waiting now to find out when this is going to be released and by whom here. I made an album with, uh, a piano album; I haven't heard it since then. It sounded all right when I heard it there, but that was some months ago." His criticisms of his playing—voiced in the third person—arose obliquely in response to a follow-up question: "It sounds great to somebody else, but it doesn't sound great to him, his conception of how he should play. He has high standards of what he should sound like."[80] I understand what Strayhorn means: there are clearly some technical errors in his execution of certain runs or fills, as well as moments in which his playing seems to fall short of his concept. Yet, to my ears, these "errors" in no way detract from the brilliance, beauty, and thoughtful eloquence of Strayhorn performing and arranging the solo Strayhorn; indeed, following Moten, we can hear these moments as "in the break," that is, as sonic instantiations of fugitive "lyrical surplus."

The Peaceful Side captures something vital about the queer collaborative energies and jazz intimacy of Strayhorn as a performing artist. Throughout his career Strayhorn seemed to regard the recording studio as a semiprivate space, an extension of the informal spaces of parties and other social gatherings of friends and (adopted) family that was his performative métier. In its merging of jazz intimacy and the nocturnal sensorium of a Parisian recording studio, the LP archives what Shane Vogel would call the queer temporalities of "afterhours," a concept that resonates with Strayhorn's love for the nighttime, "halfway to dawn." Vogel elaborates the queerness of "afterhours" in relation to Langston Hughes's queer poetics of Harlem nightlife and cabaret: Hughes's queer poetics are manifest in his "strategies of poetic closure, anticlosure, and closural allusions," and, further, these formal and expressive Black queer resources archive "certain practices and experiences" that "are actually designed to elude what counts as the official archive, and instead compel creative and inventive ways to be remembered and preserved."[81] Vogel's insight here encourages us to think about *The Peaceful Side* as an alternative Black queer sonic archive. Indeed, I contend that the LP represents a kind of compendium of Strayhorn's queer musical poetics, gathering together the various threads that I've explored throughout this book. The performances and arrangements amplify diverse registers of Strayhorn's "practices and experiences," encompassing a multidimensional concept of arranging, the ephemeral sociality of collaborative creativity, practices of care, listening, and supportive interaction, liminal and lush sounds, affect, and mood.

To widen the lens a bit further, focusing on this register crucially foregrounds the connections of affect, emotion, and mood between Strayhorn's work on the LP and the melancholic dissonant subtexts that, as I argued earlier, inhabit Strayhorn's queer music. These unsettled layers of tension—or to borrow Lena Horne's image for "A Flower Is a Lovesome Thing," "difficult beauty"—often resonate at the edges of or just beneath Strayhorn's lush, luminous surfaces. At the risk of creating a simplistic homology between music and biography, it is from this vantage point that we can draw, via the extraordinary observations of Diahann Carroll, connections between Strayhorn's practice of dissonant underscoring on *The Peaceful Side*, his lived experiences as Black queer subject, and his presentation of self. In her account of their time spent together socializing between takes on the set of *Paris Blues* Carroll recalled:

> He was a beautiful, delicate little flower, just, you know, a genius, but a tortured genius . . . His genius was so overwhelming that being in his presence was something you could never forget. You know, there's such a thing as feeling too much and hearing too much. He suffered from that. I got exactly the same feeling being in the presence of James Baldwin. Strayhorn had the ability to perceive other people better than most of us, and what he perceived wasn't always kind, particularly in relation to himself and the life he chose for himself. Strayhorn and Baldwin both knew the cruelness of the world, and that's what I thought was part of the enormous sadness beneath their exteriors.[82]

Carroll's observations—evidence of her own remarkable powers of perception—were echoed by Douglas, who said of the LP's title *The Peaceful Side*: "It was my title, and it never was right. It was really the inside of Billy Strayhorn."[83]

Shadowing Carroll's striking comparison of Strayhorn and James Baldwin is a specifically Parisian mise-en-scène, one that foregrounds a shared Black queer transnational history and attachments. As with his work for the film, Strayhorn's piano jazz LP involved a transnational and interracial collaboration that brought Strayhorn together with French jazz and classical musicians, and a German-born sound engineer. Despite significant differences in sound and style, the collaborative energies and possibilities of *The Peaceful Side* and *Paris Blues* were both shaped by and in fact stand as vital records of the complex transnational, diasporic, and interracial social formations of postwar Parisian jazz culture.

EPILOGUE

Ever Up and Onward Searching for Strayhorn in the Twenty-First Century

As originally conceived, this concluding section was to take the form of a chapter, thematically paired with chapter 5. While I've retained the idea of a shared theme—Strayhorn arranging/performing Strayhorn—the form has changed from chapter to epilogue. This revision was motivated partly by practical concerns; however, I eventually came to see the form of the epilogue as better suited to the modes of reflection, especially on historiographical matters I wanted to engage in. An epilogue also seemed like the most Strayhorn-ian way to exit this book, a closing that I think of as taking its cue from Strayhorn's motto "ever up and onward," while also alluding to its musical equivalent, the coda. In musical practice, the coda adds, remixes, and transforms central ideas and materials as it brings a song, piece, or movement to a close; likewise, where the book's chapters presented a variety of critical arrangements organized around the concept of queer collaboration in Strayhorn's music and life, the "ever up and onward" subject of the epilogue extends this theme to address the paradox of queer (in)visibility that surrounds Strayhorn's legacy. Contending with Strayhorn's legacy in this register also underscores another implicit thematic thread of the book, namely, the multiple ways in which Strayhorn's music and career push against the boundaries of dominant jazz-historical frameworks, encouraging a *reframing* of jazz that advances an expansive historicized conception.

Strayhorn's historical invisibility and marginalization has in many ways become the dominant image in narratives of his work and life. Take for example the 2013 Dutch Storyville label box set, *Billy Strayhorn: Out of the Shadows*. According to the editors, this seven-volume centennial commemoration was intended to disperse the persistent "shadows" that surround Strayhorn, who, they note, now stands in the collective jazz imaginary as "the best known 'unknown' musician in the history of jazz."[1] This statement underscores Strayhorn's paradoxical legacy: the sense of Strayhorn as a simultaneously revered and marginalized figure in jazz, of perpetually coming out of the shadows.

It goes without saying that this paradox of (in)visibility is inseparable from the commercial and canonizing forces attached to Ellington's legacy, the persistence of which might be called the Ellington-brand effect. The auteur-like framing of Ellington's genius, in this context, has often seemed to me to be inversely related to the "problem" of Strayhorn as author and co-creator. As chronicled earlier, this negative strain of Strayhorn reception informed the posthumous marginalization of Strayhorn by a handful of powerful critics and historians whose work either diminished or denied his authorial contributions, and, in some cases, infused such denials and diminishments with homophobic animus. Thankfully, twenty-first-century stories about Strayhorn's historical marginalization are largely reparative in nature, with Brian Priestly's liner notes for the Storyville box set being just one example of public-facing reparative work. Strayhorn's presumptive public invisibility is now more often read as protective and productive; this affirmative gloss forwards the idea that working behind the scenes for Ellington allowed Strayhorn to pursue his art and live the good life as an openly gay Black man in the face of rampant homophobia and racism. Such a mixture of art, protected community, queer courage, and sacrifice makes for a powerful narrative cocktail, especially so when enhanced by figurations of Strayhorn as the diminutive, self-effacing artist.

Like many critics and fans, I have found aspects of this reparative narrative both compelling and useful; yet I'm also wary of its limitations and elisions, particularly its potential to elide subjective and social complexity, or to erase the connections of Strayhorn's story of marginalization to larger contexts and histories of Black queer identity and invisibility. Throughout the book I have explored these contexts and histories in relation to specific collaborative and sonic and affective arrangements. In this epilogue, I (re)listen closely to a moment from Strayhorn's oral history archive that is frequently cited in 21st-century writings about his legacy. This moment occurred during a Vancouver radio interview with Ellington and Strayhorn for Bob Smith's CBC "Hot Air" program on November 1, 1962 (the Ellington band was in Vancouver for an engagement at Izzy's Supper Club from October 29 to November 3). My argument is that listening to voice and context in Strayhorn's interactions with Ellington and host Bob Smith has the power to disrupt presentist invisibility narratives and to talk back to the implicit silencing of Strayhorn's voice in the circulation of discourse about his legacy.

STRAYHORN'S LAUGHTER

Between January and November 1962, Strayhorn participated in at least five interviews, including a solo interview with Bill Cross for *DownBeat* magazine and a taped guest talk for the Duke Ellington Jazz Society. As documents of Strayhorn's public voice, these interviews hold an exceptional place in the Strayhorn archive, where primary biographical material of any kind—especially in the form of oral history—is extremely scarce. The guest talk with the Duke Ellington Society, for example, offers the opportunity to hear Strayhorn narrate parts of his life story in a public forum.[2] The setting for the Ellington Society interview is quite different from that of the radio interviews: he has been invited to field questions from a moderator as well as an audience of devoted and informed Ellington fans. This scenario compels Strayhorn to compose or arrange a larger narrative about his life and career in music and with Ellington. The events from his life that he chooses to share with this audience is similar, with some variation, to the life and career narrative he offered Bill Cross just weeks prior.

The string of interviews Strayhorn gave in 1962—an annual record of public speaking unprecedented in his career—closely followed the release of *The Peaceful Side* as well as another significant independent Strayhorn recording project, his 1962 collaboration with Johnny Hodges for the Verve LP, *Johnny Hodges with Billy Strayhorn and the Orchestra*. Strayhorn directed the sessions for the latter project, working with the great sound engineer Rudy Van Gelder. Of the five interviews, only Bill Cross's edited and transcribed interview published in *DownBeat* has garnered significant attention by scholars and critics. Both the quality of Cross's interview and the fact that it was widely circulated bearing the imprimatur of jazz authority are among the obvious reasons for this attention. Although far less disseminated, the audio tape for Strayhorn's Vancouver radio interview with Ellington and Bob Smith, which was recorded in a room at the Georgian Towers Hotel, documents Strayhorn's voice and allows us to listen in on the impromptu social dynamics and affective registers in an unedited (and unspliced) format. Central to my argument is the persistent absenting of these dynamics and registers—and indeed of Strayhorn's voice—in a widely cited quote about Strayhorn that arose during the interview. This moment occurs at

FIGURE 6.1 Billy Strayhorn, Duke Ellington, and Bob Smith at the Georgian Towers Hotel, Vancouver, BC (November 1, 1962). Photograph by Franz Lindner, CBC Licensing. Reproduced courtesy of CBC Licensing.

about the sixteen-minute mark in the interview tape: Ellington tells Smith that Strayhorn "lives the life I would love to live," and hails his partner as "the pure artist," able to compose music only when the "spirit strikes him," a music that is "pure Strayhorn," unadulterated, without "outside effects," by which Ellington means the external burdens, compromises, and pressures that he (Ellington) must endure performing for the public night after night (or, as he puts it in the interview, "without anybody screaming at him," in reference to a recent encounter with a disgruntled fan).

Taken out of the rich aural/oral context of the interview and interpreted through a transcription, Ellington's statement expresses a genuine validation of, and vicarious desire for, Strayhorn's access to "pure" artistic existence, in particular his alleged freedom to compose music at his leisure and only when inspired to do so. This is certainly the interpretive frame through which this quote circulates in both scholarly and popular press. To offer just one example, here is how this quote appears in Harvey Cohen's 2010 biography of Ellington (some of which I previously quoted in chapter 4):

Epilogue 185

For most of his nearly three decades with the Ellington orchestra, Strayhorn lived an enviable life, artistically satisfying and challenging with lots of international travel. "Strayhorn lives the life I'd love to live," Ellington once said. "He is the pure artist." While the band slogged it out on the road night after night, Strayhorn usually did not accompany them, remaining in New York City and Paris for long stretches, living an openly gay lifestyle (a rarity in the African American and jazz social worlds), doing his writing, and always being on call for Ellington when he needed help composing and arranging . . . Strayhorn did not yearn for fame.[3]

A close listening to this quote in the fuller context of the aural/oral script of the interview, however, includes Strayhorn's amusingly performative response about a minute later. The sonic landscape of the fuller exchange that includes Strayhorn (and Smith) introduces a much denser social texture and more ambiguous affective registers punctuated by resonant moments of theatricality, varieties of discomfort, diffidence, and laughter. Together, the complexities of voice, affect, and power evident in the aural transcript capture a complicated sociality that interrupts any straight-ahead reading.[4] Even without accounting for Strayhorn's response, it matters that he is present in the hotel room with Ellington and Smith throughout their exchange about him.

At the 12:45 mark on the tape, the door is heard opening and Ellington exclaims, "Oh here's Billy Strayhorn and Milt Grayson." Ellington then returns to the topic he was discussing with Smith before the seemingly surprise visit from Strayhorn and Grayson (he is discussing his extended composition *Black, Brown and Beige* and tells Smith, "Oh they [Strayhorn, Grayson] know all about the *Black, Brown and Beige*"). Shortly after this Smith introduces Strayhorn into his conversation with Ellington:

> SMITH: And, uh, we were delighted to meet Bill, uh, way back in fifty-two here in Vancouver when he showed up on the scene with the orchestra, and since that time it's been nothing [*inhale*] but occasional letters that have never been *answered* but, of course, he's a busy young man as we all know. I wonder, uh, what, what eh . . . eh would you say, uh that you're going to charge him with next, from the standpoint of responsibility. What is he writing *for* you, do you . . . pass things on in that way or does it just *happen* that he comes back with something to you?
>
> ELLINGTON [EL]: With Strayhorn?
>
> SMITH: Yeah.

186 *Strayhorn Performing/Arranging Strayhorn*

ELLINGTON: Well, Strayhorn, uh . . . eh . . . lives the life that I would *love* to *live*, you know. He is the *pure* artist . . . He doesn't have to uh . . . um, well he, he *writes*, you know . . . when the, uh, spirit strikes him. And what he writes is pure *Strayhorn* . . . , unadulterated . . . without any outside effects, I mean without anybody screaming at him.

Questions arise, among them: Could Ellington have been looking at Strayhorn when he proclaims him the "pure artist?" Were they looking at each other? How do Ellington's and Strayhorn's repertoire of voice, including vocal modulations, hesitations, silences, and laughter, impact how we hear and interpret this quote, as well as the larger relations of power and creative labor that shaped their partnership? What of Bob Smith's comments about and to Strayhorn?

Let's consider Ellington's "pure artist" statement first. Against the written transcript, Ellington's vocal inflections, timbre, and modulations allow us to tune into the ironic, teasing theatricality that accompanies the words. These frequencies are especially audible as Ellington's voice drops dramatically into a gravelly, low vocal fry on the words "love" and "live," and then rises with an arch staginess and faux mid-Atlantic accent for the phrase "pure artist." The collective sonic force of Ellington's delivery I hear as queering his tribute to Strayhorn, conjuring a portrait of Strayhorn-the-artist as a kind of Wildean aesthete, a portrait that simultaneously—and artfully—also works as a defense of Strayhorn against Smith's implication that Strayhorn writes only in response to Ellington's commands—in other words, not *for* Ellington (and himself).

The sonic aura of conviviality, pleasurable conversation, and normative interview etiquette created in Ellington and Smith's interaction through this exchange is thrown off course when Smith turns his attention to Strayhorn. As can be gleaned in the transcription, Smith encounters a far less obliging and cooperative interviewee in Strayhorn.

SMITH: Let's ask Billy then, through Duke, as we . . . are doing this afternoon, what his ideas are on jazz composition. We've been talking *jazz composition* . . . about the great pinnacles in Edward's life, the extended compositions of *Creole Rhapsody*, and *Reminiscing in Tempo*; and *Diminuendo and Crescendo*; *Black, Brown and Beige*, and of course your *own* thoughts on that would be interesting. Ah, I remember the one that first endeared me to you, from the standpoint of extended composition was *Overture to Jam Session*, that is probably hard to find now but a record that you younger people in the audience should try and find . . . William Strayhorn.

[*long pause*]

STRAYHORN: Ah . . . jazz composition? . . . *Oh my* [*laughs*] . . . That's a hard one . . . Well, um, what do you want me to *say*? I don't usually *talk* about composition, or about music [*laughs*] . . . I prefer to *write* it . . . or *listen* to it . . . What, what do you want me to, uh . . .

Strayhorn's refusals to hold forth on his "ideas" about "jazz composition"—at least on Smith's terms—disrupts Smith's agenda and the host becomes audibly flustered. As Strayhorn reiterates his pointed rhetorical question ("What do you want me to say?"), Smith interrupts him and rattles off a string of awkward prompts:

SMITH: Well Edward was saying that you live the life of a true artist, uh, from the standpoint of composition how does this affect you. Do you do you, like, you've come to Vancouver with the band, or you joined the band here, and what at the moment have you . . . *accomplished*, you know . . . standing over here like you're a sergeant major . . . What is your composition to date, um ah, your *rate* in Vancouver?

STRAYHORN: I haven't done a *thing* . . . [*soft laughter*] That's what he's *talkin'* about, when he says [*extended loud laughter*], when he says that, uh, *I* live the life that he would love to live. So *far* I haven't done a *thing* [*long pause*]. But I'm *thinking*.

ELLINGTON: Actually, the thinking is the most important part of it . . .

Strayhorn's outbursts of laughter throughout his response are particularly marked affective moments that I hear as a sharp riposte, in the form of a self-deprecating send-up, to Ellington's fantasy portrait of Strayhorn's life as an artist. Indeed, his unrestrained laughter and refusal to play the role of serious composer/artist comes dangerously close to short-circuiting the social scripts of the radio interview. This transgression of interview etiquette seems to embarrass Ellington, who quickly interjects with a distinctly more serious and authoritative tone, "well, actually the thinking is the most important part it."[5] It is also crucial to hear Strayhorn's transgressions (and arguably Ellington's affirmation of Strayhorn's final words) as a reaction to the condescending asides in Smith's remarks, such as his patronizing quip to Strayhorn, "you're standing there like a sergeant major" and his description of him as a "busy young man" (he was forty-seven). From this perspective, Strayhorn's vocal repertoire of refusals and deflections—first hesitations then evasiveness, and finally laughter—complicate representations of Strayhorn as a mild-mannered, deferential, and self-effacing subject. At the same time, Strayhorn's responses can also be heard as a protective maneuver, enabling him to navigate tight spaces and collaborative situations that simultaneously included and marginalized him. Either way, the aural scripts and sonic landscape of the interview work to disrupt presumptions of (or happy compliance with) invisibility, absence, and marginalization. Put another way, and extending an organizing musical metaphor in my study, listening closely for the dissonant layers in Strayhorn's interview—and across his entire oral history archive—affords alternate takes on the familiar changes of a twenty-first-century invisibility blues.

Importantly, this problematic has been thematized and explored in twenty-first-century Black queer artistic engagements with Strayhorn's life and career, such as independent filmmaker Rodney Evans's 2010 film short, *Billy and Aaron*, and choreographer David Roussève's 2018 concert dance piece, *Halfway to Dawn* (created for his dance company REALITY). Evans's film short was originally intended to serve as an experimental workshopping of scenes from his feature-length film screenplay on Strayhorn's life entitled *Day Dream* (which is currently in development).[6] Based on his research and deep dive into Strayhorn's life and career, Evans's *Billy and Aaron* stages a series of brief richly imagined and temporally layered encounters between Strayhorn (Brandon Delagraentiss) and Aaron Bridgers (Ignaro Petronilia). These encounters unfold in two scenes with dialogue intercut with musical interludes during which we see Billy alone at a grand piano performing "Lush Life." In the first scene with dialogue, for instance, we see Billy and Aaron seated at a small bar table, drinks in hand, engaged in a tense dialogue. Confronting Billy with his absence from a high-profile magazine story on Ellington (he holds up a copy of the August 20, 1956, issue of *Time* magazine with Ellington's cover image), Aaron forcefully prompts Billy to confess his desire for public recognition and credit, and to acknowledge the destructive personal and emotional effects that continually denying (or suppressing) any desire for professional recognition has had on him. Of the magazine article, Aaron asks: "Did you see it? Not one mention of you in the entire article . . . It's ridiculous." Billy initially deflects Aaron's attempts to draw him out ("Let Edward have his magazine covers and his . . . *reviews*, and everything else. What do I care?"), but eventually admits to wanting credit for his work.[7] Yet when Aaron implores Billy to "demand" the credit he deserves, Billy thumps his drink on the table and replies, "Yes, and then it's all smoke and mirrors until I die and it's damned if you do and damned if you don't. So please *stop*. 'Cause it does neither of us any good." Billy's response leads into a dramatic monologue in which he discloses the trauma of precarity, poverty, and abuse he experienced in his childhood and concludes: "So . . . unless you [Aaron] know of another job that gives me a weekly salary, and takes care of all my expenses and . . . let's me make my own schedule while doing what I love . . . I think we both need to leave well enough alone."

Evans's writing for this monologue is powerful and moving and actor Delagraentiss effectively projects the complex emotional mix and raw pain in Evans's words. While this scene references specific events in Strayhorn's biography, Evans elides linear temporality and the normative tropes of the biopic, while also pushing against narratives of happy complicity and self-marginalization that often accompany representations of the historical Strayhorn as a mild-mannered, introverted artist wary of fame and fortune. Indeed, Evans has described his concept for the feature-length narrative drama (the screenplay from which the film short was derived) as a "highly stylized fantasia incorporating a surreal aesthetic."[8]

A related Black queer creative practice also orients David Roussève's concept, choreography, and direction for *Halfway to Dawn* which, like Evans's short, critically (re)arranges biography and fiction, probing the elusive and silenced spaces and ways of knowing, being, and feeling at the border of or, more precisely, in-between fact and fiction. In his own words, Roussève's piece "redefines 'biography' as the intersection of fact, conjecture, comment, abstraction, and fantasy as it seeks to uncover the complicated emotional 'truths' of gay, African American jazz composer Billy Strayhorn's life while creating a dialogue on urgent social 'truths' of our own."[9] Through a resonant mix of postmodern movement, jazz, and social dance accompanied by a rich playlist of Strayhorn's music, newly composed soundscapes, projected text, and video, Roussève's choreographies of a Black queer history in dialogue with Strayhorn's life can here serve as a blueprint for engaging the paradoxes of invisibility around Strayhorn's legacy. Both *Halfway to Dawn* and Evans's filmic inventions remind us that centering Black queer identity and history in Strayhorn's legacy is not simply a matter of bringing him out of the shadows; it is a project that requires speculative acts of imagination and lingering with shadows—with "urgent social truths," emotional dilemmas, and complex Black queer lived experiences both past and present.

NOTES

INTRODUCTION *Queer Arrangements, Queer Collaboration*

1. The James Weldon Johnson Memorial Collection of African American Arts and Letters includes photographs that span Van Vechten's career as an amateur photographer, 1930s to 1964, the year of his death. These dates run roughly parallel to Strayhorn's career, spanning the early 1930s until his death from esophageal cancer at age fifty-one in May 1967.

2. Emily Bernard, *Carl Van Vechten and the Harlem Renaissance* (New Haven, CT: Yale University Press 2012), 2. It is also worth noting that Strayhorn's session with Van Vechten in New York occurred just seven days after the iconic *A Great Day in Harlem* photograph (in which the only Ellingtonians included were Lawrence Brown and Sonny Greer).

3. Bernard, *Carl Van Vechten and the Harlem Renaissance*, 2.

4. Geoff Dyer, *But Beautiful: A Book About Jazz* (New York: Farrar, Straus and Giroux, 1996), ix–x.

5. To stretch the parallels a bit further (and into familiar metaphorical territory for music history), portraiture has a significant history as a conceptual conceit for original compositions across the classical, jazz, and pop spectrum. I would cite here in particular Strayhorn's *Portrait of a Silk Thread* (1945) and *Portrait of Ella Fitzgerald* (1957, co-composed with Ellington).

6. Duke Ellington, *Music Is My Mistress* (New York: Doubleday, 1973; New York: Da Capo, 1976), 153.

7. David Hajdu, *Lush Life: A Biography of Billy Strayhorn* (New York: North Point Press, 1997), 79. Hajdu does not identify this interlocutor, who presumably chose anonymity. On this point, see Hajdu, *Lush Life*, 79–80.

8. Hajdu, *Lush Life*, 79.

9. See, for example, David Hajdu, "A Jazz of Their Own," *Vanity Fair* 465 (May 1999): 190–91.

10. Walter van de Leur, *Something to Live For: The Music of Billy Strayhorn* (New York: Oxford University Press, 2002).

11. After Strayhorn's death, his niece and nephew, Alyce Claerbaut and Gregory Morris (who Strayhorn named as the executor of his estate), discovered in his apartment four large steel file cabinets filled with hundreds of manuscript scores, including this significant catalog of hitherto unknown original compositions and arrangements (see A. Alyce Claerbaut and David Schlesinger, eds., *Strayhorn: An Illustrated Life* [Chicago: Agate Bolden, 2015], 32–33). The Dutch Jazz Orchestra, under the direction of Walter van de Leur, subsequently recorded these newly discovered compositions and arrangements (*Portrait of a Silk Thread: Newly Discovered Works of Billy Strayhorn*, Challenge Records CHR 70089, Compact Disc).

12. One of the first jazz-historical versions of this came in Derek Jewell's chapter on Strayhorn in in his 1977 book on Ellington, in which he characterizes Strayhorn as the "female side of an artistically joint persona" (*Duke: A Portrait of Duke Ellington* [New York: W. W. Norton, 1977], 173.)

13. See, for example, the collected essays in Nichole T. Rustin and Sherrie Tucker, eds., *Big Ears: Listening for Gender in Jazz Studies* (Durham, NC: Duke University Press, 2008). Other work on gender and sexuality in jazz include studies of women jazz musicians, dancers, and performers: see, for example, Angela Y. Davis, *Blues Legacies and Black Feminism: Gertrude 'Ma' Rainey, Bessie Smith, and Billie Holiday* (New York: Vintage, 1998); Sherrie Tucker, *Swing Shift: "All-Girl" Bands of the 1940s* (Durham, NC: Duke University Press, 2000); David Brackett, "Family Values in Music? Billie Holiday's and Bing Crosby's 'I'll Be Seeing You,'" in David Brackett, *Interpreting Popular Music* (Berkeley: University of California Press, 2000), 34–74; Farah Jasmine Griffin, *If You Can't Be Free, Be a Mystery: In Search of Billie Holiday* (New York: The Free Press, 2001); Tammy Kernodle, *Soul on Soul: The Life and Music of Mary Lou Williams* (Boston: Northeastern University Press, 2004); Laurie Stras, "White Face, Black Voice: Race, Gender, and Region in the Music of the Boswell Sisters," *Journal of the Society for American Music* 1, no. 2 (May 2007): 207–55; Jayna Jennifer Brown, *Babylon Girls: Black Women Performers and the Making of the Modern* (Durham, NC: Duke University Press, 2008); Kristin A. McGee, *Some Like It Hot: Jazz Women in Film and Television, 1928–1959* (Middletown, CT: Wesleyan University Press, 2009); Franya J. Berkman, *Monument Eternal: The Music of Alice Coltrane* (Middletown, CT: Wesleyan University Press, 2010); Yoko, Suzuki, "Two Strikes and the Double Negative: The Intersections of Gender and Race in the Cases of Female Jazz Saxophonists," *Black Music Research Journal* 33, no. 2 (2013): 207–26; special issue on Melba Liston, Hairston O'Connell, guest editor (and the Melba Liston Research Collective), *Black Music Research Journal* 34, no. 1 (2014); CJ Wells, "'A Dreadful Bit of Silliness': Feminine Frivolity and Ella Fitzgerald's Early Critical Reception," *Women and Music: A Journal of Gender and Culture*, 21 (2017): 43–65; Vanessa Blais-Tremblay, "'Where

You Are Accepted, You Blossom'": Toward Care Ethics in Jazz Historiography," *Jazz & Culture* 2 (2019): 59–83; Kimberly Hannon Teal, "Mary Lou Williams as Apology: Jazz, History, and Institutional Sexism in the Twenty-First Century," *Jazz & Culture* 2 (2019): 1–26; "The Power of Geri Allen," special issue of *Jazz & Culture* 3, no. 2 (Fall–Winter, 2020); and Daphne A. Brooks, *Liner Notes for the Revolution: The Intellectual Life of Black Feminist Sound* (Cambridge: Harvard University Press, 2021). For analyses of jazz, race, and masculinity, see Ingrid Monson "The Problem with White Hipness: Race, Gender, and Cultural Conceptions in Jazz Historical Discourse," *Journal of the American Musicological Society* 48, no. 3 (Fall 1995): 396–422; Hazel Carby, "Playing the Changes," in *Race Men* (Cambridge, MA: Harvard University Press, 1998), 135–65; David Ake, "Re-Gendering Jazz: Ornette Coleman and the New York Scene in the Late 1950s," in David Ake, *Jazz Cultures* (Berkeley: University of California Press, 2002); Krin Gabbard, "Revenge of the Nerds: Representing the White Male Collector of Black Music," in Krin Gabbard, *Black Magic: White Hollywood and African American Culture* (Rutgers, NJ: Rutgers University Press, 2004), 199–232; Patrick Burke, "Oasis of Swing: The Onyx Club, Jazz, and White Masculinity in the Early 1930s," *American Music* 24, no. 3 (2006): 320–46; Benjamin Piekut, "New Thing? Gender and Sexuality in the Jazz Composers Guild," *American Quarterly* 62, no. 1 (March 2010): 25–48; Guthrie P. Ramsey, *The Amazing Bud Powell: Black Genius, Jazz History, and the Challenge of Bebop* (Berkeley: University of California Press, 2013); and Nichole Rustin-Paschal, *The Kind of Man I Am: Jazzmasculinity and the World of Charles Mingus Jr.* (Middletown, CT: Wesleyan University Press, 2017).

14. Sherrie Tucker, "When Did Jazz Go Straight? A Queer Question for Jazz Studies," *Critical Studies in Improvisation/'Etude critiques en improvisation* 4, no. 2 (2008): 4.

15. Tucker, "When Did Jazz Go Straight?" 4.

16. E. Patrick Johnson and Mae Henderson, "Introduction: Queering Black Studies/'Quaring' Queer Studies," in E. Patrick Johnson and Mae Henderson, eds., *Black Queer Studies: A Critical Anthology* (Durham, NC: Duke University Press, 2005), 6–7. See also, Marlon Bryan Ross, *Sissy Insurgencies: A Racial Anatomy of Unfit Manliness* (Durham, NC: Duke University Press, 2022); Tavia Nyong'o, *Afro-Fabulations: The Queer Drama of Black Life* (New York: New York University Press, 2019); Kara Keeling, *Queer Times, Black Futures* (New York: New York University Press, 2019); Stephen Best, *None Like Us: Blackness, Belonging, Aesthetic Life* (Durham, NC: Duke University Press, 2018); E. Patrick Johnson, ed., *No Tea, No Shade: New Writings in Black Queer Studies* (Durham, NC: Duke University Press, 2016); Darieck Scott, *Extravagant Abjection: Blackness, Power, and Sexuality in the African American Literary Imagination* (New York: New York University Press, 2010); Roderick A. Ferguson, *Aberrations in Black: Toward a Queer of Color Critique* (Minneapolis: University of Minnesota Press, 2004); Siobhan B. Somerville, *Queering the Color Line: Race and the Invention of Homosexuality in American Culture* (Durham, NC: Duke University Press, 2002); José Muñoz, *Disidentifications: Queers*

of Color and the Performance of Politics (Minneapolis: University of Minnesota Press, 1999).

17. Fred Moten, *In the Break: The Aesthetics of the Black Radical Tradition* (Minneapolis: University of Minnesota Press, 2003). Strayhorn also referenced his role as sonic trickster in the 1957 Ellington-Strayhorn Shakespearean "tone parallel" suite, *Such Sweet Thunder*. As I discuss in part 2, Strayhorn's most extended contribution to the suite, "Up and Down, Up and Down," is a musical "parallel" to Puck, perhaps the queerest of Shakespeare's trickster figures.

18. Marlon B. Ross, "Beyond the Closet as Raceless Paradigm," in Johnson and Henderson, eds., *Black Queer Studies: A Critical Anthology*, 183.

19. Another complicating factor is the fragmented and dispersed nature of all (musical and nonmusical) Strayhorn materials embedded in the Duke Ellington Collection.

20. Hajdu, *Lush Life*, xii.

21. Ann Cvetkovich, *An Archive of Feelings: Trauma, Sexuality, and Lesbian Public Cultures* (Durham, NC: Duke University Press, 2003). Other studies that have guided my thinking about queer archives include Marion Wasserbauer, "'That's What Music is About—It Strikes a Chord': Proposing a Queer Method of Listening to the Lives and Music of LGBTQs," *Oral History Review*, 43, no. 1 (2016): 153–69; Brent Edwards Hayes, "The Taste of the Archive," *Callaloo* 35, no. 4 (2012): 944–72; Heather K. Love, "Emotional Rescue: The Demands of Queer History," in Heather Love, *Feeling Backward: Loss and the Politics of Queer History* (Cambridge, MA: Harvard University Press, 2007), 31–52; J. J. Halberstam, "What's That Smell? Queer Temporalities and Subcultural Lives," in *Queering the Popular Pitch*, ed. Sheila Whiteley and Jennifer Rycenga (New York: Routledge, 2006); José Esteban Muñoz, "Ephemera as Evidence: Introductory Notes to Queer Acts," *Women and Performance: A Journal of Feminist Theory* 8, no. 2 (1996): 5–16.

22. Cvetkovich, *An Archive of Feelings*, 8.

23. A second note reads: "Billy Strayhorn stayed with Mr. Bridgers when he was in Paris—A mug of pencil [sic] was on the piano for Billy's use." The pencils that Bridgers provided for Strayhorn appear to be Great Wall brand pencils (a line of The China First Pencil Co. Ltd, a leading pencil manufacturer in China founded in the 1930s). The pencil can be found in the Duke Ellington Collection of Ephemera and related Audiovisual Materials.

24. This interview documents aspects of Bridgers own fascinating biography as well as his poignant, if guarded, memories of Strayhorn and the Ellington-Strayhorn partnership (a far more candid remembrance of his relationship with Strayhorn is contained in Hajdu's biography). In the interview, Bridgers makes reference to a personal scrapbook and book manuscript—a memoir—both of which appear to be lost.

25. Their residence is included in the NYC LGBT Historic Sites Project (https://www.nyclgbtsites.org).

26. Billy Strayhorn, "Conversation/Interview with unidentified male," November 3, 1962 (Vancouver, BC), Ruth Ellington Collection of Duke Ellington Materials, Smithsonian Institution, Archives Center, National Museum of American History, Box 23, Item 107.

27. Georgina Born, "Music and the Social," in *The Cultural Study of Music: A Critical Introduction*, ed. Martin Clayton, Trevor Herbert, and Richard Middleton (New York and London: Routledge, 2012), 267.

28. Hajdu, *Lush Life*, 79.

29. Mark Tucker, "In Search of Will Vodrey," *Black Music Research Journal* 16, no. 1 (Spring 1996): 123–82; John Wriggle, *Blue Rhythm Fantasy: Big Band Jazz Arranging in the Swing Era* (Urbana: University of Illinois Press, 2016).

30. Tucker, "In Search of Will Vodrey," 123.

31. Wriggle, *Blue Rhythm Fantasy*, 11.

32. Wriggle, *Blue Rhythm Fantasy*, 12–13.

33. Amiri Baraka, *Blues People: Negro Music in White America* (New York: W. Morrow, 1963), 181.

34. Scott DeVeaux, "Bebop and the Recording Industry: The 1942 AFM Recording Ban Reconsidered," *Journal of the American Musicological Society* 41, no. 1 (Spring 1988): 135.

35. This model shows interesting parallels with the productive interdependence of scripts and improvisation in theater rehearsals and productions (see, for example, Zoë Svendsen, "The Dramaturgy of Spontaneity: Improvising the Social in Theater," in *Improvisation and Social Aesthetics*, ed. Georgina Born, Eric Lewis, and Will Straw [Durham, NC: Duke University Press, 2017], 288–308).

36. See, for example, the essays collected in *Jazz/Not Jazz: The Music and Its Boundaries*, eds. David Ake, Charles Hiroshi Garrett, and Daniel Goldmark (Berkeley: University of California Press, 2012), and Born, Lewis, and Straw, eds., *Improvisation and Social Aesthetics*; Scott DeVeaux, "Constructing the Jazz Tradition: Jazz Historiography," *Black American Literature Forum* 25, no. 3 (Autumn 1991): 525–60; George Lewis, "Improvised Music after 1950: Afrological and Eurological Perspectives," *Black Music Research Journal* 16, no. 1 (Spring 1996): 91–122; and David Brackett, "Jazz at the Crossroads of Art and Popular Music Discourses in the 1960s," in *The Routledge Companion to New Jazz Studies*, eds. Nicholas Gebhardt, Nichole Rustin, and Tony Whyton (New York: Routledge, 2019), 347–56.

37. Naomi Schor, *Reading in Detail: Aesthetics and the Feminine* (New York: Routledge, 2007), xlii–xliii. See also Naomi Schor, *Bad Objects: Essays Popular and Unpopular* (Durham, NC: Duke University Press, 1995). Also relevant to this discussion is Alexandra Vazquez's monograph on Cuban music/performance, *Listening in Detail: Performances of Cuban Music* (Durham, NC: Duke University Press, 2013). Vazquez extends Schor's ideas to theorize the expressive and critical powers of sonic details, which she describes

as "fugitive and essential living" sonic elements and "specific choices made by musicians and performers, that "come in infinite numbers of forms: saludos, refusals, lyrics, arrangements, sounds, grunts, gesture, bends in voice" (19). The gendered ranking of artistic authenticity signaled by the distinctions between composer and arranger can be usefully compared to similar gendered oppositions/roles in other cultural and art world spheres, such as ideologies that police distinctions between architects and interior designers or, in the fashion industry, those between tailor and seamstress.

38. Wriggle, *Blue Rhythm Fantasy*; Kernodle, *Soul on Soul*; Jeffrey Magee, *The Uncrowned King of Swing: Fletcher Henderson and Big Band Jazz* (New York: Oxford University Press, 2005); and John Howland, *Ellington Uptown: Duke Ellington, James P. Johnson, and the Birth of Concert Jazz* (Ann Arbor: University of Michigan Press, 2009).

39. Wriggle, *Blue Rhythm Fantasy*, 169. For a groundbreaking study on the centrality of Black women dancers and performers on the shaping of jazz in midcentury Montreal see Vanessa Blais-Tremblay, "Jazz, Gender, Historiography: A Case Study of the 'Golden Age' of Jazz in Montreal (1925–1955)," PhD diss., McGill University, 2018.

40. A full account of arranging and backstage labor in relation to marginalized identities in jazz is beyond the scope of this discussion. For work on the significant history of women arrangers such as Lil Hardin Armstrong, Mary Lou Williams, and Melba Liston, see, for example, Jeffrey Taylor, "With Lovie and Lil: Rediscovering Two Chicago Pianists of the 1920s," in Rustin and Tucker, eds., *Big Ears*, 48–63; Tammy Kernodle, "Black Women Working Together: Jazz, Gender, and the Politics of Validation," *Black Music Research Journal* 34, no. 1 (2014): 27–55; Lisa Barg, "Taking Care of Music: Gender, Arranging, and Collaboration in the Weston-Liston Partnership," *Black Music Research Journal* 34, no. 1 (2014): 97–119.

41. Ellington, *Music is My Mistress*, 156.

42. Van de Leur, *Something to Live For*, 103.

43. "Billy Strayhorn's Arranging Hints," quoted in van de Leur, *Something to Live For*, 65.

44. Donald Shirley, quoted in Claerbaut and Schlesinger, eds., *Strayhorn, An Illustrated Life*, 145.

45. Van de Leur, *Something to Live For*, 9–10. Following a successful premiere at Strayhorn's high school, Westinghouse High, the musical toured in and around Pittsburgh and western Pennsylvania to great acclaim (the touring production of *Fantastic Rhythm* was a significantly expanded and reworked version of the original production). The show continued to be produced for almost ten years after its first run, including productions at "navy bases throughout the Pacific" (9).

46. The other songs were an arrangement of Ellington's classic "Solitude" (1932) and the newly minted pop tune "Two Sleepy People" (Hoagy Carmichael/Frank Loesser, 1938). What was perhaps most impressive to his prospective employer, however, was Strayhorn's

daring decision to play a seemingly on-the-spot improvised arrangement of Ellington's "Sophisticated Lady." As the story goes, Strayhorn first played Ellington's version the way he had just heard it in the Stanley Theatre concert, thus demonstrating how well he could simulate Ellington's voice, then said, "Well [Mr. Ellington], this is the way I would play it" (Hajdu, *Lush Life*, 50).

47. Hajdu, *Lush Life*, 212–13.

48. For a detailed overview of Strayhorn's civil rights activism, see Bruce Rastrelli's contribution to Claerbaut and Schlesinger, eds., *Strayhorn: An Illustrated Life*, 81–131.

49. My thinking about alternative modes of jazz historiography is deeply indebted to the Melba Liston Research Collective, a feminist jazz studies research team I participated in alongside Tammy L. Kernodle, Monica Hairston O'Connell, Dianthe "Dee" Spencer, and Sherrie Tucker. The need to account for Liston's multifaceted career as a composer, arranger, trombonist, and educator demanded a collaborative research approach, one inspired by and modeled after Liston's centering of jazz practices of collaboration, interaction, care, and community. Our work with the Melba Liston Collection at the Center for Black Music Research in Chicago culminated in a 2014 special issue for the *Black Music Research Journal*. As Tucker and O'Connell eloquently summarize in the epilogue of their contribution, Liston's model enabled our research team to counter modes of jazz historiography that "have been practiced and promoted from the standpoint of authorship and subject matter as solo work" with modes that promote awareness of both jazz practice and jazz historiography as "social and interactive" ("Not One to Toot Her Own Horn(?): Melba Liston's Oral Histories and Classroom Presentations," 155–56). (See also, "Introduction: The Melba Liston Research Collective," *Black Music Research Journal* 34, no. 1 [Spring 2014], 1–8.)

ONE Arriving by "Flamingo"

Epigraph. David Hajdu, *Lush Life: A Biography of Billy Strayhorn* (New York: North Point Press, 1997), 124.

1. Hajdu, *Lush Life*, 96.

2. Hajdu, *Lush Life*, 94–95.

3. Hajdu, *Lush Life*, 94–95.

4. Matthew Tinkcom, *Working Like a Homosexual: Camp, Capital, Cinema* (Durham, NC: Duke University Press, 2002), 8–11.

5. Tinkcom, *Working Like a Homosexual*, 38. Simone's statement obviously relies on prevailing essentialist discourses of gender/sexuality difference and thus reproduces stereotypes of the "feminine" and feminized homosexual man. It goes without saying that not all gay male artists working behind the scenes embraced "soft" and "nice" col-

laborative practices. To cite just one example from the world of midcentury theater and dance, Jerome Robbins was infamously dictatorial and could be emotionally abusive to performers. I thank Jeffrey Magee for bringing this counterexample to my attention.

6. James Gavin, *Stormy Weather: The Life of Lena Horne* (New York: Atria Books, 2009), 114.

7. Gavin, *Stormy Weather: The Life of Lena Horne*, 114–15.

8. Gavin, *Stormy Weather*, 135.

9. In an interview with Gavin, Laurents described Strayhorn's professional interactions with Horne this way: "boy, did he observe . . . And he could talk to her and tell her what he saw." Gavin, *Stormy Weather*, 251–52.

10. This meeting is implied in the following quote in Horne's autobiography: "Strayhorn was often in California and we were very, very close. Roger Edens frequently dropped over in the evenings usually with a couple of people from the M-G-M music department." Lena Horne and Richard Schickel, *Lena* (New York: Doubleday, 1965), 157. For critical accounts of Ellington's role in *Cabin in the Sky*, see, for example, Krin Gabbard, *Jammin' at the Margins: Jazz and the American Cinema* (Chicago: University of Chicago Press, 1996); and Arthur Knight, *Disintegrating the Musical: Black Performance and American Musical Film* (Durham, NC: Duke University Press, 2002).

11. Tinkcom, *Working Like a Homosexual*, 36–37.

12. Walter van de Leur, *Something to Live For: The Music of Billy Strayhorn* (New York: Oxford University Press, 2002), 32.

13. Van de Leur, *Something to Live For*, 61–63.

14. Hajdu, *Lush Life*, 97. While Strayhorn and Kay Davis were good friends, he wrote little for her due to her role as Ellington's vocalese specialist.

15. See Laura Pellegrinelli, "Separated at 'Birth': Singing and the History of Jazz," in *Big Ears: Listening for Gender in Jazz Studies*, ed. Nicole Rustin and Sherrie Tucker (Durham, NC: Duke University Press, 2008), 31–47. It is also worth mentioning here that, as van de Leur reminds us, in taking on work that Ellington had neither the time for nor interest in, Strayhorn's creative labor made it possible for Ellington "to realize his goals," namely ones that we now identify with the extraordinary pieces he composed for (and with) the legendary Blanton-Webster Band of this era. Van de Leur, *Something to Live For*, 63.

16. The tune peaked at #11 on the pop charts on June 14, 1941. According to Hajdu, the tune was "discovered by Ellington's friend, Edmund Anderson, a businessman, who added the lyrics" (*Lush Life*, 86). Jeffries, however, claimed the song was given to him by the composer Grouya himself, a little-known figure then working in the music publishing division of MGM, in hope that it would get a hearing from Ellington. As he narrates it, Jeffries put the song on his dressing-room table where Strayhorn later discovered it and, within earshot of Ellington, began playing the song at the piano. Ellington liked what he heard and instructed: "Whatever you're playing, make a chart of it." Jeffries also claimed

that Grouya contacted him after "Flamingo" was charting to complain that his words had been altered, thus suggesting he had a hand in writing the lyrics. Herb Jeffries, interview, *San Diego Union-Tribune*, December 13, 1993; see also Stuart Nicholson, *Reminiscing in Tempo: A Portrait of Duke Ellington* (Boston: Northeastern University Press, 1999), 226.

17. "Herb Jeffries," accessed February 20, 2012, http://www.herbjeffries.com. The Ellington Orchestra recorded "Flamingo" on December 28, 1940, at Victor Studios in Chicago, a date that marked the end of a grueling year of cross-country travel, playing mostly one-nighters.

18. Mark Tucker, ed., *The Duke Ellington Reader* (New York: Oxford University Press, 1993), 500.

19. Hajdu, *Lush Life*, 97.

20. Allison McCracken, *Real Men Don't Sing: Crooning in American Culture* (Durham, NC: Duke University Press, 2015), 276. Writing of this effect of naturalness in Bing Crosby's baritone appeal, McCracken observes that his "exploitation of the directional mic's proximity effect should be understood as a key moment in the often conflated industrial and cultural constructions of 'natural' and 'masculine' that characterized this new era in sound media" (281).

21. A. Alyce Claerbaut and David Schlesinger, eds., *Strayhorn: An Illustrated Life* (Chicago: Agate Bolden, 2015), 88.

22. Indeed, Cole and Eckstein barely register in McCraken's historical map. A brief take on Cole, for example, appears in two footnotes, one of which aligns the complex popular cross-racial appeal of Nat "King" Cole with a "gentlemanly, romantic, but asexual presence." *Real Men Don't Sing*, 371. I should also note here that Jeffries's racial/ethnic self-identification changed over time. During this period, he self-identified as mixed race.

23. Vincent L. Stephens, *Rocking the Closet: How Little Richard, Johnnie Ray, Liberace, and Johnny Mathis Queered Pop Music* (Urbana: University of Illinois Press, 2019), 7–8. Stephens's analysis of Johnny Mathis's embodiment of the Black queer dandy provides an intriguing point of comparison for assessing the ambiguous racial/gendered presentation and vocal sound of a figure like Jeffries (*Rocking the Closet*, 115–46). For other critical studies of the Black male jazz/pop ballad voice, see, for example, Krin Gabbard, "Borrowing Black Masculinity: The Role of Johnny Hartman in *The Bridges of Madison County*," in Pamela Robertson Wojcik and Arthur Knight, eds., *Soundtrack Available* (Durham, NC: Duke University Press, 2001), 295–316; Mark Anthony Neal, "Fear of a Queer Soul Man: The Legacy of Luther Vandross" in Mark Anthony Neal, *Looking for Leroy: Illegible Black Masculinities* (New York: NYU Press, 2013), 143–67; Mark Burford, "Sam Cooke as Pop Album Artist—A Reinvention in Three Songs," *Journal of the American Musicological Society* 65, no. 1 (2012): 113–78; Andrew Flory, "The Ballads of Marvin Gaye," *Journal of the American Musicological Society* 72, no. 2 (2019): 313–61.

24. Hajdu, *Lush Life*, 73–74. Strayhorn's Francophilia also functioned as a sign of queer affiliation, a subject I explore in chapter 5.

25. Van de Leur, *Something to Live For*, 38–43. The following discussion of "Flamingo" and several other of Strayhorn's vocal arrangements during this period is indebted to van de Leur's analytical insights.

26. Van de Leur, *Something to Live For*, 67. As van de Leur puts it elsewhere, Strayhorn's "approach to popular repertory was . . . essentially *compositional*" (70).

27. Van de Leur, *Something to Live For*, 38.

28. Mark Tucker, liner notes in Duke Ellington, *The Blanton-Webster Band*, RCA Bluebird, 1986, Compact Disc.

29. Van de Leur, *Something to Live For*, 42. See also Hajdu, *Lush Life*, 86–87.

30. Quoted in Nicholson, *Reminiscing in Tempo*, 226.

31. Tinkcom, *Working Like a Homosexual*, 36–37.

32. Tinkcom, *Working Like a Homosexual*, 36–37.

33. On this point, while Tinkcom does clearly acknowledge white racial privilege in his analysis of the camp aesthetics in the MGM Minnelli/Freed Unit, he does not fully explore how this racialized environment might figure into his analyses of camp, gender, and sexuality. For a historically nuanced discussion of racism in the Freed Unit, see Donald Bogle's account of arranger Phil Moore's struggles at MGM during this period in *Bright Boulevards, Bold Dreams: The Story of Black Hollywood* (New York: Random House, 2005), 224–32. For an excellent history of the practices and cultural meanings associated with the symphonic jazz arranging tradition, see John Howland, *Ellington Uptown: Duke Ellington, James P. Johnson, and the Birth of Concert Jazz* (Ann Arbor: University of Michigan Press, 2009).

34. Van de Leur, *Something to Live For*, 39.

35. Van de Leur, *Something to Live For*, 39.

36. Lloyd Whitesell, "The Uses of Extravagance in the Hollywood Musical," in *Music and Camp*, ed. Christopher Moore and Philip Purvis (Middletown, CT: Wesleyan University Press, 2018), 20–22.

37. Here, Strayhorn's arrangement of "Flamingo" has far more in common with later jazz-oriented versions of "You Stepped Out of a Dream" such as Nat "King" Cole's 1949 recording, and the George Shearing Quintet 1959 version included on the LP *Latin Affair*.

38. Whitesell, "Uses of Extravagance," 22.

39. Whitesell, "Uses of Extravagance," 28.

40. Whitesell, "Uses of Extravagance," 28.

41. Van de Leur also singles out Strayhorn's arrangement of "I'll Remember April" for its stand-out ten-bar introduction, and "The Man I Love" for an early example of Strayhorn's technique of creating intricate contrapuntal texture based on thematic material. Most of these vocal arrangements were unrecorded during his lifetime, posthumously discovered

by van de Leur, and recorded by his Dutch Jazz Orchestra. In 1957, however, "Where or When" was recorded as an instrumental for the LP *Ellington Indigos*.

42. Van de Leur, *Something to Live For*, 68.

43. Van de Leur, *Something to Live For*, 68. As van de Leur points out, it is this midform shift, "a temporary modulation" from D♭ to the E, creates the effect of surprise (69).

44. See Frederick Nolan, *Lorenz Hart: A Poet on Broadway* (New York: Oxford University Press, 1994).

45. Indeed, this jazz modernist blend can be productively heard in relation to what Whitesell would call sonic glamour, one of several defining "style modes" that, he argues, comprise "common background modalities of style over the [twentieth] century." Whitesell, *Wonderful Design: Glamour in the Hollywood Musical* (New York: Oxford University Press, 2018). In Whitesell's account, sonic glamour "projects an aura of ethereality or sophistication by way of suave deportment, sensuous textures, elevated styles and aesthetically refined effects" (*Wonderful Design*, 40–41). As with his exploration of ironic vs. nonironic modes of queer extravagance discussed previously, Whitesell presents "You Stepped Out of a Dream" as an exemplar of sonic glamour: "'You Stepped Out of a Dream' fuses abundance, opulence, dazzlement, polish, grace, grandeur, refinement, and ornateness in a single overwhelming aesthetic experience" (*Wonderful Design*, 6–7).

46. Hajdu, *Lush Life*, 93.

47. Hajdu, *Lush Life*, 90. Kuller told Hajdu that he introduced himself to Ellington after one of the band's nightly shows at the LA ballroom, at which time he extended the initial invitation.

48. This work was copyrighted in 1946 under the title "Francesca." As of this writing, the dedicatee for this name is unknown. In 1967, the piece was posthumously repurposed under the Hindi-inspired title "Charpoy" (which means daybed) for Ellington's great memorial Strayhorn tribute LP . . . *And His Mother Called Him Bill* (see van de Leur, *Something to Live For*, 74). For more on Turner's changing star text image, see Richard Dyer, "Four Films of Lana Turner," in Richard Dyer, *Only Entertainment*, 2nd ed. (New York: Routledge, 2005), 79–110.

49. Van de Leur, *Something to Live For*, 31. Van de Leur suggests that Strayhorn also worked behind the scenes on the set for Vincente Minnelli's iconic MGM 1943 all-Black-cast film musical *Cabin in the Sky*. Based on the Broadway musical, which had a successful run in 1940, the film featured an all-star cast of Black entertainers and dancers, including the Ellington Orchestra, Lena Horne, and the Katherine Dunham dance group, along with Ethel Waters and Louis Armstrong. The majority of the filming would've taken place in the year following the making of the soundies, but I have not been able to verify Strayhorn's involvement as an arranger on the MGM set.

50. The initials in RCM are for its three founders: James Roosevelt, Sam Coslow, and Gordon Mills. The screen in the Panoram machine measured 22 x 25 inches and was placed

at eye level encased in a seven-foot-high walnut art deco-style cabinet. The speakers, which used RCA sound reproduction technology, were placed below the ground-glass screen and the movies themselves were back-projected off two mirrors. Daniel Egen has estimated that at the "height of popularity, there were approximately 4,500 Panorams operating commercially." *America's Film Legacy: The Authoritative Guide to the Landmark Movies in the National Registry* (New York: Continuum Books, 2010), 348.

51. Klaus Stratemann, *Duke Ellington: Day by Day and Film by Film* (Copenhagen: JazzMedia, 1992), 180–85.

52. Stratemann, *Duke Ellington*, 180–85. The set for "Flamingo" was also used in several of the other Ellington soundies, e.g., "Hot Chocolate (Cottontail)." Moreover, Collins and Beatty appeared in two other soundies that featured Black theater dance numbers taken from (or based on) contemporaneous Dunham productions. See also Patricia Willard, "Dance: The Unsung Element of Ellingtonia," *Antioch Review* (1999): 405–6.

53. Susan Manning, *Modern Dance, Negro Dance: Race in Motion* (Minneapolis: University of Minnesota Press, 2004), 157.

54. Manning, *Modern Dance, Negro Dance*, 157.

55. Manning, *Modern Dance, Negro Dance*, 157.

56. Manning, *Modern Dance, Negro Dance*, 145. Manning specifically argues here for a reading of Dunham's "Woman with Cigar" in terms of queer eroticism (*Modern Dance, Negro Dance*, 157–58). For a recent consideration of Katherine Dunham and/in queer dance history, see Clare Croft, "Introduction," in *Queer Dance: Meanings and Makings*, ed. Clare Croft (New York: Oxford University Press, 2017), 15–16.

57. Also in evidence here is the influence of Lester Horton's technique on Collins's dancing (she trained in modern dance with Horton). I am grateful to Susan Manning for sharing this and other insights with me. Manning, personal communication, July 11, 2011.

TWO *Difficult Beauty*

1. James Gavin, *Stormy Weather: The Life of Lena Horne* (New York: Atria Books, 2009), 3–4.

2. Gavin, *Stormy Weather*, 464. Another song on the album, the ballad "Forever Was a Day," composed by Mike Renzi and Rodney Jones, was inspired by a young gay friend of Horne's who had died of AIDS. Gavin, *Stormy Weather*, 462–63.

3. Lena Horne and Richard Schickel, *Lena* (New York: Doubleday, 1965), 124.

4. Horne, quoted by Larry Blumenfield in his review of *We'll Be Together Again*, *Jazziz* 13, no. 9 (September 1996): 55–56.

5. Gavin, *Stormy Weather*, 97.

6. Lena Horne quoted in "Lena Horne Makes Jazz Festival Debut a Tribute to Strayhorn," *Los Angeles Sentinel*, July 1, 1993, B-3.

7. To cite just one example, in giving an account of her break-out engagement at the Savoy-Plaza, the first for an African American cabaret performer at the posh hotel, she observed, "I began to spend a lot of time with Phil [Moore] and Strayhorn, working on my material. I had already begun to realize, even then, that one should always have the best musicians to work with. No matter what the sacrifice" (Horne and Schickel, *Lena*, 147). These comments act as a lead-in to the harrowing story Horne tells about repercussions of the Savoy-Plaza's refusal to let her stay at the hotel ("the hotel's strange policy of semi- or demi-segregation damn near killed me.") Ill at the time, Horne collapsed during a performance one evening during the engagement; although she was hemorrhaging, she refused to be treated by the hotel's doctor and insisted on being taken back uptown to her Harlem hotel, the Theresa. Phil Moore didn't want to move her; she "yelled at him: 'I don't care if I'm dying. Don't leave me where I'm not wanted'" (Horne and Schickel, *Lena*, 148).

8. David Hajdu, *Lush Life: A Biography of Billy Strayhorn* (New York: North Point Press, 1997), 95.

9. It was during her performances at the Little Troc in 1942 that Rodger Edens "discovered" Horne and thus began her career-making but extremely troubled history with the color line in Hollywood at MGM.

10. Horne and Schickel, *Lena*, 125; see also Hajdu, *Lush Life*, 96.

11. Horne and Schickel, *Lena*, 125. These charts were never recorded and the manuscripts appear to be lost. Horne would perform a different version of "Honeysuckle Rose" a year later in the 1943 MGM film musical *Thousands Cheer*. See Richard Dyer, "Singing Prettily: Lena Horne in Hollywood," in Richard Dyer, *In the Space of a Song: The Uses of Song in Film* (New York: Routledge, 2012), 114–44. Also, in 1943 the Ellington Orchestra included a version of the tune Strayhorn arranged for clarinetist Jimmy Hamilton in their December 1943 Carnegie Hall concert program. (The autograph score is labeled "Honey Suckle" and is held in the Billy Strayhorn Collection).

12. Gavin, *Stormy Weather*, 97.

13. R. J. Smith, *The Great Black Way: L.A. in the 1940s and the Lost African-American Renaissance* (New York: Public Affairs, 2006), 220–21. Confusingly, Gavin identifies the owners as a lesbian couple who had a taste for butch sartorial style. Gavin, *Stormy Weather*, 124–25.

14. The reasons for Strayhorn's estrangement from Ellington are detailed chapter 3.

15. Strayhorn's participation on the McCrae date was the result of McCrae's "special request": as the story goes, McRae asked an inebriated Strayhorn to accompany her on the song at a party the prior weekend (Hajdu, *Lush Life*, 138–39). The recording itself, with Wendell Holmes on bass, is a shining testament to Strayhorn's extraordinary skills as an accompanist. Marian McPartland would later name it as one of her favorite recordings ("I love his nice single notes, and those long-line fills, like flowing horn lines, and that lovely ending with its dissonant chords"). (Marian McPartland, quoted in Kevin

Whitehead, "Strayhorn the Pianist," *Blue Light: The Journal of the Duke Ellington Society UK* 22, no. 3 [Autumn 2015]: 19).

16. Hajdu, *Lush Life*, 137–42.

17. Hajdu, *Lush Life*, 120. Strayhorn took counsel from critic and producer Leonard Feather, who told Hajdu he gave Strayhorn a "crash course in the music business" (120).

18. Hajdu, *Lush Life*, 122.

19. Hajdu, *Lush Life*, 122.

20. Hajdu, *Lush Life*, 122.

21. See for example *The Duke Ellington Reader*, ed. Mark Tucker (New York: Oxford University Press, 1993), 263.

22. Lena Horne, quoted in the 1996 PBS *American Masters* documentary, *Lena Horne: In Her Own Voice*.

23. "Lena Horne Becomes 'Production Home' In New Café Routine," *Chicago Defender*, January 29, 1955, 6.

24. Marion B. Campfield, "Mostly about Women," *Chicago Defender*, February 19, 1955, 14.

25. Pianist, composer, and fellow Black queer musician and friend Donald Shirley was in the audience at one of the Chez Paree shows and would later tell Hajdu, "Billy was very intuitive and knew what the occasion was. When he played with Lena Horne, he was the best possible accompanist for Lena Horne." *Lush Life*, 132.

26. Hajdu, *Lush Life*, 132.

27. Hajdu, *Lush Life*, 132.

28. Shane Vogel, *The Scene of the Harlem Cabaret: Race, Sexuality, Performance* (Chicago: University of Chicago Press, 2009), 167–69.

29. Vogel, *Scene of the Harlem Cabaret*, 189; Horne and Schickel, *Lena*, 271–72. See also Deborah Paredez, "Lena Horne and Judy Garland: Divas, Desire, and Discipline in the Civil Rights Era," *TDR: The Drama Review* 58, no. 4 (2014): 105–19.

30. Quoted in James Gavin, "A Legend Lays Bare Her Hurt," *New York Times*, June 5, 1994, 84.

31. Horne and Schickel, *Lena*, 197; see also profile of Horne by Michiko Kakutani, "Lena Horne Aloofness Hid the Pain, until Time Cooled Her Anger," *New York Times*, May 3, 1981, https://www.nytimes.com/1981/05/03/arts/lena-horne-aloofness-hid-the-pain-until-time-cooled-her-anger.html.

32. Nichole Rustin-Paschal, "'The Reason I Play the Way I Do Is': Jazzmen, Emotion, and Creating in Jazz," in *Routledge Companion to Jazz Studies*, ed. Nicholas Gebhardt, Nichole Rustin-Paschal, and Tony Whyton (New York: Routledge, 2019), 402.

33. Another very important collaborator for Horne was the vocal arranger, vocal coach, singer, author, actor, and dancer Kay Thomas. Thomas was Horne's vocal coach in the 1940s MGM-Freed Unit (during this period Thomas also had a huge impact on Judy Garland).

As Richard Dyer notes, Horne credited Thomas for encouraging her "to find lower and edgier timbres in her delivery" for her filmic performances. Dyer, "Singing Prettily," 137.

34. According to data on the *Jazz Discography Online* (*TJD Online*), the session for "Let Me Love You" and "It's Love" took place in New York on May 31, 1955; the session for "It's All Right with Me" was on June 7, 1955. In his discussion of these sessions, Hajdu doesn't include "Let Me Love You," but notes Strayhorn's accompanying on an unreleased version of the standard—one of Strayhorn's favorites—"You Go to My Head." The only extant commercially released Horne recording for this standard I could find is from a French 1962 LP, *Lena Horne with Phil Moore & His Orchestra–L'Inimitable Lena Horne*, on the Guilde Du Jazz label.

35. Hajdu, *Lush Life*, 132.

36. Bill Cross, review of "I Love to Love," *Metronome* 71, no. 6 (June 1955): 29. That same year, Horne performed the hit on Stan Kenton's CBS TV series *Music '55*. Horne's performance simultaneously projects ferocity and despair.

37. James Gavin, *Intimate Nights: The Golden Age of New York Cabaret* (New York: Grove Press, 1991), 107–10. Notably, Howard got his start in New York as the accompanist for a legendary queer entertainer, the female impersonator Ray Bourbon. Although not as consciously progressive as Café Society Uptown, the Blue Angel, according to Gavin, "practiced a staunch policy of racial tolerance, hiring dozens of black performers and never barring a black customer." Among the many Black cabaret artists who performed there were Pearl Bailey, Josephine Premice, Barbara McNair, Diahann Carroll, and Johnny Mathis. Gavin, *Intimate Nights*, 82–83.

38. Howard served as Mabel Mercer's accompanist at another New York cabaret, Tony's, beginning in 1946. According to James Gavin, Mercer "introduced dozens of his songs to singers and fans there." As a songwriter, however, Howard is best known as the author of the standard "Fly Me to the Moon," originally titled "In Other Words." The cabaret singer Felicia Sanders debuted the song in 1954 at the Blue Angel and Kaye Ballard cut a recording of it the same year (during this period, the song was also performed regularly by Mabel Mercer, Portia Nelson, and Sylvia Syms). It was after Peggy Lee popularized the song in the early 1960s that Howard formally changed the title. Gavin, *Intimate Nights*, 108–9.

39. Indeed, Horne's version of the tune arguably inspired later midcentury jazz sides such as Blossom Dearie's 1957 version of "Let Me Love You" for the Verve label.

40. Edward Berger, David Chevan, and Benny Carter, "Bassically Speaking: An Oral History of George Duvivier," *Studies in Jazz*, 17 (Newark, NJ: Institute of Jazz Studies, Rutgers–The State University of New Jersey, 1993): 99; Duvivier, interview with Harriet Milnes for the Duke Ellington Oral History, Tape B, August 18, 1983 (Yale University: Oral History of American Music Collections. https://yale.app.box.com/s/pbiox61fi8xy6cqwqz txls1f56ooni3f). This LP also featured Horne's 1955 arrangement of "Let Me Love You."

41. David Hajdu, liner notes in Lena Horne, *We'll Be Together Again*, Blue Note, CDP 7243 8 28974 2 2, 1994, compact disc.

42. All three items are held in the Billy Strayhorn Collection.

43. Hajdu, *Lush Life*, 133.

44. If it was meant as a gift for Grove, that raises the possibility of queer repurposing of the lyric.

45. The hotel stationary draft lyric remains undated. Between 1956 and 1960, Ellington played at least eight extended engagements at the Blue Note in Chicago. An advertisement for a double-bill program featuring Billy Strayhorn (as part of a trio) and singer Lurlean Hunter appeared in the *Chicago Defender* on July 3, 1957, just days ahead of Ellington's engagement there from July 10–21 (during Strayhorn's engagement the Ellington band was at the Ravinia Festival, Highland Park, Ill.; see *Chicago Defender*, July 3, 1957, 19; Klaus Stratemann, *Duke Ellington: Day by Day and Film by Film* [Copenhagen: JazzMedia, 1992], 377).

46. Horne's recorded performances of the song on *Live from the Sands* and *We'll Be Together Again* feature some minor yet notable alterations to Strayhorn's draft lyric. The most (possibly) significant of these is Horne's replacement of the word "gay" in the line "maybe the tune will be that gay and light again," with the word "sweet." The most likely reason for Horne's reluctance to sing the word "gay" would be that by the early 1960s, it seemed out-of-date. But it is also possible that she may have been uncomfortable navigating in a public forum the word's queer connotations. This possibility is strikingly suggested in a filmed rehearsal of Horne's performance of Strayhorn's "Something to Live For" that was included in the outstanding PBS *American Masters* documentary *Lena Horne: In Her Own Voice*. In the first run-through, Horne abruptly stops singing, a knowing smile directed at the other musicians, just before the word "gay" in the lyric's line "Someone who'd take my life/And make it seem gay as they say it ought to be." But when they restart for a second take she joyfully sings the line.

47. Horne and Schickel, *Lena*, 281–82. This event took place a week before the murder of Medgar Evers and shortly after Evers's house was bombed. Horne movingly recounts her encounters with Evers, who came out to the airport to personally greet Horne and Strayhorn upon their arrival: "I'll never forget that this man, with all he had on his mind, came out to the airport to meet us when we flew in. We could not stay at his house because it had been recently bombed . . . But he saw to it that we were comfortably settled." Horne and Schickel, *Lena*, 281–82.

48. Shane Vogel, "*Jamaica* on Broadway: The Popular Caribbean and Mock Transnational Performance," *Theatre Journal* 62, no. 1 (March 2010): 1–21.

49. Hajdu, *Lush Life*, 226–27.

50. Horne and Schickel, *Lena*, 281–87.

51. Quoted in A. Alyce Claerbaut and David Schlesinger, eds., *Strayhorn: An Illustrated Life* (Chicago: Agate Bolden, 2015), 115.

52. Chillingly, Evers's murderer, the white supremacist Byron De La Beckwith Jr., was a menacing presence at this event: along "with two of his cronies he blew cigarette smoke at Lena and Billy while they performed" (they were in short order asked to extinguish their cigarettes, after which they stormed out of the church). Bruce Rastrelli, "Moral Freedoms," in *Strayhorn: An Illustrated Life*, ed. Claerbaut and Schlesinger, 117.

53. Clooney also starred in another 1954 Paramount musical, the Western parody *Red Garters* (with co-stars Guy Mitchell and Jack Carson). For a discussion of Mitch Miller's critical role in popular music during the 1950s, see Albin J. Zak III, *I Don't Sound Like Nobody: Remaking Music in 1950s America* (Ann Arbor: University of Michigan Press, 2010), 43–75.

54. Both Irving Townsend and Hajdu state that Clooney was pregnant with her fourth child; however, her fourth child, Monsita Ferrer, was born in 1958, nearly two years after *Blue Rose* was released. Her second child, Maria Ferrer, was born in 1956. See Irving Townsend, liner notes, in Rosemary Clooney and Duke Ellington and his Orchestra, *Blue Rose*, Sony, B00000JBDV, 1999, CD; Hajdu, *Lush Life*, 147.

55. Hajdu, *Lush Life*, 148.

56. The title may also have evoked associations with another blue flower pop song from the period, "Blue Gardenia," which was the title song for Fritz Lang's 1953 film noir (arranged by Nelson Riddle and sung in the film by Nat "King" Cole). The song was also recorded by Dinah Washington in 1956 for her critically acclaimed LP *The Swingin' Miss "D"* (arr. Quincy Jones).

57. To give one midcentury example, in Tennessee Williams's *The Glass Menagerie* (which debuted on stage in 1944 and was made into an MGM film in 1950), the blue rose symbolizes the various forms of "difference" embodied in the misfit character Laura Wingfield, including her retreat into a fantasy world of small glass animals and popular songs; her disability; and her extreme fragility, shyness, and inability to conform to heteropatriarchal social expectations.

58. Hajdu, *Lush Life*, 147, 149. As a parting memento of their time together and to thank him for his caregiving, Clooney presented Strayhorn with a Cartier watch with the ironic inscription "To Svengali." Hajdu, *Lush Life*, 149.

59. See, for example, Donald Bogle, *Toms, Coons, Mulattoes, Mammies, and Bucks: An Interpretive History of Blacks in American Films* (New York: Continuum International Publishing Group, 2001); Ann DuCille, "The Shirley Temple of My Familiar," *Transition* 73 (1997): 10–32; Ed Guerrero, *Framing Blackness: The African American Image in Film* (Philadelphia: Temple University Press, 1993).

60. I am using the word "nonnormative" here to signal how dominant perceptions of Strayhorn's Black masculinity align with what Roderick A. Ferguson calls the racialized logic of "nonheteronormativity"—that is, the tangle of pathologizing histories and discourses of difference ascribed to African American cultural formations broadly and,

more particularly, to internal variations of Black queer masculinity within these discourses/histories. See Roderick A. Ferguson, *Aberrations in Black: Toward a Queer of Color Critique* (Minneapolis: University of Minnesota Press, 2004), 13. See also Phillip Brian Harper, *Are We Not Men?: Masculine Anxiety and the Problem of African American Identity* (New York: Oxford University Press, 1996); and Siobhan B. Somerville, *Queering the Color Line: Race and the Invention of Homosexuality in American Culture* (Durham, NC: Duke University Press, 2000).

61. Hajdu, *Lush Life*, 147.

62. Hajdu, *Lush Life*, 149. And, indeed, only insiders would know that "Grievin'" and "I'm Checkin' Out, Goom Bye" came off Strayhorn's pen, as these two songs are credited only to Ellington on the original release, a perception emphasized by Irving Townsend in his liner notes (he identifies them as Ellington originals).

63. The manuscript is housed in the Duke Ellington Collections, of the Smithsonian Institution, Archives Center, National Museum of American History, Washington, DC.

64. Cootie Williams's trumpet solo in the original 1939 recordings does not modulate.

65. Quoted in Stanley Dance, *The World of Duke Ellington* (New York: Da Capo Press, 1970), 30.

66. Rosemary Clooney with Joan Barthel, *Girl Singer: An Autobiography* (New York: Broadway Books, 1999), 154. Following the birth of her daughter Maria in the summer of 1956, Clooney officially registered Billie Holiday as Maria's godmother. Clooney refers to the song "Blue Rose" in her autobiography as "a new number Billy [Strayhorn] wrote especially for me" (153).

67. See, for example, Will Friedwald's discussion of Clooney during this period in which he argues that Clooney's greatest affinity was with "the great male icons of the jazz-and-pop mainstream: Sinatra, Bennett and, most of all Crosby." *Jazz Singing: America's Great Voices from Bessie Smith to Bebop and Beyond* (New York: Da Capo, 1996), 415.

68. Clooney, *Girl Singer*, 131.

69. Clooney offered the following account by a reporter of the divorce court drama: "Weeping uncontrollably on the witness stand, singer Rosemary Clooney, thirty-three, today accused her husband, actor José Ferrer, forty-nine, who fathered her five children of 'having affairs with other women since the beginning our marriage' and 'violent acts of temper.'" Clooney, *Girl Singer*, 186.

70. Walter van de Leur, *Something to Live For: The Music of Billy Strayhorn* (New York: Oxford University Press, 2002), 115; see also Hajdu, *Lush Life*, 113–14.

71. Hajdu, *Lush Life*, 144. Hajdu quotes here an unidentified "black gay musician familiar with the Paris scene" who likened Strayhorn at the Mars Club in Paris to "a miniature, black Noel Coward" (145).

72. Hajdu, *Lush Life*, 145.

73. Hajdu, *Lush Life*, 145.

74. The mediating role of multitrack technology in Strayhorn and Clooney's collaboration in the recording studio is also at issue here, but is beyond the scope the present study. For an account of the recording studio as an intermundane space of "deadness" in which human, nonhuman, and other entities collaborate, see Jason Stanyek and Benjamin Piekut, "Deadness: Technologies of the Intermundane," *TDR: The Drama Review* 54, no. 1 (Spring 2010): 14–38.

75. Hajdu, *Lush Life*, 148.

76. Clooney, *Girl Singer*, 153. See also a similar account in Hajdu, *Lush Life*, 148; and Claerbaut and Schlesinger, eds., *Strayhorn*, 135.

77. See, for example, John Fass Morton, *Backstory in Blue: Ellington at Newport '56* (New Brunswick, NJ: Rutgers University Press, 2008).

78. The LP was also groundbreaking for Ellington and Strayhorn: it was the first LP in their composing partnership comprised entirely of new compositions. I discuss *A Drum Is a Woman* and *Such Sweet Thunder* in part 2.

79. These include *Irving Berlin Song Book*, *George and Ira Gershwin Song Book*, *Harold Arlen Song Book*, *Jerome Kern Song Book*, and *Johnny Mercer Song Book* (but not the 1981 *Antonio Carlos Jobim Song Book* for Pablo Records).

80. To be clear, I'm referring only to the sessions Fitzgerald recorded with the Ellington band, which were released as the first volume in a two-volume four-LP set; volume 2 comprised sessions Fitzgerald cut in a small group setting, featuring Oscar Peterson, Ray Brown, Barney Kessel, Herb Ellis, Stuff Smith, and Ben Webster, among others.

81. Van de Leur, *Something to Live For*, 101. The reissue liner notes, however, attempt to finesse the matter by offering the corrective that the LP should "in all fairness and accuracy be titled 'Ella Fitzgerald Sings the Ellington and Strayhorn Songbook,'" while also attributing the absenting of Strayhorn's name from the exterior packaging of the reissue to a mutually agreed upon "custom not oversight," Patricia Willard, liner notes in *Ella Fitzgerald Sings the Duke Ellington Song Book*, Verve Records, 1999, three compact discs.

82. As curated on in the 1999 CD reissue, the rehearsal takes appear to culminate in the officially released, master take. Despite—or perhaps because of—the aura of unfettered access (of listening-in on a private or semiprivate space of a rehearsal), the rehearsal tapes included in the reissue are nevertheless partial and selective both at the level of the taped material itself (we hear the tape fade out and back in at a number of places) and ways in which the material is framed in relation to contradictory historical and social narratives and scripts.

83. Patricia Willard, liner notes, in *Ella Fitzgerald Sings the Duke Ellington Song Book*, Verve Records.

84. Leonard Feather, liner notes, in *Ella Fitzgerald Sings the Duke Ellington Song Book*, Verve Records.

85. Monica Hairston-O'Connell and Sherrie Tucker, "Not One to Toot Her Own

Horn(?): Melba Liston's Oral Histories and Classroom Presentations," *Black Music Research Journal* 34, no. 1 (Spring 2014): 123–24.

86. Ella Fitzgerald, quoted in "An Interview with Leonard Feather," *DownBeat*, November 18, 1965, 23.

87. Hajdu, *Lush Life*, 168.

88. Hajdu, *Lush Life*, 168.

89. As Hajdu observes, Ellington tried to make amends to Strayhorn and Fitzgerald through showcasing a new three-movement composition on the LP *Portrait of Ella Fitzgerald*, co-composed by Ellington and Strayhorn. During the spoken introductions on the work (outtakes of which are also included on the reissue) Ellington pays tribute to Strayhorn, accompanied by Strayhorn extemporizing on the piano.

90. Hajdu, *Lush Life*, 167. Morgan's homophobia also resulted in Strayhorn's after-hours social exclusion. For instance, on evenings that Morgan and Ellington were seated together at the Hickory House nightclub, Strayhorn kept a safe distance, hanging out at the bar—literally and figuratively in the shadows (Hajdu, *Lush Life*, 166–67).

91. Hajdu, *Lush Life*, 171.

92. Honi Coles, quoted in *Strayhorn: An Illustrated Life*, ed. Claerbaut and Schlesinger, 98. Strayhorn was introduced to the group in the early 1950s through Charles "Cookie" Cook, who was among Strayhorn's close-knit circle of gay male friends (the group also included Coles's tap duo partner Cholly Atkins). As the lifetime president of the organization, he wrote music for their annual benefit shows (a high point on the Harlem society social calendar) for over a decade.

93. "Crazy Little Story," *Newsweek*, May 6, 1957, 66.

94. Hajdu, *Lush Life*, 171–72.

95. Indeed, Hajdu's decision to include Coles's story in his biography was clearly guided by this critical function. As he writes: "Strayhorn's feeling . . . had more levels than his calmly accommodating manner suggested. In private with his intimates, Strayhorn revealed a deepening well of unease about his lack of public recognition as Ellington's prominence grew" (Hajdu, *Lush Life*, 171).

96. Howard Pollack, *The Ballad of John Latouche: An American Lyricist's Life and Work* (New York: Oxford University Press, 2017), 189.

97. Van de Leur, *Something to Live For*, 98. One aspect of this history might suggest a queer biographical intertext for Strayhorn's engagement with Latouche's lyric in "Day Dream"—namely, longstanding rumors that Strayhorn and Latouche were briefly lovers during the production. See John Franceschina, *Duke Ellington's Music for the Theatre* (London: McFarland & Company, Inc., 1988), 211n10; Pollack, *Ballad of John Latouche*, 188–90.

98. John Latouche papers, 1930–1960, Series III, Box 1, Columbia University Libraries Archival Collections, Columbia University, New York, New York.

99. Hajdu, *Lush Life*, 103–4.

100. It is also entirely possible that Strayhorn's decision to arrange the vocal version for Fitzgerald may have been prompted by—and a response to—Pete Rugolo's 1956 arrangement of the song for June Christy (included on her LP *The Misty Miss Christy*). Given the liberties that Rugolo's arrangement makes, which include "luxe" strings and an introduction scored for solo flute (Bud Shank), one can imagine that Strayhorn's version a year later sought to sound a corrective to the record, as it were.

101. Strayhorn's manuscript draft of the lyrics for "A Flower Is a Lovesome Thing," written on staff paper, is held in the Billy Strayhorn Collection. An image of the handwritten draft is given in *Strayhorn: An Illustrated Life*, ed. Claerbaut and Schlesinger, 46.

102. As Hajdu puts it in *Lush Life*, Strayhorn's mother "took extreme measures to insulate him from his father as well as from his older brother . . . and indeed all of Homewood sending him on a series of long visits to his grandparents in North Carolina" (10).

103. Hajdu, *Lush Life*, 10.

104. Strayhorn also advocated for women jazz instrumentalists. As the featured guest in 1951 for Leonard Feather's *DownBeat* "Blindfold Test," Strayhorn hailed the pianist Beryl Booker alongside pianists such as Art Tatum: "I'm enthusiastic about some lesser-known pianists, such as Beryl Booker—she's wonderful!" (Leonard Feather, "The Blindfold Test: Swee'Pea Stays on the Scene," *DownBeat*, September 7, 1951, 12.

THREE Strayhorn's Lorcian Encounter

1. Italics original. Stanley Dance, *The World of Duke Ellington* (New York: Da Capo Press, 1970), 32. Although composed for the Shakespeare Festival in Stratford, Ontario, in September 1957, the suite was premiered at a Music for Moderns concert in Town Hall, New York, on April 28, 1957, under the title *Twelve-Tone to Ellingtonia*.

2. *A Midsummer Night's Dream*, act 3, scene 2, lines 110–15.

3. For instance, David Schiff has proposed that Strayhorn's orchestration of Puck's quotation "can heard as a gay comment on the follies of the straight world." *The Ellington Century* (Berkeley: University of California Press, 2012), 184. He sees this queer comment as a "reversal of hierarchies that perfectly matches the overturning of values" around discourses of music, race, and gender, which he discusses in two of the suite's other movements, the titular "Such Sweet Thunder" and "Lady Mac." He further compares the "covert" signaling of queeness in "Up and Down" to another famous North American queer Shakespearean appropriation from this moment—*West Side Story* by Bernstein/Robbins, which premiered only months after *Such Sweet Thunder*. Schiff, *The Ellington Century*, 184.

4. For queer literary readings of Puck and, more broadly, the comedy's stagings of perverse and same-sex desire, see, for example, Douglass E. Green, "Preposterous Pleasures: Queer Theories and *A Midsummer Night's Dream*," in *A Midsummer Night's Dream: Critical*

Essays, ed. Dorothea Kehler (New York: Garland, 1998), 369–97. Green hails Puck as his "queer hero" and argues that he "is the very possibility of the perverse operating within yet against constraints, of pleasures beyond such constraints" (386–87); Puck's character, in other words, serves as a figure for disorder in the fairy world, one that also signals "the un- or mis-recognized possibility of preposterous pleasures ("'And those things do best please me / That befall prepost'rous_y,'" 3.2.120–21)" (386–87). Green's reading of Puck builds on Jonathan Dollimore's notion of the "paradoxical perverse," which he develops in *Sexual Dissidence: Augustine to Wilde, Freud to Foucault* (Oxford: Oxford University Press, 1991). See also Richard Rambuss, "Shakespeare's Ass Play," in *Shakesqueer: A Queer Companion to the Complete Works of Shakespeare*, ed. Madhavi Menon (Durham, NC: Duke University Press, 2011), 234–44. A less affirmative view of the queer potential of Puck is argued in Alan Sinfield, *Cultural Politics—Queer Reading* (London: Routledge, 2005). For a detailed history of postwar queer performances of *Romeo and Juliet*, see Richard Burt, "No Holes Bard: Homonormativity and the Gay and Lesbian Romance with *Romeo and Juliet*," in *Shakespeare without Class: Misappropriations of Cultural Capital*, ed. Donald Hendrick and Bryan Reynolds (New York: Palgrave Macmillan, 2000), 153–88.

5. David Hajdu, *Lush Life: A Biography of Billy Strayhorn* (New York: North Point Press, 1997), 155. Eve Kosofsky Sedgwick, for example, characterized these sonnets as "a kind of floating decimal in male homosexual discourse." *Between Men: English Literature and Male Homosocial Desire* (New York: Columbia University Press), 1985, 28. See also Joseph Pequigney, *Such Is My Love: A Study of Shakespeare's Sonnets* (Chicago: University of Chicago Press, 1996); and Bruce R. Smith, "Shakespeare's Sonnets and the History of Sexuality: A Reception History," in *A Companion to Shakespeare's Works*, ed. Richard Dutton and Jean Elizabeth Howard (Malden, MA: Blackwell, 2003), 4–26.

6. Hajdu, *Lush Life*, 155.

7. Hajdu, *Lush Life*, 155.

8. Schiff, *The Ellington Century*, 4–5.

9. Other transnational Ellington-Strayhorn projects during this period include the *Peer Gynt Suite* (1960) and the *Far East Suite* (1963).

10. For specific literature related to Black gay cultural production, history, and aesthetic practices, see the notes in the introduction to this book.

11. The name "Ool-Ya-Coo" references the 1947 Dizzy Gillespie Orchestra recording "Ool-Ya-Koo." Indeed, Strayhorn's collaborator, Luther Henderson, described the musical as "a bebop musical," in spirit but not "necessarily" in sound ("but with that feeling, that coolness, that hipness"). Hajdu, *Lush Life*, 128.

12. For a history of the term *queer* in early twentieth-century homosexual subcultures in New York, see Chauncey, *Gay New York*, 15–22.

13. "New Hit, 'Lush Life!' Is Not New," *DownBeat*, August 12, 1949, 2. In his essay "Moral Freedoms," Bruce Rastrelli speculates that the earliest autograph manuscript for "Lush

Life," dated c.1934 under the original title "Life is Lonely," may have origins as a breakup song lamenting the end of Strayhorn's relationship (and musical collaboration) with musician and lyricist Raymond Wood, who Strayhorn connected with through Homewood neighborhood networks (Bruce Rastrelli, in A. Alyce Claerbaut and David Schlesinger, eds., *Strayhorn: An Illustrated Life* (Chicago: Agate Bolden, 2015), 133–36; for an earlier account of Strayhorn and Wood see Hajdu, *Lush Life*, 20–21).

14. Hajdu, *Lush Life*, 129.

15. Hajdu, *Lush Life*, 128. Another Strayhorn song from the musical "Ool-Ya-Coo," sung by Brother Big Eyes, gestures toward this queer perceptual theme, a lyric that, as Hajdu observes, "distills the central notion of *Rose-Colored Glasses* in one verse: 'Nearly everyone has a rosy view / But every now and then / It seems that something happens / Which even I can't understand / And the perspective of such nice people as these / Seems to go askew'" (130).

16. Hajdu, *Lush Life*, 129. According to van de Leur's indexing of the musical, Henderson contributed five songs. Of all the songs, only three were issued a copyright by 2000 and the remainder have never been located. Walter van de Leur, *Something to Live For: The Music of Billy Strayhorn* (New York: Oxford University Press, 2002), 278–79.

17. Hajdu, *Lush Life*, 112–13.

18. Van de Leur, *Something to Live For*, 115. See also Hajdu, *Lush Life*, 113–14.

19. Van de Leur, *Something to Live For*, 116. By comparison, Ellington's decision to cut Strayhorn's newly composed introduction to "Chelsea Bridge" in the Ella Fitzgerald *Song Book* session, detailed in chapter 2, seems like a mild violation.

20. Van de Leur, *Something to Live For*, 115. For Baldwin this would have been the years he was at work on his great semi-autobiographical novel, *Go Tell It on the Mountain* (published 1953). Neal appeared in several 1940s Broadway musicals, including "Carmen Jones," "On the Town," and "Finian's Rainbow"; however, after the war he primarily devoted his creative energies to art. Sebree continued painting/exhibiting but also branched out into playwriting—his critically acclaimed play *Mrs. Patterson*, starring Eartha Kitt (also a Dunham alum), debuted on Broadway in 1954. Beatty, the most high profile of the three artists, founded his own dance company in the early 1950s; his encounters with Strayhorn at the Neal salon led to several important collaborations, including Beatty's starring role as Carribee Joe in Ellington-Strayhorn's *A Drum Is a Woman*, broadcast on CBS in 1959, and Beatty's ballet, *The Road of the Phoebe Snow* (1959).

21. Hajdu, *Lush Life*, 117. Yet directly after his return to New York, Strayhorn had already begun to work outside the Ellington organization, most notably through his membership in the legendary society of Black tap dancers, the Copasetics, for which he served as president from the early 1950s until his death. Significantly, Strayhorn was initially brought into the group through Charles "Cookie" Cook (of the comic dance duo Cook and Brown), whom he met through "mutual friends in gay circles." As fellow Copasetic

member, the celebrated dancer Cholly Atkins commented, "I think the reason Strayhorn was so dedicated to the Copasetics was that he recognized how much love was in the Copasetics for him . . . Most people shunned people like him for being how he was, and here was a bunch of guys who were crazy about him." Hajdu, *Lush Life*, 117, 119.

22. Hajdu, *Lush Life*, 127.

23. Hajdu, *Lush Life*, 141–42. This same year, 1954, a notice in *Melody Maker* reported that Strayhorn was to collaborate with Charles Sebree on a Broadway-bound musical, a "fantasy play" by Sebree called *Fischer Boy*, which was to star Harry Belafonte.

24. Artists' Theatre flyer for the 1953–54 season.

25. See Hajdu, *Lush Life*, 126–28; van de Leur, *Something to Live For*, 121–26. While van de Leur's analyses provide a wealth of musical insights into Strayhorn's settings of García Lorca's lyrics (many of which my analyses are indebted to), he says little about queer thematic connections between music and the play, stating only that "it is not clear how the play served as a vehicle for black and gay pride" (121). In addition, van de Leur speculates that the production may have modified Lorca's text in some way to accommodate Strayhorn's conception. While this is a possibility, there is no evidence to support significant alterations to the play, although the production did take some liberties in realizing Lorca's stage directions.

26. Brent Hayes Edwards, "The Literary Ellington," in *Uptown Conversation: The New Jazz Studies*, ed. Robert O'Meally, Brent Hayes Edwards, and Farah Jasmine Griffin (New York: Columbia University Press, 2004), 326–56. The 1953 Artists' Theatre production used the 1941 translation of the play by James Graham-Lujan and Richard L. O'Connell: Federico García Lorca, *The Love of Don Perlimplín and Belisa in the Garden*, in *Lorca's Theatre: Five Plays of Federico García Lorca*, trans. James Graham-Lujan and Richard L. O'Connell (New York: Charles Scribner's Sons, 1941).

27. Hajdu, *Lush Life*, 125.

28. John D'Emilio, *Sexual Politics, Sexual Communities: The Making of a Homosexual Minority in the United States, 1940–1970* (Chicago: University of Chicago Press), 22; see also Douglas Field, *All Those Strangers: The Art and Lives of James Baldwin* (New York: Oxford University Press, 2015), 41.

29. Field, *All Those Strangers*, 41.

30. Field, *All Those Strangers*, 41.

31. Rachel Corbman, "'Next Time, the Fire in Giovanni's Room': The Critical Reception of James Baldwin's Second Novel in the Black Press," *Zeteo: Journal of Interdisciplinary Writing* (Spring 2012), 2 (reprinted in Zeteo sampler Fall 2014, http://zeteojournal.com/2012/04/11/james-baldwin-and-the-black-press/). See also, Thaddeus Russell, "The Color of Discipline: Civil Rights and Black Sexuality," *American Quarterly* 60, no. 1 (March 2008), 104–5; and Gregory Conerly, "Swishing and Swaggering: Homosexuality in Black

Magazines during the 1950s," in *The Greatest Taboo: Homosexuality in Black Communities*, ed. Delroy Constantine-Simms (Los Angeles: Alyson, 2001), 384–94.

32. Corbman, "'Next Time, the Fire in Giovanni's Room,'" 12. Corbman also discusses Alfred Duckett's "Third Sex" multipart series published in the *Chicago Defender* in 1957 (11). Interestingly, several years prior, in 1954, Duckett published a glowing profile of Strayhorn emphasizing his deep influence on the Ellington sound (Alfred Duckett, "Duke Ellington Employs a 'Stray-Horn' Not as Instrument—as an Arranger," *Chicago Defender*, August 21, 1954).

33. Hajdu, *Lush Life*, 127.

34. The group El Caracol and its director, Cipariano Rivas Cherif, were already under surveillance following their previous lesbian-themed production *El Sueño de las razón* (The Dream of Reason), subtitled *Un engendro des lesbos* (A Procreation of Lesbos").

35. The official reason given for the government's censoring of the play concerned the actor, a military officer, who played the role of Perlimplín. Being made a cuckold on the stage was thus construed as a de facto insult to the honor of the military. A long-running British production of the play directed by Joan Littlewood in the late 1940s and early 1950s also aroused much controversy. According to Gwynne Edwards, the sexual content of the play in the Theatre Workshop production (which also, like the 1953 Artists' Theatre production, used the 1941 Graham-Lujan and O'Connell translation) shocked audiences. Gwynne Edwards, "Theatre Workshop's Translations of Three Spanish Plays," *New Theatre Quarterly* 25, no. 1 (2009): 52–62.

36. *The Love of Don Perlimplín* is often grouped with several other of Lorca's plays from this period, including *The Shoemaker's Wonderful Wife*, *The Puppet Play of Don Cristóbal*, and *The Butterfly's Evil Spell*, which similarly recast in experimental terms popular traditions of farce and puppetry.

37. Jim Carmody, "Lorca's *The Love of Don Perlimplín for Belisa in the Garden*: The Perspectives Are Deliciously Wrong," in *Federico García Lorca: Impossible Theater, Five Plays and Thirteen Poems*, trans. Caridad Svich (Hanover, NH: Smith and Kraus, 2000), 20.

38. Paul McDermid, *Love, Desire and Identity in the Theatre of Federico García Lorca* (Woodbridge, UK: Tamesis, 2007), 70.

39. McDermid, *Love, Desire and Identity*, 70. McDermid also notes the "affinity" of this aesthetic approach to Buñuel's filmic "notion of 'decoupage'" (70). In addition to McDermid, for English language commentary on *Don Perlimplín* see the following: Carmody, "Lorca's *The Love of Don Perlimplín*"; Paul Smith, *The Theater of García Lorca* (Cambridge: Cambridge University Press, 1998); C. Christopher Soufas, *Audience and Authority in the Modernist Theater of Federico García Lorca* (Tuscaloosa: University of Alabama Press, 1996); Sarah Wright, *The Trickster-Function in the Theatre of García Lorca* (Woodbridge, UK: Tamesis, 2000); Maria M. Delgado, *Federico García Lorca* (London:

Routledge, 2008); Virginia Higginbotham, *The Comic Spirit of Federico García Lorca* (Austin: University of Texas Press, 1976).

40. Here, McDermid positions Lorca's use of artifice and masking in relation to Oscar Wilde's "queer artifice of the Mask." McDermid, *Love, Desire and Identity*, 202.

41. Hajdu, *Lush Life*, 127. Leslie's digital reconstruction of one scene from the production features a stylized "close-up" of the head from Diego Velazquez's portrait of *Infanta Maria Teresa* (c. 1652–53) positioned on one side of the proscenium, juxtaposed against a nocturnal landscape image after Albert Pinkham Ryders's famous moonlit seascape paintings. Alfred Leslie, personal communication with author, February 7, 2010.

42. McDermid, *Love, Desire and Identity*, 71.

43. Wright, *The Trickster-Function*, 39–61.

44. Sarah Wright, "Theatre," in *A Companion to Federico García Lorca*, ed. Federico Bonaddio (Woodbridge, UK: Tamesis, 2007), 47. Wright's observations here are made in the context of her compelling rereading of *Perlimplín* as a veiled recasting of the "Platonic version of love between men as a tale of mismatched heterosexuality." This recasting, she argues, "permits Lorca to harness a range of intertextual metanarratives . . . from the *Beauty and the Beast*, to Edmond Rostand's *Cyrano de Bergerac* (1897) and Fernand Crommelynck's *Le cocu magnifique* (1921)." Wright also sees the play as a foreshadowing of the gender inversions staged in Lorca's most explicit gay play, *El publico*, in which "a young man disguises himself as a young woman in a love story with an older man" (Wright, "Theatre," 48).

45. For the premiere production in 1933 at the Teatro Español in Madrid, Lorca used Scarlatti harpsichord sonatas. These apparently were both played as musical interludes and arranged in some way to accompany the three songs in the play.

46. Lorca, *The Love of Don Perlimplín and Belisa*, in *Lorca's Theatre*, trans. Graham-Lujan and O'Connell, 119.

47. The piano music of Francis Poulenc also serves as a resonant point of reference here. See van de Leur, *Something to Live For*, 122–23.

48. There were no recordings made of the original 1953 production. In 1995, however, the Dutch Jazz Orchestra, supervised by Walter van de Leur, recorded all four pieces. According to van de Leur, the singer, Marjorie Barnes, was uncomfortable performing the line "morning cock" in "Love, Love," so they substituted the original Spanish, "Gallo, que se va la noche," which works very well given the flamenco allusion. Of course, the word *gallo* in Spanish has as strong sexual connotations, meaning basically "stud." Walter van de Leur, personal communication with author, December 1, 2012.

49. Wright, *The Trickster-Function*, 39.

50. David Johnston, *Federico García Lorca* (Bath, UK: Absolute Press, 1988), 43.

51. Lorca, *The Love of Don Perlimplín and Belisa*, in *Lorca's Theatre*, trans. Graham-Lujan and O'Connell, 115.

52. On queer Francophilia and Euro-modernist composers, see Nadine Hubbs, *The Queer Composition of America's Sound: Gay Modernists, American Music, and National Identity* (Berkeley: University of California Press, 2004).

53. Van de Leur, *Something to Live For*, 124. Despite this similarity, van de Leur's reading of "Wounded Love" aligns it not with jazz but with the musical and expressive practices of the Early Baroque operatic lament, specifically Monteverdi (124–25).

54. Interestingly, Strayhorn sets "Wounded Love" in the same key, D♭ major, as "Lush Life," a tonal field that Strayhorn also turned to—sometimes in its B♭ minor incarnation—to write some of his most complex and, as I argue later, queerly sensuous pieces such as "Passion Flower" and "Isfahan" (from *Far East Suite*), as well arrangements of the popular songs "Flamingo" and "Where or When." I admit it is very problematic to draw any particular conclusions here, as such keys are also just good keys for the alto saxophone and are also keys favored by many jazz pianists.

55. Heather Love, *Feeling Backward: Loss and the Politics of Queer History* (Cambridge, MA: Harvard University Press, 2007), 22–23. Love's argument pivots around the need to reclaim and not disavow negative affects in the name of affirmative, post-Stonewall gay and lesbian politics.

56. Van de Leur, *Something to Live For*, 124.

57. Van de Leur dubs the recurrence of this descending minor seventh leap in the piano accompaniment the "love motive" which, he observes, acts in counterpoint to this recurring vocal motive (the "death motive") on the words "dying of love," "bleeding heart," and "take me by the hand." *Something to Live For*, 124.

58. See, for example, Robert J. Corber, *Homosexuality in Cold War America: Resistance and the Crisis of Masculinity* (Durham, NC: Duke University Press, 1997); Bruce McConachie, *American Theater in the Culture of the Cold War: Producing and Contesting Containment, 1947–1962* (Iowa City: University of Iowa Press, 2003).

59. Hajdu, *Lush Life*, 127. Later in the season, he also attended (and took friends to see) multiple performances of Jane Auer Bowles's *In the Summerhouse*, another pre-Stonewall "closet drama" with an intricate lesbian subtext. For a valuable reading of the queer "complex patterns of identification and desire" in Bowles's *In the Summerhouse*, see David Savran, "A Different Kind of Closet Drama; or the Melancholy Heterosexuality of Jane Bowles," in *A Queer Sort of Materialism: Recontextualizing American Theater* (Ann Arbor: University of Michigan Press, 2003), 155–69.

60. McConachie, *American Theater in the Culture of the Cold War*, 259.

61. John M. Clum, *Still Acting Gay: Male Homosexuality in Modern Drama* (London: Palgrave MacMillan, 2000), 116. Clum argues that the play ultimately substitutes homophobia for anticommunism. As he observes, Anderson's play "both raises and dismisses the possibility of homosexuality. In essence, it pushes its characters back in the

closet" (116). For other relevant discussions, see Alan Sinfeld, *Out on the Stage: Lesbian and Gay Theatre in the Twentieth Century* (New Haven, CT: Yale University Press, 1999); David Gerstner, "The Production and Display of the Closet: Making Minnelli's 'Tea and Sympathy,'" *Film Quarterly* 50, no. 3 (Spring 1997): 13–26.

62. McDermid, *Love, Desire and Identity*, 202–3.

63. McDermid, *Love, Desire and Identity*, 96–97.

64. On a formal level it is meant ironically to refer to the opening scene. Belisa's offstage singing is also part of the play's theatrical surrealism, in the sense that all the "action" is some elaborate metaphor or symbol of Perlimplín's tortured mind as well as another manifestation of Lorca's "meta" reflections on the dynamics of theater, spectatorship, etc. From a gender/sexuality perspective, containing her voice offstage could also be interpreted as a form of disavowal or fear of female sexuality/bodies.

65. The lyric/poem appears in his collection *Canciones*, published in 1927. Candelas Gala, "'Tôpicos Sublimados': Lorca's Female Iconographies in 'Eros Con Bastôn,'" in *Lorca, Buñuel, Dali: Art and Theory*, ed. Manuel Delgado and Alice Jan Proust (Cranbury, NJ: Associated University Presses, 2001), 99. Lorca's fondness for this lyric is evidenced by its appearance in a collection of poetry he published around the same time, titled "Serenata" (with the name "Lolita" replacing "Belisa"). Writing about the latter, Gala argues that "the meaning of this poem lies in the incongruity between the poem's sweet popular form and its dark content . . . Parallel to the seemingly unthreatening, lyrical game between stanzas and chorus, the moon is playing tricks on Lolita's unsuspecting desire" (99).

66. Smith performed the role of the Compère opposite Altonell Hines as the Commère (Hines created the role of the Commère in the original 1934 Broadway production). For analyses of race, modernism and queerness in *Four Saints in Three Acts* see Hubbs, *The Queer Composition of America's Sound*, 19–63; and Lisa Barg, "Black Voices/White Sounds: Race and Representation in Virgil Thomson's *Four Saints in Three Acts*," *American Music* (2000): 121–61.

67. *Jet* magazine, October 22, 1953, 64. A notice in *Billboard* from December 1, 1951, describes Bruce's singing on the Mundy sides as a "pop styled torcher," praising her "pleasing low pitched voice" and "warm, husky quality" (*Billboard*, 116). In 1961, according to a notice in *Jet*, Bruce was "screentested" for the lead role in a Billie Holiday biopic (*Jet*, January 19, 1961, 64).

68. Henry Hewes, *Saturday Review of Literature*, November 21, 1953, 49.

69. Brooks Atkinson, "Two Short Plays," *New York Times*, November 4, 1953, 30.

70. Lawrence Glenn Jasper, "A Critical History of the Artists' Theatre of New York," (PhD diss., University of Kansas, 1986), 135. Jasper uses Myers' critique to support his argument that Machiz made a "serious miscalculation" in "his attempt to mount this delicate period-style piece with an all-black cast of musical comedy/vaudeville performers."

Jasper leaves the reader to conclude, presumably, that being Black and coming from the world of popular music-theater precludes an ability to engage with an historical setting and Lorca's "fragile theater poetry" (134).

71. Hajdu, *Lush Life*, 127.

72. Ian Gibson, *The Assassination of Federico García Lorca* (Chicago: J. P. O'Hara, 1979), 179.

73. Langston Hughes, trans., *Bodas de Sangre* (Fate at the Wedding/Blood Wedding), 1994; Langston Hughes, trans., *Gypsy Ballads*, 1951; Bob Kaufman, "The Night That Lorca Comes," *The Ancient Rain: Poems 1956–1978*; Amiri Baraka, "Lines for Garcia Lorca," in *New Negro Poets USA*, ed. Langston Hughes (Bloomington: Indiana University Press, 1964).

74. Jonathan Mayhew, *Apocryphal Lorca: Translation, Parody, Kitsch* (Chicago: University of Chicago Press, 2009), 19.

75. Mayhew, *Apocryphal Lorca*, 27–29. Mayhew also points out the more pervasive cultural fad for Spanish culture/exotica during the 1950s, citing, for example, Miles Davis, "Flamenco Sketches" (*Kind of Blue*, 1959) and Davis/Evans, *Sketches of Spain* (1960), and John Coltrane's *Olé* (1961). While Mayhew's argument points to critical ideological issues, he tends to elide transnationalist imaginaries and histories, ignoring, for example, the frames of critical cosmopolitanism.

76. A striking example of this discourse, one that coincides with the *Perlimplín* production, comes in Ralph Ellison's 1954 essay "Flamenco"—his first published piece of music criticism. See Ralph Ellison, *Living with Music*, ed. Robert G. O'Meally (New York: Modern Library, 2001), 95–100; and Mayhew, *Apocryphal Lorca*, 30, 34–35.

77. See, for example, Mayhew's discussion of the literary responses to Lorca by Frank O'Hara, Jack Spicer, and Robert Duncan in *Apocryphal Lorca*, 41–46. As Mayhew observes, after 1955, following Ben Bellit's translation of Lorca's essay "Play and Theory of the Duende" and the collection *Poet in New York*, the responses of American poets to Lorca are overwhelmingly focused on a very selective Lorcian canon and, he argues, "creative misreadings" informed by a set of stereotyped "stock images" (48–49). Although he discusses them elsewhere, Mayhew does not include Hughes or Kaufman in his section on postwar queer poetic readings of Lorca.

78. On Bob Kaufman's pivotal role in the Beat "nexus of sexual, racial and gendered tensions," see Maria Damon, "Triangulated Desire and Tactical Silences in the Beat Hipscape: Bob Kaufman and Others," *College Literature* 27, no. 1 (Winter 2000): 139–57.

79. Both lead sheet and manuscript sketch are held in the Billy Strayhorn Collection at the Library of Congress. The two most significant alterations heard on the recording are (1) a transposition to E♭ major (although both lead sheet and manuscript sketch indicate F major); and (2) a shortened B section that deletes the final 4 mm of the original, in effect creating a symmetrical ABA form.

80. See, for example, van de Leur's analyses of "Passion Flower" and "A Flower Is a Lovesome Thing," *Something to Live For*, 30.

81. For the definitive accounting of these recordings, see van de Leur, "Appendix B: Billy Strayhorn's Works on Record," in *Something to Live For*, 194–254.

82. Given Strayhorn's queer self-portrait as the elf Puck in "Up and Down, Up and Down" from *Such Sweet Thunder*, one wonders about a similar dynamic in the ballad "Elf" (Lena Horne, Strayhorn's self-described soulmate, evoked his visage this way: "he had a face like an elf," Hajdu, *Lush Life*, 95).

83. Jack Chambers, "Lotus Eaters Unite!: The Spectral Alliance of Johnny Hodges and Billy Strayhorn," in *Sweet Thunder: Duke Ellington's Music in Nine Themes* (Canam Books, 2019), 158.

84. Chambers, "Lotus Eaters Unite!," 128–29.

85. Stanly Dance, "Interview with Cootie Williams," May 1976 (Smithsonian Institution: Washington, DC), transcript in Rutgers Jazz Institute.

86. In a rare interview in 1966, Hodges named *A Drum Is a Woman* as one of his favorite Ellington works (Johnny Hodges, interview by Henry Whiston, *Jazz Journal International* January [1966]: 9). For a related analysis of gender and sound in "Ballet of the Flying Saucers" see John Wriggle, "'The Mother of All Albums': Revisiting Ellington's *A Drum Is a Woman*," in *Duke Ellington Studies*, ed. John Howland, Cambridge Composer Studies (Cambridge: Cambridge University Press, 2017): 265–98. The apparent misogynistic images and language in the scenario, Ellington's narration, and the song lyrics have been recently reinterpreted in productive ways. See, especially, Shane Vogel, "Madam Zajj and US Steel: Blackness, Bioperformance, and Duke Ellington's Calypso Theater," *Social Text* 30, no. 4 (2012): 1–24.

87. In consultation with Strayhorn, Beatty compiled the score for the ballet from three late-1950s Ellington-Strayhorn works. In addition to *Such Sweet Thunder*, these included *A Drum Is a Woman* (in which Beatty danced the role of Carribee Joe), and the film score for *Anatomy of a Murder* (the Ellington family gave Beatty the acetate demos in advance of the film's commercial release). All three works connect to *Phoebe Snow's* themes and choreographies.

88. Hajdu, *Lush Life*, 178. Hodges grew up in Cambridge, Massachusetts, and although his mother was a skilled pianist, he was largely self-taught, learning piano and drums before switching to saxophone. During his first decade with Ellington from 1928 to 1939, he played both the soprano and alto saxophone, but after 1940 he refused to continue playing soprano because, as rumor had it, he demanded (without success) that Ellington double his pay for playing both instruments. Later, Hodges would take to reminding Ellington of his monetary value onstage, famously signing the "pay me" gesture after taking solos.

89. In his 1970 eulogy for Hodges (he died at age sixty-one from a heart attack), El-

lington hailed the paradoxes of his longtime star virtuoso: "Never the world's most highly animated showman or greatest stage personality, but a tone so beautiful it sometimes brought tears to the eyes—this was Johnny Hodges. This *is* Johnny Hodges" (Ellington, *Music is My Mistress*, [New York: Da Capo Press, 1973], 118).

90. Hajdu, *Lush Life*, 178.

91. I'm thinking here of what sociologist Erving Goffman first identified as extra or "double" social labor, coping strategies and fraught social contingencies that living with/through stigma require. See Erving Goffman, *Stigma: Notes on the Management of Spoiled Identity* (New York: Simon & Schuster, 1963), 12–19.

92. Hajdu, *Lush Life*, 178.

93. Chambers, "Lotus Eaters Unite!" 138. Interestingly, Jack Chambers credits Ellington with "orchestrating" the Strayhorn-Hodges musical alliance, citing as an origin point Ellington and Strayhorn's collaborative work on an Ellington 1940 ballad representing "quiet feminized sensuality" with its none-too-subtle vagina metaphor—"Warm Valley" (its phallus counterpart being "The Flaming Sword"). That is, Chambers claims that through their work on this ballad featuring Hodges, Ellington recognized the power of the Strayhorn-Hodges ballad alliance (Chambers, "Lotus Eaters Unite!" 134–36).

94. It would also risk asserting a reified or essentialized "gay sensibility" in Strayhorn's music.

FOUR *Black Queer Moves in the Strayhorn-Ellington* Nutcracker Suite

1. David Hajdu, *Lush Life: A Biography of Billy Strayhorn* (New York: North Point Press, 1997), 206.

2. Ibid, 203–4. This meeting occurred in March 1960, which suggests that Strayhorn worked on the arrangements sometime during an (approximately) six-week period between mid-April and June 1960. The work was recorded in Los Angeles for Columbia Records on June 3 at Radio Recorders (see Klaus Stratemann, *Duke Ellington: Day by Day and Film by Film* [Copenhagen: JazzMedia], 420).

3. Strayhorn paid tribute to (and sonically immortalized) the Logan social scene in the great uptempo "U.M.M.G." The title stands for the "Upper Manhattan Medical Group" run by Arthur Logan.

4. Hadju, *Lush Life*, 204–5.

5. Elizabeth Freeman, "Introduction," *Queer Temporalities*, special issue of *GLQ: A Journal of Lesbian and Gay Studies* 13, nos. 2–3 (2007): 159–76.

6. These are: movements 1, 2, 4, 5, 8, 9 ("Overture," "Toot Toot Tootie Toot," "Sugar Rum Cherry," "Entr'Acte," "Dance of the Floreadores," and "Arabesque Cookie"), see Walter van de Leur, *Something to Live For: The Music of Billy Strayhorn* (New York: Oxford University Press, 2002), 275–76.

7. Van de Leur, *Something to Live For*, 89; 235–36.

8. Hajdu, *Lush Life*, 204.

9. Peter Szendy, *Listen: A History of Our Ears* (New York: Fordham University Press, 2008), 65.

10. Szendy, *Listen: A History of Our Ears*, 36. While I am drawn to Szendy's notion of arranging as a type of "active, critical listening," it is also important to note that his history of arranging and arranging practices/aesthetics is focused exclusively around the perspectives and creative practices of Romantic European composers (primarily Berlioz, Liszt, and Robert Schumann). While his discussion of this repertoire mounts a rigorous and compelling defense of how arrangements restore the (lost ideal of) plasticity of authorship, it nevertheless assumes what George Lewis would call "Eurological" distinctions between an "original" and its "arrangement" (George E. Lewis, "Improvised Music after 1950: Afrological and Eurological Perspectives," *Black Music Research Journal* [1996]: 91–122).

11. Quoted in Stanley Dance, *The World of Duke Ellington* (Boston: Da Capo Press, 1970), 31.

12. Hajdu, *Lush Life*, 18,

13. Richard Dyer, *The Culture of Queers* (London and New York: Routledge, 2002), 18–21.

14. Hajdu, *Lush Life*, 18.

15. Interpreting Tchaikovsky's representation of otherness adds an extra layer of complexity. As Richard Dyer has argued with respect to the ballet, Tchaikovsky's pastiche-like approach is itself inscribed with complex forms of imitation, sympathetic fantasy, and othering (Richard Dyer, *Pastiche* [London and New York: Routledge, 2007], 144–46).

16. Jennifer Fischer, *Nutcracker Nation: How an Old-World Ballet Became a Christmas Tradition in the New World* (New Haven, CT, and London: Yale University Press, 2003), 28. The CBS production was based on Balanchine's 1954 production of the ballet.

17. Fischer, *Nutcracker Nation*, 30.

18. Mervyn Cooke develops this argument in his essay "Jazz Among the Classics, and the Case of Duke Ellington," in *The Cambridge Companion to Jazz*, ed. Mervyn Cooke and David Horn (Cambridge: Cambridge University Press, 2002), 162–71.

19. Gene Lees, "Duke Ellington—'The Nutcracker Suite' (Columbia); 'Peer Gynt Suites No.1 and 2, Suite Thursday' (Columbia)," *DownBeat* 28, May 11, 1961, 28.

20. Or, as critic Eddie Lambert later quipped, the "question of 'jazzing the classics' was a dead one in an age when Beethoven was used to advertise breadcrumbs" (Eddie Lambert, *Duke Ellington: A Listener's Guide*, Studies in Jazz Series, No. 26 [Lanham, MD, and London: Scarecrow Press, 1999], 218).

21. Walter van de Leur, ed., "Editor's Notes," *Nutcracker Suite*, arranged by Duke Ellington and Billy Strayhorn (Pittsburgh: Billy Strayhorn Songs, 1998).

22. Leonard Feather, "Blindfold Test: Shorty Rogers," *DownBeat*, April 27, 1961, 49. The striking contrast between Gene Lee's negative critical assessment of the Strayhorn-Ellington *Nutcracker* and Rogers's acclaim for its "high creative level" points to a broader divide between the "ears" of *DownBeat* critics and musicians in the reception of the LP. For example, Feather played two other sides from the LP, "Dance of the Floreodores" and "Chinoiserie," for, respectively, George Russell and Benny Golson, both of whom gave the recordings five stars ("Blindfold Test: George Russell," *DownBeat*, January 5, 1961, 43; "Blindfold Test: Benny Golson," *DownBeat*, June 22, 1961, 390).

23. Musically, this personal stamp comes through Strayhorn's revisions to form and tempo: he slows the tempo considerably and makes substantial cuts, removing, for example, the complete da capo repetition. Such cuts enable him to focus "on minute details in the original to enlarge them . . . as if looking through a magnifying glass." A brief transitional passage linking the first and second theme in Tchaikovsky, for instance, is transformed into to "a melancholic wa-wa trombone feature" (van de Leur, notes to *Nutcracker Suite*, arranged by Duke Ellington and Billy Strayhorn).

24. On Strayhorn's activism within the civil rights movement, see Hajdu, *Lush Life*, 223–31.

25. Hajdu, *Lush Life*, 72–73.

26. Henry Louis Gates Jr., *The Signifying Monkey: A Theory of African-American Literary Criticism* (New York: Oxford University Press, 1988), 46–48.

27. This possibility was, in fact, suggested in Donald Byrd's 1996 *Harlem Nutcracker*, in which the scene is staged as a nightclub act. Studies of queer Harlem Renaissance nightclub culture and its afterlives include: Eric Garber, "A Spectacle in Color: The Lesbian and Gay Subculture of Jazz Age Harlem," in *Hidden from History: Reclaiming the Gay and Lesbian Past*, ed. Martin Duberman, Martha Vicinus, and George Chauncey (New York: New American Library, 1989), 318–31; Shane Vogel, *The Scene of Harlem Cabaret: Race, Sexuality, Performance* (Chicago: University of Chicago Press, 2009); James F. Wilson, *Bulldaggers, Pansies, and Chocolate Babies: Performance, Race, and Sexuality in the Harlem Renaissance* (Ann Arbor: University of Michigan Press, 2010); Fiono Ngô, *Imperial Blues: Geographies of Race and Sex in Jazz Age New York* (Durham, NC: Duke University Press, 2014); and Kortney Ziegler, "Black Sissy Masculinity and the Politics of Dis-respectability," in *No Tea, No Shade: New Writings in Black Queer Studies*, E. Patrick Johnson, ed. (Durham, NC: Duke University Press, 2016): 196–215. Angela Davis's pioneering work on Gertrude "Ma" Rainey, Bessie Smith, and Billie Holiday centers Black feminist thought and histories of the (queer) performance and song lyrics of these iconic blueswomen (Davis, *Blues Legacies and Black Feminism* (New York: Vintage, 1998).

28. Sam See, "Spectacles in Color: The Primitive Drag of Langston Hughes," *PMLA* 124, no. 3 (May 2009): 799–802. One of See's most provocative theoretical moves lies in his

attempt to recuperate the category "natural" through his analysis of the queer performative dynamics in Hughes's *The Weary Blues*. Writing about the poem "Cross," for example, See argues that it "performs as embodied and affectively natural what it performatively exposes as unstably gendered," thus reclaiming the term "natural" for queerness from the epistemological frames of (hetero)normativity (See, "Spectacles in Color," 814). For a related reading of Hughes's poems see Anne Borden, "Heroic 'Hussies' and 'Brilliant Queers': Genderracial Resistance in the Works of Langston Hughes," *African American Review* 28 (1994): 333–45; and Martin J. Ponce, "Langston Hughes's Queer Blues," *Modern Language Quarterly* 66, no. 4 (December, 2005): 505–37.

29. Elisa F. Glick, *Materializing Queer Desire: Oscar Wilde to Andy Warhol* (Albany: State University of New York Press, 2009), 83–106. See, in fact, cites Nugent's much discussed 1926 cover for *Opportunity*, calling it "an emblematic figure of primitive drag" (See, "Spectacles in Color," 813).

30. Glick, *Materializing Queer Desire*, 87. Glick erroneously refers to the last name of the character of Paul Arbian (aka Nugent) as "Arabian"—an appealing confusion from the perspective of this article, as will become clear. For an unsurpassed account of the cultural history of Black dandyism see Monica L. Miller, *Slaves to Fashion: Black Dandyism and the Styling of Black Diasporic Identity* (Durham, NC: Duke University Press, 2009).

31. Glick, *Materializing Queer Desire*, 84, 99. Nugent's *Drawings for Mulattoes* are also examined in Susan Gubar, *Racechanges: White Skin, Black Face in American Culture* (New York and Oxford: Oxford University Press, 1997), 107–22; and Thomas H. Wirth, ed., *Gay Rebel of the Harlem Renaissance: Selections from the Work of Bruce Richard Nugent* (Durham, NC: Duke University Press, 2002), 67–71.

32. See, "Spectacles in Color," 814. While my reading of these practices emphasizes a retrospective historical connection, the play of difference and affinity I have been exploring in Strayhorn's arrangement, in particular the use of signifying practices, also resonates with queer-of-color critiques. For example, in his important essay "Toward a Black Gay Aesthetic: Signifying in Contemporary Black Gay Literature" (published in Essex Hemphill's groundbreaking 1991 collection *Brother to Brother: New Writings by Black Gay Men*), Charles Nero argues that the uses of signifying by Black gay men not only "places their writing squarely within the African American literary tradition," but "permits black gay men to revise the 'Black Experience' in African American literature and, thereby, to create a space for themselves" (Nero, "Toward a Black Gay Aesthetic," in *Brother to Brother*, ed. Essex Hemphill [Boston: Alyson Publications, Inc., 1991], 231). See also Simon Dickel, *Black/Gay: The Harlem Renaissance, the Protest Era, and Constructions of Black Gay Identity in the 1980s and 90s* (East Lansing: Michigan State University Press, 2011).

33. Vogel, *The Scene of Harlem Cabaret*, 118–19.

34. Vogel, *The Scene of Harlem Cabaret*, 119.

35. Gunther Schuller, in fact, drew an explicit parallel between "Caravan" and Tchaikovsky's "Arabian Dance": "What Tchaikovsky's *Arab Dance* from the *Nutcracker* Ballet is to classical music, Tizol and Ellington's *Caravan* is to jazz" (Gunther Schuller, *The Swing Era: The Development of Jazz, 1930–1945* [New York: Oxford University Press, 1989], 89). Interestingly, in 1955 Ellington appeared on the popular TV game show *Masquerade Party* dressed in Arab garb, a satirical gesture to the Arabian drag of "Caravan" (Harvey G. Cohen, *Duke Ellington's America* [Chicago: Chicago University Press, 2010], 262).

36. The uses of "Caravan" for theatrical exoticism during this period extend beyond the Ellington world. In her study of Black female dancers on the Montreal midcentury variety stage, Vanessa Blais-Tremblay notes that the piece served to showcase the choreographies of Black female shake dancers. As she brilliantly observes, "what connected the sound of a piece like Duke Ellington's 'Caravan' to the 'mysterious veiled world' that Mark Tucker said the piece conjured was not just the sound itself, but actually a very conspicuous practice in which black female bodies *un*veiled to the world to the particular drum pattern that introduces the piece" (Blais-Tremblay, "Jazz, Gender, Historiography: A Case Study of the 'Golden Age' of Jazz in Montreal [1925–1955]," PhD diss., McGill University, 2018, 36–39).

37. Van de Leur, *Something to Live For*, 185; see also "Billy Strayhorn and the File Cabinets," in *Strayhorn: An Illustrated Life*, ed. A. Alyce Claerbaut and David Schlesinger (Chicago: Agate Bolden, 2015), 32–33.

38. A review of the floor show in *Women's Wear Daily* refers to the entire show as "Strange Feelings" and also identifies the final production number featuring the song as "Strange Feeling" (*Women's Wear Daily*, May 28, 1943, 23). As noted in this review, the floor show was a considerably revamped version, directed by Dave Wolper, of the opening floor show at the Hurricane, which ran from April to May. (See Stratemann, *Duke Ellington: Day by Day and Film by Film*, 241–42.)

39. The decision to showcase Leticia in the floor show's dramatic finale was undoubtedly an attempt to capitalize on her notoriety as a featured dancer in the hit Broadway musical *Star and Garter*, which ran from June 1942 to December 1943 at the Music Box Theater. The musical, a vehicle for Bobby Short and burlesque star Gypsy Rose Lee, cast Leticia in a dance number titled "The Harem." Confusingly, some sources give her name as "Letitia" rather than "Leticia," a problem that is reproduced in the secondary literature. A more significant confusion in the secondary literature concerns her surname, which in both Stratemann and van de Leur is given as "Hill" (*Duke Ellington: Day by Day and Film by Film*, 241; *Something to Live For*, 94). The misidentification of her last name possibly came from a confusion with the author Constance Valis Hill, the author who discusses Leticia Jay in her important *Tap Dancing America: A Cultural History* (New York: Oxford University Press, 2010). Leticia Jay would become an influential figure in the postwar revival of tap dance. As Hill notes, in the 1960s, Jay "worked to resurrect the great tap performers who she had watched through her own career," almost all of whom were the

original members of the Copasetics—Cholly Atkins, Ernest Brown, Honi Coles, Charles "Cookie" Cook, and Chuck Green. Strayhorn, as is well known, served as the president of this legendary tap-dancing fraternity and, as mentioned elsewhere in the book, composed and arranged music for their annual benefit shows.

40. "Leticia Jay [biography]," *Performing Arts Encyclopedia*, accessed December 3, 2022, https://memory.loc.gov/diglib/ihas/loc.music.tdabio.111/default.html.

41. "Strange Feeling" is the second movement (of four) in the *Perfume Suite*. I discuss Strayhorn's arrangement of the work for *The Peaceful Side* (1961) in chapter 5.

42. "M. Ravel Discusses His Own Work: The Boléro Explained," interview by M. D. Calvocoressi, *London Daily Telegraph*, July 11, 1931; reprinted in Arbie Orenstein, ed., *A Ravel Reader: Correspondence, Articles, Interviews* (New York: Columbia University Press, 1990), 477–78.

43. Monica L. Miller, *Slaves to Fashion*, 217.

44. Wirth, *Gay Rebel of the Harlem Renaissance*, 40.

45. Wallace Thurman, *Infants of Spring* (Boston: Northeastern University Press, 1992), 45. Arbian narrates his dream to an audience of friends at the "Nigaratti Manor." The flower exotica in Thurman's simulation of Nugent's text (and Nugent's original version) offer a further queer connection to Strayhorn, specifically to his flower ballads for Hodges. For analyses of Thurman's and Nugent's texts, see Glick, *Materializing Queer Desire*, 83–105; Steven Knadler, "Sweetback Style: Wallace Thurman and a Queer Harlem Renaissance," *Modern Fiction Studies* 48, no. 4 (2002): 899–936; Joseph A. Boone, *Libidinal Currents* (Chicago: University of Chicago Press, 1998), 220–32; Wirth, *Gay Rebel of the Harlem Renaissance*, 41–56; Scott Herring, *Queering the Underworld: Slumming, Literature, and the Undoing of Lesbian and Gay History* (Chicago: University of Chicago Press, 2007), 127–44.

46. Joseph A. Boone, "Vacation Cruises; or, The Homoerotics of Orientalism," *PMLA*, 110, no. 1 (January 1995): 90. On queer orientalism and Euro-American art music see Philip Brett, "Queer Musical Orientalism," *Echo: A Music-Centered Journal* 9, no. 1 (Fall 2009).

47. Jennifer Fischer, "'Arabian Coffee' in the Land of Sweets," *Dance Research Journal* (Winter 2003–Summer 2004): 153. In 1964, however, Balanchine "made it a nonsmoking solo for a female dancer" (Fischer, *Nutcracker Nation*, 30).

48. Marjorie Garber, *Vested Interests: Cross-Dressing and Cultural Anxiety* (New York: Routledge, 1992). On the queer history of Harlem Renaissance depictions of the eroticized "sheik" figures see Somerville, "'Queer to Myself As I Am to You': Jean Toomer, Racial Disidentification, and Queer Reading," in *Queering the Color Line: Race and the Invention of Homosexuality in American Culture* (Durham, NC: Duke University Press, 2002), 131–65; Knadler, "Sweetback Style: Wallace Thurman and a Queer Harlem Renaissance"); and Benjamin Kahan, "Sheiks, Sweetbacks, and Harlem Renaissance Sexuality, or the Chauncey Thesis at Twenty-Five," *Journal of Modern Literature* 42, no. 3 (Spring 2019): 39–54.

49. Among Strayhorn's contemporaries, this list would include Paul Bowles, Tennessee Williams, Truman Capote, Allen Ginsberg, and William S. Burroughs.

50. See, for example, Penny M. Von Eschen, *Race Against Empire: Black Americans and Anticolonialism, 1937–1957* (Ithaca and London: Cornell University Press, 1997); Nikhil Pal Singh, *Black is a Country: Race and the Unfinished Struggle for Democracy* (Cambridge, MA: Harvard University Press, 2004); Bill V. Mullen, *Afro-Orientalism* (Minneapolis: University of Minnesota Press, 2004).

51. A closely related critical move can be heard in "Chinoiserie" (movement seven), a disorienting, funky photomontage-like reassembling of the *Chinese Dance*, almost certainly a product of Ellington's imagination, and one which displays well his delight in abstraction and preference for on-the-spot compositional practice. For instance, in the last section of the movement, Ellington adds a twenty-two-bar coda that is introduced by a brief four-bar piano-bass duet. Ellington strikes out a series of offbeat stacked fourths against a pentatonic bass line that parodically animates an "oriental" musical cliché. This sense of the parodic derives partly from the instrumentation, particularly the sonic quality of the bass (usually we would expect to hear a celesta or xylophone). While "Chinoiserie" shares with "Arabesque Cookie" a critical take on orientalist representation, the emotional force and sonic atmosphere of the two movements are very different.

52. David Schiff, *The Ellington Century* (Berkeley: University of California Press, 2012), 186. Schiff relates the modernist soundings of this movement to modal jazz, seeing it as a precursor to *The Far East Suite*. He also notes how the theme of interracial romance in *Such Sweet Thunder* reflects Ellington's lifelong interest—by all accounts shared with Strayhorn—in expressing racial equality through interracial romantic pairings.

53. Schiff, *The Ellington Century*, 167.

54. Widening the lens to survey the larger jazz field at this moment, Strayhorn's "Arabesque Cookie" shares a resonant sonic and affective connection to Sun Ra's 1959 multipart piece "Ancient Aiethopia," (Impulse! label), which was included in the Sun Ra and His Arkestra's LP *Jazz in Silhouette*. Recorded on March 6, 1959—a year before Strayhorn would be dancing around Marian Logan's living room—the piece's opening instrumental section conjures its own Afrofuturist, Black (queer) transnational sonic revisions of Tchaikovsky's "Arabian" dance. Although it is not an exact quotation, we hear a close resemblance between the melodic profile of the opening motive in "Ancient Aiethopia" and Tchaikovsky's "Arabian" dance. As well, Sun Ra's scoring, in particular the use of hand drums, flute, and dissonant parallel lines, recalls Strayhorn's "Half the Fun" and "Arabesque Cookie."

55. Duke Ellington, "The Race for Space," in *The Duke Ellington Reader*, ed. Mark Tucker (New York: Oxford University Press, 1993), 294.

56. On this point, I would further note the links between Strayhorn and Ellington's *Nutcracker Suite* and transnationally oriented jazz projects by other jazz figures from

the period, such as works like Miles Davis's *Sketches of Spain* (1960), and John Coltrane's "India" and *Olé* (1961), as well as Oliver Nelson's arrangement of Prokofiev's *Peter and the Wolf* featuring Jimmy Smith (1966).

57. Although exceptional in the Ellington-Strayhorn book, as an instance of African American and Russian musical-cultural translation, the jazz *Nutcracker* can be positioned within a cultural history of African American-Russian comparative musings among Black intellectuals, writers, and artists from W. E. B. DuBois, Alain Locke, Claude McKay, and Paul Robeson to Langston Hughes, Richard Wright, Ralph Ellison, and James Baldwin, all of whom explicitly drew parallels between Russian and African American cultural identity and expressive practices. In the case of DuBois, Robeson, and Hughes this involved actual travel to Soviet Union, and sustained engagement. See, for example, Kate Baldwin, *Beyond the Color Line and the Iron Curtain: Reading Encounters Between Black and Red, 1922–1963* (Durham, NC: Duke University Press, 2002); and Dale E. Peterson, *Up from Bondage: The Literatures of Russian and African American Soul* (Durham, NC: Duke University Press, 2000).

58. I would also add here the 1957 televised performance of Ellington-Strayhorn's *A Drum Is a Woman*. For an important queer reading of the work, particularly as embodied in the gender queer "transubstantiation" of the central character Madam Zajj, see Shane Vogel, "Madam Zajj and US Steel: Blackness, Bioperformance, and Duke Ellington's Calypso Theater," *Social Text* 30, no. 4 (Winter 2012): 18–21. As Vogel notes, the work of two Black queer performers in the cast, Ozzie Bailey and Talley Beatty, as, respectively, the voice and the body of Madame Zajj's love interest Calypso Joe, further contributed to the queer dimensions of the performance.

59. In a piece published in *Vanity Fair* during the Ellington centennial year, Hajdu makes a somewhat similar point but frames it as a generalized "gay sensibility" (Hajdu, "A Jazz of their Own," *Vanity Fair* [May 1999]: 196.).

60. Gunther Schuller, *The Swing Era: The Development of Jazz, 1930–1945* (New York: Oxford University Press, 1989), 135–36; James Lincoln Collier, *Duke Ellington* (New York: Oxford University Press, 1987), 273–74. Collier further characterized Strayhorn's music as "a tropical rain forest thick with patches of purple orchids and heavy bunches of breadfruit." Van de Leur also comments briefly on homophobia in Strayhorn criticism (van de Leur, *Something to Live For*, 59).

61. Lambert, *Duke Ellington: A Listener's Guide*, 187.

62. Here, a comparison could be made to the reception of Tchaikovsky in North American criticism which, like the commentary on Strayhorn, is haunted by the trope of emotional excessiveness. Indeed, one wonders the extent to which Strayhorn may have been aware of the homophobic dimensions of Tchaikovsky reception which, as Malcolm Brown has convincingly shown, informed much twentieth-century Anglo-American criticism of the composer and his music. Although it is doubtful that Strayhorn engaged

in any sustained way with this literature, it is not far-fetched to assume that, given his reputation as an intellectual, and his formal training in and life-long passion for classical music, he would have been aware of Tchaikovsky's sexual orientation. See, Malcolm Hamrick Brown, "Tchaikovsky and His Music in Anglo-American Criticism, 1890–1950s," in *Queer Episodes in Music and Modern Identity*, Sophie Fuller and Lloyd Whitesell, eds. (Urbana and Chicago: University of Illinois Press, 2002), 134–49.

63. Quoted in Nat Shapiro and Nat Hentoff, eds., *Hear Me Talkin' to Ya: The Story of Jazz as Told by the Men Who Made It* (New York: Dover Publications, 1955), 238.

64. My discussion of the Black queer critical potential of beauty and pleasure is inspired by the rich body of work on Isaac Julien's extraordinary 1989 film *Looking for Langston*, especially Kobena Mercer's foundational essay on Julien's use of beauty and the beautiful as a form of critique (Kobena Mercer, "Avid Iconographies," in *Isaac Julien*, ed. Kobena Mercer and Chris Darke [London: Ellipsis, 2001]); and Monica L. Miller's reading of Julien's "mediation" on Black gay history and aesthetics of the Harlem Renaissance ("'You Look Beautiful Like That': Black Dandyism and Visual Histories of Black Cosmopolitism," in *Slaves to Fashion*, 222–41). I pursue this connection in the relation to posthumous LBGTQ+ engagements with Strayhorn's legacy in the book's epilogue.

65. Van de Leur, *Something to Live For*, 159.

66. Van de Leur, *Something to Live For*, 157.

67. Van de Leur, *Something to Live For*, 54.

68. Van de Leur, *Something to Live For*, 157. The Dutch Jazz Orchestra, *Something to Live For: The Dutch Jazz Orchestra Plays the Music of Billy Strayhorn* (Challenge Records CHR 70089).

69. Cohen, *Duke Ellington's America*, 308. However, as Cohen is quick to point out, Strayhorn never expressed a desire for (much less envy of) Ellington's fame and, on several occasions voiced antipathy toward the trappings of the celebrity life, which he viewed as anathema to his creative self. Strayhorn's statements on this topic thus seem to frame "working behind the scenes" as a creatively and personally productive choice. This is the narrative that he chose to present about himself during the last decade or so of his life. Yet, as I examine the book's epilogue, Strayhorn's narrative elides a much more complex and ambiguous situation, one that would require us to ask what is not said or can't be said about his reluctance to pursue a more high-profile professional path.

70. Another photograph from this series—an unpublished photograph—shows the two partners at work, dressed in nothing more than their underwear, on a hotel bed strewn with manuscript pages (Ellington is actually in bed, talking on the phone). This photograph is included in Hajdu, "A Jazz of their Own," 193.

71. For an extended discussion of the *Peer Gynt Suites*, see Anna Celenza, "Duke Ellington, Billy Strayhorn and the Adventures of *Peer Gynt* in America," *Music & Politics* 2, no. 5 (Summer 2011), http://dx.doi.org/10.3998/mp.9460447.0005.205.

FIVE Paris, Halfway to Dawn, or Listening to The Peaceful Side

1. As of this writing, I've not been able to identify the club in this sequence. The clientele and employees appear to be mostly white. The final sequence of the footage, however, takes place in Chez Haynes, a "restaurant américain" and de facto community center in Montmartre for visiting and expat African American musicians, artists, and writers in the postwar years. The owner-chef of Chez Haynes, Leroy Haynes, appears behind the restaurant's bar. A former football star, Morehouse graduate, and GI, Haynes settled in Paris after the war. With the help of his French spouse, Gabrielle "Gabby" Lecarbonnier, he turned the site of a former brothel located in the 9th arrondissement into the first soul food restaurant in Europe. See Jean Segura, "Haynes's: 60 Years of an American in Paris," trans. Christine Madsen, *Rue des collectionneurs*, n.d., accessed July 30, 2020, http://www.ruedescollectionneurs.com/magazine/mag/haynes-us.php; and Tyler Stovall, *Paris Noir: African Americans in the City of Light* (CreateSpace Independent Publishing Platform, 2012), 160–62.

2. It was only through the expert guidance of the jazz archivist at the Bibliothèque Nationale de France, Anne Legrand, that I discovered this footage.

3. David Hajdu, *Lush Life: A Biography of Billy Strayhorn* (New York: North Point Press, 1997), 212.

4. Hajdu, *Lush Life*, 143.

5. Tyler Stovall, *Paris Noir*, 205. Other important Black queer expat artists during this period: Baldwin's close friend and mentor the painter Beauford Delaney, the great diva and club owner Bricktop, Shakespearean actor Gordon Heath, and the pianist Art Simmons, who, as I discuss, performed at the Mars Club, alternating with Bridgers.

6. Hajdu, *Lush Life*, 209. Another Parisian hub that nurtured and sustained the Black diasporic artistic community in the postwar era was the Left Bank bar-restaurant Chez Inez, owned by African American singer (and former assistant and literary collaborator to Duke Ellington) Inez Cavanaugh. See Rashida K. Braggs, *Jazz Diasporas: Race, Music, and Migration in Post-World War II Paris* (Berkeley: University of California Press, 2016), 92–124.

7. Hajdu, *Lush Life*, 208. Hajdu documents Strayhorn's staying at the Hôtel de la Trémoille. However, Aaron Bridgers would later remember that Strayhorn stayed with him in his Paris apartment (quoted in Maximilien Samson François, *Samson François, Histoires de . . . Mille Vies, 1924–1970* [Paris: Bleu nuit éditeur, 2002], 109–10.

8. According to the film's producer, Sam Shaw, "Billy took me out to meet Aaron, where he was playing, and I was impressed. I thought he had a great look, very strong, very handsome. Billy was very proud of him" (Hajdu, *Lush Life*, 208). While Bridgers's appearance in the scene makes reference to the Mars Club, the tiny stage in the real Mars Club could not accommodate even the small-band ensemble that appears in the film.

9. Krin Gabbard, "*Paris Blues*: Ellington, Armstrong, and Saying It with Music," in *Uptown Conversations: The New Jazz Studies*, ed. Robert O'Meally, Brent Hayes Edwards, and Farah Jasmine Griffin (New York: Columbia University Press, 2004), 300.

10. Gabbard, "*Paris Blues*," 302.

11. Hajdu, *Lush Life*, 207.

12. Braggs, *Jazz Diasporas*, 12. As Braggs reminds us, the film's depiction of Paris as a color-blind society here erased the racism surrounding the anticolonial Algerian War of Independence (1954–1962), specifically the "concurrent ill treatment and disrespect of North Africans living in Paris" (210). The "folklore" of Paris as a race-free zone underwrites the "descriptive summary" for the Gaumont newsreel, discussed at the outset, which reads in part:

> It is in PARIS that this black student walks. For her and her friends who only know the records of the jazz gods or their rhythms played by others, January will remain a great date. The blacks of the capital were able to see and hear Duke ELLINGTON and Louis ARMSTRONG, who had never before played together, up close and personal, as this document shows. In America, where some of their admirers refuse to shake hands, they had not imagined that a whole city could crowd around them in this way, a city in which, every evening, the blacks, as in another country, dream of the distant sounds of their native land, and live these haunting rhythms, these messages from the heart that they are the only ones in the world to transmit in this way. (C'est à PARIS que se promène cette étudiante noire. Pour elle et ses amis qui ne connaissent que les disques des dieux du jazz ou leurs rythmes joués par d'autres, janvier restera une grande date. Les noirs de la capitale ont pu voir et entendre de près, venus en même temps à PARIS comme lemontre ce document, Duke ELLINGTON et Louis ARMSTRONG qui jamais n'avaient encore jouéensemble. (Synchrone) . . . En AMERIQUE où certains de leurs admirateurs refusent de leur serrer la main, ils n'avaient pasimaginé que toute une ville peut ainsi se presser autour d'eux. Une ville aux quatre coins de laquelle, chaque soir les noirs comme dans une autre patrie, vont rêver aux lointaines sonorités de leur pays natal, et vivre ces rythmes obsédants, ces messages du coeur qu'ils sont seuls au monde à transmettre ainsi.)

For a related analysis of race, music, and identity surrounding *Paris Blues*, with a focus on its adaption from novel to screenplay, see Andy Fry, *Paris Blues: African American Music and French Popular Culture, 1920–1960* (Chicago: University of Chicago, 2014).

13. Braggs, *Jazz Diasporas*, 209.

14. Gabbard, "*Paris Blues*," 306–7. This underscore/nondiegetic music was recorded at Reeves Sound Studios in New York May 1 to 3, 1961. However, the composing and recording history of *Paris Blues* is quite complicated and information is incomplete. Some of the music was recorded preproduction in a Hollywood studio in the spring of 1960,

and several months later in November at Barclay Studios in Paris (under the direction of Strayhorn). A significant bulk of the prerecordings were for diegetic music—the music mimed onscreen by the actors. As Gabbard notes, these recordings were used by Newman and Poitier in preparing their roles so that they could "convincingly mime their instruments" (302).

15. Gabbard, "*Paris Blues,*" 306. Gabbard offers other compelling scenarios for interpreting the concluding music.

16. John Tynan, "Paris Blues," *DownBeat*, November 23, 1961, 16.

17. The manuscript scores for *Paris Blues* are held in the Smithsonian's Duke Ellington Collection. A controversy over the film music's authorship followed Tynan's review, and some six months later the editors of *DownBeat* published a retraction "clarifying" that, with the exception of Strayhorn's "'A' Train," Ellington was the sole creator of all the music and orchestration. *DownBeat*, May 24, 1962; Klaus Stratemann, *Duke Ellington Day by Day and Film by Film* (Copenhagen: JazzMedia, 1992), 435.

18. Tynan, "Paris Blues," 16.

19. Gabbard, "*Paris Blues,*" 306.

20. Gabbard, "*Paris Blues,*" 304. Gabbard also importantly cites Strayhorn's previous experience scoring for nontraditional jazz instruments, including oboe, for the 1946 production of *Beggar's Holiday* (303).

21. Brian Priestly, "Billy Strayhorn: Out of the Shadows" (Storyville Records, 2013), 8.

22. Hajdu, *Lush Life*, 212.

23. This point further differentiates the solo LP from the recording sessions for *Paris Blues* which, for the most part, followed traditional "live take" studio practices.

24. Hajdu, *Lush Life*, 211.

25. Aaron Bridgers, Oral History Interview with Patricia Willard, Paris 1989, Ruth Ellington Collection, Smithsonian. It is possible that Elek Bacsik played the violin part (or with overdubbing, both parts) in the string arrangements.

26. Les Double Six are now best known in connection with the Paris-based vocal jazz group the Swingle Singers: Ward Swingle and several other members of Les Double Six formed the Swingle Singers in 1962.

27. As a composer, François wrote a piano concerto (1950), scored music for a 1963 French film called *Ballade pour un voyou*, and composed music for jazz singer Peggy Lee.

28. *Billboard*, October 31, 1960, 46.

29. Aaron Bridgers, quoted in François, *Samson François*, 109–10, author's translation. The original reads:

> Au bout de dix minutes, nous discutions comme deux amis de longue date. Nous découvrîmes que nous partagions beaucoup d'intérêts en commun, bien que je fus un pianiste de bar et lui, en pianiste de musique classique. Par exemple, notre passion pour

Ravel, Chopin, Liszt et Duke Ellington! Tandis que nous évoquions Duke Ellington, il me dit qu'il avait une admiration particuliére pour les compositions de Billy Strayhorn, qui était un de ses proches collaborateurs. Je lui dis que Strayhorn était mon meilleur ami, que nous partagions un appartement á New York et que sa rencontre m'avait beaucoup motivé á devenir pianiste de jazz. Peu aprés cette premiére rencontre, de passage á New York, je découvris que Strayhorn venait d'acheter une série de disques de Samson François. Il me demanda si je le connaissais et quand je lui répondis "oui" et lui racontai notre rencontre cela le mit en joie. Un ou deux and plus tar, á Paris . . . Strayhorn vine un soir m'ecouter au Club Mars quand je vis entrer Samson François, je m'exclamai: "Enfin, j'ai le privilége de vous présenter l'un á l'autre!" Leur sympathie mutuelle fut immédiate et ils s'engagèrent bientôt dans une conversation intellectuelle sur la musique, échangeant leurs points de vue sur Bartok, etc. qui, je dois dire, me passa complétement au-dessus de la tete.

30. Aaron Bridgers, interview with Patricia Willard, *Duke Ellington Oral History Tapes*, four audio cassettes (Box 26), Smithsonian Institution, Archives Center, National Museum of American History, Washington, DC.

31. Walter van de Leur, *Something to Live For: The Music of Billy Strayhorn* (Oxford: Oxford University Press, 2002), 58. The "Chopin side" is especially audible in Strayhorn's early 1934 composition, "Valse," one of many works, including *Portrait of a Silk Thread*, discovered posthumously in a private collection that Strayhorn stored in a filing cabinet in his apartment, kept under lock and key. See, for example, A. Alyce Claerbaut and David Schlesinger, eds., *Strayhorn: An Illustrated Life* (Chicago: Agate Bolden, 2015), 65.

32. Hajdu, *Lush Life*, 66. In a different but not unrelated context, the Black gay poet, novelist, and literary critic Melvin Dixon recalled of his Francophile-oriented college education in the early 1970s: "most men who studied French were gay; so there was a connection there, and my best friends were Francophiles, and I guess, it was a way to establish one's sophistication and sissyhood and all that." Jerome de Romanet, "A Conversation with Melvin Dixon," *Callaloo* 23, no. 1 (2000): 84–109.

33. Hajdu, *Lush Life*, 236–40.

34. John S. Wilson, *New York Times*, June 7, 1965.

35. Kevin Whitehead, "Strayhorn the Pianist," in *Blue Light: The Journal of the Duke Ellington Society UK* 22, no. 3 (Autumn 2015): 18–19.

36. Whitehead, "Strayhorn the Pianist," 19. To be fair, Whitehead also includes the more appreciative—and less comparison-driven—comments of the great Marian McPartland. In her view, while Strayhorn could, when the occasion demanded it, "pound out the ballsy chords," he was essentially "a romantic in the true sense, really soulful" (ibid).

37. Hajdu, *Lush Life*, 212.

38. Hajdu, *Lush Life*, 212.

39. According to Hajdu's biography, during Strayhorn's early New York years, these informal performance settings also included an uptown gay-friendly piano bar, Luckey's Rendezvous, located at St. Nicholas Avenue and 149th Street. The filmmaker and photographer Sam Shaw reported hearing Strayhorn perform at the bar on multiple occasions, recalling that it was "one place uptown where nobody looked twice or cared about a couple of gay guys coming in. Billy and his friends could have themselves a good time out in public. And he started to get quite a following there for his piano playing" (Hajdu, *Lush Life*, 72).

40. Hajdu, *Lush Life*, 212.

41. The decision to title these sessions "The Billy Strayhorn Trio" arose as a tactic to avoid coming into conflict with Ellington's contract with Columbia Records. A decade later, Ellington cut two additional jazz trio LPs: the first one, *Piano in the Foreground*, was recorded in March 1961, two months after *The Peaceful Side* sessions; the second, *Money Jungle*, with Charles Mingus and Max Roach, was released in 1963. Like *The Peaceful Side*, the Ellington-Mingus-Roach sessions for *Money Jungle* were produced by Alan Douglas for the United Artists label (I discuss the marketing of this recording in the final section of this chapter). For a wide-ranging discussion of cultural and musical contexts in the marketing of Ellington LPs during this period see, for example, Gabriel Solis, "Duke Ellington in the LP Era," in *Duke Ellington Studies*, ed. John Howland (New York: Cambridge University Press), 197–223.

42. A pioneering touchstone for a project like *The Peaceful Side* is Mary Lou Williams's extraordinary 1945 recording of her *Zodiac Suite*, which also features duet arrangements for piano and bass.

43. Claerbaut and Schlesinger, eds., *Strayhorn: An Illustrated Life*, 74–75.

44. In 1949, the "Race Records" category was renamed R&B (Rhythm and Blues). The Delta Rhythm Boys performed a pops "foxtrot" version of the song in 1946 with Charlie Barnet and his Orchestra, also for Decca. As is well known, Lee Gaines penned a lyric in 1941 for "'A' Train," not to be confused with the much more popular 1944 lyric composed by a young Joya Sherrill for the occasion of her audition for the Ellington band. For more on the changing nomenclature of popularity charts for Black popular music during the mid-1940s, including a discussion of recordings by the Ellington Band that "crossed over" to the mainstream chart and of cover versions of Ellington recordings by white artists, see David Brackett, *Categorizing Sound: Genre and Twentieth-Century Popular Music* (Oakland: University of California Press, 2016), 175–81.

45. To clarify this point: the discographic information for the original 1945 recording is vague with respect to the arranger—the sessions on which the single was recorded credit arrangements to both Kenton and his arranger Rugolo, who was then working for Kenton. As Rugolo is fully credited for this second version/arrangement (which features the added introductory sung vocal), it is almost certain that he scored the chart used in the 1945

recording. Another context for Strayhorn's use of the added sung introduction is that by the early 1960s it had become incorporated into the tune's life as a "songbook" standard.

46. Hajdu, *Lush Life*, 110–11. For a musical analysis of the Rugolo arrangement as an exemplar of "luxe pop" aesthetics, see John Howland, *Hearing Luxe Pop* (Berkeley: University of California Press, 2021), 122–23. Notably, Rugolo also arranged "Day Dream" for Christy in 1956 for the Capitol LP *The Misty Miss Christy*.

47. Perrin and company made another recording for Alan Douglas/United Artists under the name Paris Blue Notes—a 1962 single of the folk-revival tune popularized by the Brothers Four, "Greenfields," arranged (and conducted) for orchestra and vocalese by the film music composer and producer Luchi de Jesus. For an extended discussion of Perrin's collaborative work on these transnational projects, see Benjamin Givan, "Dizzy à la Mimi: Jazz, Text, and Translation," in *Journal for the Society of American Music* 11, no. 2 (2017): 121–54. A history of French vocalese groups is given in Éric Fardet, "Les groups vocaux français de jazz," *Itamar, revista de investigación musical: territorios para el arte* 3 (2010): 69–77; see also, Fardet, *Vocal jazz groups, scat & vocalese* (Anatole France: Éditions Connaissances et Savoirs, 2018).

48. Van de Leur, *Something to Live For*, 83, 164. For example, in writing about the adventuresome "cool jazz" arrangements scored for big bands led by Boyd Raeburn and Claude Thornhill in the late 1940s, van de Leur notes it was likely that some of these arrangers "closely studied the Strayhorn arrangements that were part of the regular broadcasts of the Ellington orchestra (83)."

49. "Passion Flower" is arguably the most iconic of the signature ballads, and remained a staple in the Ellington book throughout Hodges's tenure with the band.

50. However, lyrics penned by the pianist, conductor, and arranger Milton Raskin were added to "Passion Flower" during this period, most likely in conjunction with Ella Fitzgerald's recording of a vocal version for the Verve LP *Ella Fitzgerald and Duke Ellington & His Orchestra* (reissued as *Ella at Duke's Place*). According to van de Leur the arrangement used for this session (October 18–20, 1965) repurposed the chart for the *Blue Rose* instrumental version from 1956. A new copyright was registered in the names of Strayhorn and Raskin in 1965.

51. Hajdu, *Lush Life*, 213.

52. For an analysis of the influence of mood music on jazz recording during this period, specifically as this intersection shaped the critical reception of Bill Evans, see Paul Allen Anderson, "'My Foolish Heart': Bill Evans and the Public Life of Feelings," *Jazz Perspectives* 7, no. 3 (2013): 205–49, especially 233–34. As Anderson notes, jazz critics writing for *DownBeat*, *Metronome*, and other publications spilled considerable ink "complaining" about what they saw as the corrupting commercial effects of the mood music trend on jazz artistic authenticity. See also Albin I. Zak III, *I Don't Sound Like Nobody: Remaking Music in 1950s America* (Ann Arbor: University of Michigan Press, 2010), 68–70.

53. Produced by Norman Granz (Norgran label), *Ben Webster with Strings* followed the blueprint set by *Charlie Parker with Strings* (1949–50), widely considered the most significant instrumental soloist-led prototype for ballad-centric jazz with strings recording. Importantly, the other charts for *Ben Webster with Strings* were scored by Strayhorn's friend and fellow gay jazz arranger, Ralph Burns. Another essential LP in this category is *Clifford Brown with Strings* (1955). Although beyond the scope of this chapter to fully address, "with strings" was the norm, rather than the exception, for prestige vocal jazz/pop recordings during this period. Among the abundant jazz-pop vocal recordings in this category: Ella Fitzgerald and Frank Sinatra albums with name arrangers such as Nelson Riddle, Buddy Bregman, Paul Weston (e.g., with Riddle, *Ella Fitzgerald Sings the George and Ira Gershwin Song Book* [1959], and *In the Wee Small Hours* [1955], respectively); Billie Holiday, *Lady in Satin* (1958, Claus Ogerman, arranger); Dinah Washington, *What a Diff'rence a Day Makes!* (1959, Belford Hendricks, arranger); and Sarah Vaughan's collaboration with Quincy Jones, *Vaughn and Violins* (released in 1959). Although the latter recording did not have the kind of critical and popular impact of the other LPs cited, I include it here because the 1958 sessions with Vaughan and Jones's arrangements took place in Paris at the same recording studio—Barclay Studios—as the *The Peaceful Side*, with Jones conducting a fifty-five-piece orchestra. For a compelling and wide-ranging history of the jazz-with-strings trend of the 1940s and 1950s in relation to the symphonic jazz tradition, and "glorified pop" and "lush pop" (including mood music) repertoires, see John Howland, "Jazz with Strings: Between Jazz and the Great American Songbook," in *Jazz/Not Jazz* (Berkeley: University of California Press, 2012), 111–14.

54. Strayhorn and Shirley were good friends, having been introduced through their mutual friend and colleague Luther Henderson. Dr. Shirley, now famous as the musician-subject of the 2018 film *Green Book* (played by Mahershala Ali), was an important interlocutor for *Lush Life* (Hajdu conducted several extended interviews with him). (See, Hajdu, "Dr. Funky Butt and Me: My Friendship with the Real Donald Shirley," *New York Times*, March 10, 2019, https://www.nytimes.com/2019/03/10/movies/don-shirley-david-hajdu-green-book.html.)

55. Indeed, *Polynesian Fantasy* became part of the canon of the 1990s–2000s exotica/mood music revival, rebranded as "lounge music" (or "space age bachelor pad music"). The high soprano wordless voices on "Moon Mist" were delivered by veteran studio singers Marni Nixon and Loulie Jean Norman (Norman is perhaps most remembered for her coloratura futuristic wordless singing on the vocal version of the original *Star Trek* theme song). For studies of midcentury mood music/exotica and its various "after-lives" see, for example, Francesco Adinolfi, *Mondo Exotica: Sounds, Visions, Obsessions of the Cocktail Generation* (Durham, NC: Duke University Press, 2008); Rebecca Leydon, "Utopias of the Tropics: The Exotic Music of Les Baxter and Yma Sumac," in *Widening the Horizon: Exoticism in Post-War Popular Music*, ed. Philip Hayward (Sydney: John Libbey, 1999),

45–71; Phil Ford, "Taboo: Time and Belief in Exotica," *Representations* 103, no. 1 (2008): 107–35; Shuhei Hosokawa, "Martin Denny and the Development of Musical Exotica," in Hayward, ed., *Widening the Horizon*, 72–93; David Toop, *Exotica: Fabricated Soundscapes in a Real World* (London: Serpent's Tail, 1999); and Joseph Lanza, *Elevator Music: A Surreal History of Muzak, Easy-Listening, and Other Moodsong* (New York: Picador, 1994; Ann Arbor: University of Michigan Press, 2004).

56. Fred Moten, *In the Break: The Aesthetics of the Black Radical Tradition* (Minneapolis: University of Minnesota Press, 2003), 25–42.

57. Moten, *In the Break*, 31.

58. Moten, *In the Break*, 25. This double move to Ellington via Mingus initiates the first chapter of Moten's book, "The Sentimental Avant-Garde," the first section of which takes the form of an extravagant theoretical improvisation on "the politics of the erotic and the erotics of sound in Ellington's music" (via Freud's theory of drives in *An Outline of Psycho-Analysis*) (ibid., 25–31).

59. On the Strayhorn-Mingus connection, according to Andrew Homzy, Strayhorn gifted a novel arrangement of "A Flower Is a Lovesome Thing," scored for alto sax, two trumpets, trombone, French horn, tuba, and rhythm section, to Mingus sometime in the mid-1960s. In going through Mingus's papers, Homzy discovered the original handwritten manuscript in its original envelope, marked "Pour monsieur Charles Mingus from Swee' Pea Strayhorn." (Given that the instrumentation in Strayhorn's chart matches that of ensembles Mingus worked with in 1965, Homzy dates the arrangement to that year). As documented in several interviews, Strayhorn held Mingus in the highest esteem. During a 1964 interview with an Italian jazz magazine, Strayhorn said of Mingus: "I adore him. I always admired Charlie, because he has extraordinary sensibility and courage. His sensibility is immediately recognizable in his music. And he demonstrated this by taming the audience's taste without worrying about their initial violent reactions. Mingus is both sincere and honest. He's a fantastic musician. The expression of freedom: this is the main characteristic of his music" (Strayhorn, quoted in "The Duke's Shadow," *Musica Jazz* [May 1964]).

60. Rounding out the trio—"the instrument as small band"—is French avant-garde icon Antonin Artaud. In relation to Delaney, Moten sees their encounter as "one of space-time separated coincidence and migrant imagination, channels of natal prematurity as well as black rebirth, modernism as intranational as well as international relocation, and the politico-aesthetics of a surplus of content irreducible to identity in and/or for itself, but held, rather, in identity's relation to general upheaval" (Moten, *In the Break*, 35).

61. Moten, *In the Break*, 35.

62. Moten, *In the Break*, 38.

63. Curiously, but no doubt intentionally, Moten's citing of the lyric cuts the final sixth line, "from jazz and cocktails" (Moten, *In the Break*, 39).

64. Moten, *In the Break*, 38. Moten further analogizes Strayhorn's "lyrical surplus" to Delaney's use of impasto in his paintings and Artaud's moments of poetic "glossolalia" (ibid., 38–39).

65. "Billy Strayhorn's Arranging Hints," *Music and Rhythm* 2, no. 17 (May 1942): 37.

66. Notably, Pete Rugolo also pulls out the word-painting device as a backing for this line in his 1949 vocal arrangement of "Lush Life" for Nat "King" Cole. However, the cartoonish literalness of his treatment, as well as to some extent the luxe pop sound of his arrangement overall (which features strings, bongos, flute, and harp) differentiates it from Strayhorn's intimate and much more integrated and creatively expansive concept and treatment.

67. On genre, style, and identity see Brackett, *Categorizing Sound*.

68. Zak, *I Don't Sound Like Nobody*, 50, 62.

69. Another connection worth noting here is that "Lush Life" and "A Flower Is a Lovesome Thing" are scored in their original keys of D♭ (as is "Chelsea Bridge"), a favorite ballad/mood piece key for Strayhorn.

70. Strayhorn interview with the Duke Ellington Society, New York chapter meeting, March 1962. The context for Strayhorn's statement concerns a 1949 invitation to arrange "Lush Life" for the Norman Granz-produced LP *Jazz Scene*. As Strayhorn narrates the story in the 1962 interview, he declined initially to participate in Granz's project as he "didn't like the idea" of what seemed to him a formless "collection of things." After prodding from Granz, however, he proposed arranging "Lush Life" for string quartet (which, he specified, would act as a contrast to the other works, which were scored for large orchestra), but later changed his mind, explaining, "There's only one way to do 'Lush Life,' and that's with piano."

71. On this point, as the *The Peaceful Side* was recorded at Barclay Studios with European collaborators, it also exemplified the transatlantic networks of postwar independent white-owned record labels. For an excellent history of French jazz labels during this period, see Celeste Day Moore, "Race in Translation: Producing, Performing, and Selling African American Music in Greater France, 1944–74," (PhD diss., University of Chicago, 2014).

72. Nicole Rustin-Paschal, *The Kind of Man I Am: Jazzmasculinity and the World of Charles Mingus Jr.* (Middletown, CT: Wesleyan University Press, 2017), 99. I'm grateful to Sherrie Tucker for the concept of "extractive white jazz love" (Tucker, "How Do We Sound? How Do We Listen?" [presentation, *Return to the Center: Black Women, Jazz, and Jazz Education*, Berklee Institute of Jazz and Gender Justice, Boston, MA, June 10, 2021].)

73. Rustin-Paschal, *The Kind of Man I Am*, 95–104; John Gennari, *Blowin' Hot and Cool: Jazz and Its Critics* (Chicago: University of Chicago Press, 2006); see also Herman Gray, *Producing Jazz: The Experience of an Independent Record Company* (Philadelphia: Temple University Press, 1988).

74. Rustin-Paschal, *The Kind of Man I Am*, 91.

75. *DownBeat*, March 28, 1963, 29.

76. If some of these mistakes were to be blamed on United Artists' relative inexperience in the music business, one wonders why the neglect didn't happen in other UA releases at the time such as *Money Jungle*. Strayhorn received 50 percent of the royalties. Among Strayhorn's financial records held in the BSC is a royalty statement from United Artists dated February 28, 1963, showing a balance paid to Strayhorn of $377.46 (worth about $3,320 in 2021, adjusted for inflation).

77. Hajdu, *Lush Life*, 214.

78. Hajdu, *Lush Life*, 214.

79. John S. Wilson, "Billy Strayhorn: The Peaceful Side—United Artists 15010," *DownBeat* March 3, 1963.

80. Strayhorn, interview with the Duke Ellington Society, New York chapter, March 1962.

81. Shane Vogel, *The Scene of the Harlem Cabaret: Race, Sexuality, Performance* (Chicago: University of Chicago Press, 2009), 129–30.

82. Hajdu, *Lush Life*, 210–11.

83. Hajdu, *Lush Life*, 212.

EPILOGUE *Ever Up and Onward: Searching for Strayhorn in the Twenty-First Century*

1. Brian Priestley, liner notes for *Billy Strayhorn: Out of the Shadows*, Storyville, 2013, CD, 5.

2. Bill Cross, "Ellington & Strayhorn, Inc.," *DownBeat*, June 7, 1962, 22–23, 40; Billy Strayhorn, Talk for the Duke Ellington Jazz Society (New York, March 1962), Ruth Ellington Collection, Smithsonian Institution, Archives Center, National Museum of American History, Washington, DC, Box 18, Series 11, Item 92.1-92.3.

3. Harvey G. Cohen, *Duke Ellington's America* (Chicago: University of Chicago Press, 2010), 308.

4. Monica Hairston O'Connell and Sherrie Tucker, "Not One to Toot Her Own Horn(?): Melba Liston's Oral Histories and Classroom Presentations," *Black Music Research Journal* 34, no. 1 (Spring 2014): 123–24. My approach to listening for aurality and voice with and against written transcripts is indebted to Hairston O'Connell and Tucker's analyses of Melba Liston's oral history.

5. The performative registers of Ellington and Strayhorn's interactions in this interview echo (and thus are usefully listened to alongside) their arch comments captured in a January 6, 1962, interview with Paul Werth in Los Angeles (Studios KBCA), the transcript of which serves as the opening to the preface for Hajdu's biography (David Hajdu, *Lush Life: A Biography of Billy Strayhorn* [New York: North Point Press, 1997], ix–x).

6. Evans's *Daydream* project follows up on his 2004 feature film *Brother to Brother*. This award-winning film excavates the Black gay history and legacy of the Harlem Renaissance through the perspectives of, and encounters between, an elderly, Black queer writer (modelled on Bruce Richard Nugent) and a young Black queer university student. For a wider discussion and analysis of Evans's film see Kara Keeling, *Queer Times, Black Future* (New York: New York University Press, 2019), 81–96.

7. Some of the material for this scene draws on Hajdu's account of the painful encounter, discussed in chapter 2, between Honi Coles and Strayhorn that took place in 1957 at New York's Hickory House (see Hajdu, *Lush Life*, 171–72).

8. Rodney Evans, "Synopsis," *Day Dream Project Information*, 2010, 2. Evans's *Day Dream* puts Strayhorn's life story in counterpoint to that of the New Orleans cornetist Buddy Bolden, the legendary "forefather" of jazz. As Evans writes, the film explores "the ways that alienation, improvisation, and freedom were integral to the lives of these iconoclastic men and the ways that these themes were central motifs within the music they created." Like *Brother to Brother*, then, *Day Dream* moves contrapuntally between temporalities: the film "follows jazz composer Billy Strayhorn on a quest for musical inspiration as he travels to New Orleans to investigate the life of Buddy Bolden, the forefather of modern jazz who spent the last twenty-four years of his life in a mental institution" (Rodney Evans, "2023 DAYDREAM," June 1, 2022, https://www.rodneyevansfilm.com/feature-films).

9. David Roussève "Halfway to Dawn," June 24, 2022, https://www.davidrousseve.com/halfwaytodawn. Roussève's interest in Strayhorn grew out of his work on adapting Strayhorn and Luther Henderson's unrealized musical *Rose-Colored Glasses*: "I fell in love with Billy Strayhorn—his life and his music . . . It was about 2002 that *Rose-Colored Glasses* came to an end and I said, 'I'm going to come back to Billy Strayhorn one day, but just do a totally different thing on my own terms.'" David Roussève, quoted in "A Life Lived 'Halfway to Dawn': David Roussève Celebrates Jazz Legend Billy Strayhorn," Lara J. Altunian, *LA Dance Chronicle*, October 4, 2018, accessed on December 3, 2022, https://www.ladancechronicle.com/a-life-lived-halfway-to-dawn-david-rousseve-celebrates-jazz-legend-billy-strayhorn/.

BIBLIOGRAPHY

ARCHIVAL COLLECTIONS

Duke Ellington Collection, Smithsonian Institution, Archives Center, National Museum of American History, Washington, DC.

Ruth Ellington Collection of Duke Ellington Materials, Smithsonian Institution, Archives Center, National Museum of American History, Washington, DC.

Institute of Jazz Studies, Rutgers University Libraries, New Brunswick, NJ.

John Latouche Papers, 1930–1960. Columbia University Libraries Archival Collections, New York, NY.

Billy Strayhorn Collection, ML31.S76, Library of Congress, Washington, DC.

BOOKS, ARTICLES, DISSERTATIONS, AND ESSAYS

Adinolfi, Francesco. *Mondo exotica: Sounds, Visions, Obsessions of the Cocktail Generation*. Durham, NC: Duke University Press, 2008.

Ake, David. *Jazz Cultures*. Berkeley: University of California Press, 2002.

———, Charles Hiroshi Garrett, and Daniel Goldmark, eds. *Jazz/Not Jazz: The Music and Its Boundaries*. Berkeley: University of California Press, 2012.

Anderson, Paul Allen. "'My Foolish Heart': Bill Evans and the Public Life of Feelings." *Jazz Perspectives* 7, no. 3 (2013): 205–49.

Atkinson, Brooks. "Two Short Plays." *New York Times*, November 4, 1953.

Baldwin, Kate. *Beyond the Color Line and the Iron Curtain: Reading Encounters Between Black and Red, 1922–1963*. Durham, NC: Duke University Press, 2002.

Baraka, Amiri. *Blues People: Negro Music in White America*. New York: W. Morrow, 1963.

Barg, Lisa. "Black Voices/White Sounds: Race and Representation in Virgil Thomson's *Four Saints in Three Acts*." *American Music* 18, no. 2 (2000): 121–61.

———. "Taking Care of Music: Gender, Arranging, and Collaboration in the Weston-Liston Partnership." *Black Music Research Journal* 34, no. 1 (2014): 97–119.

Berger, Edward, David Chevan, and Benny Carter. *Bassically Speaking: An Oral History of George Duvivier*. Newark, NJ: Institute of Jazz Studies, Rutgers, The State University of New Jersey, 1993.

Berkman, Franya J. *Monument Eternal: The Music of Alice Coltrane*. Middletown, CT: Wesleyan University Press, 2010.

Bernard, Emily. *Carl Van Vechten and the Harlem Renaissance*. New Haven, CT: Yale University Press, 2012.

Best, Stephen. *None Like Us: Blackness, Belonging, Aesthetic Life*. Durham, NC: Duke University Press, 2018.

Blais-Tremblay, Vanessa. "Jazz, Gender, Historiography: A Case Study of the 'Golden Age' of Jazz in Montreal (1925–1955)." PhD diss., McGill University, 2018.

Blais-Tremblay, Vanessa. "'Where You Are Accepted, You Blossom': Toward Care Ethics in Jazz Historiography." *Jazz & Culture* 2 (2019): 59–83.

Blumenfeld, Larry. "Review: Lena Horne, *We'll Be Together Again*." *Jazziz* 13, no. 9 (September 1996): 55–56.

Bogle, Donald. *Bright Boulevards, Bold Dreams: The Story of Black Hollywood*. New York: Random House, 2005.

———. *Toms, Coons, Mulattoes, Mammies, and Bucks: An Interpretive History of Blacks in American Films*. New York: Continuum International Publishing Group, 2001.

Boone, Joseph Allen. *Libidinal Currents: Sexuality and the Shaping of Modernism*. Chicago: University of Chicago Press, 1998.

———. "Vacation Cruises; or, The Homoerotics of Orientalism." *PMLA* 110, no. 1 (January 1995): 89–107.

Borden, Anne. "Heroic 'Hussies' and 'Brilliant Queers': Genderracial Resistance in the Works of Langston Hughes." *African American Review* 28 (1994): 333–45.

Born, Georgina. "Music and the Social." In *The Cultural Study of Music: A Critical Introduction*, ed. Martin Clayton, Trevor Herbert, and Richard Middleton, 261–74. New York and London: Routledge, 2012.

———, Eric Lewis, and Will Straw, eds. *Improvisation and Social Aesthetics*. Durham, NC: Duke University Press, 2017.

Brackett, David. *Categorizing Sound: Genre and Twentieth-Century Popular Music*. Oakland: University of California Press, 2016.

———. *Interpreting Popular Music*. Berkeley: University of California Press, 2000.

———. "Jazz at the Crossroads of Art and Popular Music Discourses in the 1960s." In *The Routledge Companion to New Jazz Studies*, ed. Nicholas Gebhardt, Nichole Rustin, and Tony Whyton, 347–56. New York: Routledge, 2019.

Braggs, Rashida K. *Jazz Diasporas: Race, Music, and Migration in Post-World War II Paris*. Berkeley: University of California Press, 2016.

Brett, Philip. "Queer Musical Orientalism." *Echo: A Music-Centered Journal* 9, no. 1 (Fall 2009). http://www.echo.ucla.edu/article-queer-musical-orientalism-by-philip-brett/.

Brooks, Daphne A. *Liner Notes for the Revolution: The Intellectual Life of Black Feminist Sound.* Cambridge, MA: Harvard University Press, 2021.

Brown, Jayna Jennifer. *Babylon Girls: Black Women Performers and the Making of the Modern.* Durham, NC: Duke University Press, 2008.

Brown, Malcolm Hamrick. "Tchaikovsky and His Music in Anglo-American Criticism, 1890–1950s." In *Queer Episodes in Music and Modern Identity*, ed. Sophie Fuller and Lloyd Whitesell, 134–49. Urbana and Chicago: University of Illinois Press, 2002.

Burford, Mark. "Sam Cooke as Pop Album Artist—A Reinvention in Three Songs." *Journal of the American Musicological Society* 65, no. 1 (2012): 113–78.

Burke, Patrick. "Oasis of Swing: The Onyx Club, Jazz, and White Masculinity in the Early 1930s." *American Music* 24, no. 3 (2006): 320–46.

Burt, Richard. "No Holes Bard: Homonormativity and the Gay and Lesbian Romance with *Romeo and Juliet*." In *Shakespeare without Class: Misappropriations of Cultural Capital*, ed. Donald Hendrick and Bryan Reynolds, 153–88. New York: Palgrave Macmillan, 2000.

Calvocoressi, M. D. "M. Ravel Discusses His Own Work: The Boléro Explained." In *A Ravel Reader: Correspondence, Articles, Interviews*, ed. Arbie Orenstein, 477–78. New York: Columbia University Press, 1990.

Campfield, Marion B. "Mostly about Women." *Chicago Defender*, February 19, 1955.

Carby, Hazel. *Race Men.* Cambridge, MA: Harvard University Press, 1998.

Carmody, Jim. "Lorca's *The Love of Don Perlimplín for Belisa in the Garden*: The Perspectives Are Deliciously Wrong." In *Federico García Lorca: Impossible Theater: Five Plays and Thirteen Poems*, trans. Caridad Svich. Hanover, NH: Smith and Kraus, 2000.

Celenza, Anna. "Duke Ellington, Billy Strayhorn and the Adventures of *Peer Gynt* in America." *Music & Politics* 2, no. 5 (Summer 2011). http://dx.doi.org/10.3998/mp.9460447.0005.205.

Chambers, Jack. *Sweet Thunder: Duke Ellington's Music in Nine Themes.* Milestones Music & Art, 2019.

Chauncey, George. *Gay New York: Gender, Urban Culture, and the Makings of the Gay World, 1890–1940.* New York: Basic Books, 1994.

Claerbaut, A. Alyce, and David Schlesinger, eds. *Strayhorn: An Illustrated Life.* Chicago: Agate Bolden, 2015.

Clooney, Rosemary, and Joan Barthel. *Girl Singer: An Autobiography.* New York: Broadway Books, 1999.

Clum, John M. *Still Acting Gay: Male Homosexuality in Modern Drama.* London: Palgrave MacMillan, 2000.

Cohen, Harvey G. *Duke Ellington's America.* Chicago: University of Chicago Press, 2010.

Collier, James Lincoln. *Duke Ellington*. New York: Oxford University Press, 1987.

Conerly, Gregory. "Swishing and Swaggering: Homosexuality in Black Magazines during the 1950s." In *The Greatest Taboo: Homosexuality in Black Communities*, ed. Delroy Constantine-Simms, 384–94. Los Angeles: Alyson, 2001.

Cooke, Mervyn. "Jazz Among the Classics, and the Case of Duke Ellington." In *The Cambridge Companion to Jazz*, ed. Mervyn Cooke and David Horn, 153–74. Cambridge: Cambridge University Press, 2002.

Corber, Robert J. *Homosexuality in Cold War America: Resistance and the Crisis of Masculinity*. Durham, NC: Duke University Press, 1997.

Corbman, Rachel. "'Next Time, the Fire in Giovanni's Room': The Critical Reception of James Baldwin's Second Novel in the Black Press." *Zeteo: Journal of Interdisciplinary Writing* (Spring 2012): 1–18.

Croft, Clare, ed. *Queer Dance: Meanings and Makings*. New York: Oxford University Press, 2017.

Cross, Bill. "Ellington & Strayhorn, Inc." *DownBeat*, June 7, 1962.

Cvetkovich, Ann. *An Archive of Feelings: Trauma, Sexuality, and Lesbian Public Cultures*. Durham, NC: Duke University Press, 2003.

Damon, Maria. "Triangulated Desire and Tactical Silences in the Beat Hipscape: Bob Kaufman and Others." *College Literature* 27, no. 1 (Winter 2000): 139–57.

Dance, Stanley. *The World of Duke Ellington*. New York: Da Capo Press, 1970.

Davis, Angela Y. *Blues Legacies and Black Feminism: Gertrude 'Ma' Rainey, Bessie Smith, and Billie Holiday*. New York: Vintage, 1998.

Delgado, Maria M. *Federico García Lorca*. London: Routledge, 2008.

D'Emilio, John. *Sexual Politics, Sexual Communities: The Making of a Homosexual Minority in the United States, 1940–1970*. 2nd ed. Chicago: University of Chicago Press, 1998.

de Romanet, Jerome. "A Conversation with Melvin Dixon." *Callaloo* 23, no. 1 (2000): 84–109.

DeVeaux, Scott. "Bebop and the Recording Industry: The 1942 AFM Recording Ban Reconsidered." *Journal of the American Musicological Society* 41, no. 1 (Spring 1988): 126–65.

———. "Constructing the Jazz Tradition: Jazz Historiography." *Black American Literature Forum* 25, no. 3 (Autumn 1991): 525–60.

Dickel, Simon. *Black/Gay: The Harlem Renaissance, the Protest Era, and Constructions of Black Gay Identity in the 1980s and 90s*. East Lansing: Michigan State University Press, 2011.

Dollimore, Jonathan. *Sexual Dissidence: Augustine to Wilde, Freud to Foucault*. Oxford: Oxford University Press, 1991.

DuCille, Ann. "The Shirley Temple of My Familiar." *Transition* 73 (1997): 10–32.

Dyer, Geoff. *But Beautiful: A Book About Jazz*. New York: Farrar, Straus and Giroux, 1996.

Dyer, Richard. *The Culture of Queers*. London; New York: Routledge, 2002.

———. *In the Space of a Song: The Uses of Song in Film*. New York: Routledge, 2012.

———. *Only Entertainment*. 2nd ed., New York: Routledge, 2005.

———. *Pastiche*. London; New York: Routledge, 2007.

Eagan, Daniel. *America's Film Legacy: The Authoritative Guide to the Landmark Movies in the National Registry*. New York: Continuum Books, 2010.

Edwards, Brent Hayes. "The Literary Ellington." In *Uptown Conversation: The New Jazz Studies*, ed. Robert O'Meally, Brent Hayes Edwards, and Farah Jasmine Griffin, 326–56. New York: Columbia University Press, 2004.

———. "The Taste of the Archive." *Callaloo* 35, no. 4 (2012): 944–72.

Edwards, Gwynne. "Theatre Workshop's Translations of Three Spanish Plays." *New Theatre Quarterly* 25, no. 1 (2009): 52–62.

Ellington, Duke. *Music Is My Mistress*. 2nd ed., New York: Da Capo Press, 1976.

Ellison, Ralph, and Robert G. O'Meally. *Living with Music: Ralph Ellison's Jazz Writings*. New York: Modern Library, 2001.

Evans, Rodney. "2022 Daydream." Rodney Evans, writer/director/producer. Accessed June 1, 2022. https://www.rodneyevansfilm.com/feature-films.

Fardet, Éric. "Les groupes vocaux français de jazz." *Itamar, revista de investigación musical: territorios para el arte* 3 (2010): 69–77.

———. *Vocal jazz groups, scat & vocalese: l'école française de vocalese*. Saint-Denis, France: Éditions Connaissances et Savoirs, 2018.

Feather, Leonard. "Blindfold Test: Shorty Rogers." *DownBeat*, April 27, 1961.

———. "The Blindfold Test: Swee'Pea Stays on the Scene." *DownBeat*, September 7, 1951.

Ferguson, Roderick A. *Aberrations in Black: Toward a Queer of Color Critique*. Minneapolis: University of Minnesota Press, 2004.

Field, Douglas. *All Those Strangers: The Art and Lives of James Baldwin*. New York: Oxford University Press, 2015.

Fisher, Jennifer. "'Arabian Coffee' in the Land of Sweets." *Dance Research Journal* 35–36 (Winter 2003–Summer 2004): 146–63.

———. *Nutcracker Nation: How an Old World Ballet Became a Christmas Tradition in the New World*. New Haven, CT; London: Yale University Press, 2003.

Flory, Andrew. "The Ballads of Marvin Gaye." *Journal of the American Musicological Society* 72, no. 2 (2019): 313–61.

Ford, Phil. "Taboo: Time and Belief in Exotica." *Representations* 103, no. 1 (2008): 107–35.

Franceschina, John. *Duke Ellington's Music for the Theatre*. London: McFarland & Company, 1988.

François, Maximilien Samson. *Samson François, Histoires de . . . Mille Vies, 1924–1970*. Paris: Bleu nuit éditeur, 2002.

Freeman, Don. "'Bronze Buckaroo' Is Still Singing at Age 82." *San Diego Union-Tribune*, December 13, 1993.

Freeman, Elizabeth. "Introduction." *Queer Temporalities*, Special Issue of *GLQ: A Journal of Lesbian and Gay Studies* 13, nos. 2–3 (2007): 159–76.

Friedwald, Will. *Jazz Singing: America's Great Voices from Bessie Smith to Bebop and Beyond*. New York: Da Capo Press, 1996.

Fry, Andy. *Paris Blues: African American Music and French Popular Culture, 1920–1960*. Chicago: University of Chicago, 2014.

Gabbard, Krin. *Black Magic: White Hollywood and African American Culture*. New Brunswick, NJ: Rutgers University Press, 2004.

———. "Borrowing Black Masculinity: The Role of Johnny Hartman in *The Bridges of Madison County*." In *Soundtrack Available: Essays on Film and Popular Music*, ed. Pamela Robertson Wojcik and Arthur Knight, 295–316. Durham, NC: Duke University Press, 2001.

———. *Jammin' at the Margins: Jazz and the American Cinema*. Chicago: University of Chicago Press, 1996.

———. "*Paris Blues*: Ellington, Armstrong, and Saying It with Music." In *Uptown Conversations: The New Jazz Studies*, ed. Robert O'Meally, Brent Hayes Edwards, and Farah Jasmine Griffin, 297–311. New York: Columbia University Press, 2004.

Gala, Candelas. "'Tópicos Sublimados': Lorca's Female Iconographies in 'Eros Con Bastón.'" In *Lorca, Buñuel, Dalí: Art and Theory*, ed. Manuel Delgado and Alice Jan Poust, 86–105. Cranbury, NJ: Associated University Presses, 2001.

Garber, Eric. "A Spectacle in Color: The Lesbian and Gay Subculture of Jazz Age Harlem." In *Hidden from History: Reclaiming the Gay and Lesbian Past*, ed. Martin Duberman, Martha Vicinus, and George Chauncey, 318–31. New York: New American Library, 1989.

Garber, Marjorie. *Vested Interests: Cross-Dressing and Cultural Anxiety*. New York: Routledge, 1992.

Gates Jr., Henry Louis. *The Signifying Monkey: A Theory of African-American Literary Criticism*. New York: Oxford University Press, 1988.

Gavin, James. *Intimate Nights: The Golden Age of New York Cabaret*. New York: Grove Press, 1991.

———. "A Legend Lays Bare Her Hurt." *New York Times*, June 5, 1994.

———. *Stormy Weather: The Life of Lena Horne*. New York: Atria Books, 2009.

Gennari, John. *Blowin' Hot and Cool: Jazz and Its Critics*. Chicago: University of Chicago Press, 2006.

Gerstner, David. "The Production and Display of the Closet: Making Minnelli's 'Tea and Sympathy.'" *Film Quarterly* 50, no. 3 (Spring 1997): 13–26.

Gibson, Ian. *The Assassination of Federico García Lorca*. Chicago: J. P. O'Hara, 1979.

Givan, Benjamin. "Dizzy à la Mimi: Jazz, Text, and Translation." *Journal for the Society of American Music* 11, no. 2 (2017): 121–54.

Glick, Elisa F. *Materializing Queer Desire: Oscar Wilde to Andy Warhol*. Albany: State University of New York Press, 2009.

Goffman, Erving. *Stigma: Notes on the Management of Spoiled Identity*. New York: Simon & Schuster, 1963.

Gray, Herman. *Producing Jazz: The Experience of an Independent Record Company*. Philadelphia: Temple University Press, 1988.

Green, Douglas E. "Preposterous Pleasures: Queer Theories and *A Midsummer Night's Dream*." In *A Midsummer Night's Dream: Critical Essays*, ed. Dorothea Kehler, 369–97. New York: Garland, 1998.

Griffin, Farah Jasmine. *If You Can't Be Free, Be a Mystery: In Search of Billie Holiday*. New York: The Free Press, 2001.

Gubar, Susan. *Racechanges: White Skin, Black Face in American Culture*. New York; Oxford: Oxford University Press, 1997.

Guerrero, Ed. *Framing Blackness: The African American Image in Film*. Philadelphia: Temple University Press, 1993.

Hajdu, David. "Dr. Funky Butt and Me: My Friendship with the Real Donald Shirley." *New York Times*, March 10, 2019. https://www.nytimes.com/2019/03/10/movies/don-shirley-david-hajdu-green-book.html.

———. "A Jazz of Their Own." *Vanity Fair*, May, 1999.

———. *Lush Life: A Biography of Billy Strayhorn*. New York: North Point Press, 1997.

Halberstam, J. J. "What's That Smell? Queer Temporalities and Subcultural Lives." In *Queering the Popular Pitch*, ed. Sheila Whiteley and Jennifer Rycenga, 3–25. New York: Routledge, 2006.

Harper, Phillip Brian. *Are We Not Men? Masculine Anxiety and the Problem of African-American Identity*. New York: Oxford University Press, 1996.

Heller, Michael, ed. "The Power of Geri Allen." Special issue of *Jazz & Culture* 3, no. 2 (Fall–Winter 2020).

Herring, Scott. *Queering the Underworld: Slumming, Literature, and the Undoing of Lesbian and Gay History*. Chicago: University of Chicago Press, 2007.

Higginbotham, Virginia. *The Comic Spirit of Federico García Lorca*. Austin: University of Texas Press, 1976.

Hill, Constance Valis. *Tap Dancing America: A Cultural History*. New York: Oxford University Press, 2010.

Horne, Lena, and Richard Schickel. *Lena*. New York: Doubleday, 1965.

Hosokawa, Shuhei. "Martin Denny and the Development of Musical Exotica." In *Widening the Horizon: Exoticism in Post-War Popular Music*, ed. Philip Hayward, 72–93. Sydney: John Libbey, 1999.

Howland, John. *Ellington Uptown: Duke Ellington, James P. Johnson, and the Birth of Concert Jazz*. Ann Arbor: University of Michigan Press, 2009.

———. *Hearing Luxe Pop*. Berkeley: University of California Press, 2021.

———. "Jazz with Strings: Between Jazz and the Great American Songbook." In *Jazz/Not Jazz: The Music and Its Boundaries*, ed. David Ake, Charles Hiroshi Garrett, and Daniel Goldmark, 111–47. Berkeley: University of California Press, 2012.

Hubbs, Nadine. *The Queer Composition of America's Sound: Gay Modernists, American Music, and National Identity*. Berkeley: University of California Press, 2004.

Jasper, Lawrence Glenn. "A Critical History of the Artists' Theatre of New York." PhD diss., University of Kansas, 1986.

Jewell, Derek. *Duke: A Portrait of Duke Ellington*. New York: W. W. Norton, 1977.

Johnson, Patrick E., ed. *No Tea, No Shade: New Writings in Black Queer Studies*. Durham, NC: Duke University Press, 2016.

———, and Mae Henderson. "Introduction: Queering Black Studies/'Quaring' Queer Studies." In *Black Queer Studies: A Critical Anthology*, ed. E. Patrick Johnson and Mae Henderson, 1–17. Durham, NC: Duke University Press, 2005.

Johnston, David. *Federico García Lorca*. Bath, UK: Absolute Press, 1988.

Kahan, Benjamin. "Sheiks, Sweetbacks, and Harlem Renaissance Sexuality, or the Chauncey Thesis at Twenty-Five." *Journal of Modern Literature* 42, no. 3 (2019): 39–54.

Kakutani, Michiko. "Lena Horne Aloofness Hid the Pain, until Time Cooled Her Anger." *New York Times*, May 3, 1981. https://www.nytimes.com/1981/05/03/arts/lena-horne-aloofness-hid-the-pain-until-time-cooled-her-anger.html.

Keeling, Kara. *Queer Times, Black Futures*. New York: New York University Press, 2019.

Kernodle, Tammy. "Black Women Working Together: Jazz, Gender, and the Politics of Validation." *Black Music Research Journal* 34, no. 1 (2014): 27–55.

———. *Soul on Soul: The Life and Music of Mary Lou Williams*. Boston: Northeastern University Press, 2004.

Knadler, Steven. "Sweetback Style: Wallace Thurman and a Queer Harlem Renaissance." *Modern Fiction Studies* 48, no. 4 (2002): 899–936.

Knight, Arthur. *Disintegrating the Musical: Black Performance and American Musical Film*. Durham, NC: Duke University Press, 2002.

Lambert, Eddie. *Duke Ellington: A Listener's Guide*. Studies in Jazz Series, no. 26. Lanham, MD; London: Scarecrow Press, 1999.

Lanza, Joseph. *Elevator Music: Surreal History of Muzak, Easy-Listening, and Other Moodsong*. 2nd ed. Ann Arbor: University of Michigan Press, 2004.

Lewis, George E. "Improvised Music After 1950: Afrological and Eurological Perspectives." *Black Music Research Journal* 16, no. 1 (Spring 1996): 91–122.

Leydon, Rebecca. "Utopias of the Tropics: The Exotic Music of Les Baxter and Yma Sumac." In *Widening the Horizon: Exoticism in Post-War Popular Music*, ed. Philip Hayward, 45–71. Sydney: John Libbey, 1999.

Lorca, Federico García. *The Love of Don Perlimplín and Belisa in the Garden*. In *Lorca's Theatre: Five Plays of Federico García Lorca*, trans. James Graham-Lujan and Richard L. O'Connell. New York: Charles Scribner's Sons, 1941.

Love, Heather K. *Feeling Backward: Loss and the Politics of Queer History*. Cambridge, MA: Harvard University Press, 2007.

Magee, Jeffrey. *The Uncrowned King of Swing: Fletcher Henderson and Big Band Jazz*. New York: Oxford University Press, 2005.

Manning, Susan. *Modern Dance, Negro Dance: Race in Motion*. Minneapolis: University of Minnesota Press, 2004.

Mayhew, Jonathan. *Apocryphal Lorca: Translation, Parody, Kitsch*. Chicago: University of Chicago Press, 2009.

McConachie, Bruce. *American Theater in the Culture of the Cold War: Producing and Contesting Containment, 1947–1962*. Iowa City: University of Iowa Press, 2003.

McCracken, Allison. *Real Men Don't Sing: Crooning in American Culture*. Durham, NC: Duke University Press, 2015.

McDermid, Paul. *Love, Desire and Identity in the Theatre of Federico García Lorca*. Woodbridge, UK: Tamesis, 2007.

McGee, Kristin A. *Some Like It Hot: Jazz Women in Film and Television, 1928–1959*. Middletown, CT: Wesleyan University Press, 2009.

Mercer, Kobena, and Chris Drake. *Isaac Julien*. London: Ellipsis, 2001.

Miller, Monica L. *Slaves to Fashion: Black Dandyism and the Styling of Black Diasporic Identity*. Durham, NC: Duke University Press, 2009.

Monson, Ingrid. "The Problem with White Hipness: Race, Gender, and Cultural Conceptions in Jazz Historical Discourse." *Journal of the American Musicological Society* 48, no. 3 (Fall 1995): 396–422.

Moore, Celeste Day. "Race in Translation: Producing, Performing, and Selling African American Music in Greater France, 1944–74." PhD. diss., University of Chicago, 2014.

Morton, John Fass. *Backstory in Blue: Ellington at Newport '56*. New Brunswick, NJ: Rutgers University Press, 2008.

Moten, Fred. *In the Break: The Aesthetics of the Black Radical Tradition*. Minneapolis: University of Minnesota Press, 2003.

Mullen, Bill V. *Afro-Orientalism*. Minneapolis: University of Minnesota Press, 2004.

Muñoz, José Esteban. *Disidentifications: Queers of Color and the Performance of Politics*. Minneapolis: University of Minnesota Press, 1999.

———. "Ephemera as Evidence: Introductory Notes to Queer Acts." *Women and Performance: A Journal of Feminist Theory* 8, no. 2 (1996): 5–16.

Neal, Marc Anthony. *Looking for Leroy: Illegible Black Masculinities*. New York: New York University Press, 2013.

Nero, Charles. "Toward a Black Gay Aesthetic: Signifying in Contemporary Black Gay

Literature." In *Brother to Brother: New Writings by Black Gay Men*, ed. Essex Hemphill, 229–52. Boston: Alyson Publications, 1991.

Ngô, Fiona I. B. *Imperial Blues: Geographies of Race and Sex in Jazz Age New York*. Durham, NC: Duke University Press, 2014.

Nicholson, Stuart. *Reminiscing in Tempo: A Portrait of Duke Ellington*. Boston: Northeastern University Press, 1999.

Nolan, Frederick. *Lorenz Hart: A Poet on Broadway*. New York: Oxford University Press, 1994.

Nyong'o, Tavia. *Afro-Fabulations: The Queer Drama of Black Life*. New York: New York University Press, 2019.

O'Connell, Monica Hairston, and Sherrie Tucker. "Not One to Toot Her Own Horn(?): Melba Liston's Oral Histories and Classroom Presentations." *Black Music Research Journal* 34, no. 1 (Spring 2014): 121–58.

Paredez, Deborah. "Lena Horne and Judy Garland: Divas, Desire, and Discipline in the Civil Rights Era." *TDR: The Drama Review* 58, no. 4 (2014): 105–19.

Pellegrinelli, Laura. "Separated at 'Birth': Singing and the History of Jazz." In *Big Ears: Listening for Gender in Jazz Studies*, ed. Nichole Rustin-Paschal and Sherrie Tucker, 31–47. Durham, NC: Duke University Press, 2008.

Pequigney, Joseph. *Such Is My Love: A Study of Shakespeare's Sonnets*. Chicago: University of Chicago Press, 1996.

Peterson, Dale E. *Up from Bondage: The Literatures of Russian and African American Soul*. Durham, NC: Duke University Press, 2000.

Piekut, Benjamin. "New Thing? Gender and Sexuality in the Jazz Composers Guild." *American Quarterly* 62, no. 1 (March 2010): 25–48.

Pollack, Howard. *The Ballad of John Latouche: An American Lyricist's Life and Work*. New York: Oxford University Press, 2017.

Ponce, Martin J. "Langston Hughes's Queer Blues." *Modern Language Quarterly* 66, no. 4 (December, 2005): 505–37.

Rambuss, Richard. "Shakespeare's Ass Play." In *Shakesqueer: A Queer Companion to the Complete Works of Shakespeare*, ed. Madhavi Menon, 234–44. Durham, NC: Duke University Press, 2011.

Ramsey, Guthrie P. *The Amazing Bud Powell: Black Genius, Jazz History, and the Challenge of Bebop*. Berkeley: University of California Press, 2013.

Rastrelli, Bruce. "Moral Freedoms." In *Strayhorn: An Illustrated Life*, ed. A. Alyce Claerbaut and David Schlesinger, 81–176. Chicago: Agate Bolden, 2015.

Ross, Marlon B. "Beyond the Closet as Raceless Paradigm." In *Black Queer Studies: A Critical Anthology*, ed. E. Patrick Johnson and Mae Henderson, 161–89. Durham, NC: Duke University Press, 2005.

---. *Sissy Insurgencies: A Racial Anatomy of Unfit Manliness*. Durham, NC: Duke University Press, 2022.
Roussève, David. "Halfway to Dawn." David Roussève/REALITY. Accessed June 24, 2022. https://www.davidrousseve.com/halfwaytodawn.
Russell, Thaddeus. "The Color of Discipline: Civil Rights and Black Sexuality." *American Quarterly* 60, no. 1 (March 2008): 101–28.
Rustin-Paschal, Nichole. *The Kind of Man I Am: Jazzmasculinity and the World of Charles Mingus Jr.* Middletown, CT: Wesleyan University Press, 2017.
---. "'The Reason I Play the Way I Do Is': Jazzmen, Emotion, and Creating in Jazz." In *The Routledge Companion to Jazz Studies*, ed. Nicholas Gebhardt, Nichole Rustin-Paschal, and Tony Whyton, 401–9. New York: Routledge, 2019.
---, and Sherrie Tucker, eds., *Big Ears: Listening for Gender in Jazz Studies*. Durham, NC: Duke University Press, 2008.
Savran, David. *A Queer Sort of Materialism: Recontextualizing American Theater*. Ann Arbor: University of Michigan Press, 2003.
Schiff, David. *The Ellington Century*. Berkeley: University of California Press, 2012.
Schor, Naomi. *Bad Objects: Essays Popular and Unpopular*. Durham, NC: Duke University Press, 1995.
---. *Reading in Detail: Aesthetics and the Feminine*. New York: Routledge, 2007.
Schuller, Gunther. *The Swing Era: The Development of Jazz, 1930–1945*. New York: Oxford University Press, 1989.
Scott, Darieck. *Extravagant Abjection: Blackness, Power, and Sexuality in the African American Literary Imagination*. New York: New York University Press, 2010.
Sedgwick, Eve Kosofsky. *Between Men: English Literature and Male Homosocial Desire*. New York: Columbia University Press, 1985.
See, Sam. "Spectacles in Color: The Primitive Drag of Langston Hughes." *PMLA* 124, no. 3 (May 2009): 798–816.
Segura, Jean. "Haynes's: 60 Years of an American in Paris." *Rue des collectionneurs*, trans. Christine Madsen. Accessed July 30, 2020. http://www.ruedescollectionneurs.com/magazine/mag/haynes-us.php.
Shapiro, Nat, and Nat Hentoff, eds. *Hear Me Talkin' to Ya: The Story of Jazz as Told by the Men Who Made It*. New York: Dover Publications, 1955.
Sinfield, Alan. *Cultural Politics—Queer Reading*. London: Routledge, 2005.
---. *Out on the Stage: Lesbian and Gay Theatre in the Twentieth Century*. New Haven, CT: Yale University Press, 1999.
Singh, Nikhil Pal. *Black is a Country: Race and the Unfinished Struggle for Democracy*. Cambridge, MA: Harvard University Press, 2004.
Smith, Bruce R. "Shakespeare's Sonnets and the History of Sexuality: A Reception His-

tory." In *A Companion to Shakespeare's Works*, ed. Richard Dutton and Jean Elizabeth Howard, 4–26. Malden, MA: Blackwell, 2003.

Smith, Paul. *The Theater of García Lorca*. Cambridge: Cambridge University Press, 1998.

Smith, RJ. *The Great Black Way: L.A. in the 1940s and the Lost African-American Renaissance*. New York: Public Affairs, 2006.

Solis, Gabriel. "Duke Ellington in the LP Era." In *Duke Ellington Studies*, ed. John Howland, 197–223. Cambridge; New York: Cambridge University Press.

Somerville, Siobhan B. *Queering the Color Line: Race and the Invention of Homosexuality in American Culture*. Durham, NC: Duke University Press, 2002.

Soufas, C. Christopher. *Audience and Authority in the Modernist Theater of Federico García Lorca*. Tuscaloosa: University of Alabama Press, 1996.

Stanyek, Jason, and Benjamin Piekut. "Deadness: Technologies of the Intermundane." *TDR: The Drama Review* 54, no. 1 (Spring 2010): 14–38.

Stephens, Vincent L. *Rocking the Closet: How Little Richard, Johnnie Ray, Liberace, and Johnny Mathis Queered Pop Music*. Urbana: University of Illinois Press, 2019.

Stovall, Tyler. *Paris Noir: African Americans in the City of Light*. n.p.: CreateSpace Independent Publishing Platform, 2012.

Stras, Laurie. "White Face, Black Voice: Race, Gender, and Region in the Music of the Boswell Sisters." *Journal of the Society for American Music* 1, no. 2 (May 2007): 207–55.

Stratemann, Klaus. *Duke Ellington: Day by Day and Film by Film*. Copenhagen: JazzMedia, 1992.

Suzuki, Yoko. "Two Strikes and the Double Negative: The Intersections of Gender and Race in the Cases of Female Jazz Saxophonists." *Black Music Research Journal* 33, no. 2 (2013): 207–26.

Svendsen, Zoë. "The Dramaturgy of Spontaneity: Improvising the Social in Theater." In *Improvisation and Social Aesthetics*, ed. Georgina Born, Eric Lewis, and Will Straw, 288–308. Durham, NC: Duke University Press, 2017.

Szendy, Peter. *Listen: A History of Our Ears*. New York: Fordham University Press, 2008.

Taylor, Jeffrey. "With Lovie and Lil: Rediscovering Two Chicago Pianists of the 1920s." In *Big Ears: Listening for Gender in Jazz Studies*, ed. Nichole Rustin-Paschal and Sherrie Tucker, 48–63. Durham, NC: Duke University Press, 2008.

Teal, Kimberly Hannon. "Mary Lou Williams as Apology: Jazz, History, and Institutional Sexism in the Twenty-First Century." *Jazz & Culture* 2 (2019): 1–26.

Thurman, Wallace. *Infants of Spring*. Boston: Northeastern University Press, 1992.

Tinkcom, Matthew. *Working Like a Homosexual: Camp, Capital, Cinema*. Durham, NC: Duke University Press, 2002.

Toop, David. *Exotica: Fabricated Soundscapes in a Real World*. London: Serpent's Tail, 1999.

Tucker, Mark. "In Search of Will Vodrey." *Black Music Research Journal* 16, no. 1 (Spring 1996): 123–82.

———, ed. *The Duke Ellington Reader*. New York: Oxford University Press, 1993.

Tucker, Sherrie. *Swing Shift: "All-Girl" Bands of the 1940s*. Durham, NC: Duke University Press, 2000.

———. "When Did Jazz Go Straight? A Queer Question for Jazz Studies." *Critical Studies in Improvisation/Études critiques en improvisation* 4, no. 2 (2008): 1–16.

Tynan, John. "Paris Blues." *DownBeat*, November 23, 1961.

Van de Leur, Walter. *Something to Live For: The Music of Billy Strayhorn*. New York: Oxford University Press, 2002.

Vazquez, Alexandra. *Listening in Detail: Performances of Cuban Music*. Durham, NC: Duke University Press, 2013.

Vogel, Shane. "*Jamaica* on Broadway: The Popular Caribbean and Mock Transnational Performance." *Theatre Journal* 62, no. 1 (March 2010): 1–21.

———. "Madam Zajj and US Steel: Blackness, Bioperformance, and Duke Ellington's Calypso Theater." *Social Text* 30, no. 4 (2012): 1–24.

———. *The Scene of the Harlem Cabaret: Race, Sexuality, Performance*. Chicago: University of Chicago Press, 2009.

Von Eschen, Penny M. *Race Against Empire: Black Americans and Anticolonialism, 1937–1957*. Ithaca, NY, and London: Cornell University Press, 1997.

Wasserbauer, Marion. "'That's What Music Is About—It Strikes a Chord': Proposing a Queer Method of Listening to the Lives and Music of LGBTQs." *Oral History Review* 43, no. 1 (2016): 153–69.

Wells, Christopher J. "'A Dreadful Bit of Silliness': Feminine Frivolity and Ella Fitzgerald's Early Critical Reception." *Women and Music: A Journal of Gender and Culture* 21, no. 1 (2017): 43–65.

Whitehead, Kevin. "Strayhorn the Pianist." *Blue Light: The Journal of the Duke Ellington Society UK* 22, no. 3 (Autumn 2015), 18–19.

Whitesell, Lloyd. "The Uses of Extravagance in the Hollywood Musical." In *Music and Camp*, ed. Christopher Moore and Philip Purvis, 16–30. Middletown, CT: Wesleyan University Press, 2018.

———. *Wonderful Design: Glamour in the Hollywood Musical*. New York: Oxford University Press, 2018.

Wilson, James F. *Bulldaggers, Pansies, and Chocolate Babies: Performance, Race, and Sexuality in the Harlem Renaissance*. Ann Arbor: University of Michigan Press, 2010.

Wilson, John S. "Billy Strayhorn: The Peaceful Side—United Artists 15010." *DownBeat*, March 3, 1963.

———. "Pianist Echoes Mentor in Pastels and Wit." *New York Times*, June 7, 1965.

Wirth, Thomas H., ed. *Gay Rebel of the Harlem Renaissance: Selections from the Work of Bruce Richard Nugent*. Durham, NC: Duke University Press, 2002.

Wriggle, John. *Blue Rhythm Fantasy: Big Band Jazz Arranging in the Swing Era*. Urbana: University of Illinois Press, 2016.

———. "'The Mother of All Albums': Revisiting Ellington's *A Drum Is a Woman*." In *Duke Ellington Studies*, ed. John Howland, 265–98. Cambridge Composer Studies. Cambridge: Cambridge University Press, 2017.

Wright, Sarah. "Theatre." In *A Companion to Federico García Lorca*, ed. Federico Bonaddio, 39–62. Woodbridge, UK: Tamesis, 2007.

———. *The Trickster-Function in the Theatre of García Lorca*. Woodbridge, UK: Tamesis, 2000.

Zak III, Albin J. *I Don't Sound Like Nobody: Remaking Music in 1950s America*. Ann Arbor: University of Michigan Press, 2010.

Ziegler, Kortney. "Black Sissy Masculinity and the Politics of Dis-respectability." In *No Tea, No Shade: New Writings in Black Queer Studies*, ed. E. Patrick Johnson, 196–215. Durham, NC: Duke University Press, 2016.

INDEX

Page numbers in *italics* indicate figures.

aesthetics: in arranging, 16–18, 30–32; of Black modernism, 151; of Black queer dandyism, 132; camp, 34–39, 200n33; commerce and, 166; of femininity, 16, 137; gendered nature of, 16–17; queer histories and, 21, 87; of sonic glamour, 201n45; of Strayhorn-Ellington partnership, 71, 76. *See also* queer aesthetics
Ahmed, Sarah, 8
Ailey, Alvin, 4
Anderson, Cat, 64, 66
Anderson, Edmund, 31, 198n16
Anderson, Ivie, 20, 30, 109
Anderson, Paul Allen, 235n52
Anderson, Robert, 102–3, 218n61
anticommunism, 102, 136, 218n61
Armstrong, Louis, 145–49, 201n49
Arnaud, Leo, 36, 37
arranging: aesthetics in, 16–18, 30–32; composing compared to, 16–17; critical listening and, 116–17, 222n10; devaluing of, 16, 17, 31; in film industry, 40; functions of, 2, 4, 16; improvisation and, 15–16, 52; instrumental arrangements, 20, 22, 30, 50, 63–64, 108–9, 137; in legal context, 16, 17; queer collaboration and, 14, 18, 28, 69; sociality of, 21, 29, 67, 69; Strayhorn on art of, 18–19, 117; swing-era, 15, 17. *See also* vocal arrangements

Artaud, Antonin, 237n60, 238n64
Artists' Theatre, 91–92, 105, 214n26
Atkins, Cholly, 210n92, 214n21, 226n39
authorship issues, 8, 68, 71, 76–77, 90, 151, 161

Babs, Alice, 22
Bacsik, Elek, 155
Bailey, Ozzie, 70, 228n58
Balanchine, George, 118–20, 133
Baldwin, James, 4, 91, 93, 102, 147, 181, 213n20
"The Ballad for Very Tired and Very Sad Lotus Eaters," 109
"Ballet of the Flying Saucers," 110. *See also A Drum Is a Woman*
Baraka, Amiri, 15, 16, 107
Barclay Studios, 140, 146, 155, 232n14, 238n71
Bearden, Romare, 107
Beane, Reginald, 4
Beatty, Talley: in *A Drum Is a Woman*, 70, 213n20, 228n58; at Little Troc, 48–49; at Neal salon, 91, 213n20; in *The Road of the Phoebe Snow*, 110, 213n20, 220n87; in soundies, 40–41, 43, 43–44, 202n52
bebop, 15, 89, 212n11
Beggar's Holiday, 20, 78–79
Benjamin, Satima Bea, 22
Berish, Andrew, 17
Bernard, Emily, 1–2

Billy and Aaron (film), 189–90
Black community: domestic worker narrative and, 62–63; in Jim Crow era, 32, 47, 53; leftists within, 106–7; Lorquismo and, 107; in Paris, 145–49, 230nn5–6; sexuality as expressed by, 32; Van Vechten's interest in, 1–2. *See also* civil rights movement; racism
Black feminism, 47, 53, 223n27
Black masculinity, 32, 137, 140, 207–8n60
Black modernism: aesthetics of, 151; Harlem Renaissance and, 132; *Nutcracker Suite* and, 131, 134, 135; *Paris Blues* and, 151; *The Peaceful Side* and, 147, 151, 169–70; queer, 4, 22, 46, 90, 125; *Rose-Colored Glasses* and, 89, 90
Black queer dandyism, 4, 117, 124–25, 132–33, 140, 199n23
Black queer identity: career opportunities affected by, 6–7, 14; collaborative relationships and, 81; invisibility dynamic and, 9, 183; masculinity and, 32, 207–8n60; in musical theater productions, 93; representations of, 87, 113, 132; in Van Vechten's portraits, 4
Black queer transnationalism, 22, 113, 134, 136, 181
Blais-Tremblay, Vanessa, 225n36
Blanton-Webster Band, 30, 198n15
"Bli-Blip," 40
"Blood Count," 109
Blue Angel (nightclub), 55, 205n37
Blue Rose project: cover art for, 60–61, *61*; Ellington and, 60–63, *61*, 67, 68, 165; selection of tracks for, 63, 68, 165; Strayhorn and, 21, 30, 47, 60–69, 65, 165; vocal arrangements for, 63–67, *65*, 69
Bolero (Ravel), 131
Booker, Beryl, 211n104
Born, Georgina, 13
Bowles, Jane Auer, 217n59
Braggs, Rashida, 149, 231n12
Bridgers, Aaron: on François, 156–58; Francophilia of, 158; as Mars Club pianist,
11, 22, 68, 90, 147, 148, 155; in *Paris Blues*, 147–48, 230n8; Strayhorn's relationship with, 11, 22, 68, 120, 145–47, 162
"Brother Big Eyes," 88–90. See also *Rose-Colored Glasses*
Brothers (nightclub), 49
Brother to Brother (film), 240n6
Brown, Lawrence, 35, 119
Brown, Nacio Herb, 36
Bruce, Gladys, 105–6, 218n67
Burns, Ralph, 121, 236n53

camp aesthetics, 34–39, 200n33
Campfield, Marion B., 52
"Caravan," 129–30, *130*, 225nn35–36
care ethics, 69, 81
Carney, Harry, 64, 114, 119, 121–22
Carroll, Diahann, 181
"Cashmere Cutie," 138
chamber jazz, 164, 166
Chambers, Jack, 109, 112, 221n93
Chapman, Aristide, 49
"Chelsea Bridge," 5, 70–76, 78, 108, 137
Chez Paree (nightclub), 51, 55, 204n25
Chopin, Frédéric, 156, 157
Christy, June, 161–62
civil rights movement, 23, 50, 59–60, 93, 120, 135–36, 140
classical music: as homosexual "perversion," 102; modern jazz and, 156, 158, 165, 167; in Paris, 155–56; scoring in relation to, 15; Strayhorn's passion for, 117, 229n62. *See also specific artists*
classicism, 34–35, 41, 157
Clooney, Rosemary: *Blue Rose*, 21, 30, 47, 60–69, *61*, 65, 165; marriage and family life, 67, 207n54, 208n66, 208n69; musicals starring, 60, 207n53; relationship with male jazz icons, 208n67; Strayhorn's collaboration with, 21, 30, 47, 60–64, 66–69, 162, 207n58; vocal persona of, 66, 67
Clum, John M., 217–18n61
Cohen, Harvey G., 138–39, 185–86, 229n69

256 *Index*

Cole, Nat "King," 32, 162, 199n22, 238n66
Coleman, Anthony, 159
Coles, Honi, 76–78, 210n95, 226n39
collaborative relationships: Black queer identity and, 81; creativity in, 6, 8, 13–14, 27, 180; dimensions of, 6, 47; dynamics of, 48, 54, 69–76, 151; in "Flamingo" arrangement, 31; in soundie production, 44; Strayhorn-Clooney, 21, 30, 47, 60–64, 66–69, 207n58. *See also* queer collaboration; Strayhorn-Ellington partnership; Strayhorn-Horne partnership
Collier, James Lincoln, 137, 228n60
Collins, Janet, 40–41, *43*, 43–44, 202n52, 202n57
Columbo, Russ, 31–32
composing: arranging compared to, 16–17; in legal context, 16, 17; Strayhorn on art of, 19
Cook, Charles "Cookie," 210n92, 213–14n21, 226n39
Copasetics, 50, 76, 213–14n21, 226n39
Corbman, Rachel, 93–94
Coslow, Sam, 39
Cotton Club, 123, 126
critical arrangements, 6, 182
critical listening, 116–17, 222n10
crooning, 31–32, 36, 37, 41
Crosby, Bing, 31–32, 60, 199n20
Cvetkovich, Ann, 10–11

dandyism. *See* Black queer dandyism
Davis, Kay, 30, 198n14
Davis, "Wild Bill," 112
"Day Dream," 73, 78, 79, 108, 110, 138, 167, 210n97
Day Dream (film), 189, 240n8
Dearie, Blossom, 68, 205n39
Debussy, Claude, 34, 156, 157, 166
Delaney, Beauford, 4, 169, 230n5, 237n60, 238n64
DeLavallade, Carmen, 70
D'Emilio, John, 93
DeVeaux, Scott, 15

Dicks, Lillian Strayhorn, 80
Dillard, Bill, 93
Dixon, Melvin, 233n32
Douglas, Alan, 22, 146, 154–55, 159–60, 177–79, 181
drag culture, 124
Drawings for Mulattoes (Nugent), 124–25, *125*
A Drum Is a Woman, 20, 70, 77, 110, 213n20, 228n58
Duckett, Alfred, 215n32
Duke, Vernon, 93
Dunham, Katherine, 4, 40–41, 48, 91, 201n49, 202n56
Dutch Jazz Orchestra, 192n11, 201n41, 216n48
Duvivier, George, 51, 52, 56, 164
Dyer, Geoff, 2
Dyer, Richard, 205n33, 222n15

Eckstine, Billy, 32, 199n22
Edens, Roger, 29, 198n10, 203n9
Edwards, Brent Hayes, 92
Egen, Daniel, 202n50
"Elf," 109. *See also* "Isfahan"
Ellington, Duke: absence from Van Vechten's portrait archive, 5; *Blue Rose* and, 60–63, *61*, 67, 68, 165; *Ellington Song Book* sessions and, 69–76, 78; in "Flamingo" soundie, 41, *42*; great-man narratives of, 7; Hodge's relationship with, 220–21nn88–89; Horne's relationship with, 28; jungle style of, 123, 125, 126; Kuller and, 39, 201n47; Morgan as publicist for, 76, 210n90; in Paris, 140, 145–46; *Paris Blues* film music and, 140, 147–51, 153; *Portrait of Ella Fitzgerald* and, 210n89; on racism in United States, 136; Sacred Concert by, 58; Smith's interview with, 183–89, *185*. *See also* Ellington Orchestra; Strayhorn-Ellington partnership
Ellington, Marie, 30
Ellington, Mercer, 45, 160, 167
Ellington Orchestra: Carnegie Hall performance, 130, 165, 203n11; classicism and, 34; improvisation in, 6; interpretive

Index **257**

sonic filter of, 18; in musical theater, 29, 201n49; at Newport Jazz Festival, 70; shaping of sound by Strayhorn, 5; State Department Tours, 141; vocal arrangements for, 21, 30–34; West Coast tour by, 39

Evans, Rodney, 189–90, 240n6, 240n8

Evers, Medgar, 59, 206n47, 207n52

exotica: artistic figurations of, 113; at Brothers nightclub, 49; in "Flamingo" arrangement, 33; in *Infants of the Spring*, 132; in "Love, Love," 97; modern jazz and, 167, 168; in *Nutcracker Suite*, 131, 135; queer aesthetics and, 21, 87; in "You Stepped Out of a Dream," 37

Fantastic Rhythm, 20, 196n45

Far East Suite, 109, 110, 141

Feather, Leonard, 51, 72, 120, 160, 204n17

feminism, Black, 47, 53, 223n27

Ferguson, Roderick A., 207–8n60

Ferrer, José, 62, 67, 208n69

Field, Douglas, 93

film industry: arranging in, 40; queer labor in, 28–29, 34; soundies in, 39–44, 42–43, 202n52

Fischer, Jennifer, 118

Fitzgerald, Ella: agency as collaborator, 73, 74; *Ellington Song Book* sessions, 21, 30, 47, 69–76, 78, 79; *Portrait of Ella Fitzgerald*, 210n89; Strayhorn's collaboration with, 20, 21, 30, 47, 69–76, 78, 79; Van Vechten's portrait archive and, 5; vocal arrangements for, 20, 30, 70–75, 78, 79

"Flamingo" arrangement, 30–44; aesthetic practices in, 31, 32; bridge section of, 35, 36, 43; collaborative relationships in, 31; improvisation in, 35, 44; introductory section of, *33*, 33–34; Jeffries and, 21, 30–32, 35, 40, 198–99n16; queer collaboration in, 44; queer histories of, 21, 30; soundie produced from, 39–44, 42–43; stylistic extravagance of, 35–38, 41; transition section of, 35, 43; trombone solo in, 35,

43–44; van de Leur on, 32–34; wind motive in, 35, 43

"A Flower Is a Lovesome Thing," 45–47, 79–80, 108, 137, 155, 160, 165, 167, 169, 176, 211n101

"The Flowers Die of Love," 103–5, *104*, 137

François, Samson, 156–58, 165, 166, 232n27

Francophilia, 32, 99, 158, 200n24, 233n32

Freed Unit (MGM studios), 28–29, 34–37, 200n33, 204n33

French modernism, 22, 99, 131, 134, 157

Friedwald, Will, 208n67

fugitivity, 9, 10, 96, 168, 169, 180, 196n37

Gabbard, Krin, 148–51, 153, 232n14

Gaines, Lee, 161, 163, 234n44

Gala, Candelas, 218n65

Garland, Judy, 37, 204n33

Gaudry, Michel, 155, 161, 163, 165

Gavin, James, 29, 45, 47, 205nn37–38

gay persons. *See* homosexuality

gender: aesthetics and, 16–17; artistic authenticity and, 16, 196n37; Black domestic worker narrative and, 62–63; collaborative creativity and, 14; crooning voices and, 31–32; heteropatriarchal codes of, 28; jazz intimacy and, 48; in jazz studies, 8, 16; stereotypes related to, 73; visual economy and, 140. *See also* women in jazz

Gennari, John, 177

Gibson, Ian, 106

Gillespie, Dizzy, 78, 212n11

Giovanni's Room (Baldwin), 93

The Glass Menagerie (Williams), 207n57

Glick, Elisa, 124–25, 132

Goffman, Erving, 221n91

Goldberg, Francis, 68

Golson, Benny, 233n22

Gonsalves, Paul, 86, 119, 121–23

Granz, Norman, 71–73, 236n53

Grappelli, Stephane, 22

great-man narratives, 7, 8

Green, Douglass E., 212n4

Greenlee, George, 6, 14

258 *Index*

Greer, Sonny, 39
"Grievin'," 63–67, 65, 208n62
Grouya, Ted, 31, 198–99n16
Grove, Bill, 57–58

Hajdu, David: on Clooney, 62, 207n54; dismantling of myths by, 7; on Ellington's undermining of Strayhorn, 50; on Grove's relationship with Strayhorn, 57; on Hodge's personality, 111; on homophobia of Morgan, 76; interviews conducted by, 10, 27; on social life in Paris, 147; on Strayhorn as openly gay, 5–6, 9; on Turner's meeting with Strayhorn, 39
Halfway to Dawn (Roussève), 189, 190
Hamilton, Chico, 51–53, 56, 164
Hamilton, Jimmy, 78, 86, 114, 119, 131, 203n11
Harlem Renaissance, 107, 113, 124, 132, 240n6
Haynes, Leroy, 230n1
Hayton, Lennie, 46, 47, 50, 54
Heath, Gordon, 40, 230n5
Henderson, Joe, 45
Henderson, Luther, 11, 50, 89–91, 212n11
Henderson, Mae, 9
heteronormativity: in jazz studies, 8; Lorca's rejection of, 94; masculinity and, 32, 207–8n60; of *The Nutcracker* ballet, 118; sexuality and, 103; women in jazz and, 67
heteropatriarchy, 28, 126, 207n57
Hewes, Henry, 106
Hill, Constance Valis, 130, 225–26n39
Himes, Chester, 49
Hinton, Milt, 2
Hodges, Cue, 111
Hodges, Johnny: "Ballet of the Flying Saucers" and, 110; "Day Dream" and, 78, 108, 110; Ellington's relationship with, 220–21nn88–89; "Flamingo" and, 44; "A Flower Is a Lovesome Thing" and, 79–80, 108; instrumental arrangements for, 20, 63, 108–9, 137; *Nutcracker Suite* and, 119, 132; *Paris Blues* and, 150, 151; "Passion Flower" and, 63, 108, 110, 165; personality of, 111–12;

Such Sweet Thunder and, 85–86, 110, 135; "Wounded Love" and, 99, 108, 110–11
Holiday, Billie, 67, 208n66
homophobia: in Cold War era, 93, 134; in critical assessments of Strayhorn, 137, 228n60; fear-mongering and, 94; Lorca's murder as reflection of, 106; in McCarthyite era, 102; of Morgan, 76, 210n90
homosexuality: Black press coverage of, 93–94; heteronormative fears of, 103; Kinsey reports on, 93; of Lorca, 21, 87, 94, 106; in musical theater productions, 93; openness regarding, 5, 6; representations of, 102; of Tchaikovsky, 21, 87. *See also* "queer" entries
Homzy, Andrew, 237n59
Horne, Lena: Black feminism and, 47, 53; civil rights activism of, 50, 59–60, 140; documentary on, 45–46, 206n46; Ellington's relationship with, 28; *It's Love*, 54–56; Joint Negro Appeal performance by, 52; JVC Jazz Festival performance, 45; "Let Me Love You," 54–56, 205n34, 205n39; musicals featuring, 59, 201n49; performative impersona of, 53–54; Svaoy-Plaza engagement, 203n7; Van Vechten's portrait archive and, 5; *We'll Be Together Again*, 45, 46, 56, 79, 206n46. *See also* Strayhorn-Horne partnership
Horton, Lester, 202n57
Howard, Bart, 54, 55, 205nn37–38
Howland, John, 17
Hughes, Langston, 4, 107, 124, 126, 180, 224n28

"I Got It Bad (and That Ain't Good)," 63, 67, 109
"I'll Remember April," 38, 200n41
"I'm Beginning to See the Light," 56
"I'm Checkin' Out, Goom Bye," 63, 69, 208n62
improvisation: arranging and, 15–16, 52; in Ellington Orchestra, 6; in "Flamingo," 35, 44; in "Grievin'," 64, 66; in musical theater, 195n35; in *Nutcracker Suite*, 119, 131, 132; in *The Peaceful Side*, 147, 158; in theater rehearsals, 195n35

Index **259**

Infants of the Spring (Thurman), 132–33, 226n45
instrumental arrangements, 20, 22, 30, 50, 63–64, 108–9, 137
interracial relationships, 135–36, 148–49, 151
In the Summerhouse (Bowles), 217n59
intimacy. *See* jazz intimacy; queer intimacy
invisibility dynamic: Black queer identity and, 9, 183; queer archival method and, 10; in Strayhorn-Ellington partnership, 5, 9, 23, 71, 183
"Isfahan," 109. See also *Far East Suite*

Jacobs, Phoebe, 76
Jasper, Lawrence Glenn, 218–19n70
Jay, Leticia, 130, 225–26n39
jazz intimacy, 27, 44, 46–48, 146, 155, 160, 180
jazz music: authenticity of, 16, 196n37; bebop and, 15, 89, 212n11; blues values in, 15; chamber jazz, 164, 166; cultural prestige of, 119; great-man narratives and, 7, 8; Hollywood framing of, 154; multitrack recording of, 62, 209n74; queer histories and, 7–11, 18, 21, 170; swing-era, 15, 17, 63; symbolic capital of, 21; vocalese in, 35, 63, 72, 154, 155, 163–64; West Coast, 164. *See also* arranging; composing; modern jazz; scoring; women in jazz; *specific artists*
Jeffries, Herb: crooning by, 31, 32, 35, 41; in Ellington Orchestra, 21, 30; in "Flamingo" soundie, 40–43, *42*; Francophilia of, 32; Grouya and, 198–99n16; racial self-identification by, 199n22; vocal persona of, 31; West Coast tour described by, 39
Jenkins, Gordon, 176
Jim Crow era, 32, 47, 53
Johnson, E. Patrick, 9
Joint Negro Appeal fundraising campaign, 52
Jump for Joy, 20, 30, 39, 40, 48, 109
jungle style, 123, 125, 126
"Just A-Settin' and A-Rockin'," 161–63

Kahn, Gus, 36
Kaufman, Bob, 107

Kenton, Stan, 161–62, 164, 234n45
Kinsey, Alfred, 93
Kuller, Sid, 39, 201n47
Kyser, Kay, 36–37

Lamarr, Hedy, 37
Lambert, Eddie, 137, 222n20
"Lana Turner," 39
"Lately," 110, 135
Latouche, John, 73, 78–79, 93, 210n97
Laurents, Arthur, 29, 198n9
Lee, Gene, 119, 223n22
Lehner, Gerhart, 159, 170, 176
Leslie, Alfred, 95, 106, 216n41
"Let Nature Take Its Course," 20
Lewis, George, 222n10
Liston, Melba, 72, 197n49
Little Troc (nightclub), 29, 48, 203n9
Lockhart, June, 118, 133
Logan, Arthur, 115, 221n3
Logan, Marian, 115, 117
Lorca, Federico García: *Blood Wedding*, 107; *Gypsy Ballads*, 107; homosexuality of, 21, 87, 94, 106; murder of, 106; *Poet in New York*, 107, 219n77; "Serenata," 218n65; theatrical modes and devices used by, 94, 97, 216n40; transformative nature of works by, 103. See also *The Love of Don Perlimplín for Belisa in Their Garden*
Love, Heather, 99–100, 217n55
"Love, Love," 96–100, *98*
"Love Like This Can't Last," 45
The Love of Don Perlimplín for Belisa in Their Garden (Lorca), 94–106; all-Black cast in, 20, 92, 106; censorship of, 94, 215n35; as experimental production, 20, 87, 91; "The Flowers Die of Love" in, 103–5, *104*; "Love, Love" in, 96–100, *98*; masking and, 94–97, 99; plot overview, 94–96; press reviews of, 106; queer transnationalism and, 21, 92; set and costume design for, 95, 106; "Sprite Music" in, 97–99, *99*; translations of, 214n26; "Wounded Love" in, 99–102, *101*

"Lover Man," 38

"Lush Life": expressions of truth in, 6; on failed/impossible love, 99–100, 172, 176; as lyrical tribute to Paris, 22; mood music features in, 167; origins of, 213n13; *The Peaceful Side* version of, 167–76, *171*, *174–75*; popularity of, 5, 20; queer aesthetics in, 137, 168; queer topics in, 89, 111, 112, 147; Rugolo arrangement of, 162, 238n66

Machiz, Herbert, 92–94, 106, 219n70
Mackey, Nathaniel, 107
Magee, Jeffrey, 17
"The Man I Love," 38, 200n41
Manning, Susan, 40–41, 202n56
Mars Club, 11, 22, 68, 90, 146–48, 155–57, 208n71
Martin, Tony, 36
masking, 21, 87, 94–97, 99
Mathis, Johnny, 199n23, 205n37
Maxwell, Jimmy, 54
"Maybe," 45, 56–58, *59*
Mayhew, Jonathan, 107, 219n75, 219n77
McCracken, Allison, 31–32, 199n20
McDermid, Paul, 95, 103, 216n40
McEachern, Murray, 150
McPartland, Marian, 203n15, 233n36
McRae, Carmen, 50, 203n15
Mercer, Mabel, 55, 205n38
A Midsummer Night's Dream (Shakespeare), 85–86, 135
Miller, Glenn, 36–37
Miller, Mitch, 60, 176
Miller, Monica A., 132
Mingus, Charles, 168–69, 177–78, 237n59
Minnelli, Vincente, 28–29, 200n33, 201n49
Mitchell, Arthur, 4, 133
modernism. *See* Black modernism; French modernism
modern jazz: characteristics of, 37–39; classical music and, 156, 158, 165, 167; exotica and, 167, 168; mood music and, 166–68, 235n52; piano trio recordings within, 160–61; sonic glamour and, 201n45; Strayhorn in shaping sound of, 5; third-stream projects and, 164, 166; trends in production of, 23, 146, 176–77

Money Jungle advertisement, 178, *178*
"Mood Indigo," 56, 151
mood music, 166–68, 235n52
Moore, Phil, 49, 54, 200n33
Morgan, Joe, 76, 210n90
Moten, Fred, 9, 168–69, 180, 237n60, 238n64
"Multi-Colored Blue," 164
multitrack recording, 62, 209n74
musical theater: *Beggar's Holiday*, 20, 78–79; Black queer identity in, 93; *Cabin in the Sky*, 29, 41, 93, 201n49; *A Drum Is a Woman*, 20, 70, 77, 110, 213n20, 228n58; Ellington Orchestra in, 29, 201n49; *Fantastic Rhythm*, 20, 196n45; improvisation in, 195n35; *Jamaica*, 59; *Jump for Joy*, 20, 30, 39, 40, 48, 109; *Rose-Colored Glasses*, 11, 20, 87–91, 213n15, 240n9; stylistic extravagance in, 36; *Ziegfeld Girl*, 36–37. *See also The Love of Don Perlimplín for Belisa in Their Garden*
Myers, John Bernard, 92, 106
"My Little Brown Book," 20

Nance, Ray, 86, 114
National Association for the Advancement of Colored People (NAACP), 58–60, 140
Neal, Dorcas, 91
Neal, Frank, 91, 213n20
Nero, Charles, 224n32
Nugent, Bruce Richard, 4, 124–25, *125*, 132–33
The Nutcracker (ballet), 113, 118, 133
Nutcracker Suite (Strayhorn and Ellington), 114–40; "Arabesque Cookie," 119, 126–37, *127–29*, 227n54; "Chinoiserie," 227n51; cover art for, 133, *134*, *139*, 139–40; "Entr'acte," 119; genesis of, 114–15, 117; improvisation in, 119, 131, 132; "Overture," 119–21; precompositional phase of, 85, 116; queer collaboration in, 115; queer histories of, 125, 130–31, 135; queer transnationalism and,

Index **261**

21, 87, 113, 136; renaming of dance titles in, 117–18; reviews of, 119, 120, 223n22; "Sugar Rum Cherry," 120–26, *122*; "Waltz of the Floreodores," 119

O'Connell, Monica Hairston, 72, 197n49
"Oo! (You Make Me Tingle)," 11, 51
orchestrations: expressive framework through, 2; internal logic of, 33; in *Nutcracker Suite*, 128, 131; in *Paris Blues*, 150; vocal background, 34
orientalism, 126, 130, 132–34
Oshei, Bernard, 94, 95, 106
Othello (Shakespeare), 135

Panoram machines, 40, 201–2n50
Paris Blues (film), 22, 140, 146–53, 230n8, 231–32n14, 232n17
Parker, Charlie, 109
Parks, Gordon, 139
"Passion Flower," 5, 63, 68, 108, 110, 165, 235nn49–50
patriarchy, 28, 81, 126, 207n57
Patterson, Bill, 57, 58
The Peaceful Side (Strayhorn): Barclay Studios recording of, 140, 146, 155, 238n71; Black modernism and, 147, 151, 169–70; cover art for, *178*, 178–79; improvisation in, 147, 158; jazz intimacy and, 155, 160, 180; "Lush Life" and, 167–76, *171*, *174–75*; mood music features in, 166–68; positioning within jazz field, 160–67; queer collaboration in, 22–23, 146–47, 155, 160, 162, 177; race and power in production of, 177; Strayhorn's perception of, 179–80; track selection for, 154, 159–60, 165, 177
Peer Gynt Suites Nos. 1 and 2, 140
Perfume Suite, 130, 165, 226n41
Perrin, Mimi, 155, 163, 170, 235n47
Pollack, Howard, 78
Popwell, Albert, 79
"Prelude to a Kiss," 109
"Pretty Girl," 109, 110

Priestly, Brian, 154, 183
Procope, Russell, 86
Puck (Shakespearean character), 85–86, 194n17, 211–12nn3–4

queer aesthetics: exotica and, 21, 87; flower-themed compositions and, 80; in "Lush Life," 137, 168; of primitive drag, 124; stylistic extravagance and, 37–38; in *Such Sweet Thunder*, 86
queer collaboration: arranging and, 14, 18, 28, 69; conceptual dimensions of, 13–14, 19; dynamics of, 48, 69; Ellington-Strayhorn, 14, 18, 168; ethics of care in, 69, 81; in "Flamingo" arrangement, 44; Hodges-Strayhorn, 112; Horne-Strayhorn, 21, 28; in *Nutcracker Suite*, 115; in *Paris Blues*, 151; in *The Peaceful Side*, 22–23, 146–47, 155, 160, 162, 177
queer histories: aesthetic practices and, 21, 87; Black, 6, 22, 126, 132, 135, 167, 190; blue rose as figure in, 62; of drag culture, 124; failed/impossible love in, 21, 87, 89; of "Flamingo" arrangement, 21, 30; jazz music and, 7–11, 18, 21, 170; masking in, 21, 87; of *Nutcracker Suite*, 125, 130–31, 135
queer identity. *See* Black queer identity
queer intimacy, 18, 28, 55, 139
queer labor, 28–29, 34
queer subculture: cabarets and, 22, 68; camp aesthetics and, 34–35; drag performance and, 124; Lorquismo and, 107; in Paris, 147; terminology used in, 89; transnational, 22
queer temporality, 116, 126, 180
queer transnationalism, 21–22, 87, 92, 113, 134, 136, 181

race: collaborative creativity and, 14; crooning voices and, 32; heteropatriarchal codes of, 28; interracial relationships, 135–36, 148–49; jazz intimacy and, 48; jazz record production and, 177; in jazz studies, 8, 16. *See also* Black community

racism, 32, 107, 110, 135–36, 183, 200n33, 231n12
Rastrelli, Bruce, 60, 213n13
Ravel, Maurice, 34, 99, 131, 156, 157
Robbins, Jerome, 198n5
Robeson, Paul, 107
Rogers, Shorty, 118–20, 164, 223n22
Rose-Colored Glasses, 11, 20, 87–91, 213n15, 240n9
Ross, Marlon B., 9
Roussève, David, 189, 190, 240n9
Rugolo, Pete, 162, 234–35n45, 238n66
Russell, George, 164, 233n22
Rustin-Paschal, Nichole, 54, 177–78

Salinger, Connie, 36, 37
same-sex relationships. *See* homosexuality
Sanders, John, 78, 86
Satie, Erik, 96, 157
Savage, Archie, 4, 40, 41
Schiff, David, 86, 135, 211n3, 227n52
Schor, Naomi, 16
Schuller, Gunther, 137, 225n35
scoring: critical perspectives of, 15; expressive framework through, 2; jungle style, 126; multidimensional, 127; for singers, 21, 49, 75
Scrima, Michael "Micky," 117
Sebree, Charles, 91, 213n20, 214n23
See, Sam, 124, 224n28
sexuality: Black domestic worker narrative and, 62–63; Black male expressions of, 32; collaborative creativity and, 14; crooning voices and, 32; feminized, 110; heteronormativity and, 103; heteropatriarchal codes of, 28; identity and, 80, 87, 89, 102, 132; jazz intimacy and, 48; in jazz studies, 8, 16; Kinsey reports on, 93. *See also* homosexuality; "queer" entries
Shaw, Sam, 148, 230n8, 234n39
Sherrill, Joya, 30, 70, 234n44
Shirley, Donald, 19, 167, 204n25, 236n54
Short, Bobby, 45
Simmons, Art, 155, 230n5
Simone, Lela, 28, 29, 197n5

singers: scoring for, 21, 49, 75; vocal coaching for, 21, 29, 30, 47, 48, 204n33; vocal persona of, 31, 66, 67, 80. *See also* vocal arrangements; *specific artists*
"Skylark," 38
Smith, Bob, 183–89, *185*
Smith, Elwood, 105, 218n66
Smith, R. J., 49
"Solitude," 196n46
"Something to Live For," 5, 20, 45, 99, 111, 206n46
sonic glamour, 201n45
"Sophisticated Lady," 63, 197n46
"So This is Love," 20
soundies, 39–44, *42–43*, 202n52
Spanish Civil War, 106–7
"Sprite Music," 97–99, *99*
Stephens, Vincent L., 32, 199n23
Stovall, Tyler, 147
"Strange Feeling," 165–66
Stratemann, Klaus, 40
Strayhorn, Billy: archival collections related to, 7, 9–11, 194n19; on art of arranging and composing, 18–19, 117; Black queer dandyism and, 4, 117, 140; *Blue Rose* and, 21, 30, 47, 60–69, *65*, 165; Bridgers's relationship with, 11, 22, 68, 120, 145–47, 162; character-composer parallels in works of, 85–86, 88–89; civil rights activism of, 23, 59–60, 120, 140; Clooney's collaboration with, 21, 30, 47, 60–64, 66–69, 162, 207n58; creative individuality of, 7, 22, 146; critical assessments of, 137–39, 158–59, 228n60; death of, 5, 137, 191n1; discovery of unknown works by, 7, 192n11; *Ellington Song Book* sessions and, 21, 30, 47, 69–76, 78, 79; family background, 80, 211n102; Fitzgerald's collaboration with, 20, 21, 30, 47, 69–76, 78, 79; Francophilia of, 32, 99, 158, 200n24; Grove's relationship with, 57–58; JVC Jazz Festival tribute to, 45; legacy of, 6, 7, 9, 182–84, 190; manuscript pencil used by, 11, *12*, 194n23; *Paris Blues* film music and, 22, 140, 146–51,

Index **263**

153; personality of, 28, 111–12; *Portrait of Ella Fitzgerald* and, 210n89; professional identity of, 6, 50, 90; queer dilemma faced by, 5–6; Smith's interview with, 183–89, *185*; solo concert performances by, 158–59; Van Vechten's portraits of, *xiv*, 1–4, *3*, 191n2. *See also* arranging; composing; musical theater; *The Peaceful Side*

Strayhorn-Ellington partnership: aesthetics of, 71, 76; authorship issues in, 8, 68, 71, 76–77, 90, 151, 161; critical perceptions of, 113, 138–39; division of labor in, 30; Ellington on, 13, 18; financial issues in, 50–51; invisibility dynamic in, 5, 9, 23, 71, 183; myths surrounding, 7–8; queer collaboration and, 14, 18, 168; queer intimacy in, 18, 139; Strayhorn on, 5–6, 13; tensions within, 50–51, 68, 76, 90, 91

Strayhorn-Horne partnership: Beatty on, 49; beginnings of, 27, 48; Hamilton on, 52–53; Horne on, 27, 28, 46–49, 52, 198n10; *It's Love* album and, 54–56; Laurents on, 198n9; performance engagements, 48–49, 51–52, 59–60; posthumous archive of, 45–46; queer collaboration and, 21, 28; star-sapphire ring as symbol of, 4; vocal arrangements and, 28, 30, 47, 56; vocal coaching in, 21, 29, 30, 47, 48, 204n33

stylistic extravagance, 35–38, 41

subculture. *See* queer subculture

subjectivity, queer, 10, 34, 37

Such Sweet Thunder, 70, 77, 85–86, 110, 135, 194n17, 227n52

swing-era jazz, 15, 17, 63

The Swingin' Nutcracker (Rogers), 118–19

Szendy, Peter, 116–17, 222n10

"Take the 'A' Train," 5, 7, 20, 78, 155, 160, 167

Tchaikovsky, Peter Ilych: "Arabian Dance," 126–27, *127*, 131, 135–36, 225n35, 227n54; homosexuality of, 21, 87; otherness represented by, 118, 222n15; "Sugar Plum Fairy," 123, 125

Tea and Sympathy (Anderson), 102–3

Terry, Clark, 85, 86

Thiele, Bob, 177

third-stream projects, 164, 166

Thomas, Kay, 204–5n33

Thurman, Wallace, 124, 132–33, 226n45

Tinkcom, Matthew, 28, 29, 34, 35, 37, 200n33

Townsend, Irving, 61–62, 68, 207n54, 208n62

transnationalism. *See* queer transnationalism

Tropics and Le Jazz "Hot" (Dunham Troupe), 41

Tucker, Mark, 14, 34, 225n36

Tucker, Sherrie, 8, 72, 197n49

Turner, Lana, 37, 39

"Two Sleepy People," 196n46

Tynan, John, 150

Tynes, Margaret, 70

"U.M.M.G.," 221n3

United Artists, 146, 149, 177–79, *178*, 239n76

"Up and Down, Up and Down," 85, 138, 194n17

van de Leur, Walter: on artistic conflicts, 90; on "Day Dream," 78; dismantling of myths by, 7; Dutch Jazz Orchestra of, 192n11, 201n41, 216n48; on "Flamingo" arrangement, 32–34; on French modernist sound, 157; on multilayered formal design, 138; on *Nutcracker Suite*, 116, 119–20; on *The Peaceful Side*, 161, 164–65; on Strayhorn-Ellington works, 18; on "Where or When" arrangement, 38; on "Wounded Love," 99, 217n53

Van Vechten, Carl, *xiv*, 1–5, *3*, 40, 191nn1–2

Vazquez, Alexandra, 195–96n37

vocal arrangements: aesthetic practices in, 29–32; for *Blue Rose*, 63–67, *65*, 69; for Ellington Orchestra, 21, 30–34; for Fitzgerald, 20, 30, 70–75, 78, 79; for Horne, 28, 30, 47, 56; innovative approaches to, 33; queer collaboration and, 28; queer intimacy in, 28; stylistic extravagance of, 35–38, 41. *See also* singers

vocal coaching, 21, 29, 30, 47, 48, 204n33
vocalese, 35, 63, 72, 154, 155, 163–64
vocal persona, 31, 66, 67, 80
Vodery, Will, 14
Vogel, Shane, 53, 54, 59, 126, 180, 228n58

Waters, Ethel, 124, 201n49
The Weary Blues (Hughes), 124, 224n28
Webster, Ben, 50, 161, 236n53
Welles, Orson, 90, 92
West Coast jazz, 164
"Where or When," 38–39, 201n41
Whitehead, Kevin, 159, 233n36
Whitesell, Lloyd, 35–38, 201n45
Willard, Patricia, 11, 71, 156
Willett, Chappie, 17
Williams, Cootie, 109, 208n64
Williams, Henry "Brother," 49
Williams, Tennessee, 92, 102, 207n57
Wilson, John S., 158–59, 179

women in jazz: challenges for, 81; gendered stereotypes of, 73; heteronormative expectations of, 67; as instrumentalists, 211n104; marginalization of, 17, 30. *See also* gender; *specific artists*
Wood, Raymond, 213n13
Woode, Jimmy, 74–75
Woodyard, Sam, 75, 121, 135
"Wounded Love," 99–102, *101*, 108, 110–11, 137, 217nn53–54
Wriggle, John, 14, 15, 17
Wright, Sarah, 96, 216n44

Young, Felix, 29, 48
"You're the One," 45, 46, 54, 56, 57
"Your Love Has Faded," 20
"You Stepped Out of a Dream" arrangements, 36–37, 39, 201n45

Zak, Albin, 173–76

MUSIC / CULTURE
A series from Wesleyan University Press
Edited by Deborah Wong, Sherrie Tucker, and Jeremy Wallach
Originating editors: George Lipsitz, Susan McClary, and Robert Walser

The Music/Culture series has consistently reshaped and redirected music scholarship. Founded in 1993 by George Lipsitz, Susan McClary, and Robert Walser, the series features outstanding critical work on music. Unconstrained by disciplinary divides, the series addresses music and power through a range of times, places, and approaches. Music/Culture strives to integrate a variety of approaches to the study of music, linking analysis of musical significance to larger issues of power—what is permitted and forbidden, who is included and excluded, who speaks and who gets silenced. From ethnographic classics to cutting-edge studies, Music/Culture zeroes in on how musicians articulate social needs, conflicts, coalitions, and hope. Books in the series investigate the cultural work of music in urgent and sometimes experimental ways, from the radical fringe to the quotidian. Music/Culture asks deep and broad questions about music through the framework of the most restless and rigorous critical theory.

Marié Abe
Resonances of Chindon-ya: Sounding Space and Sociality in Contemporary Japan

Frances Aparicio
Listening to Salsa: Gender, Latin Popular Music, and Puerto Rican Cultures

Paul Austerlitz
Jazz Consciousness: Music, Race, and Humanity

Shalini R. Ayyagri
Musical Resilience: Performing Patronage in the Indian Thar Desert

Christina Baade and Kristin McGee
Beyoncé in the World: Making Meaning with Queen Bey in Troubled Times

Lisa Barg
Queer Arrangements: Billy Strayhorn and Midcentury Jazz Collaboration

Emma Baulch
Genre Publics: Popular Music, Technologies, and Class in Indonesia

Harris M. Berger
Metal, Rock, and Jazz: Perception and the Phenomenology of Musical Experience

Harris M. Berger
Stance: Ideas about Emotion, Style, and Meaning for the Study of Expressive Culture

Harris M. Berger and Giovanna P. Del Negro
Identity and Everyday Life: Essays in the Study of Folklore, Music, and Popular Culture

Franya J. Berkman
Monument Eternal: The Music of Alice Coltrane

Dick Blau, Angeliki Vellou Keil, and Charles Keil
Bright Balkan Morning: Romani Lives and the Power of Music in Greek Macedonia

Susan Boynton and Roe-Min Kok, editors
Musical Childhoods and the Cultures of Youth

James Buhler, Caryl Flinn, and David Neumeyer, editors
Music and Cinema

Thomas Burkhalter, Kay Dickinson, and Benjamin J. Harbert, editors
The Arab Avant-Garde: Music, Politics, Modernity

Patrick Burkart
Music and Cyberliberties

Julia Byl
Antiphonal Histories: Resonant Pasts in the Toba Batak Musical Present

Corinna Campbell
Parameters and Peripheries of Culture: Interpreting Maroon Music and Dance in Paramaribo, Suriname

Alexander M. Cannon
Seeding the Tradition: Musical Creativity in Southern Vietnam

Daniel Cavicchi
Listening and Longing: Music Lovers in the Age of Barnum

Susan D. Crafts, Daniel Cavicchi, Charles Keil, and the Music in Daily Life Project
My Music: Explorations of Music in Daily Life

Jim Cullen
Born in the USA: Bruce Springsteen and the American Tradition

Anne Danielsen
Presence and Pleasure: The Funk Grooves of James Brown and Parliament

Peter Doyle
Echo and Reverb: Fabricating Space in Popular Music Recording, 1900–1960

Ron Emoff
Recollecting from the Past: Musical Practice and Spirit Possession on the East Coast of Madagascar

Yayoi Uno Everett and Frederick Lau, editors
Locating East Asia in Western Art Music

Susan Fast and Kip Pegley, editors
Music, Politics, and Violence

Heidi Feldman
Black Rhythms of Peru: Reviving African Musical Heritage in the Black Pacific

Kai Fikentscher
"You Better Work!" Underground Dance Music in New York City

Ruth Finnegan
The Hidden Musicians: Music-Making in an English Town

Daniel Fischlin and Ajay Heble, editors
The Other Side of Nowhere: Jazz, Improvisation, and Communities in Dialogue

Wendy Fonarow
Empire of Dirt: The Aesthetics and Rituals of British "Indie" Music

Murray Forman
The 'Hood Comes First: Race, Space, and Place in Rap and Hip-Hop

Lisa Gilman
My Music, My War: The Listening Habits of U.S. Troops in Iraq and Afghanistan

Paul D. Greene and Thomas Porcello, editors
Wired for Sound: Engineering and Technologies in Sonic Cultures

Tomie Hahn
Sensational Knowledge: Embodying Culture through Japanese Dance

Edward Herbst
Voices in Bali: Energies and Perceptions in Vocal Music and Dance Theater

Deborah Kapchan
Traveling Spirit Masters: Moroccan Gnawa Trance and Music in the Global Marketplace

Deborah Kapchan, editor
Theorizing Sound Writing

Max Katz
Lineage of Loss: Counternarratives of North Indian Music

Raymond Knapp
Symphonic Metamorphoses: Subjectivity and Alienation in Mahler's Re-Cycled Songs

Victoria Lindsay Levine and Dylan Robinson, editors
Music and Modernity among First Peoples of North America

Noel Lobley
Sound Fragments: From Field Recording to African Electronic Stories

Laura Lohman
Umm Kulthūm: Artistic Agency and the Shaping of an Arab Legend, 1967–2007

Preston Love
A Thousand Honey Creeks Later: My Life in Music from Basie to Motown—and Beyond

René T. A. Lysloff and Leslie C. Gay Jr., editors
Music and Technoculture

Ian MacMillen
Playing It Dangerously: Tambura Bands, Race, and Affective Block in Croatia and Its Intimates

Allan Marett
Songs, Dreamings, and Ghosts: The Wangga of North Australia

Ian Maxwell
Phat Beats, Dope Rhymes: Hip Hop Down Under Comin' Upper

Kristin A. McGee
Some Liked It Hot: Jazz Women in Film and Television, 1928–1959

Tracy McMullen
Haunthenticity: Musical Replay and the Fear of the Real

Rebecca S. Miller
*Carriacou String Band Serenade:
Performing Identity in the
Eastern Caribbean*

Tony Mitchell, editor
*Global Noise: Rap and Hip-Hop
Outside the USA*

Christopher Moore and
Philip Purvis, editors
Music & Camp

Rachel Mundy
*Animal Musicalities: Birds, Beasts,
and Evolutionary Listening*

Keith Negus
*Popular Music in Theory:
An Introduction*

Johnny Otis
*Upside Your Head: Rhythm and Blues
on Central Avenue*

Jeff Packman
*Living from Music in Salvador:
Professional Musicians and the
Capital of Afro-Brazil*

Kip Pegley
*Coming to You Wherever You Are:
MuchMusic, MTV, and Youth Identities*

Jonathan Pieslak
*Radicalism and Music: An Introduction
to the Music Cultures of al-Qa'ida, Racist
Skinheads, Christian-Affiliated Radicals,
and Eco-Animal Rights Militants*

Thomas M. Pooley
*The Land Is Sung: Zulu Performances
and the Politics of Place*

Matthew Rahaim
*Musicking Bodies: Gesture and Voice
in Hindustani Music*

Matthew Rahaim
*Ways of Voice: Vocal Striving and Ethical
Contestation in North India and Beyond*

John Richardson
*Singing Archaeology:
Philip Glass's Akhnaten*

Tricia Rose
*Black Noise: Rap Music and Black Culture
in Contemporary America*

David Rothenberg and
Marta Ulvaeus, editors
*The Book of Music and Nature:
An Anthology of Sounds, Words, Thoughts*

Nichole Rustin-Paschal
*The Kind of Man I Am: Jazzmasculinity
and the World of Charles Mingus Jr.*

T. Sankaran, Matthew Harp Allen,
and Daniel Neuman, editors
The Life of Music in South India

Marta Elena Savigliano
*Angora Matta: Fatal Acts
of North-South Translation*

Joseph G. Schloss
*Making Beats: The Art
of Sample-Based Hip-Hop*

Barry Shank
*Dissonant Identities: The Rock 'n' Roll
Scene in Austin, Texas*

Jonathan Holt Shannon
*Among the Jasmine Trees: Music and
Modernity in Contemporary Syria*

Daniel B. Sharp
*Between Nostalgia and Apocalypse:
Popular Music and the Staging
of Brazil*

Helena Simonett
Banda: Mexican Musical Life across Borders

Mark Slobin
Subcultural Sounds: Micromusics of the West

Mark Slobin, editor
Global Soundtracks: Worlds of Film Music

Tes Slominski
Trad Nation: Gender, Sexuality, and Race in Irish Traditional Music

Christopher Small
The Christopher Small Reader

Christopher Small
Music of the Common Tongue: Survival and Celebration in African American Music

Christopher Small
Music, Society, Education

Christopher Small
Musicking: The Meanings of Performing and Listening

Andrew Snyder
Critical Brass: Street Carnival and Musical Activism in Rio de Janeiro

Maria Sonevytsky
Wild Music: Sound and Sovereignty in Ukraine

Tore Størvold
Dissonant Landscapes: Music, Nature, and the Performance of Iceland

Regina M. Sweeney
Singing Our Way to Victory: French Cultural Politics and Music during the Great War

Colin Symes
Setting the Record Straight: A Material History of Classical Recording

Steven Taylor
False Prophet: Field Notes from the Punk Underground

Kelley Tatro
Love and Rage: Autonomy in Mexico City's Punk Scene

Paul Théberge
Any Sound You Can Imagine: Making Music/Consuming Technology

Sarah Thornton
Club Cultures: Music, Media, and Subcultural Capital

Michael E. Veal
Dub: Songscape and Shattered Songs in Jamaican Reggae

Michael E. Veal and E. Tammy Kim, editors
Punk Ethnography: Artists and Scholars Listen to Sublime Frequencies

Robert Walser
Running with the Devil: Power, Gender, and Madness in Heavy Metal Music

Dennis Waring
Manufacturing the Muse: Estey Organs and Consumer Culture in Victorian America

Lise A. Waxer
The City of Musical Memory: Salsa, Record Grooves, and Popular Culture in Cali, Colombia

Mina Yang
Planet Beethoven: Classical Music at the Turn of the Millennium

ABOUT THE AUTHOR

Lisa Barg is associate professor of Music History and Musicology at the Schulich School of Music at McGill University and associate dean of Graduate Studies. She has published articles on race and modernist opera, Duke Ellington, Billy Strayhorn, Melba Liston, and Paul Robeson. She is currently principle investigator for a research project funded by the Social Sciences and Humanities Council of Canada (SSHRC) titled "Collaborative Creativity: Sound Recording and Music Making." She is co-editor-in-chief of *Women and Music: A Journal of Gender and Culture*. As a member of the Melba Liston Research Collective, she served as a guest co-editor for a special issue of the *Black Music Research Journal* devoted to the career and legacy of Melba Liston.